KT-451-138

Modern Moral Philosophy

This book is to be returned on or before
the last date stamped below.

17. MAR. 1997
27. JAN. 1998

10. JUN. 2002

14 SEP 2013

MODERN INTRODUCTIONS TO PHILOSOPHY
General Editor: D.J. O'CONNOR

Modern Moral Philosophy

Second Edition

W. D. Hudson

MACMILLAN

First edition 1970
Reprinted twice
Second edition 1983

Published by
MACMILLAN PRESS LTD
Houndmills, Basingstoke, Hampshire RG21 2XS
and London
Companies and representatives
throughout the world

ISBN 0–333–35773–6

A catalogue record for this book is available
from the British Library.

14 13 12 11 10 9   8   7   6
03 02 01 00 99 98 97 96 95

Printed in Hong Kong

TO ROSEMARY

CONTENTS

Contents

PREFACE

I should like to express my sincere thanks to those who have helped me in the writing of this book and, in particular, to the following persons.

Professor D. J. O'Connor, Head of the Department of Philosophy in this University, added to the many debts of gratitude which I owe him by his willingness to discuss with me, from time to time, points which arose in the planning and preparation of this book. I am most grateful for his unfailing help and encouragement.

Professor R. M. Hare, White's Professor of Moral Philosophy in the University of Oxford, very kindly read and talked over with me a first draft of Chapter 5 and of parts of Chapter 6. I am greatly indebted to him, not only for his many helpful comments, but for the generosity with which he has made available to me some of his unpublished papers and has allowed me to refer to them in my treatment of prescriptivism.

It hardly needs to be added that neither of the philosophers whom I have named must be held in any way responsible for what I say in this book or for any mistakes which I may have made.

The former secretary to this department, Mrs. Ann Smith, cheerfully and painstakingly attended to much of the typing and my thanks are due to her; as they are also to the faculty secretary, Mrs. E. Ridgeon, who helped me with the proof-reading.

My wife has also helped me greatly and to her I dedicate the book.

Department of Philosophy   W. D. HUDSON
University of Exeter

PREFACE TO SECOND EDITION

The first five chapters of this book have been taken over unchanged from the first edition. But the original Chapter 6, called simply "Descriptivism", has been replaced by the present Chapters 6, 7 and 8. In the first edition, the original Chapter 7 dealt with philosophical problems concerning action and responsibility. I have omitted it here because it was something of a digression from the main story that I have to tell.

I must make it quite clear what that story is. During the present century a number of philosophers, who belong to what is commonly called the analytical tradition, have engaged in a continuing discussion concerning the meaning of moral judgments. I attempt to clarify and relate what seem to me to have been the principal moves and counter-moves in this discussion. It is, in my opinion, the most important intellectual discussion concerning the nature of morality that has gone on, and continues to go on, in modern times. But, of course, it is not the only one. Many recent writers, who would be called moral philosophers, receive no mention here. It has not been my intention to provide an encyclopaedic survey of everything that passes for modern moral philosophy. This is partly because that task would be impossible to fulfil within one volume; but chiefly because I think it is usually more rewarding in philosophy to follow through carefully one line of argument and counter-argument within a branch of the subject than to attempt aerial pictures of whole fields of thought.

Since this book was first published in 1970, there have been considerable developments in the branch of the subject with which it is concerned. That is why I have expanded my account of the most recent ones into three chapters. It has not been possible to deal with every significant development in analytical moral philosophy but I hope that what has emerged is a reasonably balanced and comprehensive picture of the lively exchanges which have taken place in recent attempts to understand what we are doing when we deliver moral judgments.

It has been my good fortune, in preparing this second edition, to have had the advice and assistance of three people who gave me their help in preparing the first. Professor D. J. O'Connor gave me his invaluable editorial guidance. Professor R. M. Hare looked over what I have written about his most recent views. And Mrs. E. Ridgeon, as ever, gave me much painstaking secretarial assistance. It goes without saying that none of them are in any way responsible for this book's defects but I should like to place on record my sincere thanks to them.

University of Exeter   W. D. HUDSON
1983

ABBREVIATIONS USED IN THIS VOLUME

RG: *The Right and the Good* by W. D. Ross (Oxford, 1930)

RM: *Reason and Morality* by A. Gewirth (Chicago and London, 1978)

T: *Tractatus Logico-Philosophicus* by L. Wittgenstein (1961 translation by Pears and McGuinness)

VV: *Virtues and Vices* by Philippa Foot (Oxford, 1978)

CHAPTER 1. MORAL DISCOURSE AND MORAL PHILOSOPHY

This book is not about what people ought to do. It is about what they are doing when they *talk* about what they ought to do. Moral philosophy, as I understand it, must not be confused with moralizing. A moralist is someone who uses moral language in what may be called a first-order way. He, qua moralist, engages in reflection, argument, or discussion about what is morally right or wrong, good or evil. He talks about what people ought to do. I suppose the expression "moral philosopher" is sometimes used to mean a particularly wise or well-informed moralist. But I shall not so use it. By a moral philosopher I mean someone who engages in what may be called second-order discourse. Qua moral philosopher, he thinks and speaks about the ways in which moral terms, like "right" or "good," are used by moralists when they are delivering their moral judgments. What are the defining characteristics of moral language as such? How is it like, and how unlike, language used for other purposes, such as for stating empirical facts or uttering commands? What *are* people doing when they talk about what they ought to do? That is the moral philosopher's concern. The distinction which I draw here is sometimes expressed by saying that a moralist, as such, is interested in ethics; and a moral philosopher, as such, in metaethics.

An Example of Moral Discourse

As an example of first-order moral discourse, let us take the Parliamentary debate which, as I write, has just occurred at an all-night sitting of the House of Commons when the Divorce Reform Bill (1969) was receiving its second and third readings.[1] This bill recognized the breakdown of marriage as the sole ground for divorce. To put the matter summarily, there have been hitherto in England four main grounds on which one party to a marriage could petition for divorce from the other party, viz. adultery, desertion, cruelty, and insanity. The "guilty" party could, in no instance, petition for divorce on the ground of his own "guilt." The new bill abolishes this distinction between "guilty" and "innocent" parties. It allows either party to petition for divorce on the ground of the break-down of the marriage. What constitutes breakdown is, within certain limits, for the divorce court judge to decide. Five years' separation, other things being equal, could mean that the marriage had broken down. If a husband (or wife) walked out on his (or her) spouse, then, after five years he (or she) could, if this bill becomes law, petition for divorce with considerable chance of success.

The moral question which arises is: ought divorce law to be reformed along these lines? That was the question debated at the all-night sitting to which I have referred. We may safely take this debate as an example of moral discourse. The participants put forward what purported to be their own answers to a moral question. They supported these with what they considered reasons appropriate to the settlement of a moral issue.

What were they doing when they talked through the night about what they ought to do? That is the question which would interest a moral philosopher, as I have defined him. He would not wish to participate in the first-order debate; not, that is, qua philosopher. Nor would he want to reopen the moral question, when the debate was ended, by discussing whether or not the House ought really to do what those present had said that it ought to do about divorce. It is the logical features of the debate itself which would interest him, as a philosopher. What had these people been doing when they talked about what they ought to do? I will indicate one or two points which I think might have occurred to a moral philosopher as he reflected upon that question.

[1] See *Weekly Hansard* No. 798, June 16–19, 1969, pp. 1798–2074.

He might have asked himself, for instance, whether they were trying to make some sort of discovery or to reach some sort of decision. Which of these would be the more appropriate account of what had occurred? Some philosophers would say that trying to answer a moral question is trying to make a discovery. Some others would say that it is trying to reach a decision. Whichever answer he gave, however, a philosopher would recognize that what goes on in moral discourse is not quite like what goes on in other contexts where it is appropriate to talk about making discoveries or reaching decisions. In science, for example, men claim to make discoveries. It is true enough that when they claim to have done so, they are sometimes mistaken; and that when they really have done so, it sometimes takes other scientists a long time to agree that they have. Nevertheless, in science, there are accepted objective tests for determining when a discovery has really been made and when it has not. Moreover, you cannot be a scientist unless you are willing to submit your claims to these tests. In morals, however, there seems to be no counterpart to such tests. Moralists, it appears, can go on disagreeing with one another forever. It is not a necessary condition of being a moralist that one should be willing to submit one's claim to have made a discovery to certain specific, agreed, objective tests which verify, or falsify, it.

Turning now to the taking of decisions, compare what goes on in morals with what goes on, say, in a sport. In a sport, decisions have to be taken. A coin is tossed, for instance, to decide who shall bat first. If any captain came back from the tossup claiming that it had not really decided who should bat first, what could we make of that? It wouldn't be cricket, not only in the sense that we should take a poor view of the man's sportsmanship, but because it would be opting out of the game. Unless you abide by the tossup you cannot (logically) play cricket, since one of the rules of the game is that the tossup decides who shall bat or bowl—or perhaps it would be more accurate to say decides who shall decide, since it is the captain winning the toss who chooses to do one or the other. The point to take is that the tossup is the recognized "authority" which settles the matter. This is a very simple ex-

ample of decision-making. But, in far more complicated examples, the same point can be observed. In trying a criminal
or deciding a lawsuit, for instance, there is a recognized authority to which appeal is made. All who participate in such
legal activities accept this authority. It is true, of course, that
lawyers may disagree as to what the law says about some sort
of case, as captains of cricket teams can hardly disagree as
to whether an upturned coin is "heads" or "tails." But the
point remains that, without the law to appeal to, there could
(logically) be no trials and no lawsuits. Now, where is the
"authority" to which appeal is made in taking moral decisions? In morals, there appears to be no counterpart to the
authority of the tossup or the law. It is not a necessary condition of being a moralist that one should be prepared to
decide things by invoking a recognized authority. Cricketers,
as such, abide by the tossup, and lawyers, as such, by the
law; but where is the authority, the invoking of which makes
a moralist a moralist?

Such reflections as these suggest that moral discourse, while
in many ways resembling other sorts of discourse, nevertheless has something distinctive about it. Most modern moral
philosophers, whether they think of a moral judgment as a
discovery or a decision, conceive of it as *sui generis*. What
reflections confirm them in that opinion?

I turn for an answer to the Parliamentary debate upon
which we are supposing a moral philosopher to be reflecting.
(It should be recognized that those members of Parliament
whom I quote had all far more to say than I indicate. The
quotations which I give should not be taken to represent their
entire, or indeed their most important, remarks on the subject
of divorce reform.) Take at random two things which were
said in the course of the debate. Sir Tufton Beamish, member
for Lewes, who opposed the bill, said: "It is bound to have
the effect of unnecessarily increasing the number of broken
homes"; and under it, a woman "would suffer . . . the
misery that is part and parcel of being a deserted wife and
of course in many cases the children would stand to suffer
as well." Another opponent of the bill, Sir Lionel Heald,
member for Chertsey, was troubled by the passage in it which

deals with financial provision by the petitioner for the respondent. Such provision, says the bill, must be reasonable and fair "or the best that can be made in the circumstances." Sir Lionel said of the words in quotation marks, "I have never seen anything like that in a statute," and implied that they introduced a new principle into British law.

The appeal of both Sir Tufton and Sir Lionel was to *fact*, or putative fact. Sir Tufton appealed to what, as a matter of fact, in his opinion, would happen to some women and children if the bill became law. Sir Lionel appealed to what, as a matter of fact, can or cannot be found in the statute book of England. Both speakers could conceivably have been mistaken in what they took the facts to be. And indeed, so far as Sir Tufton was concerned, that is the argument with which Mrs. Lena Jeger, member for Holborn and St. Pancras, South, in effect, countered his remarks. She said that a law which made breakdown of marriage the sole ground of divorce would raise the status of both parties to a marriage. So far from it increasing the miseries of women, the women of the future would rejoice in it because it would give them greater equality with men.

All of this might suggest that the only difference between supporters and opponents of the bill lies in what they take the facts of the matter to be. A moral philosopher, reflecting upon such remarks as I have quoted, will ask himself: does this tell us what supporters of the bill *meant* when they said that it ought to become law, or opponents when they said that it ought not? Did the supporters mean by "ought" simply that, if the bill becomes law, it will, in fact, increase the happiness of the women of the future, or that its terms are not, in fact, unique in the statute book, or something like that? Did its opponents mean, by "ought not," the opposite? It may seem, superficially, that the answer is yes, because so much of the debate about what ought or ought not to be done was concerned with matter of fact. But the moral philosopher, as such, will not leave it there. He will notice that it *made sense*, when someone agreed with the bill's opponents as to the facts but said that nevertheless it *ought* to become law; and again, when someone agreed with the bill's supporters as to the facts

but said that it *ought not*. In the course of the debate, for example, the Solicitor General, Sir Arthur Irvine, appeared to
agree in effect with Sir Lionel Heald that the words "or the
best that can be made in the circumstances" would be new
to the statute book, but spoke *in favor* of the bill. Again,
Quintin Hogg, member for St. Marylebone, agreed with supporters of the bill that it would end misery for many people;
nevertheless, he inclined to the view that the bill ought not
to be passed into law. To the ordinary listener in the public
gallery, neither the Solicitor General nor Mr. Hogg would
have appeared to be contradicting themselves. But the former
would certainly have done so if "ought to be done," as ordinarily used, *meant* "is not new to the statute book," and
the latter, if it *meant* "will prevent misery."

Considerations such as these suggest to the moral philosopher that the meaning of "ought" and "ought not" must be
very carefully distinguished from the meaning of expressions
such as "is new to the statute book," "prevents misery," and
so on. He may wonder, of course, whether the trouble is
simply that he has not yet come across the expression of this
kind which *is* equivalent in meaning to "ought (or ought
not) to be done." He may try other expressions not unlike
"is new to the statute book" or "prevents misery." Many
moral philosophers have tried to find some such factual description with which to replace moral terms like "ought." But
many of them have come to the conclusion that none can
be found. Just as it makes sense to say "Ought what prevents
misery to be done?" or "Ought what is new to the statute
book to be enacted?" so, whatever expression is suggested as
equivalent in meaning to "ought," or "ought not," some such
question can be asked. When I say that it "can" be asked,
I use "can" in a logical sense. The point is that none of such
questions would seem to somebody who uses English normally
to be self-answering. But at least one of them would have to
do so (logically), if there were some factual description which
could be substituted, without loss or change of meaning, for
a moral judgment. *If* "ought to be done" *meant* "is X,"
where X is some matter of fact, then "Ought what is X to be
done?" would be self-answering. It would be meaningless in

the sense that it was a question which there is no point in raising because anyone who knew the meaning of the words used to ask it would thereby know the answer. But this question *is* meaningful. People who know the meaning of all the expressions used may differ as to the answer. Some may say that what is X ought to be done, some that it ought not. We may, of course, *disagree* with either side. But we should not consider that those who said that what is X ought to be done were merely uttering a *tautology*, or those who said that it ought not were *contradicting* themselves. This applies, be it emphasized, *whatever* matter of fact X refers to.

Reflections upon these lines lie behind the view now widely held among moral philosophers that it is logically impossible to define moral language in terms of nonmoral, or to derive "ought" from "is." "Ought to be" or "ought to be done" does *not mean* that something is, or is not, the case.

What then does it mean? What are people doing when they talk about what they ought to do, if not stating some specific fact about the consequences of doing it, or what some authority says on the subject, etc?

In this connection there is one thing which a philosopher, reflecting upon the Parliamentary debate about divorce reform, would have noted. Let us take, as an example of it, what Peter Mahon, member for Preston, South, had to say, when speaking against the bill. "This is legislation for marital pandemonium, or if you prefer it, the law of the jungle. . . . With the bill we are trying to pledge this country to eternal promiscuity. . . . If the bill makes its mark, Britain will indubitably be a philanderer's paradise." Mr. Mahon did not like the bill and wanted others not to like it; hence, his emotionally-charged language. "Marital pandemonium," "the law of the jungle," "eternal promiscuity," "a philanderer's paradise"—these are angry noises. They give vent to what Mr. Mahon feels on the subject and are intended to arouse similar feelings in others. The member for Preston, South, was doing what people often do in the heat of moral argument. He was using language in the way that propagandists and advertisers frequently use it, to play upon the emotions of his hearers rather than to appeal to their reason. Who wants "pandemonium" or a return to "the jungle"? Who would wish to be thought "promiscuous"—eternally so, to boot—or a "philanderer"? Mr. Mahon's intention was clearly to saddle the bill with these descriptions and so to direct upon it the opprobrium incapsulated within them. Anyone who uses English normally and who assents to Mr. Mahon's description of the bill will necessarily feel some disgust for it. He will be assenting, not so much to description, as to abuse.

The moral philosopher notices this emotive element in moral discourse, but he asks: is that all there is to it? He may well decide that it is not. The great majority of those members of Parliament who participated in the debate did not use Mr. Mahon's sort of language. They gave reasons for their judgments. And they worked with these reasons, to some degree at least, as rational men work with reasons in universes of discourse other than the moral. In a word, they recognized the need for *consistency*.

As an example of one thing which I have in mind here, let us take what Kenneth Lewis, member for Rutland and Stamford, said following upon Sir Lionel Heald's remarks referred to above. He claimed that it was self-contradictory to say that provision for a divorced wife should be "fair" and "reasonable," as the bill does, and then to go on to add "or the best that can be made in the circumstances." His point was that for the bill to say that the provision must be "fair and reasonable" and then, as he claimed it did, to say that the provision may be *either* that *or* "the best that can be made in the circumstances" *is* self-contradictory, because the latter expression admits the possibility of an unfair and unreasonable provision being made. One cannot meaningfully offer as a reason for action that which is self-contradictory. Anything follows from a contradiction. And where anything follows, no reason has been given for one thing rather than another.

The recognition of reason, or consistency, in the debate, however, went much further than this demand that the phrasing of the bill should not be self-contradictory. In effect, every speaker who offered a reason for saying that the bill ought, or ought not, to become law was appealing for consistency. Sir Tufton Beamish, as we saw, said that if it does become law it will cause unnecessary misery to many women. In effect, he was saying: "You believe, do you not, that whatever causes unnecessary misery to women is morally wrong? I am pointing out that this bill will cause it. I call on you, as rational men, to be consistent and oppose the bill." Mrs. Jeger, in her turn, was saying in effect: "You believe, do you not, that whatever gives women greater equality with men is morally right? I am pointing out that this bill will do so. I invite you, as reasonable men and women, therefore, to support it."

A distinction can be drawn between reasons which appeal for consistency in moral beliefs which everyone does, as a matter of fact, hold and those which appeal for consistency in beliefs which only some hold. Sir Tufton's appeal is an instance of the former. It may make sense to ask: ought one to do what will cause misery? But this is not a question which normal people *do*, in fact, ask. One can safely assume that, other things being equal, any member of our society will profess assent to the principle that one ought not to cause unnecessary misery. Sir Tufton was invoking a principle to which everybody who is not sick subscribes. Whether he was correct in saying that the passing of the Divorce Reform Bill would cause misery is, of course, another matter. But his appeal was for consistency in what everybody believes. Contrast it with the appeal which Mr. Emery, member for Honiton, made. He claimed, in effect, that the bill ought to become law because in divorce, there is never just one guilty party. But many people would say that if a bill is based on this belief it ought not to become law. "We ought to do whatever instantiates the opinion that, in divorce, there is never just one guilty party" is not a principle to which everyone, by any means, subscribes. Mr. Emery was setting up, rather than using, a standard of what ought to be done. Here the question which arises for the moral philosopher is: can moral discourse claim to be based in reason, as other types of discourse (e.g., scientific) are, if, as we have just seen, it allows those who participate in it to set up their own standards of what ought, or ought not, to be done? What should we make of a scientist who said: "I have my own method of determining what is true or false. Many scientists have other methods. But I am consistent in adhering to mine. So my discourse is grounded in reason"? Moral judgments, since they appear to allow those who pass them to make up their own reasons for doing so, are not like scientific hypotheses.

Such reflections may well lead the moral philosopher to another, and a deeper, question. Namely: how, then, are the reasons which are given for moral judgments related to them? I pointed out above that there seems to be a logical gap of some kind between factual reasons such as "This will prevent misery" and moral judgments such as "This ought to be done." Is there really such a gap between "is" and "ought"; and if so, how is it to be bridged? Are we to say that "the passing of this bill will prevent misery," though it has the appearance solely of a statement of fact concerning a particular bill, is really such a statement *together with* an incapsulated universal principle to the effect that whatever prevents misery ought to be done? Or are we to say that the expression "prevents misery" states a fact of a peculiar kind, a morally-loaded fact so to speak, such that, when you have said that anything "prevents misery" you have said that it ought to be done? If we take the former line, we are saying that there certainly *is* a logical gap between "is" and "ought." We are saying that an ought conclusion can only follow from an ought premise. No one could, therefore, get from the factual premise "This bill will prevent misery" to the ought conclusion "This bill ought to become law" without the aid of a major premise, "Whatever will prevent misery ought to become law." People do argue from the factual premise to the ought conclusion and what they say does not have the appearance of nonsense. What they are really saying, therefore, must include the major premise. If we take the latter of the above lines, on the other hand, we are, in effect, saying that there *is no* logical gap between "is" and "ought," in some instances at any rate. To say "X is what prevents misery" is to say "X ought to be done." Moral philosophers are at present busily engaged in debating the relative merits of these two ways of explaining what men are doing when they talk about what they ought to do.[2]

I hope that the *kind* of question with which the moral philosopher, as I have defined him, deals, will now have been made clear. In this book I shall be concerned with the sort of questions which we have seen would arise for a moral philosopher who reflected on the Parliamentary debate about the Divorce Reform Bill. Recall some of these questions.

Are moral judgments more like discoveries than decisions, or vice versa? We shall see why the intuitionists said that they are more like the former; and the prescriptivists, more like the latter.[3]

Can moral judgments be replaced, without loss or change of meaning, by any statements of nonmoral fact? We shall see why some philosophers, ethical naturalists as they may be called, have thought that the answer is yes; while others—intuitionists, emotivists, prescriptivists—have thought that the answer is no.[4]

Is the appeal in moral discourse primarily to emotion or to reason? This question raises many issues with which I shall deal in due course. We shall see what emotivists have meant when they said that the meaning of moral language is primarily emotive; and we shall see what criticisms can be brought against their point of view.[5] We shall see what pre-scriptivists mean when they say that reasoned argument on moral questions is possible.[6] And we shall see that their critics, the descriptivists, think that prescriptivism does not show this to be so because, on the prescriptivist analysis of moral discourse, it is logically possible for anyone who participates not only to form his own opinion on a moral issue but to choose for himself what shall, or shall not, count as evidence, and this, they hold, is not reasoning.[7] Descriptivists claim to have found a firmer ground in reason for moral discourse than the prescriptivists. There are, they maintain, certain specific con-

---

[2] See Chap. 6.
[3] Chaps. 3 and 5.
[4] See especially pp. 69—71.
[5] Chap. 4.
[6] Chap. 5.
[7] Chap. 7.

siderations, or kinds of consideration, which must (logically) count as evidence for, or against, a moral judgment in the minds of all reasonable men. We shall see that their view, in its turn, has not gone unchallenged by contemporary philosophers who hold fast to emotivism or prescriptivism.[8]

In all of this, the fundamental question is: what is the *meaning* of *moral* discourse? That will be our main concern throughout this book. Behind the question just stated, however, lies another and an even more fundamental one, namely: what *is* meaning? We can hardly see the meaning of moral discourse, if we have no view of meaning as such. First of all, then, I shall consider in the next chapter some of the theories of meaning to which modern moral philosophers have subscribed. I shall go on to show in subsequent chapters how these theories of meaning respectively form the background to the main types of modern metaethical theory.

The story which I have to tell in this book is of a discussion which has gone on for more than fifty years. It has become more interesting with each decade. At the present time, one of the liveliest areas of philosophical debate is that concerned with the meaning of moral language. I shall of necessity have to tell the story as it appears to me, selecting for attention those thinkers and developments which seem to me to have most notably advanced the subject. No two philosophers, I suspect, would tell the story in exactly the same way, for opinions are bound to differ as to what has been, or what is, most notable in modern moral philosophy. I can only hope that I shall be able to tell the story in sufficient detail and with enough accuracy and fairness for the reader to understand what, in the main, has been going on and to form a judgment of his own on some, at least, of the crucial points which have been, and are, at issue.

Is There a Connection between Moral Philosophy and First-Order Moral Discourse?

I have differentiated very sharply between moral philosophy and first-order moral discourse in this chapter—some may

[8] *Ibid.*

feel, too sharply. Even as I define it, is there not a connection between moral philosophy and what has been called first-order moral discourse?

I stand by my insistence that the two must not be confused. When we come to consider prescriptivism, I shall refer to the criticism that its foremost exponent mixes up what is called "the universalizability thesis" with the liberal principle that one ought to apply to oneself the same standards as one applies when judging others.[9] The thesis referred to is a *logical* one; the principle, a *moral* one. The former is a theory about what people are doing when they talk about what they ought to do; the latter is what some people say that they ought to do. One belongs to moral philosophy, the other to what may be called (in an entirely non-pejorative sense) moralizing. Below, I shall discuss this particular criticism of prescriptivism and argue that it is not well founded. All I wish to point out at the moment is that if anyone were unaware of the fact that it is one thing to make the moral judgment "We ought to be impartial," and quite another to offer the logical analysis "Moral judgments, as such, are universalizable," he would, indeed, be guilty of a great confusion. The two activities are quite distinct.

However, where two activities are distinct, the one may nevertheless imply the other. Is there any such connection between moral philosophy and first-order moral discourse? Obviously, there is. Just because philosophy is second-order talk, it implies the existence of the first-order talk which it is about. In that sense, moral philosophy implies moralizing. It is perhaps worth emphasizing something which follows from this. A moral philosopher, as such, needs to know as much as possible about what goes on in first-order moral discourse. If he has not taken part in very much moral argument or discussion, there is a presumption that he will not be a very good moral philosopher. There is always a danger that philosophers will go astray because they do not know enough about what they are talking *about*. It is notorious, for example, that in the philosophy of science and the philosophy

9 See pp. 230–31.

of religion, the instances of first-order discourse upon which philosophers, specializing in these fields, base their analyses, often strike practicing scientists and religious believers respectively as naive to the point of misrepresentation. A philosopher who writes about the logic of scientific discovery without having been a scientist, or who sets out to analyze religious belief without knowing at firsthand what it is like to be, or at least to have been, a believer, must, to say the least, be careful. The same point can be made about moral philosophy. Here, perhaps, there is much less possibility of a philosopher not really knowing what he is talking about. One could know little of science, and have no acquaintance with religious belief, but still feel quite at home in our contemporary society. But one would hardly feel at home if one were totally inexperienced in moral discourse. There is some distaste for such discourse nowadays, it is true, but it would be difficult to find anyone who has managed to opt out of moralizing, however pejorative that word may have become in his usage.

This connection, then, exists between moralizing (in my non-pejorative sense) and moral philosophy. The latter presupposes the former. Although I have said that it is an advantage for a moral philosopher to participate in first-order moral discourse, I must make it quite clear that I am not saying that he must (logically) do so in order to be a moral philosopher. I am only saying that he must have some acquaintance with what it is that he exists to analyze. If he reads a newspaper, watches television, or listens to people on trains and buses, he will not lack for material. He can (logically) know what he is talking about simply by listening to other people moralizing. It remains true that, for any individual, to philosophize about moral discourse is to do one thing and to moralize is to do another.

However, it may be instructive to pursue a little further the question: can the opinions which someone holds, as a moral philosopher, make any difference to any views, other than purely philosophical ones, which he holds where moral discourse is concerned? I am taking the "can" here to be a logical "can." It is very important, of course, to keep clearly in mind the distinction between *understanding* a universe of discourse and *participating* in it. But, given that distinction, does the understanding which anybody thinks that he has gained from moral philosophy have any important logical consequences beyond the realm of moral philosophy? In concluding this chapter, I shall refer to three respects in which I think that it does, or rather that it may.

First, from the opinions which a moral philosopher, as such, holds there will follow certain opinions as to what constitutes moral education and as to how the latter should be conducted. I am not saying, for a moment, that anybody has to be a moral philosopher in order to be a moral educator. Many parents and teachers make excellent moral educators without knowing anything about the sort of questions with which this book will deal. But if they do happen to be interested in moral philosophy, then from their opinions on certain philosophical questions, conclusions necessarily follow as to what it is *in* which they are educating their pupils. From these, in turn, there will follow certain conclusions as to how one must go about giving a moral education.

Take, for example, the very basic question: what makes a judgment moral? Some philosophers contend that it is the *form* of the judgment, or rather of the reasoning in support of it, which does so; others, that it is the *content*. I shall be writing at length about these two points of view in the sequel.[10] All I want to point out here is that if anyone thinks that what makes a piece of thinking moral is its *form*, then it would be logical for him to say that moral education is education in that form of reasoning. He might say, "We must give our pupils every opportunity to practice arguing with one another in the specifically moral way and it doesn't matter what they are arguing about." On the other hand, if anyone thinks that what makes a piece of thinking moral is its *content*, that for instance it is about the interests or wants which human beings have, then it would be logical for him to say that a moral education ought to make those who receive it aware of the interests or wants which people have. He might say, "We must

[10] See Chaps. 5, 6, 7 and 8.

show our pupils what miseries such-and-such things (e.g., apartheid, divorce, drugs, war, or whatever) cause." Perhaps, in practice, the difference noted here in moral philosophy will not make all that much difference to what anyone does in a moral education class. But it is enough for my purpose if it could make some difference. And I have tried to show that it could. From one's answer to the question "What makes a judgment moral?" there follows logically a certain answer to the question "What must we do in order to give a moral education?" There is, then, that connection between moral philosophy and training in first-order moral discourse. But it should be born clearly in mind that the question to which I have just referred, viz. "What must we do in order to give a moral education?" is an educational or a logical question, but *not* a moral one. The same goes for any answers to it. We have not here shown that a conclusion in first-order moral discourse can be derived from a premise in moral philosophy.

Secondly, the opinions which a moral philosopher, as such, holds may provide him with what he sees as a logical foundation for a point of view within first-order moral discourse. Take, for example, a philosopher who holds what is called "the universalizability thesis." We have already noted that this is a metaethical theory about what makes discourse moral, and I shall have much more to say about it below.[11] Putting things crudely for the moment, it is the theory that a judgment is moral if, and only if, the reasons given for it could conceivably apply to other cases than that which is being judged. If, for example, we give the fact that we are in situation S as a reason why we ourselves ought (morally) to do a certain action, A, we imply that anyone else in a situation of the same kind as S ought to do an action of the same kind as A. That is, we cannot (logically) make exceptions in our own case, if we are judging morally. From which it could conceivably follow that we are not judging *morally* unless we are judging a situation from a utilitarian point of view, i.e., the view that the greatest happiness ought to be aimed at and, in

[11] Chap. 5.

assessing it, everybody ought to count for one and nobody for more than one. This conclusion has been drawn by some. What does their inference amount to? It may look as though a philosophical view (the universalizability thesis) has implied a moral point of view (the greatest happiness principle). But has it? Let us assume that it can be shown that a judgment is not moral unless it is delivered from a utilitarian point of view. If it can, it is important to be clear what has been shown and what has not. So to speak, the rules of the moral "language-game," i.e., first-order moral discourse, have been made clearer. It has been shown that it is a rule of that "game" that unless we are judging with a view to what will maximize happiness we are not judging morally. In other words, if anyone says that something ought morally to be done, but does not support what he says by reasons which have regard to the maximization of happiness, then what he has said will make no sense. In moralizing, as in any other "game," we must (logically) keep the rules or the game is at an end. But we should bear clearly in mind that enunciating the rules of a game is different from playing it. To explain the conditions under which a goal may be scored is not to score one. To show what would constitute a reason within moral discourse is not to give a reason within that discourse. Once again, it has not been shown that a conclusion in first-order moral discourse can be drawn from a premise in moral philosophy.

Thirdly, it is generally true that philosophical reflection upon any type of first-order discourse can (logically and empirically) enable one to participate in such discourse more effectively. We may safely assume that this is so where moral discourse is concerned. I am not saying that a moral philosopher will always be a better moralist than a non-philosopher —far from it. In any " game," to draw that analogy once more, there are some who know the rules of the game but are very inexpert in playing it. If a team is playing football badly, what it needs is not more people who know the rules (every well-informed spectator does), but some better players. Similarly, if a society is deteriorating morally, what it needs is not more moral philosophers but more good men.[12] However, understanding what one is doing is seldom a disadvantage and, as I have said, we may assume that this applies to morality. A moral philosopher, as we have seen above, draws distinctions within moral discourse between matters of fact and matters of evaluation. He recognizes the points at which consistency is vital, if moral thinking is not to fall apart. He reflects on what considerations make a reason a *moral* reason. He is alive to the emotive nature of the language often used in moral argument, and so on. After all this, he ought to be able to think in a reasonably clearheaded way about moral issues, if he chooses to do so. Everyone knows, of course, that philosophers are frequently just as prejudiced and irrational in their moral opinions as anybody else. But not always. It was fashionable, a little time ago, for moral philosophers to say that they had nothing to do with first-order moral questions, and to leave these alone. There is some evidence that moral philosophers are turning their attention again to practical problems, such as what we ought to do about sex or war.[13] Such problems will not concern us directly in this book. But one may venture to hope that a reader who has worked through this book will be able to think about such matters more clearly than he might otherwise have done.

[12] I realize, of course, that, whereas a good football player may be defined simply as someone who plays football well, there is more to being a good man than being a good moralizer. Nevertheless, it would make sense to say that one of the necessary conditions of being a good man is that one should engage effectively in first-order moral discourse and the form of life which it constitutes. The fact that the word "effectively" in the last sentence covers a nest of metaethical problems does not affect this point.

[13] See, e.g., R. F. Atkinson, *Sexual Morality* (1965); and R. M. Hare's lecture *Peace* (Canberra, 1966). I am currently editing a series of monographs, *New Studies in Practical Philosophy*, to be published by Macmillan, which will include *inter alia* studies by analytical philosophers of a number of practical moral problems.

CHAPTER 2. MORAL DISCOURSE AND THEORIES OF MEANING

We saw in the last chapter that the main question with which modern moral philosophers have concerned themselves is: what is the meaning of moral language? Their differing answers to it have taken shape under the influence of theories about the meaning of language in general, not simply of moral discourse. During the period of philosophy with which I am concerned in this book there have been important developments in the general theory of meaning. For an understanding of modern moral philosophy it is essential to have some knowledge of these. In this chapter, therefore, my aim will be threefold. Within the limited space available, I will try: (i) to outline the theories of meaning which lie behind the main types of modern ethical theory; (ii) to show why some of them are mistaken; (iii) to give some indication of the influence upon modern moral philosophy which each theory of meaning has had.

Each of the theories of meaning to which I shall refer has been the subject of long and detailed argument among philosophers. To do these theories justice would require a whole book rather than a chapter. I can only hope that my treatment will not appear too superficial or hasty. But even at the risk of that, some attempt at an exposition of the relevant theories of meaning must be made. We cannot get into a position to assess the merits or demerits of the different types of modern ethical theory without considering the general theories of meaning to which they are related. In order to answer the question "What is the meaning of moral language?" it is necessary not only to be clear what moral discourse is, but also to have an opinion as to what meaning is.

The word "mean" and its cognates have many differing uses. It is important to emphasize that the sense in which I am using "mean" in this chapter is that in which it applies to *language*. Consider the following examples of other uses. In the case of each I will provide a synonym for "mean" or its cognate.

I mean to go. (intend)
Excess of expenditure over income means bankruptcy. (results in)
Life has lost its meaning for me. (purpose)
What is the meaning of your lateness? (explanation)
If he takes the 6:30, that means that he will be there before us. (implies)

There are numerous other uses, in which, as in these examples, "mean" and its cognates are used to talk about persons, actions, events, or things. But the sense of "mean" etc. which concerns us is different from all of these. To take one of the above examples, it is perfectly clear that there is a sense in which "excess of expenditure over income" does *not* mean "bankruptcy," because, if anyone substituted one of these expressions for the other in a speech-act, he would change its meaning. The quotation marks indicate that what we are talking about here is the *words* "excess of expenditure over income" and "bankruptcy." It is with the meaning of words, phrases, sentences, as used in speech-acts, that we are concerned in this chapter. Language is used to communicate something. Through it something is, or is not, understood. Its *meaning* is what it communicates, what is, or is not, understood. But to the question: what precisely *is* meaning in this sense? philosophers have given differing answers. Some of these I shall consider.

First, I shall turn to the referential theory of meaning, which seems to lie behind the ethical theory of those recent moral philosophers who are called intuitionists and, with a different result, behind the early Wittgenstein's views on ethics. Next, the verificationist and the causal, or psychological, theories of meaning will be discussed. These may be said to undergird the ethical theory called emotivism. The verificationist theory undergirds the emotivism of the early logical positivists; the causal, or psychological, theory, that of Professor C. L. Stevenson. In the final section, called *Meaning as Use,* I shall turn to some of the opinions about language held by the later Wittgenstein and J. L. Austin respectively. These opinions form a foundation for the ethical theories of the prescriptivists and descriptivists.

I. THE REFERENTIAL THEORY

Simplest Form of the Theory

This is the theory that the meaning of language is that which it names or to which it refers. There are different ways of indicating what language means, of course. We can define it ostensively, i.e., by pointing to its referent; or we can define it verbally, i.e., by naming, or referring to, its referent in other terms. If anyone asks what "the Prime Minister of Great Britain," for example, means, we may either point to a certain individual or say something like "the man who presides over the Cabinet." Language is about things, activities, qualities of objects, states of affairs, relations, etc.; but it all, according to the theory which we are now considering, means that to which it refers. If, in the last analysis, there is nothing in existence which a word names, then it has no meaning.

Some immediate objections to this theory spring to mind. It is sometimes represented as the theory of meaning which reflection on the ordinary use of language most naturally suggests. But, even with expressions which from the point of view of this theory are least problematic, i.e., the names of objects or persons, an appeal to ordinary language soon shows that the meanings and the referents of such expressions are not, in such language, to be equated. To take examples which others have used, according to the referential theory the meaning of the expression "the morning star" is the planet Venus. But whereas it would mean one thing to say "Venus has just exploded" or "The object referred to by the expression 'the morning star' has just exploded," it would surely mean something different, if indeed it meant anything at all, to say "The meaning of the expression 'the morning star' has just exploded." We might say naturally enough on some occasion "The person called N has gone away," or with the same meaning, simply "N has gone away," but it would be unnatural to the point of nonsense to say "The meaning of the name 'N' has gone away."[1] Two pieces of language may have the same referent but different meanings; or, again, the same meaning but different referents.[2] For example, the expressions "the son who was born to James Herbert and Ethel Wilson on March 11, 1916" and "the man who became Prime Minister of this country in October 1964" have the same referent. But that their meanings are different is clear from the fact that "the son who was born to James Herbert and Ethel Wilson on March 11, 1916, became Prime Minister of this country in October 1964" is not tautologous. For example again, the expression "Prime Minister" at this moment has at least two referents, viz. Harold Wilson and Ian Smith. But, as it stands, its meaning is the same with reference to either of them. "Harold Wilson is Prime Minister" and "Ian Smith is Prime Minister" convey the same information about their different subjects.

A More Sophisticated Version of the Theory

The referential theory of meaning is said to be capable of a formulation which avoids the sort of objections just noted. This "more sophisticated view" of it has been given as follows: "that the meaning of the expression is to be identified with the relation between the expression and its referent, that the referential connection constitutes the meaning."[3] One instance of this more sophisticated formulation, sometimes quoted, is Bertrand Russell's remark: "When we ask what constitutes meaning . . . we are asking, not who is the individual meant, but what is the relation of the word to the

---

[1] Cf. F. Waismann, *The Principles of Linguistic Philosophy* (London, 1965), pp. 312–13.

[2] Cf. W. P. Alston, *Philosophy of Language* (Englewood Cliffs, N.J., 1964), p. 13.

[3] Alston, *op. cit.*, pp. 12–13.

individual which makes the one mean the other."[4] Let us consider again the expression "Prime Minister." We saw that its meaning cannot be equated with any individual referent because it will have the same meaning when it refers to some other individual. We must note further that its meaning cannot be the *class* of Prime Ministers. If we wished to say "The class of Prime Ministers isn't what it was," we could not render this as "Prime Minister isn't what it was."[5] But, despite such considerations, it is in line with the more sophisticated version of the referential theory of which I am now speaking, to hold that the meaning of "Prime Minister" consists in the referential relation which subsists between this expression and the persons whom it denotes or connotes. The expression "Prime Minister" can be applied to all members of the class of Prime Ministers, whereas it cannot, to the members of any other class of persons (denotation). A necessary and sufficient condition of its being asserted correctly of anyone that he is a Prime Minister is (if the verbal definition suggested above is accepted) that he should preside over a Cabinet (connotation). The referential theory, in this sophisticated form, is to the effect that the meaning of language is made clear only by indicating that in the world to which it applies, or of which it can be asserted. You cannot say baldly that the meaning *is* the referent. But you can say that the meaning of language is not known until the persons or things, of whom or of which the language is asserted, are known.[6]

There seem to be at least two objections to this more sophisticated version of the referential theory. (i) If language is meaningful, only when there is that in the world of which it can be asserted, what are we to make of such elements in language as prepositions, conjunctions, or the modal auxiliaries of verbs? What things in the world are there to which words like "at" or "in" refer; or words like "and" or "but"; or "would" in "He would do it if he could?" These words are not meaningless and any theory which implies that they are

[4] Cf. Alston, *op. cit.*, p. 14; from B. Russell, *Analysis of Mind* (1921), p. 191.
[5] Cf. Alston, *op. cit.*, pp. 14–15.
[6] Cf. Alston, *op. cit.*, pp. 16–18.

must be mistaken. (ii) But even if there is some way of over-
coming that objection, the referential theory oversimplifies
the concept of meaning. Take the speech-act "X is good," as
an example. It might, with certain safeguards, be true to say
that it is meaningless, if it is not *about* anything, i.e., if there
is no such thing as X. But you have not revealed what its
meaning is when you have simply shown *what* it is about.
How is it about what it is about? Is it about X in the way that
a commendation is about its subject matter, or in the way that
a description is, or in what way? Until you have shown, not
simply *what* a piece of language is about, but *how* it is about
it, you have not shown the meaning of that piece of language.
The referential theory puts all the emphasis on "what about."
We are entitled, therefore, in the light of the distinction just
drawn, to say that it oversimplifies the concept of meaning.

Wittgenstein's "Picture Theory"

One extremely sophisticated version of the referential
theory of meaning is that developed by Ludwig Wittgenstein
in his *Tractatus Logico-Philosophicus* (completed in 1918
and first published in German in 1921 and in English in 1922).

Wittgenstein's earliest recorded remark concerning this picture theory is to be found in his *Notebooks 1914–16* and runs,
"In the proposition a world is, as it were, put together experimentally. (As when in the law-court in Paris a motor accident
is represented by means of dolls, etc.)" (entry dated Septem-
ber 29, 1914).[7] It is said that this picture theory occurred to
Wittgenstein while he was serving in the trenches as a member of the Austrian army. He there read a magazine which
contained an account of how an accident had been represented in the above way during a lawsuit. To the making of
any such model three things would go, namely: (i) objects
such as dolls, toy cars, etc. which symbolize the vehicles,
persons, or whatever, involved; (ii) a certain arrangement,
or configuration, of these symbols which represents the arrangement of the vehicles, persons, or whatever, in the
modeled situation; (iii) a convention, understood and ac-

[7] Cf. *T* 4.031.

cepted by all who use the model, whereby its several elements are related to their counterparts in the actual situation. (Where objects such as dolls and toy cars are used, of course it is obvious what they symbolize; but a model could be constructed in which, for example, matchsticks represented people, ink pots stood for cars, and so on). Wittgenstein claimed that language models, mirrors, or pictures reality as that model in the law courts represented the accident. It *refers* to the world in a similar way. A proposition presents a *logical picture* of a situation. What follows, concerning (a) language and (b) the world, from this theory of meaning?

(a) So far as language is concerned, Wittgenstein said that all meaningful language is analyzable into "elementary propositions."[8] He defined an elementary proposition as a "concatenation of names."[9] By "names" here he meant logically proper names; in that sense, a name is a simple sign which does not describe but designates, or denotes, that of which it is the name. Names are the elements of language. Each of them refers to one element in reality and to no other; and each element in reality has one name and no other. Of course, the propositions expressed in language, as it is normally used, are far from elementary in Wittgenstein's sense. The terms used in them can be replaced by other terms without loss or change of meaning, and these in their turn by yet others, and so on. But this replacing of words with words must have an end. Wittgenstein said: "A proposition has one and only one complete analysis."[10] A point will be reached eventually in the analysis of a proposition's meaning at which the signs used to express it are "simple" signs. That is, there is a one-to-one correspondence between each of them and some element of reality. It is logically necessary that we should reach such a point before we can know the precise meaning of a proposition. "The requirement that simple signs be possible," said Wittgenstein, "is the requirement that sense be determinate."[11] Language consists, in the last analysis, of elemen-

[8] *T* 4.221.
[9] *T* 4.22.
[10] *T* 3.25.
[11] *T* 3.23.

tary propositions, which in turn consist of simple signs or names.

(b) What follows from Wittgenstein's theory of meaning concerning the world to which language is taken to refer? Just as language consists of simple signs, so the world must consist of—to use Wittgenstein's term for the elements of reality—simple "objects." These "objects" are simple in the sense that we can refer to them only by naming them: we cannot describe them because this would only be possible if they were analyzable into other elements, as for instance a watch can be reduced to its parts. If there is to be meaning at all, on Wittgenstein's theory, then, just as language must break down into elements which determinately refer to reality, so reality must logically consist of elements to which determinate reference can be made. "Objects," said Wittgenstein, "make up the substance of the world."[12] He did not, however, think that they exist in isolation. He said: "The world divides into facts";[13] that is, into *Sachlagen* (situations or molecular facts) and, in the last analysis, into *Sachverhalten* (states of affairs or atomic facts). An atomic fact is a "combination of objects."[14] Language reduces, in the last analysis, to elementary propositions, i.e., "concatenations of names"; the world, to atomic facts, i.e., "combinations of objects."

A point, with regard to both language and the world, which we may note in passing, is that there is a difference, according to Wittgenstein, in the way that elementary propositions and names respectively refer to the world. He marked this difference by saying that names have *Bedeutung,* and elementary propositions, *Sinn*. In the light of this distinction he said: "The meanings (*Bedeutungen*) of simple signs (words) must be explained to us, if we are to understand them. With propositions, however, we make ourselves understood. It belongs to the essence of a proposition that it should be able to communicate a *new* sense (*Sinn*) to us."[15] What this means is as follows. We need to be told to what object a name refers

[12] *T* 2.021.
[13] *T* 1.2.
[14] *T* 2.01.
[15] *T* 4.026, 4.027.

but names do not change their meanings. If, however, we know to what objects the names within a proposition refer, then, even though we have never encountered these names in this particular configuration before, we can understand what the proposition means. A name which does not refer to an existing object has *no Bedeutung;* but a proposition which does not correspond to reality, provided the names of which it is composed are the names of existing objects, may nevertheless have *Sinn.* If there is in reality no object X, then the name "X" is meaningless; but though a proposition, e.g., "Exeter is in Cornwall," is false it is not thereby necessarily meaningless. "The world divides into facts": and facts may not only change, they may be imagined to be other than they really are. We can construct a world as it were experimentally. "Objects are what is unalterable and subsistent; their configuration is what is changing and unstable."[16]

I mentioned three elements which would go to the making of a model such as that used in the Paris court. We are now in a position to see that these correspond to the three conditions which according to Wittgenstein must be fulfilled if a proposition is to be, as he said it was, a logical picture of a situation or state of affairs. These conditions are:

(i) "In a proposition there must be exactly as many distinguishable parts as in the situation that it represents."[17] In the last analysis, a proposition consists of names only and it can therefore only represent a situation (which, in the last analysis, consists of atomic facts, these in turn consisting only of objects) if for every object in the situation there is a name in the elementary proposition which pictures it.

(ii) "The configuration of objects in a situation corresponds to the configuration of simple signs in the propositional sign."[18] This is illuminated by Wittgenstein's remark: "Only facts can express a sense, a set of names cannot."[19] The proposition pictures reality only because its elements (names) have the configuration which they do have, this configuration

[16] *T* 2.0271.
[17] *T* 4.04.
[18] *T* 3.21.
[19] *T* 3.142.

corresponding to that of the elements (objects) of the situation.

(iii) ". . . A proposition is a propositional sign in its projective relation to the world."[20] A proposition is not a propositional sign *simpliciter*. A propositional sign consists of words which express the proposition. This does not mean that a proposition, according to Wittgenstein, is a mysterious metaphysical entity. A proposition, he said, is a propositional sign (i.e., a sentence, written or spoken) *intended and understood to refer to reality*. He spoke of a "law of projection."[21] The elements of the propositional sign are related by laws, or rules, of projection with the elements of reality—as, for instance, certain notes on a musical score are related by convention to certain sounds. By intending the signs to have such references in the particular configuration which they have in this propositional sign, we "think of the sense of the proposition,"[22] i.e., we think of the situation which it represents.

It is important to remember that what Wittgenstein was concerned with was the analysis of the concept of meaning. He deemed his conclusions to follow with logical necessity from that concept. If there was to be meaning, then language and the world *must* consist in the last analysis of the "simples" of which he conceived. Asked for examples of a "name" or an "object," he replied that it was no part of his business, as a logician, to supply them.[23] He considered that he had fulfilled his analytical task simply when he had shown that "names" and "objects" there must be, if there is to be meaning.

I noted, in the last subsection, two objections to the sophisticated version of the referential theory of meaning; viz.: (i) it fails to explain the meanings of words like "in," "and," "would," etc.; (ii) it oversimplifies the concept of meaning. Wittgenstein was alive to the former of these at the time when he wrote the *Tractatus,* and we shall see how he tried to

[20] *T* 3.12.
[21] *T* 4.0141.
[22] *T* 3.11.
[23] N. Malcolm, *Ludwig Wittgenstein: a Memoir* (1958), p. 86.

dispose of it in that book. To the latter objection he became increasingly alive after the *Tractatus* was written, and eventually, in view of this objection, rejected his "picture theory" of meaning. I will say something about his treatment of each of these objections in turn.

(a) Prepositions, conjunctions, and modal auxiliaries, i.e., words like "in," "and," "would," etc., appear to correspond to nothing in the world but they are undoubtedly meaningful. What, on a referential theory, can their meaning be? Wittgenstein was clear in the *Tractatus* that words like "and," "not," "or," "if—then"—logical constants or connectives as they are sometimes called—are "not representatives."[24] Take "not" for instance. If "not" represented something, then the situation referred to by the expression "not not p" would contain two more things than that represented by "p" on its own. But "not not p" and "p" are normally taken to mean the same. Again, take "and" as an example. The proposition (A) "Fred is in his car and Bill is on his bike" may be analyzed into two more elementary propositions (A1) "Fred is in his car" and (A2) "Bill is on his bike." If (A1) is true and (A2) is true, then (A) is true. If (A1) is false or (A2) is false, or both are, then (A) is false. So the truth value of (A) depends only on the truth values of (A1) and (A2) respectively. We do not need to ask whether or not there is anything which "and" represents before we can know that A is true, if we know that (A1) and (A2) are true.

(b) In *Philosophical Investigations* (completed in 1949 and published posthumously in 1953) Wittgenstein realized that the *Tractatus* had oversimplified the concept of meaning. He set out the following objections among others to his own picture theory. I will arrange the following objections so as to show their bearing upon the three elements which go to the making of a model such as that used in the Paris law court, and upon the three conditions, corresponding to these, which, I said above, must be fulfilled if a proposition is to present a logical picture of a situation.

(i) It makes no sense, Wittgenstein said, to speak of an ab-

[24] *T* 4.0312.

solute one-to-one correlation between the simples of language and those of reality because reality cannot be broken
down *absolutely* into simples. "What are the simple constituent parts of which reality is composed?" he queried. "What
are the simple constituent parts of a chair?—The bits of wood
of which it is made? Or the molecules, or the atoms?—'Simple' means: not composite. And here the point is: in what
sense 'composite'? It makes no sense at all, to speak absolutely
of the 'simple parts of a chair.'" He pointed out that "we
use the word 'composite' (and therefore the word 'simple')
in an enormous number of different and differently related
ways." The visual image of a tree, for example, cannot be
said to consist of one kind of simples. You could break it
down into the different colors of which it is composed or alternatively into the tiny straight lines of which its outline is
composed. It makes sense to ask what the simples of any given
piece of reality are only when we have decided what kind
of simplicity is in question. "Is the color of a square on a
chessboard simple, or does it consist of pure white and pure
yellow? And is white simple or does it consist of the colors
of the rainbow?—Is this length of 2 cm. simple, or does it
consist of two parts, each 1 cm. long? But why not of one bit
3 cm. long, and one bit 1 cm. long measured in the opposite
direction?"[25] Questions which presuppose—as the picture theory presupposed—absolute complexity and simplicity, quite
apart from context, are unanswerable.

(ii) When you have analyzed a complex proposition into
elementary propositions—i.e., into simpler configurations of
words—you have not, said Wittgenstein, necessarily made the
sense of the original proposition thereby clearer. According
to the theory of meaning which he is now rejecting, the statement "My broom is in the corner" could be "further
analyzed," according to Wittgenstein, into a statement giving
the position of the stick and the position of the brush. "If the
broom is there, that surely means that the stick and the brush
must be there, and in a particular relation to one another."
This analysis is, as it were, "hidden in the sense of" the first

[25] *PI*, 47.

statement and "is *expressed* in" the *analysans*. But now he questions all this. "Then does someone who says that the broom is in the corner really mean: the broomstick is there, and so is the brush, and the broomstick is fixed in the brush? —If we were to ask anyone if he meant this he would prob- ably say that he had not thought specially of the broomstick or specially of the brush at all. And that would be the *right* answer, for he meant to speak neither of the stick nor of the brush in particular. Suppose that, instead of saying 'Bring me the broom,' you said, 'Bring me the broomstick and the brush which is fitted on to it!' Isn't the answer: 'Do you want the broom? Why do you put it so oddly?'—Is he going to un- derstand the further analyzed sentence better?"[26] The answer is, obviously, that he is not.

(iii) The *Tractatus* had said in effect that meaning is given to a proposition by a mental act, distinct from the publishing of the propositional sign, namely by "thinking of the sense of the proposition."[27] It would seem to follow from this that any sign could be used to mean anything, provided some such mental act gives it this meaning. Wittgenstein now said: "Make the following experiment: *say* 'It's cold here' and *mean* 'It's warm here.' Can you do it?"[28] He thought not. You cannot take a remark out of its appropriate language- game and give it any meaning you decide upon simply by thinking of that sense for the proposition.

With such arguments, then, Wittgenstein expressly repudi- ated his earlier referential theory of meaning and replaced it by one which takes account, not only of what language is about, but of *how* it is about what it is about. We shall turn to this later theory below.

The Referential Theory and Moral Discourse

There are two ways in which, given the referential theory of meaning, it is possible to deal with a moral judgment, such as "X is good." One of these ways was taken by the intuition- ists, whose moral philosophy will be considered below in

[26] *PI*, 60.
[27] *T* 3.11; cf. above, p. 28.
[28] *PI*, 510.

Chapter 3. The other was taken by the early Wittgenstein, to whose opinions about ethics I shall refer in the early part of Chapter 4.

If one subscribes to the former of the two ways of dealing with "X is good," one has to say that "good" must refer to something. The judgment "X is good" is meaningful. Given the referential theory, then, there must be some quality to which "good" refers. But whatever goodness may be, it is not a quality or property which can be apprehended by the physical senses, like redness or sweetness. It must, then, be assumed: (a) that there are such things as "nonnatural" qualities or properties of actions or states of affairs, to which words used in moral discourse, like "right," "good," "obligatory," refer; and (b) that men possess a faculty which apprehends these and which is distinct from the physical senses, that is, the faculty commonly called conscience and conceived of either as reason or as a peculiar "moral sense." The intuitionists believed that these assumptions can be justified. We shall consider in Chapter 3 how well founded that belief was.

According to the other way of dealing with "X is good," it is possible to say that "X is good" must be meaningless. It is a value judgment. As such, it is about what *ought* to be the case. If you hold to a picture theory you hold to the view that language is meaningful only when it refers to reality. But reality is what *is*, not what ought to be, the case. Therefore, a value judgment is not about reality and so it cannot (logically) be meaningful. In Chapter 4 we shall look more closely at Wittgenstein's development of this line of thought about ethics.

II. THE VERIFICATIONIST THEORY

Logical Positivism

The verificationist theory was propounded by the logical positivists. Originally, they were a group of philosophers, scientists, and mathematicians, who during the 1920's gathered around Moritz Schlick, professor of philosophy at Vienna, and became known as the Vienna Circle. Many of those who belonged to this Circle became renowned in philosophy, e.g., Carnap, Waismann, Neurath, Feigl, and others.

Wittgenstein was never a member but he associated with Schlick; and the Circle were deeply influenced by his *Tractatus*. The best-known British exponent of logical positivism is Professor A. J. Ayer, who attended the meetings of the Circle during the early 1930's. With the rise of the Nazis and the outbreak of war, the Vienna Circle dissolved.

Logical positivism has had a profound influence on philosophy during the past fifty years and this influence has extended to moral philosophy. To appreciate its influence on moral philosophy we need to understand the verficationist theory of meaning, to which the logical positivists subscribed, and of that theory I will offer a brief account.

Its classic formulation is that the meaning of a proposition is the mode of its verification. What precisely does that mean? Ayer expanded it thus: "A statement is held to be literally meaningful if and only if it is analytic or empirically verifiable."[29] By "literally meaningful" he intended "capable of being shown to be true or false." Put very summarily, what the logical positivists said about meaning comes to this. Analytic statements are verified, or falsified, simply by appeal to the definitions of the signs used in them. If they turn out to be tautologies, on such appeal, they are true; if contradictions, false. Mathematical and logical statements are of this kind. All other meaningful statements are such as can be verified, or falsified, by empirical observation, i.e., by the evidence of our physical senses. They are, in effect, hypotheses concerning future experience. If I say "There is a policeman in the garden," I am predicting that any normal person will, if he goes into the garden, see a policeman. If I say "There was a policeman in the garden yesterday," I am predicting what anyone would experience who set out to test this statement. If, for example, he did so by questioning my neighbors, he would hear the reply "Yes, there was." The statements of science, history, and common sense are meaningful by this criterion.

There has been a great deal of philosophical discussion about the verification principle, as the logical positivists' criterion of meaning is usually called. Two main questions have been raised concerning it. The first is: what is its correct formulation? The logical positivists themselves ran into great difficulties when attempting a formulation of it which would be neither too exclusive nor too inclusive. Scientific laws are universals to the effect that all A's are B. In order to verify this conclusively, one would need to observe all the A's in the universe; but it is logically impossible to be certain that one has ever done so. There may always be an A somewhere which is not B. It follows, if statements are meaningful only when they can be verified, that scientific laws are meaningless. If we substitute for the notion of verification that of falsification, the problem is not solved completely. A scientific law will then be one which can be empirically falsified; e.g., "All A's are B" is falsified if we find one A which is not B. We may then say that scientific laws are universal propositions which have hitherto escaped falsification. But this formulation of the criterion, though it may leave science intact, seems to play havoc with common sense. For, while it would allow us to say meaningfully, "There are no A's which are B" since this could be falsified by finding one A which was B, it would not allow us to say "There are some A's which are B" because that could not be falsified.[30] To avoid such conclusions, the verification principle was reformulated to the effect that a statement is meaningful if some observation statement can be deduced from it in conjunction with certain other premises, without being deducible from these other premises alone ("observation statement" here meaning a statement which records an actual or possible empirical observation). Will this do? Let us take the metaphysical statement "The Absolute is pure spirit" as the example. If this is conjoined with the premise "If the Absolute is pure spirit, then all cats are black," we may validly deduce from these two premises, though not from the latter alone, the observation statement "All cats are black." It follows that the metaphysical statement "The Absolute is pure spirit" is, by the reformulated principle,

[30] Cf. K. R. Popper, *The Logic of Scientific Discovery* (1959), *passim*.

meaningful.[31] All these conclusions, however, were repugnant to the logical positivists. The whole point of their movement was to laud science and common sense and to discredit metaphysics. The last thing they wanted from their criterion of meaning was that it should exclude the former and include the latter. We need not go further into the intricacies of the debate. Suffice it to remark that the dilemma does not seem ever to have been resolved satisfactorily. Ayer himself in his introduction to *Logical Positivism* recognizes that the verification principle has never been adequately formulated.[32]

The second question raised concerning this principle is: does it purport to be a lexical or a stipulative definition of "meaning"? Clearly it is not the former; in the ordinary sense of the word, ethical or metaphysical statements undeniably have meaning. Ayer recognizes this and remarks:

> It seems to me fairly clear that what they [the logical positivists] were in fact doing was to adopt the verification principle as a convention. They were propounding a definition of meaning which accorded with common usage in the sense that it set out the conditions that are in fact satisfied by statements which are regarded as empirically informative. Their treatment of *a priori* statements was also intended to provide an account of the way in which such statements actually function. To this extent their work was descriptive; it became prescriptive with the suggestion that only statements of these two kinds should be regarded as either true or false, and that only statements which are capable of being either true or false should be regarded as literally meaningful.[33]

Ayer conceded that it does not follow necessarily that we should accept this prescription; but he points out quite justifiably that metaphysicians have often posed as men doing the same sort of work as scientists only doing it more profoundly, whereas, in fact, it can be shown that, since their statements are neither analytic nor empirically verifiable, they are not. If the metaphysicians are not doing what the scientists

---

[31] See Ayer, *op. cit.*, pp. 11–12.
[32] Ayer, *Logical Positivism* (Glencoe, Ill., 1959), p. 14.
[33] *Ibid.*, p. 15.

are doing, then it is up to them to make it clear just what
they are doing and, in particular, how this differs from what
poets, preachers, or writers of fiction do.[34]

The Verification Principle and Moral Discourse

What, then, of moral judgments? It seems fairly clear
that they can be verified in neither of the approved ways. They
cannot be shown to be true or false by definition. "X is good"
is not to be verified by showing that "good" means X. Some
philosophers have in the past argued that it is, but we shall see
in Chapter 3 that they made a serious mistake. Briefly, this
was the mistake of overlooking the fact that whatever definition (D) you give of, for example, "good," the question "Is
what is D good?" is never self-answering. Again, goodness, as
we have already noted in this chapter, whatever it may be, is
certainly not a property which can be seen, smelled, tasted,
touched, or heard. We may speak figuratively of apprehend-
ing it in one or other of these ways, but we do not "see" goodness as we see tables and chairs, and similarly with reference
to the other senses. If "X is good" is not verifiable—or falsifi-
able—analytically or empirically, then, by the logical positivist
theory of meaning, it is meaningless. Great scandal was
caused when early logical positivists announced that ethics is
nonsense. It seemed a monstrous thing to say. Really, though
they did not always make this clear, they were using "nonsense" as a technical term. Ethics is "non-sense": i.e., it has
to do with that which cannot be observed by sense. Its judgments, according to the logical positivists, are therefore unin-
formative; they cannot be shown to be true or false, they lack
literal meaning. This, of course, does contradict the views
of those who believe in an objective moral order, i.e., objective
in the same sense as the physical world, and in moral truths
apprehended by intuition. But it does not exclude the possibility that moral judgments have some kind of meaning,
albeit not literal meaning. We shall see in Chapter 4 that the
emotivist theory appealed to Ayer and other logical positivists

[34] Cf. A. J. Ayer, "The Vienna Circle" in *The Revolution in Philosophy*
(1956), p. 76.

as the correct account of the meaning of moral judgments. However, Stevenson, the foremost exponent of emotivism, subscribed to a theory of meaning different from theirs. To this I shall now turn.

III. THE CAUSAL, OR PSYCHOLOGICAL, THEORY

Two Senses of Meaning

According to this theory, the meaning of language is its disposition to be caused by, or to cause, the occurrence of certain psychological processes in the speaker or the hearer respectively.

The psychological processes which cause, or are caused by, language can, of course, be investigated; and numerous investigations into this subject matter have been, and are being, carried on by psychologists. They are doubtless of absorbing theoretical interest; and profitable practical application is made of their results by advocates and advertisers of every sort. The question which concerns us, however, is not simply what psychological causes or effects language has. It is whether or not these psychological causes and effects of the use of language can be logically equated with its meaning.

We noted at the beginning of this chapter that there are different kinds of meaning, different ways in which the expression "to mean" and its cognates can be used. There are some ways in which "to mean" does appear to be equivalent to "to be caused by, or to cause, the occurrence of certain psychological processes." For example, suppose a headmaster puts on the school notice board the words "All those who were absent from prayers must see me at once." As they read it, the boys may say to each other, "That means he's in a rage." This remark is equivalent to "his saying that is caused by his rage." Again, suppose two people listen to a piece of music and afterward one of them says to the other, "That was full of meaning, wasn't it?" The meaning to which he refers is certain psychological effects, e.g., tranquillity, excitement, etc., which the music has had upon him and which he expects it to have had upon his companion. Such senses as these of "to mean" and its cognates undoubtedly exist; but we must differentiate them very sharply from another sense of "to mean" and its cognates which is quite distinct. This other sense is the one in which philosophers are primarily interested. That meaning in this other sense is logically distinct from the psychological causes or effects of the use of language can be shown, I think, in at least three ways, as follows. These considerations will make it clear what this other sense of meaning is.

(i) The meaning of a speech-act may be said to remain, whatever the psychological causes or effects of its occurrence are. Let us consider these examples of speech-acts:

(a) A command: "Get out."
(b) A statement: "He got out."
(c) A judgment: "He ought to get out."

A moment's reflection, and we realize that a speaker's utterance of any one of these might be caused by the occurrence of any one of a wide variety of psychological processes within him, e.g., anger, fear, envy, love, etc. Similarly each of the above speech-acts might, according to the nature and the circumstances of the hearer, have any one of a wide variety of psychological effects upon him, e.g., astonishment, amusement, delight, dismay, etc. The point to grasp is that, whatever the psychological process which causes, or is caused by, any of the above speech-acts, the meaning of the speech-act remains the same. "Get out" would mean the same, whether it was said because of the speaker's hatred or love for the hearer and whichever of these emotions it caused the hearer to have toward the speaker. Of course, "Get out" may not always mean the same thing. My point is not that it does. It is rather that any given meaning of this speech-act could logically remain constant, whatever variety in the psychological causes or effects of its utterance there might be. And as with commands, so with statements, judgments, and any other speech-acts. It follows that the meaning of the speech-act cannot be equated with any psychological processes whose occurrence it is caused by, or causes.

(ii) If the psychological theory of meaning were correct, some absurd consequences would follow. Consider what, if that theory were correct, it would mean to disobey a command, to disbelieve a statement, or to disagree with a judgment. According to the psychological theory of meaning (leaving aside possible refinements of this account), the meaning of a command is the activity which it causes, the meaning of a statement is the belief which it occasions, and the meaning of a judgment is the assent which it gains. Now, to disobey a command is not to act upon it; to disbelieve a statement is not to believe it; and to disagree with a judgment is to withhold assent to it. But, if the psychological theory of meaning were correct, a command which was disobeyed, a statement which was disbelieved, and judgment which occasioned disagreement, would all be meaningless. They would not cause to occur the psychological processes which constitute their meaning and so they could have no meaning. This is manifestly a *reductio ad absurdum*. For it just is not open to anyone, in this way, to make what is said to him meaningless. Suppose I said to a hearer "Get out" and he stayed where he was; or I said "He got out" and my hearer disbelieved it; or I said "He ought to get out" and my hearer replied "I don't agree." In no instance, on these suppositions, does my speech-act become meaningless. There is, then, a sense of "meaning" in which it is absurd to suggest that a speech-act could be evacuated of its meaning by any effects which followed, or failed to follow, from it.

(iii) The meaning of language (in the sense of meaning which I am here attempting to distinguish and clarify) is discovered through its logical, not its causal, explanation. To see the difference between these two types of explanation, recall the command, the statement, and the judgment instanced under (i) above. Someone might ask, in each case, why the speaker says what he does. This question can, on the one hand, be taken to seek a causal explanation. What caused him to say what he has said? The answer will reveal the mechanism which produced—that is, the train of psychological events which resulted in—the utterance, by such-and-such a man at such-and-such a time in such-and-such circumstances, of this remark. Psychologists do build up hypotheses about what

such-and-such kinds of people at such-and-such times say
in such-and-such circumstances, and then apply these generalizations to particular instances. The final appeal throughout is to the empirical observation of causally connected
psychological events. That is causal explanation.

On the other hand, when we ask why someone says what
he says, we may be seeking something else, namely its logical
explanation. We want to know, that is, not what its cause was
but what the *reason* was for saying it rather than something
else. It is true, of course, that the word "reason" is sometimes
used loosely with the same meaning as "cause." But there is
a use of "reason" in which it is logically distinct from "cause";
and that is the sense in which I am using the word here. Why
does a given speaker say X? The logically explanatory answer will be: because he purports to utter a command, or
state a fact, or express a judgment, or to perform whatever
speech-act X purports to be, *and X is how to do it.* That is the
reason for saying X rather than anything else. This explanation of what has been said appeals, not to hypotheses as to
what people *do* say, but to rules or norms concerning what
to say. A logical explanation of language explains it by showing that what the speaker is doing with it is the thing to do
with it, if you purport to communicate to your hearers what
the speaker is taken to purport to communicate. When and
only when we have shown that a speaker is doing with language the thing to do with it—that is, is using it in accordance
with such-and-such rules or conventions—have we shown that
it has meaning and what its meaning is, in the sense of meaning which I am here seeking to distinguish and to clarify.

The psychological, or causal, theory of meaning has perhaps continued to attract adherents because it is, despite all
I have been saying, nevertheless true to say that language is
meaningful when it produces a certain effect in those who
hear it. But this effect, note well, is *understanding.* The important point to take against the psychological theory is that
producing understanding in one's hearers is logically quite
unlike getting them to act on a command, or believe a statement, or agree with a judgment. Professor J. R. Searle points

this out by considering what it is to understand the sentence "Hello." He writes:

1. Understanding the sentence "Hello" is knowing its meaning.

2. The meaning of "Hello" is determined by semantic rules, which specify both its conditions of utterance and what the utterance counts as. The rules specify that under certain conditions an utterance of "Hello" counts as a greeting of the hearer by the speaker.

3. Uttering "Hello" and meaning it is a matter of (a) intending to get the hearer to recognize that he is being greeted, (b) intending to get him to recognize that he is being greeted by means of getting him to recognize one's intention to greet him, (c) intending to get him to recognize one's intention to greet him in virtue of his knowledge of the meaning of the sentence "Hello."

4. The sentence "Hello" then provides a conventional means of greeting people. If a speaker says "Hello" and means it he will have intentions (a), (b), and (c), and from the hearer's side, the hearer's understanding the utterance will simply consist in those intentions being achieved. The intentions will be achieved in general if the hearer understands the sentence "Hello," i.e., understands its meaning, i.e., understands that under certain conditions its utterance counts as a greeting.[85]

The appeal in this explanation is not to empirically observed causal connections between the utterance of language and the occurrence of psychological processes, but to rules or norms for the use of language.

F. Waismann in *The Principles of Linguistic Philosophy* sums up what I have been endeavoring to say thus: "We look upon language not as a mechanism but as a calculus."[86] He gives, as instances of transition according to a calculus, moves in chess, addressing envelopes from a list of addresses, passing from the name of a color to that color on a chart, solving

[85] J. R. Searle, *Speech Acts: An Essay in the Philosophy of Language* (Cambridge, 1969), p. 48–49.
[86] Waismann, *op. cit.*, p. 124.

an algebraic equation by transforming it step by step according to the rules of algebra, and drawing a conclusion from premises according to the propositional calculus. Then he says:

> What, then, is the difference between a causal connection and a transition in a calculus? What is the difference between a calculation formed by a machine, and that made by a person? Or else between a musical box playing a tune and person playing it? One point at any rate is this: the playing or calculation of a person can be justified by rules which he gives us when asked; not so the achievements of a machine, where the question "Why do these keys spring out?" can *only* be answered by describing the mechanism, that is by describing a causal nexus. On the other hand, if we ask the calculator how he comes to his results, he will explain to us what kind of calculation he is doing and then adduce certain laws of arithmetic. He will not reply describing the mode of action of a hidden machine, say, a machine in his brain.[37]

Language *can* operate as a mechanism, as we noted at the beginning of this subsection. A speech-act may be connected with certain psychological processes in the hearer or speaker in such a way that its utterance releases, or is released by, their occurrence, in much the same way that a switch can be operated by, and in its turn operate, other parts of a machine. But, says Waismann, speaking for philosophers who share his approach to the theory of meaning, "we do not *regard* language in its mechanical aspect, but in its aspect as a calculus, that is in so far as it is guided by rules."[38] The rules to which he refers are such as lay it down that "red," for instance, is the sign for a certain color. When we use the word in accordance with that rule it has meaning. It may, of course, have other meanings: there may be other rules according to which it is the word for a Communist. But if there is no rule by reference to which we can read off its meaning, then it has no meaning.

[37] *Ibid.*, p. 122.
[38] *Ibid.*

It would be one thing for a philosopher to point out that there are different kinds of meaning and, as examples, to contrast the use of the word "meaning" in the remark quoted earlier in this subsection with regard to music ("That was full of meaning, wasn't it?") with "meaning" in the sense in which I have been attempting to distinguish and clarify it later on in this subsection. But this is *not* the kind of thing which proponents of the psychological theory of meaning have done. They have entered a discussion, going on among philosophers, which, when examined carefully, is seen to be about meaning in the latter of the two senses to which I have just referred, a discussion, that is, about what it is to understand language, about its logical explanation. Then they have, in effect, said that meaning *in this sense* is equivalent to meaning in another sense: the sense in which the headmaster's notice meant that he was angry or in which the music was full of meaning for one of its hearers. And that is simply a confusion.

The Psychological Theory and Moral Discourse

Professor C. L. Stevenson, the foremost exponent of the ethical theory called emotivism, subscribes to the psychological theory of meaning. This makes it possible for him to recognize that it is not enough to ask what language is about. If we wish to get at its meaning we must ask also *how* it is about what it is about. When we ask that question about moral judgments we see that they have a dynamic character. They do not, or not simply, describe nonnatural states of affairs. Moral judgments exert a "magnetism," to use Stevenson's word; that is to say, if anyone sincerely assents to the judgment "X is good" he must *ipso facto* acquire thereby a stronger tendency to act favorably toward X. Again, moral judgments, to use Stevenson's phrase, "create an influence"; to tell anyone that X is good is to bring a kind of pressure to bear upon him, where X is concerned, so that he will act favorably toward it. This view of moral discourse ties in with the theory that the meaning of language is its disposition to cause, or be caused by, certain psychological processes in the hearer or speaker respectively. But, like all adherents of the psychological theory, Stevenson, as we shall see in Chapter 4, failed to distinguish between the causal, and the logical, explanation of language. He recognized that the question to ask is: how is moral language used? But he confused the causes of, with the reasons for, the use to which moral discourse is put.

IV. MEANING AS USE

In this section I want to say something about ideas concerning language which have been held by the later Wittgenstein and J. L. Austin. These ideas have been highly influential in contemporary analytical philosophy. To give an adequate account of either the later Wittgenstein or Austin would require far more space than is available here. In the case of each, two questions arise: what precisely did this thinker take meaning to be? and, was he correct in so far as we are able to discern what he took it to be? These questions are still being investigated in depth by modern philosophers and alternative answers to them, debated. I hope that I can say enough about them to give some impression of how the most recent developments in moral philosophy are related to the ideas about language found in Wittgenstein's *Philosophical Investigations* (Oxford, 1953) and J. L. Austin's *How To Do Things with Words* (Oxford, 1962).

The Later Wittgenstein and the Need to Look *at the Use to Which Language Is Put*

The central idea in Wittgenstein's picture theory of meaning was as follows: "What any picture, of whatever form, must have in common with reality, in order to be able to depict it—correctly or incorrectly—in any way at all, is logical form, i.e., the form of reality."[39] Wittgenstein eventually rejected this basic idea that, for language to be meaningful, it must represent some configuration of "objects," some "logical form," which exists in the objectively real world.

Professor Norman Malcolm in his *Memoir* on Wittgen-

[39] *T* 2.18.

stein tells a story about how the latter was weaned away
from his picture theory by his friend, P. Straffa, a lecturer in
economics at Cambridge. To the stimulus of Straffa's criticism, by the way, Wittgenstein attributes the most consequential ideas of his *Investigations* in his preface to that book.
Malcolm's story is that Straffa and Wittgenstein were travel-
ing on a train one day during the early 1930's and Wittgenstein was insisting that a proposition and what it describes
must have the same "logical form." Malcolm goes on: "Straffa
made a gesture, familiar to Neapolitans as meaning something like dislike or contempt, of brushing the underneath of
his chin with an outward sweep of the fingertips of one hand.
And he asked: 'What is the logical form of *that?*' Straffa's
example produced in Wittgenstein the feeling that there was
an absurdity in the insistence that a proposition and what
it describes must have the same 'form.' This broke the hold
on him of the conception that a proposition must literally
be a 'picture' of the reality it describes."[40] Wittgenstein's
reasons for eventually abandoning that theory—or some of
them—have already been indicated briefly.[41] We must now
see what he put in place of the picture theory of meaning.

Wittgenstein believed that he had been wrong in the *Tractatus* because he had tried to impose on language a preconceived idea of what its meaning ought to be. He came to think
that what he should have done instead is to *"look at* its use
and learn from that."[42] He added: "The difficulty is to remove the prejudice which stands in the way of doing this."[43]
When one does overcome prejudice and takes such a look at
language, one sees, said Wittgenstein, that there are a great
many different uses to which it is in fact put. He compared
words to tools and said that the functions of language are
as diverse as those of the tools in a toolbox.[44] "Look at the
sentence as an instrument," he wrote, "and at its sense (*Sinn*)

[40] Malcolm, *op. cit.*, p. 69; Malcolm notes that this story exists in
differing versions.
[41] Above, pp. 29–31.
[42] *PI*, 340.
[43] *Ibid.*
[44] *PI*, 11.

as its employment."[45] Again, he spoke of these different
uses to which language may be put as so many "language-
games." The following quotation sums up in terms of "language-games" the point of view at which Wittgenstein had
arrived when he wrote his *Investigations*.

But how many kinds of sentence are there? Say, assertion, question, and command?—There are *countless* kinds:
countless different kinds of use of what we call "symbols,"
"words," "sentences." And this multiplicity is not something
fixed, given once for all; but new types of language, new
language-games, as we may say, come into existence, and
others become obsolete and get forgotten. (We can get a
rough picture of this from the changes in mathematics.)
Here the term "language-*game*" is meant to bring into
prominence the fact that the *speaking* of language is part
of an activity, or of a form of life. Review the multiplicity
of language-games in the following examples, and in others:
Giving orders, and obeying them—
Describing the appearance of an object, or giving its
measurements—
Constructing an object from a description (a draw-
ing)—
Reporting an event—
Speculating about an event—
Forming and testing a hypothesis—
Presenting the results of an experiment in tables and
diagrams—
Making up a story; and reading it—
Play-acting—
Singing catches—
Guessing riddles—
Making a joke; telling it—
Solving a problem in practical arithmetic—
Translating from one language into another—
Asking, thanking, cursing, greeting, praying.
—It is interesting to compare the multiplicity of the tools in
language and of the ways they are used, the multiplicity of
kinds of word and sentence, with what logicians have said

[45] *PI*, 421.

about the structure of language. (Including the author of the *Tractatus Logico-Philosophicus*.)[46]

Philosophical perplexity arises, said Wittgenstein, where there is confusion between language games. An example of what he meant—though not one which he used—occurs when anyone asks with what sense moral rightness is perceived. If such a question were asked about redness or hardness, instead of moral rightness, it would be easy to understand and to answer. The person who asks this question about moral rightness assumes that to speak of the latter is to do the same kind of thing as to speak of redness or hardness. That is his mistake and the occasion of his perplexity. Since it is apparent that we do not apprehend moral rightness with one of our physical senses—as we apprehend redness with sight or hardness with touch—he concludes that there must be some other sense with which we do so. A great deal of discussion has gone on in the past among moral philosophers as to what this "moral sense" might be. But it is all based on a confusion which is, at bottom, a confusion between the language game of sense perception and that of moral judgment. A question is asked which would fit well enough into the former of these, and it is assumed that an answer to it must therefore be discoverable in the latter. We shall look into this particular confusion about "moral sense" more carefully in Chapter 3.

Depth Grammar, Forms of Life, and Moral Discourse

Wittgenstein spoke of philosophy in *Investigations* as "a battle against the bewitchment of our intelligence by means of language."[47] The sort of bewitchment which he had in mind was the kind of confusion to which I have just been referring. In two ways particularly, according to Wittgenstein, the bewitchment is effected. (i) We can be tempted "to draw some misleading analogy,"[48] or, in other words, be held

[46] *PI*, 23.
[47] *PI*, 109.
[48] Wittgenstein, *The Blue and Brown Books* (Oxford, 1960), p. 48.

captive by a picture. A famous example of this is St. Augustine's puzzlement as to how time can be measured. In effect, Augustine pictured time as a stream flowing past us. If we lay a measuring rod alongside this stream, in order to measure time, the task is impossible for the following reasons. Our measuring, whenever we do it, will necessarily be done in the (then) present. We cannot, therefore, measure an interval of time in the (then) past because it is no longer there in the (then) present to be measured. For the same reason, neither can we measure an interval of time in the (then) future. Moreover, the present which, in that it is the (then) present, we could measure, cannot, in fact, be measured because it is not more than a point. We cannot, therefore, measure past, present, or future. So we cannot measure time at all. This is a logical "cannot." As a matter of fact, however, we *do* measure time—we say "It took four hours," "I'll come for tea at four fifteen," and so on. How can these things be? Now, such puzzlement arose simply because Augustine succumbed to the temptation to draw a misleading analogy, viz. between how space is measured and how time is. We take spatial measurements by laying a measuring rod alongside the objects to be measured. But we measure time by agreeing that such-and-such natural events, e.g., the rising and setting of the sun, or such-and-such artificially contrived events, e.g., the point-by-point unwinding of a spring, shall constitute *termini a quo* or *ad quem*. Units in the time span are marked off by the occurrence of such events, not by laying a measuring rod against something called time.[49] Once we free ourselves from captivity to the picture of spatial measurement, the puzzle about how time can be measured dissolves.

(ii) The second way in which the bewitchment of our intelligence by means of language takes place is through the confusion of what Wittgenstein called respectively "surface grammar" and "depth grammar."[50] By the former he meant the way in which words are used in the course of a sentence; by the latter, he meant, I think, the use to which words are char-

---

[49] Wittgenstein refers to Augustine on time; *ibid.*, p. 26.
[50] *PI*, 664.

acteristically put in their own language game. As I pointed out in the last subsection, an example of philosophical perplexity or "bewitchment"—though not one which Wittgenstein himself used—can be found in moral discourse. The sentence "X is right" is syntactically similar to "X is red"—i.e., similar in "surface grammar." A noun, X, is coupled by the third person singular present indicative of the verb "to be" with an adjective. This sentence "X is red" describes X; it attributes to it a feature which is visible to the normally sighted. This is its "depth grammar." It is a sentence which belongs within the language game of describing physical objects in terms of their colors. Now, there is a temptation to think of "X is right" as though it were similar in depth grammar as well as surface grammar to "X is red." Of course, everyone knows that rightness is not visible as redness is. But "X is right" looks like a description of X just as much as "X is red" does. Because they have assumed that this is what it must be, "moral sense" philosophers and intuitionists generally have assumed: (a) that rightness must be a property of some kind; and (b) that we must "see" it in some sense of the word. But what if the basic error lies in regarding "X is right" as a description? Its "surface grammar" could have "bewitched" philosophers into mistakenly supposing that such was its "depth grammar." We shall find reason in Chapter 3 to think that this is just what happened.

Two further points which Wittgenstein made about language games were as follows. One concerns what he calls "forms of life." He said: ". . . the term 'language-*game*' is meant to bring into prominence the fact that the *speaking* of language is part of an activity, or of a form of life."[51] The other concerns the "tacit presuppositions" on which, according to Wittgenstein, language games are based. He said: ". . . what we do in our language-game always rests on a tacit presupposition."[52] I will take them in turn.

(i) Language does not exist in a vacuum. It is, to use Wittgenstein's own word, "woven"[53] into other activities.

[51] *PI*, 23.
[52] *PI*, p. 179.
[53] *PI*, 7.

There is a cryptic remark toward the end of *Investigations:* "If a lion could talk, we could not understand him."[54] Dr. G. Pitcher endeavors to illuminate it as follows:

> Suppose a lion says "It is now three o'clock" but without looking at a clock or his wristwatch—and we may imagine that it would be merely a stroke of luck if he should say this when it actually *is* three o'clock. Or suppose he says "Goodness, it is three o'clock; I must hurry to make that appointment," but that he continues to lie there, yawning, making no effort to move, as lions are wont to do. In these circumstances—assuming that the lion's general behavior is in every respect exactly like that of an ordinary lion, save for his amazing ability to utter English sentences—we could not say that he has *asserted* or *stated* that it is three o'clock, even though he has uttered suitable words. We could not tell what, if anything he has asserted for the modes of behavior into which his use of words is woven are too radically different from our own. We would not understand him, since he does not share the relevant forms of life with us.[55]

The point which is being made here applies to moral language. Try to imagine somebody who utters the sentence "X is morally good," but there is nothing else whatever in his behavior which we would recognize as expressive of moral approval toward X; nothing, in what the speaker does himself or refrains from doing; nothing, in his attitudes toward other people. It is true, of course, that many people fail to practice what they preach. But what I now ask the reader to imagine goes far beyond what we mean by that. It is a man whose entire behavior indicates that the putative fact that X is morally good which his judgment announces does not make any difference to him beyond the utterance of "X is morally good." Should we not naturally say of such a man that he does not mean, or does not understand, what he is saying?

[54] *PI*, p. 223.
[55] G. Pitcher, *The Philosophy of Wittgenstein* (Englewood Cliffs, N.J., 1964), p. 243.

To take an example, let us imagine a small party of Martians[56] arriving on earth and speaking in terms of "moral" approval or disapproval about matters which we never think of discussing in such terms. Should we understand them or not? Some philosophers, we shall find, are inclined to say that we should not be able to recognize their discourse as moral in our sense of the word at all, because what makes our discourse "moral" is its content. Other philosophers hold that, for all its difference of content, if the Martians' discourse had the same *form* as our moral discourse, then we should certainly recognize it as moral. What respectively these philosophers take the content and the form of moral discourse to be we shall see in due course. All I wish to say at the moment is this. If Wittgenstein was right about language being woven into forms of life—and I am inclined to think that he was—then, even if a Martian's "moral" discourse had both the same content and the same form as ours, unless there was something in his behavior, besides the utterance of sentences in moral terms, which indicated moral approval, then he would resemble Pitcher's lion in our eyes. We should not be able to recognize what he was engaging in as moral discourse at all. He would not share the relevant form of life with us.

(ii) What of Wittgenstein's view that language games, or forms of life, are, based on "tacit presuppositions"? I think the point to take here is that the demand for a justification of what is said has to stop somewhere. Every language game goes down in the last analysis to certain concepts, or rules of inference, or both, which are tacitly presupposed and which logically constitute that universe of discourse. An example would be the concept of a physical object. The empirical evidence, on the basis of which we talk about physical objects, is discontinuous. Now we see the table; now we go into the next room and see it no longer; now we return and there it is. Though there has been a break between our observations of it, we nevertheless think of it as identical on the two occasions. Someone may raise the question: are we entitled to do so? In ordinary discourse, there are accepted ways of de-

[56] Cf. Chap. 7. iv.

ciding that question: conditions which must normally be fulfilled if a table which we see on one occasion is to be taken for the same table as we saw on another. But even where such conditions are fulfilled, our questioner may persist with his question. We make statements about physical objects on the strength of our experience of them. In doing so, we speak of these objects as continuous existents, for physical objects are always so conceived though their continuity may be of short duration. But our observation of physical objects is, if not invariably, at least characteristically, discontinuous. There is a logical gap here, then, between evidence which is *discontinuous* and what it is invoked to support which is *continuous*. Are we entitled to jump this gap as we do? asks our persistent questioner. Professor P. F. Strawson, dealing with the skeptic who answers that question in the negative, points out that "a *condition* of our having this conceptual scheme is the unquestioning acceptance of particular-identity in at least some cases of non-continuous observation."[57] The skeptic, says Strawson, ". . . pretends to accept a conceptual scheme, (*sc.* that of common sense or natural science in which we speak of physical objects on the strength of empirical observation) but at the same time quietly rejects one of the conditions of its employment. Thus his doubts are unreal, not simply because they are logically irresoluble doubts, but because they amount to the rejection of the whole conceptual scheme within which alone such doubts make sense."[58] Doubts about whether or not we are entitled to regard our observations as observations of the same object make sense within the scheme of common sense or natural science, where there are accepted ways of deciding whether or not they are well founded. But doubts which strike at the rules of inference tacitly presupposed by, and constitutive of, this whole conceptual scheme itself, are in Strawson's sense "unreal." That is, they are doubts which reject any settlement of them in the only place where that kind of doubt

[57] P. F. Strawson, *Individuals* (1959), p. 35.
[58] *Ibid.*

could be settled, namely the language game in which we speak of physical objects.

All modern moral philosophers—even those who antedate the later Wittgenstein—have aimed at clarifying the ultimate concept(s) and the rules of inference of the moral universe of discourse. They have asked: in the last analysis, what *is* moral obligation? The intuitionists believed it to be something which we discover, grounded in objective reality. The emotivists have taken it for a feeling which we have toward certain courses of action. The prescriptivists have judged it to be a decision which we make. The descriptivists or neo-naturalists have thought of it as, to say the least, essentially connected with certain natural properties which objects or actions have. Again, modern moral philosophers have asked: in the last analysis, what is the logical structure of moral reasoning? Does it proceed by invoking decisions of moral principle, one, or some, of which are the ultimate logical constituents in any moral judgment? Or are there moves, e.g., from what men in fact *want* to have or do to what they *ought* to have or do, which, though questioned by some skeptics, are such that their rejection amounts, to recall Strawson on skeptics, "to the rejection of the whole conceptual scheme" of moral discourse? Some say that, if the fact that all men want something does not count with you as a reason for saying that one ought to attain it, then whatever your reasoning may be, it is not moral reasoning. Others, we shall see, stoutly deny this.

The later Wittgenstein's influence becomes more and more apparent as the story of modern moral philosophy unfolds. The most recent moral philosophers have tried to take his advice and *look* at moral discourse with eyes unprejudiced by any preconceived theory of meaning. They have asked: what is moral language *for?* What job does it do? How is this job like, and how unlike, other uses to which language is put?[59] They have tried to avoid any "bewitchment" of their intelligence by means of language which would mislead them

[59] E.g., P. H. Nowell-Smith, *Ethics* (1954), pp. 95–100 and *passim.*

into oversimplifying the meaning of moral discourse or confusing it with discourse of other kinds.

J. L. Austin and What We Do with Words

In *How to Do Things with Words*[60] Austin distinguished three kinds of thing which we can do with words, calling these respectively locutionary, illocutionary, and perlocutionary acts. Much use of this distinction has been made in modern discussions about the theory of meaning. In particular, the question as to which of them, or which combination of them, constitutes the meaning of a speech-act has been, and is still being, debated. I can do little more than scratch the surface of the matter here, but I will try to give some account of it, and, in particular, to give some indication of the effects which Austin's threefold distinction, and the questions which it raises, has had on contemporary moral philosophy. First, the three kinds of thing which we can do with words must be differentiated.

(i) The locutionary action, or the locution, is the act of saying something. It is, said Austin, in effect a combination of three acts. These are: (a) a phonetic act, i.e., an act of uttering certain noises; (b) a phatic act, i.e., the uttering of certain vocables or words, i.e., noises of certain types, belonging to and as belonging to, a certain vocabulary, conforming to and as conforming to a certain grammar; (c) a rhetic act, i.e., the performing of an act of using those vocables with a certain more or less definite sense and reference. An example of a report of a phatic act would be: "He said 'The cat is on the mat.'" An example of a report of a rhetic act: "He said that the cat was on the mat."[61] This latter reports, not simply the giving vent to certain significant sounds, but the making of an assertion. That brings us to the next thing which we can do with words.

(ii) Of the illocutionary act, or illocution, Austin wrote: "To perform a locutionary act is in general, we may say, also

---

[60] J. L. Austin, *How to Do Things with Words* (Oxford, 1962), see especially Lecture VIII.
[61] Austin, *op. cit.*, p. 95.

and *eo ipso* to perform an illocutionary act, as I propose to call it. To determine what illocutionary act is so performed we must determine in what way we are using the locution."[62] The illocutionary act is what we do *in* saying something, as opposed to the locutionary act *of* saying something. "For example," wrote Austin, "it might be perfectly possible, with regard to an utterance, say 'It is going to charge,' to make entirely plain 'what we were saying' in issuing the utterance, in all the senses so far distinguished, and yet not at all to have cleared up whether or not in issuing the utterance I was performing the act of *warning* or not."[63] If we perform the act of saying something, then the question can always be raised as to what we are saying *in* saying that, the type of answer looked for being that which will make it clear whether we are answering a question, issuing a warning, making a statement, or whatever. Austin gives a list of possible illocutionary acts which is, in many ways, reminiscent of the list of the uses of language, given by Wittgenstein in *Investigations* and quoted above (p. 46). Austin's list runs:

asking or answering a question,
giving some information or an assurance or a warning,
announcing a verdict or an intention,
pronouncing a sentence,
making an appointment or an appeal or a criticism,
making an identification or giving a description.

This list is not, of course, exhaustive. These different kinds of function which language may be used to fulfill are sometimes referred to by Austin as its illocutionary "forces."[64]

(iii) When Austin spoke of a *perlocutionary* act, or of perlocutionary force, what he had in mind was as follows. "Saying something will often, or even normally, produce certain consequential effects upon the feelings, thoughts, or actions of the audience, or of the speaker, or of other persons:

[62] *Ibid.,* p. 98.
[63] *Ibid.*
[64] *Ibid.*

and it may be done with the design, intention, or purpose of
producing them; and we may then say, thinking of this, that
the speaker has performed an act in the nomenclature of
which reference is made either (C.*a*) only obliquely, or even
(C.*b*) not at all, to the performance of the locutionary, or
illocutionary act. We shall call the performance of an act of
this kind the performance of a *perlocutionary* act or *perlocution.*" [65]

Austin offered, among others, the following examples of reports of locutionary, illocutionary, and perlocutionary acts.

> *Locution:* He said to me "Shoot her!" meaning by "shoot"
>   shoot and referring by "her" to *her.*
>
> *Illocution:* He urged (or advised, ordered, etc.) me to
>   shoot her.
>
> *Perlocution:* (What he calls above C.*a*) He persuaded me
>   to shoot her.
>   (What he calls above C.*b*) He got me to (or
>   made me, etc.) shoot her. [66]

How do we know the illocutionary and perlocutionary
force of anything which is said? Austin brings out an important difference between them here. [67] Consider how we
tell that an utterance is, for instance, a warning. Suppose the
utterance is "It is going to charge." The most obvious way
in which we can tell that this is a warning is if the speaker pre-
fixes it with what Austin would have called the explicitly performative formula, "I warn you that. . . ." But there are
other possible ways as well. For instance, tone of voice or
emphasis could tell us that "It is going to charge" was a warning. In other examples, the mood of the verb (the fact, for
instance, that it is imperative, indicating that a command is
being issued) is sometimes a sufficient clue to illocutionary
force. Adverbs or adverbial phrases can serve this purpose
too: e.g., "I'll come without fail" indicates that a promise is
being made. Connecting particles may do the job: e.g., "still"

[65] *Ibid.,* p. 101.
[66] *Ibid.,* pp. 101–2.
[67] *Ibid.,* p. 103.

can have the force of "I insist that"—"Still, do it"; and "therefore" can show that a conclusion is being drawn. Gestures (e.g., winks or frowns), ceremonial nonverbal actions (e.g., bowing as one speaks), or the circumstances of the utterance (e.g., "Coming from *him*, that was an order"), may all determine illocutionary force.[68] The important point to take here is that all these are conventional devices, or *rules* for the use of language. It is by reference to these that we know what the illocutionary force of an utterance is. But the case is quite different when we turn to perlocutionary force. The psychological effects which utterances, or kinds of utterance, produce can be discovered only by empirical observation of what happens to hearers when they are said. Linguistic rules constitute illocutionary force, but not perlocutionary force. In the light of what has already been said above (p. 42), this fact leaves open the possibility that the illocutionary force of a speech-act may have something to do with its meaning, whereas its perlocutionary force does not.

Meaning, Illocutionary Force, and Moral Discourse

We will turn now to consider something of the influence which Austin's differentiation of locution, illocution, and perlocution has had upon modern moral philosophy. One part of it is easy to understand and we have already foreshadowed it.. Austin himself wrote: "to speak of the 'use' of language can . . . blur the distinction between the illocutionary and perlocutionary act."[69] The emergence of interest in the use to which moral language is put has been, as we noted, very important. It could be said with some truth that the transformation which has taken place in moral philosophy over the last fifty years reflects that which took place in the thought of Wittgenstein. Moral philosophers have been weaned away from the belief that moral discourse pictures some objective reality and from the consequent puzzlement which afflicted their philosophical forebears as to what that reality is and how we apprehend it. They have come to concern them-

[68] *Ibid.*, pp. 73–76.
[69] *Ibid.*, p. 103.

selves rather with the use, or uses, to which moral language
is put. But to leave the matter there would blur the distinction between some modern moral philosophers, the emotivists,
who conceive of this "use" as perlocutionary force, and
others, the prescriptivists, who conceive of it as illocutionary
force. In dealing with the psychological theory of meaning,
we have already seen, following Waismann, that the meaning
of language requires that it be considered, not as a mechanism, but as a calculus. This is much the same distinction as
that between perlocutionary and illocutionary force. We shall
see in Chapter 5 what advances were made when philosophers
recognized that the question about the meaning of moral language is not to be answered by considering its perlocutionary
force.

But now we must turn to a much more complicated and
difficult question: can the meaning of moral discourse be
equated with its illocutionary force? Austin himself, at first
sight anyway, seems to have thought not. He does not consider moral language in particular, but what he would have
said in its case follows from what he said in general terms.
He said explicitly: "I want to distinguish *force* (*sc*. illocutionary force) and meaning in the sense in which meaning
is equivalent to sense and reference. . . ."[70] Sense and reference Austin located in the locutionary act as we have already seen. However, it is arguable that Austin's whole object
was to show that philosophers had failed at all fully to understand how language works just because they have been held
captive by, and concentrated far too much attention on,
meaning as sense and reference. When Austin said, as he
did, that the expression "meaning" "can blur the distinction
between locutionary and illocutionary acts,"[71] it is at least
arguable that he was making a point against the traditional
interpretation of meaning as sense and reference rather than
putting up the shutters against any attempt to equate meaning and illocutionary force. Austin's intention, it would not be
absurd to suppose, was to clarify the concept of meaning and

[70] *Ibid.,* p. 100.
[71] *Ibid.,* p. 103.

deliver it from the misunderstandings of traditional philosophers. His scant use of, and seeming distaste for, the word
"meaning" would be in line with this.

Different disciples of Austin, at any rate from among those
who have turned their attention to moral philosophy, tend to
claim either (a) that they are following him by maintaining
a sharp distinction between meaning and illocutionary force
or, alternatively, (b) that they are following him by enlarging
the concept of meaning so as to include illocutionary force,
and even by equating meaning with the latter. G. J. Warnock
and R. M. Hare are respectively cases in point.

Warnock seems to take the former course (at least it is
Hare's charge against him that he does).[72] In his *Contemporary Moral Philosophy*, he argues that what is definitive of
moral discourse is that it has, as such, a particular content;
and in one place he gives this as: "human happiness or interests, needs, wants, or desires."[73] Given this subject matter,
then, according to Warnock, speakers in making moral judgments may be doing as many different things as they may be
doing in discourse at large.[74] He thinks it is a great mistake
of prescriptivists to conceive of moral judgments as having
only one kind of illocutionary force. There are dozens of
things which those who employ moral words may *therein* be
doing, says Warnock, and goes on: "They may be prescribing,
certainly; but also they may be advising, exhorting, imploring;
commanding, condemning, deploring; resolving, confessing,
undertaking; and so on and so on."[75] Approvingly, Warnock
quotes P. H. Nowell-Smith: "The words with which moral
philosophers have especially to do . . . play many different
parts. They are used to express tastes and preferences, to express decisions and choices, to criticise, grade, and evaluate,
to advise, admonish, warn, persuade and dissuade, to praise,
encourage and reprove, to promulgate and draw attention to

[72] See Hare's review of Warnock's *Contemporary Moral Philosophy*
in *M* LXXVII (1968), 437.
[73] G. J. Warnock, *Contemporary Moral Philosophy* (1967), p. 55.
[74] *Ibid.*, p. 40.
[75] *Ibid.*, p. 75.

rules; and doubtless for other purposes also."[76] I doubt if it could be said that Warnock follows Austin here in conceiving of the meaning of moral discourse as its sense and reference. But he is clearly drawing, or at least implying, a distinction between meaning and illocutionary force. For if the illocutionary forces of moral judgments can be as diversified as those of speech-acts in discourse as a whole, then what makes a judgment a moral judgment cannot (logically) be its illocutionary force. Whatever illocutionary force we fastened on as constituting its meaning we could adduce counterexamples of speech-acts with a different illocutionary force which were nevertheless moral.

Hare takes the latter of the two courses which, I suggested above, a disciple of Austin's might take. He goes so far as to equate illocutionary force and meaning.[77] Austin located meaning in the locutionary act. But can we know the meaning of a speech-act before we know its illocutionary force? Take the example "You will arrive at six thirty." This could be either an order or a statement. Do we know its meaning until we know which it is? The answer is clearly that we do not, and that, I think, is why Hare insists, as we shall see that he does, upon his point that no speech-act is complete without what he calls its "tropic."[78] The latter, in Hare's terminology, is the logical particle which gives a speech-act its illocutionary force. Most obviously, this may be the sign of mood (hence the word "tropic"). In the example "You will come at six thirty" the mood of the verb is indicative and normally that would mean that a statement is being made. However, emphasis, e.g., "You *will* come at six thirty," or circumstances, e.g., the fact that it is said by an officer to a private, can make this seeming statement into a command. Notice that, even in the case of "Come at six thirty," where the mood is imperative, we cannot, without reference to something beyond the mood of the verb, be sure whether it is a command, a request, or a piece of advice. Its "tropic" may be a complicated element in a speech-act. Hare does not deny this. He simply in-

[76] *Ibid.*, p. 40; Nowell-Smith, *op. cit.*, p. 98.
[77] See *M* LXXVII (1968), 438.
[78] See below, p. 232.

sists that no speech-act is complete, i.e., meaningful, without a tropic. If this is so, then meaning cannot logically be separated altogether from illocutionary force. This shows that Austin was wrong to locate it exclusively in the locutionary act. But it does not show that there is nothing more to meaning than illocutionary force.

Against Warnock's contention, or what Hare takes to have been his contention,[79] that the meaning of moral discourse cannot be equated with its illocutionary force because the latter is as diverse in moral discourse as it is in discourse at large, Hare claims that a distinction can be drawn between a genus, and its species, of illocutionary force. He says that all the speech-acts listed by Warnock and Nowell-Smith (see above) can be regarded as species of one genus, which it is legitimate to call "prescribing." In Chapter 5, relying upon hitherto unpublished papers of Hare's, I shall consider his defense of his own position against those who contend that there are, in ordinary language, numerous examples of words such as "good" being used with their literal meaning, but without being used to prescribe or commend. If Hare's position here can be sustained, it still does not prove that the meaning and the illocutionary force of moral discourse can be equated, but it does dispose of the particular argument, attributed above to Warnock, as to why they cannot.

It has been argued[80] that, in the case of an explicitly performative speech-act, e.g., the warning, "I warn you that it is going to charge," *no* distinction can be drawn between the illocutionary force of such an utterance and its meaning. To say "I warn you that it is going to charge" is not to report or describe your warning. It is simply to warn. If your speech-act is to be assigned a meaning at all, then this meaning must be of a performative, or illocutionary, kind. Your meaning lies solely in the issuing of the warning. Where else could it lie? If somebody asked, "What did you say?" and you replied, "I warned him that it was going to charge," is not that a per-

[79] Cf. *M* LXXVII (1968), 438.
[80] Cf. L. J. Cohen, "Do Illocutionary Forces Exist?" *PQ* 14 (1964), 122.

fectly satisfactory answer? Do you need to separate out a
locution, viz. "It is going to charge," because the meaning of
what you said resides in that, as distinct from what you were
doing in saying that?

Considerations of this kind might suggest that the difference between meaning and illocutionary force can be eliminated. To anticipate matters which will occupy our attention
in Chapter 5, the sense and reference of a speech-act can be
located in what Hare called its "phrastic," i.e., the logical
particle of a speech-act which may be common to speech-
acts with differing illocutionary force. For instance, the
phrastic "Going by you to the station" is common to the
statement "You go to the station" and the command "Go to
the station." Everything except what Hare called the "tropic"
can (logically) be located in the phrastic. Now, phrastics by
themselves have no meaning because they are incomplete
as speech-acts. Meaning resides in the complete speech-act.
This is evident from the fact that we do not learn the meanings of individual words and then learn how to string them
together in speech-acts. Language, however primitive, consists
of speech-acts, and it is learned—can only be learned—by par-
ticipation in these speech-acts. Phrastics, then, have meaning
when, and only when, tropics are added to them. It is the
tropic which completes the speech-act and so gives it meaning. The tropic makes it possible to reply to the question
"What did you say?" with "I warned him that . . . ," "I
asked him whether . . . ," etc. And such replies, as we have
noted, can legitimately be taken to give the meanings of the
utterances concerned.

However, the question with which this discussion began—
can the meaning of moral discourse be equated with its illocutionary force?—cannot, I think, be regarded as finally settled.
Illocutionary force is undoubtedly a necessary condition of
meaning, but is it a sufficient? True, phrastics by themselves
are meaningless. But are not tropics by themselves equally so?
While the meaning of a speech-act lies in the whole speech-
act, is it not legitimate to draw distinctions between elements
in that meaning—e.g., between *what* the speech-act is about

and *how* it is about what it is about? Considerations such as these give one pause. Perhaps we cannot give an unqualified yes in reply to the question: can the meaning of moral discourse be equated with its illocutionary force? Even so, those who have said yes to this question, it seems to me, are much nearer the mark than those who hold that the meaning of a speech-act resides in a locutionary act which is logically quite distinct from its illocutionary force. Of that point of view I would say, not that it may need some qualification, but that it is flatly mistaken and should be rejected.

CHAPTER 3. THE INTUITIONIST THEORY

In the early part of the present century, the main point at issue in British moral philosophy was that which arose between ethical naturalists and nonnaturalists. "Ethical naturalist" is the name given to a thinker who has—or is taken to have—defined moral words, such as "good" or "right," in terms of natural properties. Anyone who defined "good" or "right" as, for examples, "producing happiness," "conducing to evolution," or "fulfilling the will of God," would be an ethical naturalist. G. E. Moore set himself to refute those whom he took to have defined "good" in these, or similar, ways. The book in which he attempted to do so, *Principia Ethica* (London, 1903), has a good claim to be regarded as the *terminus a quo* of modern moral philosophy. The point of view which Moore defended in it may be described as ethical nonnaturalism.

In the opening pages of *Principia Ethica,* Moore said that his sole business was with "that object or idea" which the word "good" "is generally used to stand for."[1] It is dangerous to generalize, but I think it would be true to say that the referential theory of meaning, in some form or other, is largely taken for granted in the work of those ethical naturalists and nonnaturalists whom we shall consider. The former believed that moral terms mean, i.e., refer to, certain natural properties of actions or states of affairs and that these properties can be observed by one or other of the physical senses. Nonnaturalists, by contrast, believed that moral terms mean,

[1] *PE,* p. 6. I take this to imply a referential theory of meaning, but I do not suggest, of course, that no other theory is to be found in Moore's writings.

i.e., refer to, nonnatural properties which can only be apprehended by moral intuition.

In this chapter, I will first outline what I take to have been Moore's conception of the mistake which ethical naturalists make and for which he coined the expression "the naturalistic fallacy." I will then consider some of the questions which arise in this connection. Next, two other thinkers, H. A. Prichard and W. D. Ross, will engage our attention. They held views similar to Moore's but, as I shall try to show, extended them more widely over the field of moral language than he had done. Finally I shall ask whether or not the underlying assumption of the type of ethical theory with which this chapter is concerned, namely, the assumption that moral right and wrong, good and evil, can be known by intuition, is well founded.

I. MOORE AND THE REJECTION
OF ETHICAL NATURALISM

The principal discovery which Moore claimed to have made concerning "that object or idea" which the word "good" is generally used to stand for, was that it is *indefinable*. We must try first to answer two questions: (i) what precisely did Moore mean when he said that "good" stands for something indefinable? and (ii) what precisely were his grounds for saying so? I will take them in turn.

Good as Indefinable
Moore differentiated three kinds of definition.[2] The first two were stipulative and lexical definition respectively. He recognized that on the one hand, anyone could, logically and empirically, stipulate a meaning of his own for "good"; and on the other hand, that if one looked in a dictionary one would find that there are generally accepted rules for the use of the word. But he held that there is definition of a third kind which is much more important than either of these other two. Definitions of this third kind "describe the

[2] *PE*, p. 8.

real nature of the object or notion denoted by a word, and
. . . do not merely tell us what the word is used to mean."[3]
The point to grasp, Moore contended, is that such definitions
"are only possible when the object or notion in question is
something complex."[4] He went on to explain what he meant.
"You can give a definition of a horse, because a horse has
many different properties and qualities, all of which you can
enumerate. But when you have enumerated them all, when
you have reduced a horse to his simplest terms, then you can
no longer define those terms. They are simply something
which you think of or perceive, and to anyone who cannot
think of or perceive them, you can never, by any definition,
make their nature known."[5] He noted the possible objection
to this, that we are able to describe things to people which
they have not previously thought of or perceived; but maintained that such things are always composed of parts, with
which we and they are familiar, combined in ways with which
we and they are also familiar. Moore continued:

> "Good" then, if we mean by it that quality which we
> assert to belong to a thing, when we say that the thing is
> good, is incapable of any definition, in the most important
> sense of that word. The most important sense of "defini-
> tion" is that in which a definition states what are the parts
> which invariably compose a certain whole; and in this
> sense "good" has no definition because it is simple and has
> no parts. It is one of those innumerable objects of thought
> which are themselves incapable of definition, because they
> are the ultimate terms by reference to which whatever *is*
> capable of definition must be defined. That there must be
> an indefinite number of such terms is obvious, on reflec-
> tion; since we cannot define anything except by an analysis,
> which, when carried as far as it will go, refers us to some-
> thing, which is simply different from anything else, and
> which by that ultimate difference explains the peculiarity
> of the whole which we are defining: for every whole con-
> tains some parts which are common to other wholes also.

[3] *PE*, p. 7.
[4] *Ibid.*
[5] *Ibid.*

There is, therefore, no intrinsic difficulty in the contention
that "good" denotes a simple and indefinable quality. There
are many other instances of such qualities.[6]

Yellow was one such instance to which Moore referred. "My
point is," he said, "that 'good' is a simple notion, just as
'yellow' is a simple notion; that, just as you cannot, by any
manner of means, explain to any one who does not already
know it, what yellow is, so you cannot explain what good is."[7]
All things which are yellow do produce a certain kind of
vibration in the light; and similarly all things which are good
may be things which produce pleasure. But Moore maintained,
just as "yellow" *does not mean* "productive of a certain kind
of vibration in the light," so "good" *does not mean* "productive of pleasure." He recognized it as the aim of ethics to discover the other property, or properties, besides being good,
which all good things possess. But he argued that "far too
many philosophers have thought that when they named those
other properties they were actually defining good." For this
mistake he invented the name "the naturalistic fallacy,"[8] and
we shall return to it shortly.

It may further illuminate what Moore meant by saying
that good is indefinable, if we recall two distinctions which
he drew. The first is that between analytic and synthetic propositions. The former can be shown to be true simply by reference to the definitions of the terms used (e.g., "A bachelor
is an unmarried male"); the latter cannot. Moore said:
"Propositions about the good are all of them synthetic and
never analytic."[9] The reference here to "the good" brings
us to the other distinction which Moore drew, namely, that
between the substantive "the good" and the adjective "good."
The good (that which is good) is what the adjective "good"
applies to; but, said Moore, "if it is that to which the adjective
will apply, it must be something different from that adjective

[6] *PE*, pp. 9–10.
[7] *PE*, p. 7.
[8] *PE*, p. 10.
[9] *PE*, p. 7.

itself."[10] Moore recognized that "the good" is certainly definable: we can indicate what it is by denotation or connotation. We can, for instance, enumerate all those things which produce pleasure and say "These are what 'the good' denotes"; and we can show what "the good" connotes by saying such things as "Whatever produces pleasure is also either part or the whole of the good." Moore's crucial point is that it does not follow from this that "good" is definable; *indeed the very reverse follows*. For "there is no meaning in saying that pleasure is good unless good is something different from pleasure."[11] We shall see the force of this remark if we turn now to the second of the questions which, I said, we must try to answer.

The Naturalistic Fallacy

This was the question: what precisely were Moore's grounds for saying that "good" stands for something indefinable? He held that there are two, *and only two*, conceivable alternatives to such a view and "a simple appeal to the facts" will show that neither is tenable.[12] These alternatives were: (i) that "good" denotes "a complex, a given whole, about the correct analysis of which there may be disagreement" and (ii) that "good" "means nothing at all, and there is no such subject as Ethics."[13] He attempted to establish his own view by a *reductio ad absurdum* of these alternatives.

The former, said Moore, is seen to be incorrect from the fact that "whatever definition be offered, it may be always asked, with significance, of the complex so defined, whether it is itself good."[14] This is now sometimes referred to as "the open-question argument."[15] It runs as follows. Take any proposed definition of "good," e.g., "good" means produces pleasure. Given this definition, if we ask whether or not any-

[10] *PE*, p. 9.
[11] *PE*, p. 14.
[12] *PE*, p. 15.
[13] *Ibid.*
[14] *Ibid.*
[15] G. C. Kerner, *The Revolution in Ethical Theory* (Oxford, 1966), p. 16.

thing is good, we shall be asking in effect whether or not it produces pleasure. But suppose someone asks "Is what produces pleasure good?" If the foregoing definition is correct, this question will be self-answering; that is, it will be equivalent to "Does what produces pleasure produce pleasure?" Of course, it could (logically) be the case, that whatever produces pleasure is always also good; but that is beside the present point. The force of the argument lies here: would even a hedonist suppose that anyone who doubted whether what produces pleasure is really good simply be wondering whether what produces pleasure produces pleasure? Moore thought it perfectly clear that he would not. Whatever *definiens* of "good" were proposed, he went on to say, it would make perfectly good sense to doubt whether this *definiens* was good; and "the mere fact that we understand very well what is meant by doubting it, shows clearly that we have two different notions before our minds,"[16] viz. the *definiens* in question and goodness. To put the same point another way, no one—least of all a hedonist—would consider the proposition "whatever produces pleasure is good" to be an insignificant tautology, meaning no more than "whatever produces pleasure produces pleasure." But if "good" *means* produces pleasure, then "whatever produces pleasure is good" *is* an insignificant tautology.

Moore saw that moralists have frequently made a move which is self-defeating. He had in mind writers such as Bentham or Mill, Spencer, and Green, whom he believed to have been guilty of this move, or at least to have been "influenced" by it.[17] They have tried to win assent to their particular view about what is good by the knockdown argument that this view follows from the very meaning of the word "good" and so it cannot (logically) be denied. True enough, if "good" means X, then anyone who says "X is not good" will be guilty of self-contradiction. But, by the same token, anyone who says "X is good" will then be uttering an analytic triviality, a remark which is undeniable simply because it is uninforma-

16 *PE*, p. 16.
17 *PE*, p. 49.

tive. Moore saw that the very last thing which any of the moralists whom he had in mind would have wanted to say was that a statement of their view—"Maximizing happiness is good," "Conduct is better as it is more evolved," "What satisfies desire is good," or whatever it might be—amounted to nothing more than an insignificant tautology. He said, with hedonists particularly in mind, "When they say 'Pleasure is good' we cannot believe that they merely mean 'Pleasure is pleasure' and nothing more than that."[18] Moralists cannot have it both ways; the statement of their view cannot be both a significant and informative remark and at the same time true by definition of the word "good."

The second of the alternatives, to his own view, which Moore said was conceivable, is the view that "good" means nothing at all and there is no such subject as ethics. Against this Moore appealed to what he thought any man may observe by introspection. "But whoever will attentively consider with himself what is actually before his mind when he asks the question 'Is pleasure (or whatever it may be) after all good?' can easily satisfy himself that he is not merely wondering whether pleasure is pleasant. And if he will try this experiment with each suggested definition in succession, he may become expert enough to recognise that in every case he has before his mind a unique object, with regard to the connection of which with any other object, a distinct question may be asked. Every one does in fact understand the question 'Is this good?' When he thinks of it, his state of mind is different from what it would be, were he asked 'Is this pleasant, or desired, or approved?' "[19] The point is that for a man to feel the difference between goodness and other things there must be some "unique object" before his mind and so there must be some subject matter for ethics. A man may not be aware of this difference without being put on the alert for it; but according to Moore it is the point of analysis to make him alert to it.

[18] *PE*, p. 12.
[19] *PE*, pp. 16–17.

Moore's Predecessors

We have seen, then, what Moore meant by saying that
"good" is indefinable and what his grounds were for saying
it. Before considering these arguments any further, some comment is called for on Moore's remarks about other philosophers. He said, it will be remembered, that "far too many"
moral philosophers have been guilty of the naturalistic fallacy.[20] Another remark which he made was that only one
writer had anticipated him in his arguments for the indefinability of good, and against the naturalistic fallacy, namely
Henry Sidgwick.[21] Both of these remarks can be challenged.
The latter is certainly mistaken, as we shall see in a moment.
As for the former, it has recently been argued that at least
some of those to whom Moore attributed the naturalistic fallacy were not guilty of it. Mill was Moore's particular target,
and in the next subsection I shall refer to some recent attempts to defend Mill against his criticisms.

But first: did only Sidgwick anticipate Moore? No. If
Moore had read *A Review of the Principal Questions in
Morals* by the eighteenth-century rational intuitionist, Richard
Price, for instance, he would have found his own distinction
between a significant ethical generalization and the definition
of an ethical term as clearly drawn in Price's early pages as
in those of the *Principia*, and the doctrine that basic ethical
terms are simple and indefinable defended by a *reductio ad
absurdum* of its denial which exactly paralleled his own. It
is true that Price wrote about the word "right" rather than
"good," but that does not affect the claim that he was alive
to what Moore called the naturalistic fallacy. Price wrote:
"As to the schemes which found morality on self-love, on
positive laws and compacts, or the Divine will; they must
either mean, that moral good and evil are only other words
for *advantageous* and *disadvantageous, willed* or *forbidden.*
Or they relate to a very different question; that is, not to the
question, what is the nature and true account of virtue; but,

---

[20] See note 8.
[21] *PE*, p. 17; Moore refers to H. Sidgwick's *Methods of Ethics* I. iii. 1
(6th ed.).

what is the *subject matter* of it." This parallels Moore's distinction between what "good" means and what things are good. Price wrote again: "Right and wrong when applied to actions which are commanded or forbidden by the will of God, or that produce good or harm, do not signify merely, that such actions are commanded or forbidden, or that they are useful or hurtful, but a *sentiment* concerning them and our consequent approbation or disapprobation of the performance of them. Were not this true, it would be palpably absurd in any case to ask, whether it is *right* to obey a command or *wrong* to disobey it; and the propositions, *obeying a command is right,* or *producing happiness is right,* would be most trifling, as expressing no more than that obeying a command, is obeying a command, or producing happiness, is producing happiness."[22] This parallels exactly Moore's grounds for saying that good is simple and indefinable.

Other classical moral philosophers besides Price were aware that what is morally good, right, or obligatory cannot be proved to be so by appeal to definitions of these terms. In the eighteenth century both sides of the great debate between rational intuitionists and the "moral sense" school, despite all their differences, were at one in their opposition to Hobbes's social compact theory of morals on the ground that it is one thing to say that men have contracted together to obey the will of a sovereign but quite another to say that what this sovereign wills or commands is good or bad, right or wrong, what ought to be done or not done. It is interesting to see that they rejected such a view, even supposing the sovereign to be God. On the "moral sense" side we find Shaftesbury saying: "If the mere will, decree, or law of God be said absolutely to constitute right or wrong, then are these latter words of no significancy at all";[23] and Hutcheson, in similar vein: "To call the laws of the Supreme Deity good, or holy,

[22] Price, *Review,* edited by D. D. Raphael (Oxford, 1948), pp. 16–17. For "most trifling" Price's first edition reads "most triflingly identical." For a critical study of Price's *Review* see my *Reason and Right* (London, 1970).
[23] *Inquiry concerning Virtue or Merit* I. iii. 2; quoted by A. N. Prior, *Logic and the Basis of Ethics* (Oxford, 1949), p. 96.

or just, if all goodness, holiness and justice be constituted by
laws or by the will of a superior any way revealed, must be
an insignificant tautology, amounting to no more than this,
'That God wills what he wills.' "[24] On the rational intuitionist
side, besides Price, we find Cudworth contending that, if moral
terms are defined as meaning willed or commanded by any
agencies, human or divine, then they become "mere names
without any signification, or names for nothing else, but willed
and commanded."[25] It is, then, simply not true that only
Sidgwick anticipated Moore on this point.

Did Mill Commit the Naturalistic Fallacy?

Is it true that those to whom Moore attributed the naturalistic fallacy actually committed it? Some of them did so, but
in the case of others, doubts can be raised. It is not possible
to examine each case in depth. There has been much controversy about John Stuart Mill and so I will confine the question to his case. Mill's *Utilitarianism* provides, according to
Moore, "as naive and artless a use of the naturalistic fallacy as
anybody could desire."[26] Was Moore fair to Mill? The offending passage in *Utilitarianism* ran thus:

> The only proof capable of being given that a thing is
> visible, is that people actually see it. . . . In like manner,
> I apprehend, the sole evidence it is possible to produce that
> anything is desirable, is that people do actually desire it. If
> the end which the utilitarian doctrine proposes to itself
> were not, in theory and in practice, acknowledged to be an
> end, nothing could ever convince any person that it was so.
> No reason can be given why the general happiness is de-
> sirable, except that each person, so far as he believes it to
> be attainable, desires his own happiness. This, however, be-
> ing a fact, we have not only all the proof which the case
> admits of, but all which it is possible to require, that happi-
> ness is a good: that each person's happiness is a good to

[24] *Inquiry concerning Virtue or Moral Good* VII. vi; L. A. Selby-Bigge,
British Moralists, p. 173; quoted by Prior, *op. cit.*, p. 96.
[25] Quoted by Prior, *op. cit.*, p. 17.
[26] *PE*, p. 66.

that person, and the general happiness, therefore, a good to the aggregate of all persons.[27]

Moore, and countless critics following him, have claimed that these words of Mill's contain a mass of confusions. For one thing, while it undoubtedly follows from the fact that X is actually seen that X is visible, because "visible" means "able to be seen," Mill should have realized that "desirable" does not mean "able to be desired" but "ought to be desired" or "deserves to be desired"; and it is, to say the least, not obvious that this follows from "is actually desired." Again, Mill commits the fallacy of composition in supposing that, from the fact, if it is a fact, that A's happiness (AH) is a good to A, B's happiness (BH) a good to B, C's happiness (CH) a good to C, it follows that the entity, AH plus BH plus CH, is a good to each of A, B, and C respectively. But Mill's most serious error, Moore contended, was that he here defined "desirable" as "desired" and so rendered "X is good" equivalent in meaning to "X is desired." If this is so, then all Moore's reasons for contending that good is indefinable can be marshaled against Mill's utilitarianism.

Recently, however, some philosophers[28] have objected that to accuse Mill of committing the naturalistic fallacy is to misunderstand the above passage. It is pointed out that Mill expressly rejected the possibility of such a proof as he is accused of having fabricated: he said that questions of ultimate ends do not admit of proof in the ordinary meaning of the term.[29] Moreover, in his *System of Logic* he showed why. He differentiated quite clearly between propositions which "assert that anything is" and those which "enjoin or recommend that something should be." The latter form "a class by themselves." So "a proposition of which the predicate is expressed by the words *ought* or *should be* is generically different from

[27] Fontana edition, edited by M. Warnock (1962), pp. 288–89, cf. 254–55. Quoted and criticized by Moore, *PE*, pp. 66 ff.

[28] E.g., M. Warnock's introduction to the Fontana edition of Mill's *Utilitarianism*, pp. 25–26; A. Ryan, "Mill and the Naturalistic Fallacy," *M* LXXV (1966).

[29] Mill, *op. cit.*, pp. 254, 288.

one which is expressed by *is* or *will be.*[30] He could hardly
have been more explicit about the logical gap between "is"
and "ought," between statements of natural or empirical fact
and moral judgments. Did Mill then change his mind when
he came to write *Utilitarianism?* Such a possibility is excluded by the fact that Mill revised his *System of Logic* after
writing *Utilitarianism* but without altering any of the relevant
passages in it.[31] Only two possibilities, then, remain: either
Mill was simply inconsistent in the two works; or his meaning
in *Utilitarianism* has been misunderstood by Moore and those
who echo his criticisms. The former does, admittedly, seem
unlikely. But if we exclude it, we are left with the question,
what precisely did Mill mean by the passage from *Utilitarianism* which has given such offense? None of the answers which
have been proposed to that question seems to me to defend
Mill altogether satisfactorily against Moore's criticism.

Attention has been called by his defenders to the fact that
Mill said that he was offering a proof, not in an "ordinary"
sense of the word, but in "a larger meaning" of it. According
to this larger meaning, said Mill, "the subject is within the
cognizance of the rational faculty" because "considerations
may be presented capable of determining the intellect either
to give or withhold its assent to the doctrine; and this is equivalent to proof."[32] The first thing to say in reply to this is that
it is one thing to present considerations which "determine the
intellect" in the sense of persuading people to believe something and quite another to present considerations which show
the belief in question to be rational. If the contention of Mill's
defenders is that the former was what he was doing, then
against them it suffices to say that he may well have been, but,
once the logical flaw in his argument is pointed out, it will
cease to be persuasive, at least with rational men. However,
Mill's defenders seem to be saying that the latter of the above
alternatives was what Mill purported to be doing, namely presenting considerations which show the belief in question (the

[30] VI. xii. 6, quoted by Ryan, *op. cit.,* p. 422; italics mine.
[31] Ryan, *op. cit.,* p. 423.
[32] Mill, *op. cit.,* pp. 255, 288.

greatest happiness of the greatest number is the ultimate end)
to be rational. How do they support this contention?

Mrs. Warnock, in her introduction to Mill's *Utilitarianism*,
writes:

> When Mill uses his much-criticised argument from the
> analogy between "visible" and "desirable," he is attempting
> to establish what things are good. He holds that, if people
> did not already regard some things as ends, and therefore
> desire them, it would be impossible to prove to them that
> these things were ends. He asks "How is it possible to prove
> that health is good?" The answer is that it is not possible,
> but neither is it necessary. For everyone knows that it is
> good, and shows this by desiring it. When he says that "the
> sole evidence it is possible to produce that anything is de-
> sirable is that people actually desire it," he is making the
> same point. He is not trying to *prove* that happiness is good
> but to produce evidence that people already know, without
> waiting for any proof, that it is good. You can find out
> what people recognise as ultimate ends by finding out what
> they desire. What they desire, Mill goes on to say, is hap-
> piness.[33]

Here presumably the "proof" which Mill is *not* trying to effect
is proof in the "ordinary" meaning of the word; and the "evidence" which he *is* trying to produce is that which constitutes
proof in the "larger" meaning of the word. But what does
this "larger" "proof" amount to? Mrs. Warnock says that he
is producing evidence that people already "know" that happiness is good. But the only sense which it seems possible to give
to "know" here is "firmly believe." If Mill was grounding his
case in the putative fact that people firmly believe that happiness is good, what about the distinction between true belief
and mere opinion? This appears to have been obliterated. It
could be that Mill was right and there is no possibility of prov-
ing that anything is, or is not, desirable; in which case the most
we might hope to show would be whether or not any given
end is, or is not, *thought* to be desirable. But this would then
be entirely a psychological discovery, not an ethical one. If all

[33] Warnock, *op. cit.*, p. 26.

we can talk about is what men think desirable without any means of deciding whether their opinions are correct or mistaken, then—to recall Moore's second alternative to his own view—there is no such subject as ethics. I find it hard to believe that Mill would have been content to accept that as the point which he was making in his *Utilitarianism*.

Other possible interpretations of Mill's offending passage in *Utilitarianism* have been suggested.[34] According to one of these, Mill was attempting to deduce the greatest happiness principle from (a) every man's natural desire for his own happiness, and (b) the principle of universalizability. On this interpretation, Mill's argument purported to be as follows.

> As a sentient being, every man has a desire for his own happiness.
> As a rational being, every man recognizes that all others have as much right to their happiness as he has to his own.
> As both a sentient and a rational being, therefore, every man must (logically) recognize that the ultimate moral end is the greatest happiness equitably distributed.

According to another interpretation of Mill's offending passage, he was attempting to show that morality is logically connected with human happiness; or, more precisely, that if a rule is a *moral* rule, then it follows from the meaning of the word "moral" that it will be a rule directed to the maximization of happiness and its equal distribution.

It seems to me far from proved—perhaps far from provable —that Mill intended to put forward either of these arguments in the passage in which he was accused by Moore of committing the naturalistic fallacy. At best, one would have to say that if he was putting either of them forward, he was doing so with far less than his customary clarity. It is true, as we shall see in due course, that, in more sophisticated forms, both these latter arguments, attributed to Mill, have been put forward by modern moral philosophers in support of utilitarian-

[34] See Ryan, *op. cit.*, pp. 424–25.

ism. There is something very like the former of them in Professor R. M. Hare's writings,[35] and something very like the latter in Mrs. P. Foot's.[36] But this is to anticipate matters which will concern us in later chapters. All that need be said at the moment is that attempts so far made to absolve Mill from Moore's accusations, by reinterpreting the offending passage, do not seem to me to be convincing.

Are Moore's Arguments Good Ones?

We must now consider whether the case which Moore made out for the indefinability of good is convincing or not. He rested it, remember, upon the contention that there are only two possible alternatives to his own view and both of them are untenable. The first of these unacceptable alternatives was that "good" denotes a complex object; the second, that men do not have a unique object before their minds when they think or speak of good. I will consider them in a moment.

But first a brief word about Moore's "open question" argument (see above, p. 69). In ordinary discourse, there are contexts where no *definiens* will serve as a substitute for "good" without loss or change of meaning. If for the evaluative question "Was his action good?" we substitute "Did his action produce pleasure (conduce to evolution, fulfill the will of God, etc.)?" then we change the meaning of the question. This is seen, as Moore rightly pointed out, from the fact that the further question "But is what produces pleasure (etc.), good?" always makes sense. If "good" meant "produces pleasure" or any of the alternatives referred to by "etc.," that question would not make sense. There is, then, a logical gap of some kind between "good," used in this evaluative sense, and any such naturalistic description as "produces pleasure (etc.)." A great deal of modern moral philosophy has been concerned with this gap between naturalistic, or supernaturalistic, description and moral evaluation. Does it really exist? What precisely is its nature? And so on. Moore may justly be

[35] See below, pp. 227–30.
[36] See Chap. 7.

said to have given ethics in this century its direction by his "open question" argument. It called attention to a problem which has been discussed ever since and is still not finally settled. When, however, we turn to Moore's own reasons for thinking that the gap referred to exists, they do not seem to have been very good ones. If we recall the two alternatives to his own view which he considered untenable, we shall see what those reasons were.

The first appears to have been that we see what the nature of the gap is, and we know that it exists, when we recognize that "good" denotes a simple, not a complex, object. Moore himself says explicitly that there are as good grounds, and the same sort of grounds, for holding that "yellow" denotes a simple object as for holding that "good" does so. Moreover, he sees that it follows from this that any attempt to define "yellow" will be "the same fallacy"[37] as any attempt to define "good." Now, it is obviously impossible to establish that a gap exists between what "good" denotes and what any naturalistic description denotes by means of an argument which simply brings out the logical similarity between "good" and "yellow" because "yellow" is a naturalistic description. No doubt, because he was alive to this fact, Moore himself tried to establish some difference between "good" and "yellow." He said that, if anyone attempted to define "yellow," the *definiens* and *definiendum* would both denote "natural objects"; and so this could not be called a case of the naturalistic fallacy, i.e., the fallacy of defining naturalistically something which is nonnatural. But "good," he contended, is different: ". . . if [anyone] confuses 'good,' which is not in the same sense a natural object, with any natural object whatever, then there is reason for calling that a naturalistic fallacy; its being made with regard to 'good' marks it as something quite specific, and this specific mistake deserves a name because it is so common."[38] This leaves the crucial question unanswered, namely, what *is* the reason for saying that "good" denotes something nonnatural? That question is certainly not an-

[37] *PE*, p. 13.
[38] *Ibid.*

swered by an argument which simply shows that what "good" denotes is simple, in the sense in which what "yellow" denotes is simple.

Moore's second reason for thinking that a logical gap exists between what "good" denotes and what any naturalistic description denotes appears to have been his belief that we know this by intuition. The second alternative to his own view, viz. the opinion that there is nothing to which "good" refers, is, he held, untenable because we all know, when we look into our own minds, that what "good" denotes is "a unique object." In other words, we know by intuition that this object is logically different from whatever is denoted by expressions such as "producing happiness," "conducing to evolution," "fulfilling the will of God," etc.

I will digress for a moment to consider a question which arises at this point. Was Moore really an intuitionist? There is considerable room for doubt. He says himself in the preface to *Principia Ethica:* "I am not an 'Intuitionist,' in the ordinary sense of the term."[39] From what he goes on to say it is clear what he means. First, he denies, in effect, that he is a deontological intuitionist, i.e., one who thinks that judgments concerning *right* or *duty* are incapable of proof by consideration of the results to which different courses of action lead, or would lead. He does *not* believe in the intrinsic rightness or obligatoriness of certain kinds of action. We shall consider in the next section contemporaries of Moore who did, namely H. A. Prichard and W. D. Ross. But the Moore of the *Principia* certainly did not, though, as we shall see, in his later book *Ethics* he seems to have been coming around to a view similar to that of Ross and Prichard. In *Principia* Moore judged actions right or wrong, our duty or otherwise, in accordance with how much good they effected or failed to effect. Moore also dissociated himself from intuitionism thus: "I would wish it observed that, when I call such propositions [*sc.* propositions as to what kind of things ought to exist for their own sakes] 'Intuitions,' I mean *merely* to assert that they are incapable of proof; I imply nothing whatever as to the

[39] *PE*, p. x.

manner or origin of our cognition of them."[40] The classical
intuitionists of the seventeenth and eighteenth centuries engaged in a great debate concerning the nature of the moral
faculty.[41] Some, like Shaftesbury and Hutcheson, believed it
to be a kind of sense; others, like Cudworth, Clarke, Balguy,
and Price, believed it to be reason. Prichard and Ross appear,
on the whole, to have sided with the latter school of thought
and are generally classified as rational intuitionists. Moore,
however, was not interested in this question of how moral
intuitions originate and had nothing to say on the subject.

The third aspect of intuitionism from which Moore dissociated himself was the claim that moral intuition is infallible.
He said, "Still less do I imply (as most Intuitionists have
done) that any proposition whatever is true, *because* we cognise it in a particular way or by the exercise of any particular
faculty: I hold, on the contrary, that in every way in which it
is possible to cognise a true proposition, it is also possible to
cognise a false one."[42] This seems to reject what is surely the
bedrock belief of intuitionism, namely the belief that men
have a faculty which is unerring in its apprehension of certain
truths. This faculty, it is conceded by most intuitionists, may
be impaired or obstructed by certain conditions, but, given
the nonfulfillment of these conditions, it cannot err. I think
the important questions are two: does Moore's view that it is
possible to cognize falsely, as well as truly, by intuition, avoid
any of the problems concerning the claim to know by intuition which arise in the case of traditional intuitionism, and,
does Moore consistently adhere to this view? The answer in
both cases appears to be no.

As we shall see in the next section, the difficulty about the
claim to know X by intuition is how this can amount to more
than the claim to believe X. Moore thinks intuition may be
true or false. This does not lessen the difficulty of differentiating it from mere belief. Indeed all Moore has done is to add a
further problem: how are we to differentiate between true

[40] *Ibid.*
[41] Cf. my *Ethical Intuitionism* (1967), Chap. VII.
[42] *PE*, p. x.

and false intuitions? His view that they may be either does not make intuitionism more credible. Did he adhere to his view consistently? When we recall what he said in the *Principia* about "the Ideal," it is hard to reconcile this with his view that intuitions may be true or false. He wrote: "No one, probably, who has asked himself the question, has ever doubted that personal affection and the appreciation of what is beautiful in Art or Nature, are good in themselves." He describes this as "the ultimate and fundamental truth of Moral Philosophy," and goes on, "It is only for the sake of these things—in order that as much of them as possible may at some time exist—that any one can be justified in performing any public or private duty; . . . they are the *raison d'être* of virtue; . . . it is they . . . that form the rational ultimate end of human action and the sole criterion of social progress. . . ." He does add that "these appear to be truths which have been generally overlooked"; but he does not appear to conceive it possible that they are *not* truths at all.[43]

I return from this digression to Moore's reason for thinking that there is a logical gap between "good" and any naturalistic description. That reason was, in effect, that we all know by intuition that there is such a gap because we all apprehend that to which "good" refers as a unique object. Two points can be made against this. First, do all men have before their minds this unique object when they think about good? In order to answer that we would have to do two things: one, to decide what are the appropriate criteria for determining when a man has this unique object before his mind and when he has not; and the other, to test all men by these criteria in order to see whether or not they all do have that unique object before their minds when they think of good. It is difficult to decide what such criteria could be; and certainly no one has ever conducted the consequent investigation. If anyone says, therefore, that he does not have a unique object before his mind when he thinks of good—and we shall see in the next sub-section that some say this—then we cannot refute him. The logical gap between "good" and any naturalistic descrip-

[43] *PE*, pp. 188–89.

tion cannot be established by Moore's appeal to introspection.

But, even if that appeal were successful, what would it prove? If all men did have a unique object before their minds when they thought of "good," this would not prove that to fail to have such an object before one's mind when one thinks of good is to be guilty of a fallacy. It would show simply what is the case, not what logically must be the case. The logical gap between "good" and naturalistic descriptions concerns something which cannot (logically) be said. One cannot (logically) say "good" and mean "producing happiness." If this is so, it is so because of the rules for the use of these expressions. It is not so because of anything which does or does not happen inside men's minds. Introspection may lead to psychological discoveries. But it cannot settle questions of logical validity.

Is Ethical Naturalism Defensible?

It is instructive to ask how an ethical naturalist might attempt to counter Moore's attack upon his position. He could, as we have already noted, deny that he is aware of good as a unique object. Before such a denial, in default of any satisfactory method of testing the claim that all men are aware of "good" as such, Moore would have been helpless.

Can an ethical naturalist equally effectively dispose of the rest of Moore's case against him? Moore rejected the view that "good" refers to a complex object on the ground that, if it does, some analytic propositions about good will be true, and the "open question argument" shows that none, in fact, are. In other words, nothing is true *by definition* of "good." To this, the ethical naturalist may reply that, given what *he* himself means by "good," certain propositions about good *are* true analytically, or by definition. Suppose he says that by "good" he means "producing happiness." Then it is analytically true that anything which is good produces happiness. But Moore, in his turn, could have pointed out, in reply to this, that the naturalist's definition of "good" is stipulative. Of course anyone can (logically) stipulate whatever definition he chooses for "good," as for any other word. Moore never denied it. All he did say was, in effect, that anyone who stipulates a definition of "good" is thereby opting out of the ordinary use to which "good" is put. Lexically, as distinct from stipulatively, "good" is indefinable.

It has been suggested[44] that the ethical naturalist could return to the attack by contending that there is a simple explanation of the fact that "good" is lexically indefinable. This is the explanation which Mill offered. Mill said that a word may be "first applied to one thing, and then extended by a series of transitions . . . from one object to another, until it becomes applied to things having nothing in common with the first things . . . so that it at last denotes a confused huddle of objects, having nothing whatever in common; and connotes nothing, not even a vague and general resemblance."[45] This, the ethical naturalist might say, is what has happened in the case of "good." It is just because so many definitions of "good" are, in fact, current, that it appears to be indefinable. Mill went on to argue that, when a word has fallen into this state, "it has become unfit for the purposes either of thought or of the communication of thought; and can only be made serviceable by stripping it of some part of its multifarious denotation and confining it to objects possessed of some attributes in common, which it may be made to connote."[46] In a similar vein, the ethical naturalist may go on to claim that all he is attempting to do is to tidy up the lexical definition of "good." He is not trying to define the indefinable. He is simply proposing that the sense and reference of "good" should be restricted to one object, or type of object, rather than to a "confused huddle" of objects. He may further claim that the restricted use which he proposes is, in fact, the most common use of the word. In the interests of clarity of thought and communication, he could go on, it is desirable that the "multifarious denotation" of "good" should be stripped away from it and its meaning restricted as he proposes to restrict it. Prima facie this line of argument seems plausible.

[44] Cf. Prior, *op. cit.*, pp. 10–11.
[45] *System of Logic* I. viii. 7, quoted by Prior, *op. cit.*, p. 10.
[46] *Ibid.*

Against ethical naturalists, however, Moore had one very powerful argument, as we have already seen (above, pp. 70–71). He accused them with justice of inconsistency. They contended that "good" means "produces happiness" (etc.); and, in effect, they also contended that the statement, "what produces happiness (etc.) is good," is more than an insignificant tautology. Both these propositions cannot be true. The ethical naturalists believed that they had a triumphant argument in their point that "good" means whatever, as utilitarians, evolutionists, etc., they took it to mean. If "good" means "produces happiness (etc.)," then to say "what produces happiness (etc.) is *not* good" is to contradict oneself. By making this point, they thought that they had shown the position of anyone who rejected their utilitarianism, evolutionism, or whatever, to be irrational. But when, on their platforms and in their pamphlets, they advocated courses of action which produce happiness (etc.) *as good,* they intended to say more than that what produces happiness (etc.) simply does what it does. They intended to say that it is the end to be chosen, sought, achieved. But this they could *not* say by using "good," if their own definition of "good" was correct. All they could say was that what produces happiness (etc.) produces happiness (etc.). Moore may have been wrong about what "good" and similar words mean but he saw clearly that to call anything good cannot be to give it a naturalistic description. And he saw that there was a fundamental inconsistency in those ethical naturalists who thought that it can. He made the point in his own way:

> They [*sc.* ethical naturalists] are all so anxious to persuade us that what they call good is what we really ought to do. "Do, pray, act so, because the word 'good' is generally used to denote actions of this nature": such . . . would be the substance of their teaching. And in so far as they tell us how we ought to act, their teaching is truly ethical, as they mean it to be. But how perfectly absurd is the reason they would give for it! "You are to do this, because most people use a certain word to denote conduct such as this." . . . My dear sirs, what we want to know

from you as ethical teachers, is not how people use a word
. . . what we want to know is simply what *is* good.[47]

The ethical naturalists set themselves up as able to do two
things with the word "good": viz., (i) to point out that it was
used only to describe certain natural properties; and (ii) to
use it in ethical teaching. Moore's achievement was to see
that they could not (logically) do both.

II. THE INTUITIONISM OF PRICHARD AND ROSS

Moore was a teleologist whereas many intuitionists have
been deontologists. The difference, summarily put, between
these two types of ethical thinkers is that teleologists consider
the moral value, positive or negative, of actions to be determined by the end to which such actions are a means; while
deontologists hold that the rightness or wrongness, goodness
or evil, of an action is intrinsic to the action itself. Moore, as I
say, held the former view. He argued that all men, if they
reflect carefully on the nature of goodness, will discern by
intuition that "by far the most valuable things, which we know
or can imagine, are certain states of consciousness, which may
be roughly described as the pleasures of human intercourse
and the enjoyment of beautiful objects."[48] Personal affections
and aesthetic enjoyments constitute ends to the attainment or
fulfillment of which actions may be the means. Actions are
right or *wrong,* such as *ought,* or *ought not* to be done, as they
maximize, or fail to maximize, the pleasures of human inter-
course or the enjoyment óf beautiful objects. Here is what
Moore had to say on the subject in *Principia Ethica:* "What I
wish . . . to point out is that 'right' does and can mean nothing but 'cause of a good result,' and is thus identical with 'useful'; whence it follows that . . . no action which is not justified
by its results can be right. . . . Our 'duty' . . . can only be defined as that action which will cause more good to exist in
the Universe than any possible alternative. And what is 'right'
or 'morally permissible' only differs from this, as what will not

[47] *PE,* p. 12.
[48] *PE,* p. 188.

cause *less* good than any possible alternative."[49] On Moore's
view we know by intuition the ends which are good. But, of
course, this does not mean that it will be self-evident in any
situation what it is right to do or what we ought to do. We
shall have to work that out. What courses of action are open
to us? What amount of good will each cause to exist? Only
when we have discovered the answers to such questions by
discursive reasoning shall we be able to say where our duty
lies or what it is morally permissible to do.

Over against Moore, within intuitionism, stood his contemporaries H. A. Prichard and W. D. Ross. Prichard's most important work has been collected in his *Moral Obligation* (Oxford, 1949) and in *Moral Obligation and Duty and Interest*
(Oxford, 1968), edited by J. O. Urmson. Ross's moral philosophy is contained in his *The Right and the Good* (Oxford, 1930) and *Foundations of Ethics* (Oxford, 1939).
Prichard and Ross were deontologists. They built, however,
on the foundation which Moore had laid. Ross pointed out
that Moore's arguments for the indefinability of "good" apply
equally in the case of "right" or "obligatory." Whatever *definiens* (D) is proposed for "right" or "obligatory," the question "Is what is D right or obligatory?" is not self-answering
and the proposition "What is D is right or obligatory" is not
tautologous. We see this in the case of "right" and "obligatory"
just as clearly as in the case of "good," whether we appeal to
our own intuitions or to the ordinary use of words. Ross
claimed moreover, that Moore, in his later book *Ethics* (London, 1912), was coming around to this way of thinking.[50] In
Principia Ethica Moore had said, "If I ask whether an action
is *really* my duty or *really* expedient, the predicate of which I
question the applicability to the action in question is precisely
the same."[51] But in *Ethics* we find him saying that we cannot discover "any characteristic, over and above the mere fact
that they are right, which belongs to absolutely *all* voluntary
actions which are right, and which at the same time does not

[49] *PE*, pp. 147–48.
[50] *RG*, pp. 10–11.
[51] *PE*, p. 169.

belong to any except those which are right."[52] And he arrives at the conclusion that "it is, indeed, quite plain, I think, that the meaning of the two words [*sc.* 'duty' and 'expediency'] is *not* the same; for, if it were, then it would be a mere tautology to say that it is always our duty to do what will have the best possible consequences."[53]

H. A. Prichard

Prichard contended that with regard to any situation, we can know by intuition what action would be right or obligatory within it, but a certain amount of discursive reasoning may be necessary first in order to clear the ground for this intuition. Prichard defined the rightness of an action thus: it "consists in its being the origination of something of a certain kind A in a situation of a certain kind, a situation consisting in a certain relation B of the agent to others or to his own nature."[54] We may need to think out carefully what the action would originate. To quote his example: "We may not appreciate the wrongness of telling a certain story until we realize that we should thereby be hurting the feelings of one of our audience."[55] And in order thus to appreciate what an action would originate we may need to look into the facts of the situation to ensure that we have in mind every relevant relation of the agent to others or to his own nature. To quote Prichard again: "For instance, we may not appreciate the obligation to give X a present, until we remember that he has done us an act of kindness."[56] Getting all this clear— what the action originates, how the agent is related to himself or others—demands what Prichard called "general thinking." But having got it clear, we perceive what ought to be done by what he calls an act of "moral thinking." He explains what he means by moral thinking thus: "This apprehension is immediate, in precisely the sense in which a mathematical

---

[52] *Ethics* (1947 pagination), p. 13.
[53] *Ethics*, p. 107.
[54] "Does Moral Philosophy Rest on a Mistake?" *M* XXI (1912), reprinted in *MO*.
[55] *MO*, pp. 7–8.
[56] *MO*, p. 8.

apprehension is immediate, e.g., the apprehension that this
three-sided figure, in virtue of its being three-sided, must have
three angles. Both apprehensions are immediate in the sense
that in both, insight into the nature of the subject directly
leads us to recognise its possession of the predicate; and it is
only stating this fact from the other side to say that in both
cases the fact apprehended is self-evident."[57] These quotations are from an article entitled "Does Moral Philosophy
Rest on a Mistake?" first published in *Mind* in 1912. Prichard's answer to the question in his title was that moral philosophy *does* rest on a mistake in so far as moral philosophers
have tried to answer the question "Is there really a reason
why I should act in the ways in which hitherto I have thought
I ought to act?"[58] There is, he held, no such reason. It is not
possible to prove what is right or what ought to be done; this
"can only be apprehended directly by an act of moral
thinking."[59]

It occurred to Prichard that there are possible objections to
his view that duty is self-evident.[60] How, in the light of it, are
we to explain irresoluble differences of opinion about what
ought to be done? And if obligations are self-evident, how are
we to know what to do when they conflict as, not infrequently,
they do? His answer to the former question was: men are at
varying degrees of moral development and some have clearer
intuitions than others. Failure to recognize a particular obligation is usually due to some mistake in the preliminary "general" thinking. Even the best men are sometimes blind to
their obligations because the general thinking which has to be
done in order to be aware of every obligation is so extensive
and complicated. Granted Prichard's basic assumption—that
discerning duty is like discerning that two plus two equals
four—his answer to this first objection seems reasonable
enough. It is, of course, rather odd to say that something is
self-evident and then to add that many men cannot see it even
when told where to look, and not even the best men can see it

[57] *Ibid.*
[58] *MO*, p. 1.
[59] *MO*, p. 16.
[60] *MO*, p. 9 n.

altogether clearly and consistently. Nevertheless, Prichard could have countered any such objection by pointing out that many people are unable to perform elementary mathematical calculations even after instruction; and even the greatest mathematicians are sometimes stumped by a problem. Just as these latter facts, in themselves, do not impugn a Cartesian account of mathematics, so the fact that intuition is sometimes defective does not, in itself, preclude an intuitionist account of moral thinking.

Prichard's answer to the latter of the two above objections —how are we to know what to do when obligations conflict?— does not, at first, seem so defensible. It ran: "To the second objection I should reply that obligation admits of degrees, and that where obligations conflict, the decision of what we ought to do turns not on the question 'Which of the alternative courses of action will originate the greater good?' but on the question 'Which is the greater obligation?' "[61] Against this it might be said that, in fact, we often do decide between conflicting obligations by asking which will realize the greater good. However, I think Prichard would—or could—have replied thus. The obligation to realize the greater good is *one* obligation among others and even if, unlike any other obligation, it is instantiated in *every* situation where a moral question arises, nevertheless it cannot just be taken for granted that the question "Which action will originate the greater good?" settles conflicts of obligation. We may well decide that it is the question to ask; but if we do so, we have, in effect, answered the logically prior question: which is the greatest of obligations?

A difficulty about conflicting obligations remains, of which Prichard does not appear to have been aware. He said, as we noted, that the sense in which moral intuitions are immediate or self-evident is "precisely" the same as that in which mathematical ones are. But, in fact, there is a difference. In the mathematical case, these self-evident apprehensions never conflict. If two or more axioms are instantiated in one example, we never have to choose between them as we some-

[61] *Ibid.*

times have to choose between conflicting obligations in a given situation. It may well be, even if we reject Cartesian intuitionism, that there is a close parallel between mathematical and moral thinking. But there is also the divergence to which I have just referred, and Prichard does not account for it, even on his own presuppositions.

Prichard developed in later writings the views of his 1912 paper with great subtlety, but never changed them substantially at any rate in his hitherto published work.

W. D. Ross

In the writings of W. D. Ross we find careful distinctions drawn between right, duty, and moral goodness.

"'Right'" he said, "means 'suitable, in a unique and indefinable way which we may express by the phrase "morally suitable," to the situation in which an agent finds himself.'"[62] To this situation there are two aspects. The *objective* aspect which consists of certain morally relevant *facts* about the persons or things involved, and the *subjective* aspect which consists of certainly morally relevant *thoughts* of the agent's about the persons or things involved.[63] A number of questions arise concerning this account of right, some of which take us on to a consideration of the related concept, duty. We will deal with these questions in turn.

(i) The first of them is: what renders the facts or thoughts just referred to, in differentiating subjective and objective rightness, morally relevant? Ross believed that there are certain general principles of conduct—prima facie duties or obligations as he called them—which all men of developed moral consciousness intuit, such as promise-keeping, fidelity (i.e., not lying), reparation, gratitude, justice, beneficence, self-improvement, non-maleficence. He compared these prima facie obligations to mathematical axioms.[64] Expressly, he repudiated any claim to finality or completeness for his list; presumably because he thought that he might have over-

[62] *FE*, p. 146.
[63] *FE*, Chap. VII.
[64] *RG*, pp. 29–30.

looked some prima facie obligations which are apparent to other people. But if they are self-evident, would it not be strange if anyone who had reflected on morality as much as Ross had done, had overlooked any prima facie obligations? Alternatively, he might have thought that some further prima facie obligations, which no one had so far perceived, might eventually come to light. But again this would be strange, if they are comparable to mathematical axioms, for what should we make of it if someone said that he had just perceived an axiom of Euclid which no one had known before?

(ii) How did Ross explain the relationship between, for example, the natural property of being the fulfillment of a promise and the ethical property of being right or being one's duty? His way of differentiating between natural and ethical properties was to call the former *constitutive* characteristics and the latter *consequential*. But he does not offer any explanation of how, for instance, being the fulfillment of a promise constitutes rightness, or why rightness is a consequence of it. He thinks of the connection simply as perceived by intuition. We "see" that if X is the keeping of a promise, then X is right. Ross, like Prichard, compares this to mathematics, to seeing that if a triangle is equilateral it is equiangular. But Ross did realize that there is one difference: the relation in the case of triangles is reversible (if equilateral, then equiangular; if equiangular, then equilateral); but it is not in the case of actions (if keeping a promise, then right; but not necessarily, if right, then keeping a promise).[65]

(iii) How did Ross conceive of the relationship between rightness and duty? It will be recalled that he differentiates subjective from objective rightness. Is it our duty to do the objectively right, or the subjectively right, action? Ross originally held that it is our duty to do the former but under Prichard's influence he changed his mind.[66] In any given case it is possible to perform actions which are right in one or other of four senses:

[65] Cf. *RG*, p. 121.
[66] See *FE*, pp. 148 ff. It was Prichard's "Duty and Ignorance of Fact," Hertz Lecture 1932, reprinted in *MO*, which changed his opinion.

(a) an act which is *in fact* right in the situation as it *in fact* is;
(b) an act which the agent *thinks* right in the situation as it *in fact* is;
(c) an act which is *in fact* right in the situation as the agent *thinks* it to be;
(d) an act which the agent *thinks* right in the situation as he *thinks* it to be.

Which of these is it the agent's duty to perform? Ross, following Prichard, held that the answer is the fourth. If any of the other three were one's duty, then before I could (logically) know what any agent ought to do, I would need to have complete knowledge of what, in the case of each of the actions open to him, he would be doing, i.e., what this action would do to him and everyone else concerned; and, logically prior to this, I should need complete knowledge also of the situation in which each of such acts would have to be done, so that I would be perfectly certain that no morally relevant feature of it was being overlooked. But such completeness of knowledge is unobtainable, if not in principle then at least in practice. We do not have the time or the facilities to obtain it. If, therefore, in order to know what ought to be, or to have been, done, one needs to possess such knowledge, two consequences necessarily follow: viz., an agent can never know what his duty is; and he may do, or fail to do, his duty without knowing that he is doing, or failing to do, it.[67] An analysis of the concept of duty which lands us with these conclusions must be mistaken. They are so plainly at variance with the word "duty" as normally used. Ross pointed out that, if we consider that it is an agent's duty to do what is right in sense (d) above, we do not thereby obliterate the distinction between what an agent *really* ought to do and what he thinks that he ought to do.[68] We should consider that he ought *really* to do what is right in sense (d) above. Someone else may think that an agent ought to do what is right in senses (a), (b), or (c); but we would not concede that the

[67] Cf. *FE*, pp. 149–50.
[68] See *FE*, p. 156.

fact that he thinks this, makes it so. Such a person would, in our view, simply be mistaken. The belief that there is a correct opinion, as distinct from mistaken ones, can (logically) only be held where the distinction is preserved between what really is the case and what is merely thought to be so. Ross did not forego that distinction.

(iv) How did Ross relate prima facie rightness or obligatoriness to rightness or obligatoriness *sans phrase?* Prima facie rightness or obligatoriness, i.e., tendency to be right, or one's duty, he said, is a "parti-resultant attribute" of an action—"i.e. one which belongs to an act in virtue of some one component in its nature." Being right or obligatory *sans phrase,* on the other hand, is a "toti-resultant attribute"—i.e., "one which belongs to an act in virtue of its whole nature and of nothing less than this."[69] An action could, for instance, be right in that it was the keeping of a promise but wrong in that it was a case of maleficence. In such an instance its morally relevant features have to be "weighed" against one another. An act is right [or obligatory] when "of all acts possible for the agent in the circumstances, it is that whose *prima facie* rightness [or obligatoriness] in the respects in which it is *prima facie* right [or obligatory] most outweighs its *prima facie* wrongness [or disobligatoriness] in any respects in which it is *prima facie* wrong [or disobligatory]."[70] The difficulty which immediately arises about this view is as follows: upon what *scales,* so to speak, is this "weighing" to be done? We must weigh certain features of an act against one another, but how? Ross's answer is: by intuition. The man of developed moral consciousness, he thinks, will simply "see" in which act rightness most outweighs wrongness.

(v) What is a "tendency to be" right, or one's duty? Reference was made to this a moment ago. If an action is, for example, the fulfillment of a promise or an act of gratitude, then each of these particular features of it instantiates a prima

[69] *RG,* p. 28.
[70] *RG,* p. 46; cf. *FE,* p. 85, which differs in reading "obligatoriness" where *RG* reads "rightness" and "disobligatoriness" where *RG* reads "wrongness."

facie obligation and gives it what Ross called "a tendency to be one's duty."[71] He seemed to think that "tendency to be one's duty" is some sort of positive property which an action may have. But, as Professor P. F. Strawson has pointed out, it is not. To say, for instance, that all acts of gratitude have a tendency to be right is simply to say that most, but not all, of the class, acts of gratitude, are right.[72] It is, therefore, self-contradictory to say that *all* acts which are acts of gratitude have a tendency to be right, which is what Ross wished to say.

Before turning from right and duty to moral goodness we should note a point about duty which Prichard made and Ross took up. Duty or obligation is not really a property of actions but a fact about agents. Prichard put it: "But, as we recognize when we reflect, there are no such characteristics of an action as ought-to-be-doneness and ought-not-to-be-doneness. This is obvious; for, since the existence of an obligation to do some action cannot possibly depend on actual performance of the action, the obligation cannot itself be a property which the action would have, if it were done. What does exist is the fact that you, or that I, ought, or ought not, to do a certain action, or rather to set ourselves to do a certain action. And when we make an assertion containing the term 'ought' or 'ought not,' that to which we are attributing a certain character is not a certain activity but a certain man."[73] This point is valid and important. We might well say of some possible, but as yet unperformed, action that it would be *right, if it were done*. But we should not say that an act would be our duty, *if it were done;* we should say that it is our duty to do this act (period).

Another important distinction which Ross usefully brought out is that between moral goodness and right or duty. Moral goodness, he said, is a characteristic: (a) of certain kinds of voluntary actions, such as those done from a desire to fulfill

---

[71] *RG*, p. 28.

[72] Strawson, "Ethical Intuitionism," *P* XXIII (1949).

[73] "Duty and Ignorance of Fact" in *MO*, p. 37; quoted approvingly by Ross, *FE*, p. 155.

duty, to relieve pain, to extend knowledge, etc.; (b) of the
desire for such ends even when it fails to issue in action; (c)
of the satisfaction experienced at seeing such ends attained,
or dissatisfaction at seeing them not realized; and (d) of dispositions, embodied in character, to act for the sake of such
ends. All these, according to Ross, we call morally good.[74]
We see that moral goodness is distinct from right or duty
when we recognize that it is possible to do one's duty from a
bad motive as well as a good; for instance, to give one's weak
or promising pupils extra tuition, not from a desire to assist
them or to justify one's salary but in order to embarrass a col-
league. Equally, one may do what is morally good and thereby
fail in one's duty; for instance, toil at one's research from a
desire to extend knowledge and in the process neglect one's
teaching function. An agent's motives—with which moral
goodness always has to do—are not under his control as his intentions—with which rightness and duty have to do—are. He
can set himself to perform a certain action and carry this intention through as far as circumstances permit; but he cannot,
at will, find one end desirable and another not so. He may indeed set himself to cultivate good motives or dispositions; he
will then do whatever he thinks will achieve that result. But
"ought" implies "can"; and we cannot desire whatever we
choose to desire. It would not make sense to say that one
ought to love knowledge as it would to say that one ought
to pursue it.

Ross, then, highlights the distinctions between moral
goodness, right, and duty. But there are basic similarities in
his accounts of each of the three. These similarities are as
follows. All are discerned intuitively. All are indefinable.
All are nonnatural characteristics consequential upon constitutive, natural characteristics. All may require us to
"weigh" certain morally relevant considerations against others.
This brief attempt to clarify Ross's position has been sufficient to show that, in his case as in Moore's and Prichard's, at
every vital point in the analysis of moral thinking, a claim
is made to knowledge gained by intuition. In the next main

[74] See *FE,* Chap. XII.

section we shall challenge the view that there is any such knowledge.

A Predecessor of Prichard and Ross

We noted above that the eighteenth-century British moral philosopher Richard Price anticipated Moore's argument against "the naturalistic fallacy" in his *Review*. In that work, he also anticipated the leading ideas of Prichard and Ross.

The former's contention, that moral thinking, like mathematical, consists, in the last analysis, of the immediate apprehension by intuition of self-evident truths, he clearly enunciated. Price differentiated two acts of the understanding: "deduction," by which he meant discursive reasoning and under which he classified what we should call induction as well as what we call deduction; and "intuition" (i.e., Cartesian intuition).[75] Taking Locke's view that it is the work of the understanding to perceive agreement or disagreement between ideas and that this produces knowledge, Price contended that the ideas of such agreement or disagreement are themselves new simple ideas. For example, the equality between the two angles, made by any right line standing in any direction on another, and two right angles is a new simple idea clearly and distinctly perceived by the understanding, wholly different from that of the angles compared and denoting self-evident truth. He went on to claim that, besides such mathematical ideas, logical ideas (e.g., necessity), physical ideas (e.g., cause) and *moral ideas* (e.g., right, fit, good, duty) are likewise new simple ideas perceived by the understanding. Such ideas shine by their own light. They are the ultimate constituents of knowledge and without them all reasoning would be impossible. To such self-evident truths the last appeal in reasoning must always be made.[76]

Ross's views are also paralleled in Price. Price gives a list of "heads of virtue," as he calls them, which is very similar to Ross's list of prima facie obligations.[77] And the underlying

[75] Price, *op. cit.*, p. 18 n.

[76] Price, *op. cit.*, pp. 97–103. Price drew very largely on the Cambridge Platonist, Ralph Cudworth, for his leading ideas. See my *Reason and Right* for a full-length study of R. Price's moral philosophy.

[77] Price, *op. cit.*, Chap. VII.

idea is the same in both authors: that these general principles are directly intuited and one or more of them is instantiated in every moral situation. Ross's idea that the right or obligatory action is that which "suits" or "fits" its situation in a way which is intuited after weighing against each other the prima facie obligations, or "heads of virtue," which the situation instantiates, is also to be found in Price.[78] The objections to this view and a possible line of defense against them can be seen in the case of both authors.

First, the objections. Hume, Price's contemporary, charged rational intuitionists, like Price, with having simply assumed that virtue is some kind of relation, viz., fitness or suitableness, and vice its opposite, because they took it for granted that the moral faculty is the understanding. He contended that if virtue, or vice, does consist in a relation, then, whatever this relation might be, it could conceivably hold between material objects or animals just as well as between human beings. A sapling overtopping its parent tree must then be morally like a child crushing its parent; and incest between animals, the same kind of occurrence morally as it is between human beings. We do not believe objects and animals to be "susceptible of the same morality" as ourselves, and so the relational account of virtue and vice must be mistaken.[79] A further possible objection is that, if moral rightness is some sort of relation, such as fitness, we end in absurdity. An act, to be relationally fit, must be fit, for example, as an instance of a standard. But the question inevitably arises: is this standard right? If this question means "Is it fit?" further or higher standards are implied. Eventually, however, we come to our ultimate standard. We wish to say—and indeed need to say or all our moral judgments are forfeit—that this too is right. But what sense does that make, on the present view, unless there is some higher standard still? And, by definition, there can be none in the case of an ultimate standard.

What defense can be offered, on behalf of Price or Ross, to such objections? It is important to distinguish between two

[78] Price, *op. cit.*, p. vi.
[79] *A Treatise of Human Nature* III. i. 1; Selby-Bigge edition, pp. 464–68.

possible conceptions of moral rightness from the rationalist's
viewpoint. One is that such rightness is simply a *relation* between acts and situations or persons, comparable to mathematical equality; the other, that it is a property of acts, in situations, *entailed* by certain of their nonmoral properties, comparable to the equilaterality entailed by equiangularity in
triangles. The latter conception has certain advantages over
the former; and I think that there is good reason to say
that it is the view to which Price[80] and Ross[81] subscribed.
If rightness is, as these authors evidently thought, what Ross
calls a consequential characteristic entailed by what he calls
constitutive characteristics, such as being the fulfillment of
a promise, then the latter characteristics can (logically) be
so defined that they restrict the entailment to instances where
persons are concerned. Trees and animals do not for instance
make promises. I think the rational intuitionists would be
unanimous on the point that the grounds of rightness *always*
involve persons in some way or other; and so they safeguard
themselves in advance against Hume's objection. As we have
just interpreted their view, it is proof also against the other
objection given above. The entailment of rightness by the
grounds of rightness is the same entailment in the case of the
ultimate standard as in that of the particular instance. In so
far as there is promise-keeping, for example, there is rightness;
we intuit this in the same sense of "intuit," whether we are
thinking in general terms of a prima facie obligation or engaged in "weighing" out the rightness of a particular act. This
interpretation does not involve any regress into absurdity.

III. THE CLAIM TO KNOW BY MORAL
INTUITION

We must now call in question the very idea of knowing
by intuition. All ethical intuitionists—and this includes Moore
even though he thought that intuition may sometimes be
mistaken—subscribe to the belief that there are moral truths
known to us by intuition. They would say that we know there

[80] Cf. Raphael's introduction, Price, *op. cit.*, pp. xxxii–xxxiii.
[81] See above, p. 93.

to be a nonnatural property of goodness or rightness and that it attaches to such-and-such acts or states of affairs. In assessing this claim, we must first consider what it means to say that we *know* that something is the case; and then whether it is consistent with this to speak of knowing *by intuition*.

What conditions must be fulfilled before I can say "I know that X"? If we follow A. J. Ayer,[82] these appear to be three in number. (i) It must be true that X. I cannot know, for example, that two and two make five or that Brazil is in Europe. Of course, ways of establishing the truth or falsity of propositions vary and some of these may be questionable in themselves. But, given whatever it is that we usually mean by saying that X is true, we must be able to say this, if we are going to say "I know that X." (ii) I must believe that X. It would be nonsense, whatever value we gave to X, to say "I know that X but I don't believe that X." This is self-contradictory, not, of course, because "know" and "believe" mean entirely the same thing, but because part of what I am saying in saying that I know anything to be the case is that I believe it to be such. (iii) I must be able to give an appropriate answer to the question: how do you know that X? There are, in a phrase of Ayer's, "accredited routes to knowledge."[83] These differ. The route to discoveries in mathematics or logic is different from that to discoveries in the natural or social sciences. Epistemologists have to make clear what an appropriate answer to "How do you know?" would amount to in any given instance. They also have to show us exactly where we are when we have arrived at "knowledge" by any accredited route, for these routes do not all lead to the same destination. Analytical and empirical knowledge are clearly not the same thing, and there may be further distinctions which need to be drawn within the concept of knowledge. Nevertheless, when all such qualifications have been added, I think it remains true that, when I say I know that something is the case, I must be prepared to say how I know.

I ask the reader now to consider two illustrations. The first is of a mother who says that she knows her son is alive even

[82] *The Problem of Knowledge* (1956), pp. 31 ff.
[83] *Ibid.*, p. 33.

though he has been classified as killed in action. "But *how* do you know?" asks a somewhat insensitive person with whom she has the misfortune to be acquainted. "I can't answer that," she replies. "I just know." In such a case there is no doubt that she believes her son to be alive; and so one of the necessary conditions of a claim to know is fulfilled—viz., (ii) above. Suppose it turns out that her son was incorrectly classified as killed and she is told that he is in fact a prisoner of war. "There you are," she says, "I knew it all along." This seems a natural enough use of the verb "to know," but I think it seems so only because a distinction, which it is perfectly legitimate to draw, namely that between true belief and knowledge, is so commonly blurred in ordinary discourse. Even in the latter, if someone says "She didn't really know. She only guessed right," that will not seem an odd, or in any way a puzzling, remark.

This brings us to the second illustration. An entertainer invites members of his audience to select cards from a pack unseen by him and each time tells them correctly which card they have taken. In such a case there are certain possibilities. (i) He may have planted an assistant who can observe the denominations of the cards and communicate these to him secretly. He could, then, answer the question "How do you know?" if he chose to do so. (ii) He may—a fantastic supposition no doubt, but conceivable—have formerly made some such arrangements but then, through the operation of unusual psychological factors, now no longer be aware of having made such arrangements or of their operation. If asked, "How do you know the cards?" he will reply, "I just do." (iii) We, observing his performance, may be aware that either one or other of the foregoing possibilities is realized and if asked, "How does he know?" be able to explain accordingly. (iv) We may be unaware of any explanation, and if asked, "How does he know?" be unable to say anything beyond, "He just does."

It is important to notice that "By intuition" purports to give an answer to "How do you know?" comparable to that which the entertainer might give if possibility (i) were realized, or to "How does he know?" comparable to that which we might give if possibility (iii) were realized. Intuition, it is claimed, *entitles* a speaker to say that he knows that X; or it *explains* how it comes about that he knows that X. But, when we examine the notion of intuition carefully, both these claims evaporate. If, to take them in reverse order, when we are asked, "How does this entertainer know which cards members of his audience have selected?" we reply to the effect that either of possibilities (i) or (ii) above is realized, what are we doing? We are setting this particular event—his getting the cards right—within a framework of covering laws physical, psychological, or both. We are not just saying that this event occurred, but tying it in with what we know about the way the world, as a whole, works. For this is what it means, in common speech, to explain such an event. But if we say that the entertainer knows *by intuition* which card is selected each time, what more have we said than that he knows which card is selected each time (period)? All that which we would be saying amounts to is that he is the sort of man who gets cards right. But we know that already. It is like saying that opium sends people to sleep because it has a *virtus dormitiva*.

Does "By intuition" fare any better as an answer to "How do *you* know?" That is, does it *entitle* a speaker to claim that he knows such-and-such to be the case? Does it give him, in another of Ayer's phrases, "the right to be sure"?[84] Let us look back to the mother in the first of our two illustrations. Suppose that she had answered the question "But how do you know?" with "By intuition." This reply would have been unsatisfactory for the following reasons.

Firstly, we can form no clear idea of what more she would have said by this than if she had said only that she firmly believed her son to be alive, or "knew" him to be alive in that sense of the verb "to know." The answer "By intuition" to the question "How do you know?" in such a case simply reiterates what was given above as the second condition which must be fulfilled if one is to say "I know that X," namely, the speaker must believe that X. But the whole point of the

[84] *Ibid.*

third condition—that the speaker must be able to give an appropriate answer to the question "How do you know that X?"—is to take us beyond the fulfillment of the second condition. What *more* than "I believe that X" does "I know by intuition that X" tell us? The answer seems to be that it tells us nothing more.

Secondly, we supposed in the above illustration that the mother's belief that her son was alive turned out to be true. But now conceive of the alternative, that it turned out to be false. How would the mother's intuition—her feeling of certainty, that is—have differed in the two cases? Can she herself tell us? Can we discover, apart from what she may say, any distinction in the intuition itself as between the two cases? There are numerous examples of people feeling absolutely sure of something and being right; and apparently equally numerous examples of them so feeling and being wrong. But, as far as any evidence that is available to us may go, there does not seem to be anything necessarily different about the intuition, i.e., the feeling of certainty, in the two kinds of examples.

Thirdly, if the mother's belief that her son was alive had turned out to be false, if evidence had come to light which convinced even her that he had died—as for instance the discovery of a body which she could not but identify as his—what would she have said? Surely not, "I knew before that he was alive, but now I know that he is dead." Rather she would have said, "I felt sure he was alive but now I know that he is dead." Only crazy people insist that their intuitions are correct if evidence against them comes to light which, along some accredited route, leads to what would be generally accepted as knowledge.

The *moral* intuitionist is really in an even more exposed position than these considerations about intuition in general place him. The entertainer mentioned above, if he had said that he knew by intuition which cards members of his audience had selected, would have been claiming to know by this route what could be shown by other accredited routes to be, or not to be, the case. That A has in his hand the six of diamonds is, or is not, a fact, and whether it is, or is not, can be ascertained by appeal to something other than the entertainer's intuition. But the ethical intuitionists do not claim that men know by intuition what can be shown in any other way to be, or not to be, the case. There is, in their opinion, no check beyond intuition on what ethically is, or is not, the case. That promise-breaking is wrong, for example, can be known, and only known, by intuition. Intuitionists say, in effect, that, when it comes to moral values, men are like an entertainer who does not give the names *of* the cards which his audience select but gives names *to* the cards; and he then claims that his names for them are the correct ones. If he says a card is the six of diamonds, it *is*, quite apart from any other considerations. To claim that any such process is an accredited route to the knowledge that something is the case is obviously fantastic.

The casualty here is not, of course, morality, but only a particular account of it. This discredited account starts from the assumption that, if we talk about right and wrong, good and evil, we must be referring to properties of actions or states of affairs which, nonnatural though they be, are objectively there. If such a starting point is accepted, it follows—since we do talk about right and wrong, good and evil—that there must be some way in which we know that they are there, some faculty which apprehends them. Thus moral intuition was conceived of. The difficulties which we have exposed in any claim to know by this faculty make it hardly surprising that Moore did not wish to be identified *tout court* with the intuitionists. But it is not just the conclusion—that we know moral truths (or, *pace* Moore, falsehoods) by intuition—which is at fault. The starting point—viz., that the meaning of language in general, and ethical language in particular, is that to which it refers—is mistaken. What is needed is a new point of departure. We have seen that there are other theories of meaning besides the referential theory. We shall see in subsequent chapters to what ethical theories these have given rise.

CHAPTER 4. THE EMOTIVIST THEORY

I. THE REJECTION OF NONNATURALISM

The intuitionists disposed of ethical naturalism. But they replaced it by a nonnaturalism which most modern philosophers have found equally repugnant. Two main lines of criticism[1] have been directed against their nonnaturalism. (i) It shrouds the matter in mystery. Moral terms are taken to refer to metaphysical entities, mysterious supersensible properties of actions or state of affairs apprehended by an equally mysterious supersensory faculty of intuition. (ii) It fails to explain one essential feature of moral language, namely its close connection with action, or what may be called its essentially dynamic character.

Wittgenstein and the Logical Positivists

The first line of criticism proceeds from certain assumptions about meaning and, carried through to its conclusion, seems to render moral discourse meaningless. The early Wittgenstein and the logical positivists were protagonists in this line of attack.

We saw in the second chapter that, according to Wittgenstein's picture theory, meaningful language, as such, mirrors what *is* the case. Its elements refer to the simples of reality. Ethical discourse, however, has to do with value rather than fact. If it were to refer to anything, it would have to refer to what *ought* to be the case and this is logically different from what *is* the case. As Wittgenstein wrote in the *Tractatus*: "If there is any value that does have value, it must lie outside

[1] Cf. J. O. Urmson, *The Emotive Theory of Ethics* (1968), Chap. 2.

the whole sphere of what happens and is the case."[2] In that sense, he held, "ethics is transcendental."[3] It follows—given the picture theory of meaning—that ethical statements must be meaningless. In concluding a public lecture on ethics, which he delivered in Cambridge at the end of the thirties, Wittgenstein considered the possibility that, since we are constantly tempted to speak in ethical terms, they cannot be dismissed as meaningless, and so his own perplexity about their meaning might be due to the fact that he had not yet discovered the correct logical analysis of that meaning. To this he replied:

> Now when this is urged against me, I at once see clearly, as it were in a flash of light, not only that no description that I can think of would do to describe what I mean by absolute value, but that I would reject every significant description that anybody could possibly suggest, *ab initio*, on the ground of its significance. That is to say: I see now that these nonsensical expressions [*sc.* moral judgments] were not nonsensical because I had not yet found the correct expressions, but that their nonsensicality was their very essence. For all I wanted to do with them was just *to go beyond* the world and that is to say beyond significant language. My whole tendency and I believe the tendency of all men who ever tried to write or talk Ethics . . . was to run against the boundaries of language. This running against the walls of our cage is perfectly, absolutely hopeless. Ethics so far as it springs from the desire to say something about the ultimate meaning of life, the absolute good, the absolute valuable, can be no science. What it says does not add to our knowledge in any sense. But it is a document of a tendency in the human mind which I personally cannot help respecting deeply and I would not for my life ridicule it.[4]

All this seems to point clearly to the conclusion that ethical statements are meaningless; but it is difficult, perhaps impossible, to be sure that Wittgenstein was, in fact, drawing

[2] *T* 6.41.
[3] *T* 6.421.
[4] "A Lecture on Ethics," *PR* LXXIV (1965), 11–12.

that conclusion. Rush Rhees interprets the remark quoted a moment ago—"if there is any value that does have value, it must lie outside the whole sphere of what happens and is the case"—to mean: "because of what judgments of good and evil *do* mean . . . it is pointless to look for their meaning in any events or facts that might be found by science."[5] On this interpretation, so far· from designating ethical judgments meaningless, Wittgenstein would have been simply clarifying their real meaning; that is, drawing a line between the logic of moral discourse and the logic of scientific. It is tempting so to interpret him, especially in the light of his later philosophy. But where the picture theory of the *Tractatus* is accepted, it seems impossible to avoid the conclusion that ethics is "transcendental" in the sense of meaningless.

The logical positivists were less problematic in their treatment of ethics. We considered their theory of meaning in Chapter 2. They had only to turn to the intuitionists for arguments which showed that moral judgments are neither analytic nor empirically verifiable. Moore's arguments against the naturalistic fallacy had established: (i) that there is no moral judgment which is true by definition; (ii) that there is nothing natural, i.e., empirically observable, to which moral terms such as "good" or "right" refer. On the logical positivists' presuppositions, it followed that moral judgments are literally meaningless. As Ayer expressed it:

> The fundamental ethical concepts are unanalysable, inasmuch as there is no criterion by which one can test the validity of the judgments in which they occur. . . . The reason why they are unanalysable is that they are mere pseudo-concepts. The presence of an ethical symbol in a proposition adds nothing to its factual content. Thus if I say to someone "You acted wrongly in stealing that money," I am not stating anything more than if I had simply said "You stole that money." In adding that the action is wrong, I am not making any further statement about it.[6]

---

[5] "Some Developments in Wittgenstein's View of Ethics," *ibid.*, p. 17; italics mine.

[6] Ayer, *Language, Truth and Logic* (2nd ed., 1946), p. 107.

A moral judgment because it has no literal meaning can be neither true nor false, valid nor invalid. It cannot, therefore, be argued about. Ayer, in drawing this conclusion, realized its paradoxical nature, for it is a fact of common experience that moral judgments are disputed. He claimed, however, that such disputes are not really ever about a question of value but always one of fact. In contesting a man's moral opinions, we call his attention to matters of fact which we think he must have overlooked; for instance, the motives, effects, or circumstances, of particular actions or classes of action, which he has judged to be right or wrong. Underlying our argument is the assumption that fundamentally our opponent has the same moral attitudes as ourselves. Since he usually lives in the same social order and will usually have received much the same moral education as we have, this assumption is, as a rule, justified. But if ever we find so great a radical disagreement between ourselves and an opponent that, although he agrees with every factual consideration which we can bring forward, he still does not share our moral assessment of the action or situation in question, then, says Ayer, "we abandon the attempt to convince him by argument."[7]

It is important to remember that the logical positivists directed their opinions against ethical subjectivists and objectivists alike. According to the former, moral judgments are equivalent in meaning to factual statements about the feelings of those who utter them, e.g., "This is good" means "I (We) have a feeling of liking or approval for this." According to objectivists, moral judgments state facts of a *sui generis,* nonnatural kind. Both subjectivists and objectivists believe that moral judgments have what Ayer called "literal meaning," and it was this which the logical positivists were concerned to deny. They did not say that moral judgments are nonsensical in the way that the gibbering of a madman or the rhymes of a nonsense poet are. Some said that moral judgments should be understood as imperatives of a sort; others, as ejaculations of a kind; yet others, as a combination of the two. "Go!" is not meaningless; neither is "Ugh!" It seemed, however, to

[7] *Ibid.,* p. 111.

the logical positivists, important to point out that it would be nonsensical to reply to either of those remarks with talk of truth or falsity. The collocutions:

"Go!"

"Is that true?"

and

"Ugh!"

"You lie."

make no sense. And it seemed equally clear to them that, in the last analysis, any claim that a moral judgment is the valid, or invalid, conclusion of an argument can be shown to have begged the question. Whatever factual considerations are adduced in its support, talk of the wrongness of stealing, for instance, is grounded ultimately in assumption, not proof. It is based on commitment to some principle, or principles, from which it follows. For instance, if we say that stealing is wrong because it undermines peace and order in the society and therefore diminishes human happiness, the wrongness of what diminishes human happiness is, so to say, brought to this argument, not derived from it. We shall have to consider eventually whether the fact that it boils down in the last analysis to assumptions of that kind makes moral thinking different in principle from thinking of other kinds, such as mathematical, scientific, historical, etc.[8] But enough has been said to serve our present purpose of showing how nonnaturalism was rejected along the first of the two lines of criticism mentioned above—i.e., the criticism that it took moral terms to refer to metaphysical entities.

The Dynamic Character of Moral Discourse

The second line of criticism—that nonnaturalism fails to account for the essentially dynamic character of moral judgments—opened up the way for a discussion of the kind of meaning which moral judgments really do have.

Two points seem clear. (i) When a *fact* has been stated, it is logically possible to say that any attitude whatever has been adopted toward it, or any action taken with regard to it. Of

[8] See below, e.g., pp. 192–93.

course we may think the attitude or action concerned foolish or irrational but that is beside the point. Given that X is the case, we can (logically though not, as a rule, empirically) adopt any attitude whatever or take any course of action we choose with regard to X. (ii) When a *moral* judgment has been delivered, it would be, to use Professor P. H. Nowell-Smith's expression, "logically odd" in ordinary speech to add certain remarks.[9] For example, if I say that X is wrong, it would be, not a formal contradiction, but nevertheless odd for me to add, "Now shall I do X?" Again, if I said that state of affairs Y is good, it would, similarly, be odd if I added, "Shall I seek to bring it about?" The same sort of oddness would attach to any recommendation that others should perform X or not pursue Y. True, a *ceteris paribus* clause needs adding in each case, for we can conceive of circumstances in which it might not be logically odd to say these things. We do, in practice, sometimes ask ourselves whether or not we should do what we think wrong, or try to bring about what we think morally good; and sometimes we urge others to do what we think wrong or to spurn what we would say is good. But these considerations do not dispose of the point that *in* judging X to be wrong or Y to be good one commits oneself to certain attitudes or courses of action with regard to them. I must make it clear that it is not the *moral* principles, that one ought to be sincere or practice what one preaches, which I am invoking here. It is a logical point about moral language to which I am referring. The connection between "X is wrong" and "Shall I do X?" or between "Y is good" and "Shall I seek to obtain it?" is *not*, as I have already recognized, that the latter, in each case, formally contradicts the former. Nevertheless, there *is* a logical connection between them in the sense that, in each case, if the latter is said, once the former has been said, it is as though one were reopening a subject which has been closed, or asking a question which has just been answered. This is one thing at least which is meant by the dynamic character of moral judgments: they commit those who utter them to certain attitudes or courses of action.

[9] Cf. P. H. Nowell-Smith, *Ethics* (1954), pp. 83–84.

What is the relevance of all this to the rejection of non-naturalism? From the two points indicated in the last paragraph it follows that an utterance cannot be both (i) factual and (ii) dynamic. Moral judgments, for the reasons given in the last paragraph, are clearly dynamic. It was the mistake of the nonnaturalists to think that they can also be statements of (nonnatural) fact.

If nonnaturalism is thus disposed of, the question which remains to be answered is: what is the correct logical analysis of this essentially *dynamic* character of moral discourse? To that question emotivists, and Stevenson in particular, addressed themselves.

II. STEVENSON'S ACCOUNT OF EMOTIVISM

Origins of Emotivism

The theory known as emotivism, according to J. O. Urmson's recent study *The Emotive Theory of Ethics* (London, 1968), was adumbrated by a number of English-speaking philosophers[10] who were interested only incidentally in ethics, before it found definitive expression in the work of C. L. Stevenson. The first to propose it appear to have been I. A. Richards and C. K. Ogden in their *The Meaning of Meaning* (London, 1923). They wrote:

> "Good" is alleged to stand for a unique, unanalyzable concept . . . [which] is the subject matter of ethics. This peculiar ethical use of "good" is, we suggest, a purely emotive use. When so used the word stands for nothing whatever. . . . Thus, when we so use it in the sentence, *"This is good,"* we merely refer to *this,* and the addition of "is good" makes no difference whatever to our reference . . . it serves only as an emotive sign expressing our attitude to *this,* and perhaps evoking similar attitudes in other persons, or inciting them to actions of one kind or another.[11]

[10] A form of it had been developed by the Swedish philosopher A. Hagerstrom (1868–1939), but his work does not appear to have been known to those named here.

[11] I. A. Richards and C. K. Ogden, *The Meaning of Meaning* (2nd ed., 1946), p. 125.

Urmson also refers to the following early forms of emotivism. In a short paper in *Analysis,* 1934, W. H. F. Barnes suggested that "value judgments in their origin are not strictly judgments at all. They are exclamations expressive of approval." C. D. Broad, in a contribution to the *Proceedings of the Aristotelian Society,* 1934, entitled "Is 'Goodness' the Name of a Simple Non-natural Property?" attributed to A. S. Duncan-Jones an emotivist theory of ethics. Others, e.g., Susan Stebbing and Karl Britton, were thinking at the time along similar lines.[12] As we have seen, A. J. Ayer in *Language, Truth and Logic* (1934) rejected the literal meaning of ethical judgments. He went on to offer suggestions as to the meaning which they do have and these are still considered by many the best brief statement of the case for emotivism. That theory came to complete expression in the writings of C. L. Stevenson, particularly in his two articles "The Emotive Meaning of Ethical Terms" (*Mind,* XLVI, 1937) and "Persuasive Definitions" (*Mind,* XLVII, 1938) and in his book *Ethics and Language* (New Haven and London, 1944). To Stevenson's views we now turn.

Stevenson's Three Features of Moral Discourse

Stevenson's starting point was what he called "observations of ethical discussions in daily life."[13] What do people actually do with moral language? This was the question which opened up the way for all the important developments in recent moral philosophy. Stevenson must be given full credit for having made it his point of departure. He maintained that any account of the meaning of ethical terms, which accords with typical usage, must allow for the following three features of moral discourse:[14]

(i) *The fact that genuine agreements and disagreements occur within it.*

[12] See S. Stebbing, *A Modern Introduction to Logic* (7th ed., 1965), pp. 16–19; K. Britton, *Communication* (1939), pp. 8–10 and Chap. IX.
[13] *EL,* p. 13.
[14] "The Emotive Meaning of Ethical Terms," *M* XLVI (1937), reprinted in C. L. Stevenson, *Facts and Values* (New Haven, 1963), p. 15.

(ii) *The fact that moral terms have, so to speak, a "magnetism."*

What he had in mind here was the dynamic character of moral language which we have already noted. He explained his term "magnetism" thus: "A person who recognizes X to be 'good' must ipso facto acquire a stronger tendency to act in its favour than he otherwise would have had."[15]

(iii) *The fact that the scientific, or empirical, method of verification is not sufficient for ethics.*

In explanation of this feature, he recalled Moore's objection to naturalistic definitions of "good," and in effect rejected the ethical naturalist's reply that "good" refers to "a confused huddle" of objects.[16] Stevenson said:

> G. E. Moore's familiar objection about the open question is chiefly pertinent in this regard. No matter what set of scientifically knowable properties a thing may have (says Moore in effect), you will find, on careful inspection, that it is an open question to ask whether anything having these properties is *good*. It is difficult to believe that this recurrent question is a totally confused one, or that it seems open only because of the ambiguity of "good." Rather we must be using some sense of "good" which is not definable, relevantly, in terms of anything scientifically knowable. That is, the scientific method is not sufficient for ethics.[17]

Stevenson's moral philosophy was an attempt to provide a clarification of the meaning of ethical terms which would allow full recognition of each of these three features. I will arrange my exposition of his ethical theory in three subsections, corresponding to these three features, though, of necessity, there will be some overlap between one subsection and another.

[15] *Ibid.,* p. 13.
[16] See above, p. 85.
[17] Stevenson, *op. cit.,* p. 15. On the word "relevantly" cf. Stevenson's comment: "A defined meaning will be called 'relevant' to the original meaning under these circumstances: Those who have understood the definition must be able to say all that they then want to say by using the term in the defined way. They must never have occasion to use the term in the old, unclear sense" (*ibid.,* p. 11).

Disagreement in Attitude and Belief

The first feature of moral discourse which Stevenson wished to explain was the possibility of genuine agreement and disagreement within it. In order to do so he drew a distinction between *beliefs* and *attitudes*.

We took note above[18] of Ayer's view that men never really dispute about value but only about fact; that, if we cannot show our opponent in a moral argument that he is mistaken on some matter of fact, we abandon our attempt to convince him. Though he does not dissent fundamentally from Ayer's view, it seemed to Stevenson that the matter is somewhat more complicated than Ayer's bald statement makes it appear. There are, said Stevenson, *two* sorts of agreement or disagreement in moral argument. The one is in belief; the other, in attitude. Only by differentiating them and recognizing the presence of both can "a full picture" of "the varied functions" of ethical language, which is "in touch with practice," be drawn.[19]

The difference is obvious enough. For instance, in his highly controversial encyclical *Humanae Vitae* (1968), Pope Paul gave, as one reason for his refusal to declare the use of contraceptives licit, the fact that, were he to do so, governments might apply "to the solution of the problems of the community those means acknowledged to be licit for married couples in the solution of a family problem." Presumably, this means compulsory sterilization. He takes it for granted that, if this consequence occurred, it would constitute a "lowering of morality." We can disagree with the Pope here on either, or both, of two counts: (i) His *belief* that his declaring licit the use of contraceptives might have had such a consequence may not be one which we share. (ii) His *attitude* of total disapproval toward compulsory sterilization may not be one with which we sympathize. Stevenson argued that, whenever a moral judgment is voiced, it is possible to draw this kind of distinction: between (i) what is said, or assumed, to be the factual state of affairs under judgment, and (ii) the

18 P. 110.
19 *EL*, pp. 11–13.

positive or negative evaluation which is placed upon that state of affairs.

Concerning agreement and disagreement in attitude, it is important to emphasize that Stevenson took moral judgments to *express*—not to *report*—attitudes. He compared two simple "working models" of the analysis of "This is good," insisting that the former, not the latter, corresponded to his own theory. They were: (i) "I approve of this; do so as well" and (ii) "I approve of this and I want you to do so as well" (where the last clause is taken to have simply descriptive, not any imperative, force). If moral disagreements are to be genuine, the former analysis is required for the following reason. When A says "This is good" and B says "It is not" then, on the first analysis, there *is* a disagreement between them: one is saying "Approve of this!" the other is saying "Don't!" By contrast, on the second analysis, there is *no* neccessary disagreement between them: one is saying "I want you to approve of this" and the other, "I don't," and each of them could acknowledge both these statements to be true without self-contradiction.[20]

It is of course customary for persons who share the same beliefs to share the same attitudes, or vice versa, and a great deal of moral argument is concerned to secure agreement in belief concerning the facts of the case. Opponents of the Pope, to revert to our example, have spent a lot of time arguing that he is mistaken about the probable effect of his making contraceptives licit. Even though it is undeniable that two disputants may be at one in their beliefs concerning the object of moral judgment, while remaining divided in their attitudes to it, we can never be quite certain that further discussion would not reveal that there are relevant factual beliefs which one of them holds while the other does not. For example, those who do not sympathize with the Pope's abhorrence of compulsory sterilization, while agreeing with him that it would have been a probable effect of permitting contraception, might well be found, if a more exhaustive investigation were conducted, to differ significantly from the

[20] *EL*, Chap. II.

Pope in their beliefs concerning what is involved in, or consequent upon, compulsory sterilization. Stevenson nowhere
denied that, *in practice,* certain beliefs and attitudes do go
so closely together that frequently, perhaps invariably, if you
bring anyone to accept the beliefs, you bring him to adopt the
attitudes, and vice versa. But, nevertheless, he insisted that
the connection between agreement or disagreement in belief
and in attitude "is always factual never logical." It is always
logically possible that the beliefs concerned should be adopted
and the attitudes rejected or vice versa. In moral judgment,
every attitude is, no doubt, accompanied by some belief about
its object, but the beliefs which attend opposed attitudes, or
the attitudes which attend opposed beliefs, need not be incompatible. "Since it may . . . happen that both sorts of disagreement occur conjointly, or that neither should occur, the
logical possibilities are all open."[21]

This logical distinction between disagreement in belief and
in attitude, if it really exists, implies that, wherever a moral
disagreement occurs, the disagreement in belief (if any) can
(logically) always be stated without any reference to attitudes.
But is this so? Take, for example, the Pope's words in the
encyclical to which we have already referred: "It is also to
be feared that the man, growing used to the employment of
anti-conceptive practices, may finally lose respect for the
woman and, no longer caring for her physical and psychological equilibrium, may come to the point of considering
her as a mere instrument of selfish enjoyment and no longer
his respected and beloved companion." This purports to be
simply a statement of belief about one probable consequence
of permitting the use of contraceptives; but such expressions
as "respect," "equilibrium," "mere instrument," "selfish enjoyment," are clearly attitude-impregnated. However, on
Stevenson's view, it should be possible to rewrite the above
passage in attitude-free terms, thereby stating the precise factual belief which the Pope affirms and which those who disagree with him (i.e., those who differ from him at this point
not only in attitude but also in belief) deny. Can that be done?

[21] *EL,* p. 6.

Let us try. "It is probable that the man will have sexual inter-course with the woman more frequently than she desires." This, we may say, is the Pope's factual belief which those who disagree with him deny. But it is important to remember that there are two ways at least in which people may disagree as to the facts: (i) they may make two factual statements, the only difference between them being that one is the as-sertion of X and the other the denial of X; (ii) they may be unable to accept any common statement of fact (X) which one wishes to assert and the other to deny. Confronted by our rewriting of the Pope's belief, his defenders, for example, may well say, "You haven't adequately stated his belief" and perhaps add, "If only you appreciated what he is saying, you would be more ready to agree with him." So let us suppose that we try again and rewrite the Pope's words thus: "It is probable that the man will have sexual intercourse with the woman more frequently than she desires and this will cause her nervous distress and will make the man insensitive to her feelings." Is that what the Pope means? "No," his defenders may say again, "he means more than that." Now, how long can this go on? We want to get at the Pope's precise factual belief so that we can test it for truth or falsity; we want to know whether or not, on the available evidence, there is a significant degree of probability that permitting the use of contraceptives will have the effects which he thinks likely. His defenders may go on blocking all our attempts to state these effects in attitude-free terms, declaring any statement which we propose to be inadequate to state the full content of the Pope's belief. The interesting question is: could they con-ceivably be right? Stevenson says very confidently that the connection between belief and attitude is always factual, never logical; but what if this is simply dogmatism on his part? Is it conceivable that in order to agree with the Pope about the facts of the case, you must agree to some degree with his attitudes? Are there some statements of fact which cannot· be made in what Stevenson would have called attitude-free terms? Here I simply point out that the question can be raised.

I shall return to it[22] when we consider the views of some, in recent moral philosophy, who think that there are such facts.

Leaving that for the time being, how did Stevenson conceive of the logical structure of the argument by which agreement is reached, and disagreement resolved, in ethics? It seemed to him beyond question that the "reasons" given for moral judgments do not support them in the way that scientific hypotheses or mathematical theorems are supported. He was left with the question whether or not there is, as he phrases it, "a *different sort* of proof": "whether there is some 'substitute for proof' in ethics, some support or reasoned argument which, although different from a proof in science, will be equally serviceable in removing the hesitations that usually prompt people to ask for a proof."[23] He thinks that there is and we shall go into his account of its methodology more fully below.[24] At the moment notice the main feature of this "support" or "reasoned argument" which Stevenson had in mind. He said that it "describes the situation" which the moral judgment concerned seeks to alter or preserve, or the new situation which it seeks to bring about, and if something in this description promises to satisfy "a preponderance of the hearer's desires," he will hesitate to agree no longer.[25] That is to say, in ethics, "a reasoned agreement . . . is theoretically possible only to the extent that agreement in belief will *cause* people to agree in attitude."[26] It will be seen at once that this is indeed "a substitute for proof." There is the world of difference between providing one's hearer with *reasons* for adopting an attitude (or for anything else) and saying things which will *cause* him to do so. This is the feature which characterizes, and vitiates, Stevenson's whole ethical theory.

---

[22] See the discussion of "institutional facts" below, pp. 282 ff. The expression "to lose respect," for example, as used by the Pope, may well be similar to the expression "to promise," discussed in Chapter VI. Both expressions state "institutional facts." If it follows that when anything is a promise it ought to be kept, it may follow that when anything is the losing of respect it ought not to be done.

[23] *EL*, p. 27.

[24] See below, pp. 126 ff.

[25] *EL*, p. 27.

[26] *EL*, p. 31; italics mine.

Subtle and, in many ways, illuminating as that theory is, in the last analysis it fails because it reduces logical to psychological considerations.

The Meaning of Moral Judgments

The second feature of moral discourse which seemed to Stevenson to be evident from its ordinary use was its dynamic character, or to use his word, the "magnetism," which it has. He said that a person who recognizes X to be good thereby acquires a stronger tendency to act in its favor than he would otherwise have. In saying that X is good, that is, I am not simply expressing a belief about it; what I am really doing is expressing, and seeking to evoke, an attitude toward it. The "major use" of moral judgments, Stevenson declared, "is not to indicate facts but to *create an influence.*"[27] What, therefore, is in need of explanation is how such expression, or evocation, of an attitude can be part of the *meaning* of moral judgment. Stevenson deliberately turned for the answer from the notion of meaning as referent to that of the use which is made of language.[28] But he located this answer, not primarily in the rules or conventions in accordance with which language is used, but in the psychological processes of those who use it or on whom it is used. He attempted to show: (i) that this is a correct account of the genus, meaning; and (ii) that the meaning of moral discourse is a combination of two species of it, viz., *descriptive* and *emotive* meaning, the former corresponding to the expression of belief; the latter, of attitude. According to Stevenson, the relation between a sign and the psychological processes of those who use it, or hear it used, is causal. The meaning of the sign, however, is not some specific psychological process which serves as the cause, or effect, of its use at any one time, for such causes or effects may vary widely from person to person and time to time; and the meaning of signs must not vary unless there is to be wholesale confusion. The meaning of a sign, therefore, is "a dispositional property" of the sign to cause, or be caused by,

[27] *Facts and Values,* p. 16.
[28] *EL,* pp. 13 and 42.

certain psychological processes in hearers and speakers of it respectively.[29] This dispositional property can be called its "meaning" "only if it has been caused by, and would not have developed without, an elaborate process of conditioning which has attended the sign's use in communication."[30] Stevenson explains in detail what he means by an unchanging disposition and he is careful to recognize such points as that the statement "This sign has such-and-such a meaning" is elliptical for "This sign has such-and-such a meaning for people of such-and-such a kind."[31]

How does Stevenson apply this general psychological or causal theory of meaning to the particular case of moral discourse? In his "working model"[32] of an analysis of "This is good," namely "I approve of this; do so as well," belief and attitude, that is, descriptive and emotive meaning, are combined. But he hastened to point out that both are, to some extent, misrepresented, or at least oversimplified, in this analysis. "I approve of this" describes only the speaker's own attitude; but the descriptive meaning of moral terms may have far wider reference than that. When I say that something is good, I may be describing the motives from which it springs, the consequences which it has, the standards to which it conforms, etc. Again, ". . . do so as well" is a straightforward imperative, but emotive meaning is not simply imperative force. Stevenson said, "Emotive terms present the subject of which they are predicated in a bright or dim light, so to speak, and thereby *lead* people, rather than command them, to alter their attitudes."[33]

In accordance with his general "psychological" theory of meaning, Stevenson held that the *descriptive* meaning of a sign is its disposition to affect cognition. By cognition he meant such mental activities as believing, thinking, supposing, presuming, etc. And he tended to the behaviorist view that the

[29] *EL*, p. 54.
[30] *EL*, p. 57.
[31] *EL*, p. 56.
[32] See above, p. 117.
[33] *EL*, p. 33.

latter are dispositions to action.[34] The most interesting part of his discussion, however, for our purposes is concerned with the question: how does descriptive meaning become as precise as it does? The answer, he thought, lies in linguistic rules which relate signs to each other. For instance, a child may learn first that "100" means simply many; but this sign comes to have a more precise meaning as he learns, albeit by rote, that "100" means "10 times 10." Dictionary definitions, similarly, fix precisely the reference of descriptive signs.

This possibility of precise descriptive meaning, effected by linguistic rules, has two consequences which, we shall see, are important in Stevenson's emotivism. The linguistic rules referred to: (i) make possible a distinction between what a sign means and what it suggests;[35] and (ii) help us to measure change in a sign more exactly by providing precise criteria for the use of the sign at any given time.[36] The distinction between what a sign means and what it suggests applies, according to Stevenson, to descriptive, but not to emotive, meaning. The latter is simply a "flexible mechanism of *suggestion*."[37] Emotive words, like "Bah!" do not mean anything more than they suggest. Two of Stevenson's oft-quoted definitions of *emotive* meaning are as follows. "Emotive meaning is a meaning in which the response (from the hearer's point of view) or the stimulus (from the speaker's point of view) is a range of emotions."[38] "The emotive meaning of a word is the power that the word acquires on account of its history in emotional situations, to evoke or directly express attitudes, as distinct from describing or designating them."[39] Both these are in line with Stevenson's general causal theory of meaning. It will be noted that in the first he speaks of *emotions* and in the second of *attitudes*. He is well aware that these two expressions are not synonymous and warns against confusing them. "Emotion" or "feeling" he takes to designate "an affective

[34] *EL*, pp. 62–63; but cf. p. 66.
[35] On this see below, pp. 142–43.
[36] *EL*, pp. 68–71.
[37] *EL*, p. 33.
[38] *EL*, p. 59.
[39] *EL*, p. 33.

state that reveals its full nature to immediate introspection";
"attitude," "a complicated conjunction of dispositional properties . . . marked by stimuli and responses which relate to
hindering or assisting whatever it is that is called the 'object'
of the attitude."[40] Urmson[41] is right, however, to criticize
Stevenson for not drawing the distinction between emotion
and attitude more firmly than these definitions do. Stevenson
recognized that it is a more complicated business to express, or
evoke, an attitude than it is an emotion. But he did not bring
out the "category differences" between emotion and attitude
which are apparent in the ordinary usage of these terms. It
makes sense to speak of deliberately choosing, or taking up,
one's attitudes, or of being responsible for them, as it does
not, of one's emotions; and again, of maintaining, being consistent in, being argued into or out of, attitudes, as it does
not, emotions. Stevenson calls an attitude a "disposition" to
act in certain ways and to experience certain feelings;[42] but
even this is not altogether satisfactory for we do not normally
speak of choosing, maintaining, being argued out of, dispositions. If Stevenson had been more sensitive to these logical
differences between emotions and attitudes, he might not have
been so ready to accept the conclusion that arguments for or
against moral judgments, as attitude-directing, cannot be either valid or invalid.[43] Emotions, unlike attitudes, are often
thought of as lying beyond reason; consider how naturally a
man, if asked why he had certain feelings, would recount
what had *caused* them, whereas if asked why he had certain
attitudes, would give the *reasons* for them. It is easy to persuade oneself that no questions of validity arise in connection
with moral judgments, if like Stevenson, one thinks of the
"attitudes" which they express as like emotions or dispositions.

A moral judgment has *both descriptive and emotive* meaning, according to Stevenson. How does he relate them within
it? Both kinds of meaning are said to grow up over a period

[40] *EL*, p. 60.
[41] Urmson, *op. cit.*, pp. 40–48.
[42] *EL*, p. 90.
[43] See below, pp. 145–47.

of time and may change. Frequently they grow up together, but it does not follow that they change together. It is this latter fact which Stevenson had in mind when he spoke of the "inertia" of meaning.[44] "Democracy" is used to illustrate what he meant. This word has a descriptive meaning: "government by the people, direct or representative." It also has an emotive meaning, i.e., the power to express, or evoke, an attitude. Its emotive meaning may change while its descriptive remains constant: for instance, in the eighteenth century "democracy" meant, as now, government by the people, but writers and preachers used it then with strong pejorative overtones. Now, by contrast, the emotive meaning of the word is universally laudatory, but its descriptive meaning is very different in Communist countries from what it is in the West.

Stevenson differentiated three possibilities so far as the dependence of emotive upon descriptive meaning is concerned. (i) Emotive meaning may be *dependent* on descriptive; that is to say, changes in the latter may be followed immediately, or very soon, by changes in the former. (ii) Emotive meaning may be *independent* of descriptive to varying degrees. Expressions such as "Hurrah!" or "Boo!" have an emotive meaning which is absolutely independent, cut off from all anchorage in descriptive meaning. Most emotive expressions, however, are such that a point may always come when a change in the descriptive meaning disturbs the inertia of the emotive. (iii) Emotive meaning may be *quasi-dependent* on descriptive. In this case it is contingent upon what Stevenson calls the "cognitive suggestiveness of a sign"[45] rather than on its precise descriptive meaning. For example, the emotive meaning of "pig" in "That man is a pig" is dependent, not on the precise definition of "pig" but upon what, when applied metaphorically to men, it suggests.[46] We shall return in a moment to this subject of the relationship between emotive and descriptive meaning when we consider persuasive definitions.

[44] *EL*, p. 72.
[45] *EL*, p. 78.
[46] *EL*, p. 75.

Stevenson's Patterns of Analysis and the Methodology of Moral Argument

We come now to the third feature of ordinary moral discourse which Stevenson noted: that the scientific method of verification is not sufficient for ethics. The key to this methodological difference between science and ethics lies in the fact that moral judgments have *both* emotive *and* descriptive meaning and not only the latter. Stevenson brought this out in both his *patterns of analysis* of a typical moral judgment. He said that two patterns of analysis, not just one, are necessary because only so could justice be done to the "flexibility" of moral discourse.[47] They were intended to be complementary to one another. He uses "good" to illustrate his analyses, but he said that they applied equally to other ethical terms, such as "right," "ought," and their opposites and cognates.

(i) The first pattern is based on his working model that "This is good" means "I approve of this; do so as well." "I approve of this" constitutes the descriptive meaning; and ". . . do so as well," the emotive. (We have already noted his caveat that this analysis oversimplifies both.)[48] Stevenson said that emotive meaning, because it does not mean more than it suggests,[49] cannot be defined but only "characterised."[50] An example of such characterization is the dictionary definition of "nigger": "negro—now usually contemptuous." This cannot be defined "Negro-bah!" because the "bah!" does not tell us how the precise force and quality of the contempt varies from one occasion of use to another.

(ii) Stevenson stated his second pattern of analysis thus: "'This is good' has the meaning of 'This has qualities or relations X, Y, Z . . . ,' except that 'good' has as well a laudatory emotive meaning which permits it to express the speaker's approval, and tends to evoke the approval of the hearer."[51] He pointed out, (a) that here again the emotive

[47] *EL*, p. 89.
[48] Above, p. 122.
[49] Cf. above, p. 123.
[50] *EL*, p. 82.
[51] *EL*, p. 207.

meaning has to be characterized rather than included in the definition, (b) that reference to the speaker's attitudes is not mentioned here, though it is suggested by the presence of emotive meaning, and (c) the variables "X, Y, Z . . ." must be replaced by ordinary words before the above schema serves as a definition of "good."

Not just any ordinary words, however, can be substituted for these latter variables. If that were so, Stevenson remarks, " 'good' would be a possible synonym for any term in the language which has both a laudatory and a descriptive meaning; and although 'good' is vague, it is not so vague as that."[52] The terms replacing these variables must lie within the "boundaries of common usage,"[53] though, of course, what constitutes common usage may vary. "Good" does not have any descriptive meaning unless there are accepted standards or criteria of goodness, but these differ from age to age, community to community, locale to locale, occasion to occasion. It does not follow that the emotive meaning of "good" is, to any degree, lost. But it does follow that, whereas, according to Stevenson's first pattern of analysis, attitudes are altered only by the expression of approval or disapproval directed to things or classes of things, according to his second pattern, there is an additional way in which they can be, and frequently are, altered, namely by "persuasive definition." It is one of the chief merits of Stevenson's work that he brought out so clearly the role which such definitions play in moral discourse.

He defined persuasive definition as follows: "In any 'persuasive definition' the term defined is a familiar one, whose meaning is both descriptive and strongly emotive. The purport of the definition is to alter the descriptive meaning of the term, usually by giving it greater precision within the boundaries of its customary vagueness; but the definition does *not* make any substantial change in the term's emotive meaning. And the definition is used, consciously or unconsciously, in an effort to secure, by this interplay between emotive and

[52] *Ibid.*
[53] *EL,* p. 208.

descriptive meaning, a redirection of people's attitudes."[54]
The illustration which he uses is two men, A and B, arguing
as to whether a mutual acquaintance, C, is "cultured" or
not. A points out C's limited education, inelegant manner of
expressing his thoughts, lack of subtlety in argument, and
claims that he is uncultured. B concedes that C has all these
defects, but insists that he is cultured, claiming that in the
true sense of the word a cultured man is one who has imaginative sensitivity and originality, and that C possesses these
qualities to a higher degree than many men who are better
educated, etc., than he is.[55] Here, as in many instances, the
persuasive definition which B offers of "culture" is doubly
persuasive: it seeks to take A's attitude of approval away from
one thing *and* to attach it to another, to take it away from
education, elegant forms of speech, subtlety of mind, and to
attach it to imaginative sensitivity and originality.

It will be seen that the effect of such persuasive definitions is
achieved by a combined use of descriptive and emotive meaning. In its emotive meaning the relevant word commends or
discommends, while in its descriptive, it indicates the object
upon which this praise or condemnation is bestowed. The
former gives persuasion force; the latter, direction.[56] The
emotive meaning must, in some degree, be both dependent
upon, and independent of, the descriptive; the former in the
sense that, when descriptive meaning changes, the emotive
changes direction accordingly; the latter in the sense that such
changes in descriptive meaning do not destroy the emotive
meaning's force. Persuasive definitions are possible only where
the emotive meaning of a word is strong and its descriptive
meaning, in a measure, vague. The former condition must be
fulfilled, if the persuasive definition is to result in any significant redirection of attitude; the latter must be fulfilled to allow
room for the maneuver of persuasive definition to take place
at all. "Culture" is one word which has the requisite strength
and vagueness. Stevenson claims that there are hundreds of

[54] *EL*, p. 210.
[55] *EL*, p. 211.
[56] *EL*, p. 227.

words like it in this respect. Where persuasive definition is taking place there is frequently talk of the "true" or "real" meaning of words. What is true democracy? What is the real meaning of culture? And so on. Stevenson rightly remarks that "true" and "real" themselves, in such contexts, have persuasive force.[57] People usually accept what they consider true, and rely upon what they think real, and so these words carry with them the persuasive force "to be accepted" or "to be relied upon." In philosophy itself persuasive definition is not at all uncommon. Philosophical illustrations of it which Stevenson gives are Socrates' definition of "justice," Spinoza's of "God," and the logical positivists' of "meaning."[58]

Such then, were Stevenson's two patterns of analysis, but what was the relationship between them? His central thesis, remember, was that the point of all moral judgments is to exert an influence, to direct attitudes. This may be done by *predication*, as in the first pattern, or by *definition*, as in the second, either by predicating "good" of X or defining "good" as X. If we take the second course, however, we thereby implicitly predicate "good" of X, for as Stevenson remarks, words like "culture" are "prizes which each man seeks to bestow on the qualities of his choice."[59] The two patterns are alternatives, but it seems that, to Stevenson's mind, the first is logically prior to the second.

What difference did Stevenson see between the analysis of "good" ("right," "ought," etc.) in a *moral*, and in a *nonmoral*, sense? He said that "morally good" refers not to *any* kind of favor that the speaker has, but only to the kind that is "marked by a special seriousness or urgency."[60] This seems quite inadequate to mark the difference. Stevenson was presumably thinking of feelings of guilt and responsibility which burden those of sensitive conscience, but these can hardly serve as a sufficient criterion of morality. They often attach to objects which are not really matters of moral obligation:

[57] *EL*, pp. 213–14.
[58] *EL*, pp. 224–26; cf. "Persuasive definitions," *M* XLVII (1938), reprinted in *Facts and Values*, pp. 41–48.
[59] *Facts and Values*, p. 35.
[60] *EL*, p. 90.

for instance, to avoiding the cracks in the pavement or going back again and again to make sure that one has locked the door. Not only other people, but even the victims of such obsessions themselves, while still feeling guilt and responsibility in connection with them, can say with good sense that they are not really part of morality.[61]

Stevenson said that there are two main ways of resolving moral disagreement, the logical and the psychological. Within the latter he drew a distinction between rational and non-rational methods.[62]

The *logical* way calls in question the consistency either of the predication (first pattern) or of the use of the definition (second pattern) of "good." Suppose I say "X is good" and when asked why, reply, "Because X is P." If then, although Y is also P, I deny that Y is good, I am guilty of inconsistency. A great deal of moral argument, though not the whole of it by any means, is, Stevenson said, concerned with pointing out this sort of inconsistency.

The *rational psychological* way calls in question (a) the *comprehensiveness* of the reasons which are given for the predication, or definition, of "good" or (b) the *truth* of the beliefs which these reasons express; or both. Suppose I say that X is good because it is P. Is there something else—call it Q, etc.—about X, other than the fact that it is P, which, if I took a more *comprehensive* view, would lead me to say that X is not good? Again: is it *true* that X is P (and, if applicable, Q, etc.)? In predicating "good" of X, or defining "good" as X, one may not have taken into account, or be mistaken about, such matters as the nature and consequences of X, the motive from which X is done, the origin of one's attitude to X, how X stands in the judgment of some authority, etc. When it is pointed out that one has not taken account of, or been mistaken about, such matters, one can, and should, revise one's judgment that X is good.

All these are matters of *belief*. But, as Stevenson notes, the assumption throughout is certain logically fundamental

[61] Cf. G. J. Warnock, *Contemporary Moral Philosophy* (1967), p. 53.
[62] *EL*, pp. 111–15, 231–37.

attitudes to which appeal is being made. They are attitudes of approval or disapproval toward P (and if applicable, Q, etc.). It is only where these are presupposed that whether or not X is P (or, if applicable, Q, etc.) becomes relevant to whether or not X is good. If, and only if, there is this presumption of attitude do the beliefs that X is, or is not, P (or Q, etc.) become reasons for or against X's goodness.

The *nonrational psychological* way of supporting predications or definitions of "good" relies upon the emotive force of language entirely. An example, according to the first pattern, which Stevenson gives is:[63]

A: He has no right to act without consulting us.
B: After all, he is the chairman.
A: Yes, but not the dictator.

Here the emotive force of "dictator" is brought to bear upon B in order to change his attitude toward the chairman. In the case of the second pattern, persuasive definitions are in themselves examples of the same technique, viz. cashing in on the emotive force of the language used. It should be noted, however, that they can be supported by reasons, i.e., by statements of belief about matters of fact.[64] In seeking to persuade you that X is good by presenting it to you as really Y, where Y is something of which you approve, I make a statement about X which is either true or false and can be tested in whatever is the appropriate way.

Disagreements in ethics are resolved by all these methods, not only as between individuals, but in the case of any given individual himself when he has to make up his mind on a moral issue. He may put to himself, so to speak, considerations similar to any of those which we have just considered, calling in question his own consistency or the comprehensiveness and truth of the reasons which he would give for his judgment. And he may present the situation to himself in highly emotional language. Rationalization, as psychologists call it, is a species of persuasive definition.

[63] *EL*, p. 141.
[64] *EL*, p. 235.

III. CRITICISM OF EMOTIVISM

The emergence of emotivism was one of the most important developments in ethical theory of modern times. It provided a point of new departure. Its exponents led moral philosophy out of the blind alley of nonnaturalism and directed
it along new lines of inquiry into the dynamic character of
moral discourse. Stevenson asked the right question: to what
use is moral language put? If he made mistakes in answering
it, they were fruitful ones, the sort from which other philosophers have learned. The significant developments in ethical
theory which have occurred since, such as prescriptivism and
neo-naturalism, can only be understood, explained, and evaluated against the back cloth of emotivism.

In the remainder of this chapter I shall attempt a critical
assessment of emotivism. I shall dispose first of one very
superficial and mistaken criticism. Next I shall correct a couple of confusions about the emotivism of Stevenson and
others. Then I shall consider whether or not Stevenson was
self-consistent. Turning from defense to attack, I shall finally
marshal what appear to me to be some major objections, first
to Stevenson's theory of meaning in general, and then to his
account of moral discourse in particular.

Moral Effects of Emotivism

Emotivists have been charged with undermining morality.
Their theory, it has been said, produces within those who
accept it a loss of interest in, or of seriousness about, moral
issues. Some would have us think that if the meaning of moral
judgments is basically emotive, then, it follows, and is taken
by emotivists to follow, that in the realm of morals, anything
goes. As one critic wrote with emotivism in mind:

> If we accept in bitter earnest the theory that all differ-
> ences of opinion about what is morally good and morally
> evil are merely differences of personal taste, we shall find
> ourselves driven to the unhappy conclusion that it is im-
> possible to justify on rational grounds the conviction that
> any particular form of conduct is really any better than

any other, however apparently barbarous that other may be. Further we shall be unable to offer any rational defence for our own national or international policies, when they conflict with the purely aggressive policies of leaders like Hitler or Stalin. In the final resort this would seem to imply that conflicting policies that arise from differences of opinion can only be settled by an appeal to force. . . . In short, we seem to be driven to accept the motto of all dictators, "Might is Right." There are very few who will be prepared to accept such a conclusion with an easy mind.[65]

Indeed there are. But are we really driven to accept that conclusion, if we accept emotivism?

A distinction must be drawn between the questions: (a) have some people, as a matter of fact, been driven to it? and (b) does anyone, as a matter of logic, need to be driven to it? The answer to the former is perhaps yes. I have had pupils who claimed that the study of emotivism had robbed them of their assurance about what is right or wrong, good or evil. Sometimes they have offered this claim as the explanation of their own conduct where most people would have said that the latter was irresponsible or immoral, and one has had the choice of accepting their claim as either the true explanation or a mere rationalization. All I am saying is that it could conceivably have been the former. If you have been taught a certain code of conduct by instructors who claimed that it embodied the law of nature, or if you have been conditioned in arguments about morals to appeal to conscience, conceived as a faculty which intuits objective moral truths—and such is the context within which many people have their first thoughts about morals—then it is understandable if emotivism appears to you to knock the bottom out of morality. From which it may well follow, not that emotivism is morally objectionable, but that objectivist theories of morality are.

The answer to the second of our two questions—Does anyone as a matter of logic have to accept such conclusions as "might is right," if he accepts emotivism?—is emphatically no.

[65] R. Corkey, *A Philosophy of Christian Morals for Today* (1961), pp. 22~23.

Rejecting any such implication, Ayer remarked, "In fact the
[emotivist] theory only explores the consequences of a sound
and respectable point of logic which was already made by
Hume; that normative statements are not derivable from descriptive statements, or, as Hume puts it, that 'ought' does not
follow from 'is.' To say that moral judgments are not fact-
stating is not to say that they are unimportant, or even that
there cannot be arguments in their favour. But these arguments
do not work in the way that logical or scientific arguments
do."[66] It may be debatable, as we shall see below in
Chapter 6, whether Hume's point of logic is as sound and
respectable as all that, but, whether it is or not, there is certainly no inconsistency in denying the foundations of morality
which objectivists persuade themselves that they have discovered and at the same time holding, with reasoned conviction, some moral views rather than others. Theories such as
emotivism are metaethics, not ethics.[67] The very existence of
emotivism as a theory of morality entails the existence of morality. It is as absurd to say that emotivism destroys morality
as it would be to say that some cartographer had drawn a
map of a country which showed that the country was not
really there.

As a matter of fact some of the foremost exponents of
various forms of emotivism have shown themselves almost
fanatical in their seriousness about moral issues. Witness Ayer
marching down the Strand in a procession to protest against
apartheid, or Bertrand Russell depositing his aged bones on the
London pavement in protest against the manufacture of nu-
clear armaments.[68]

Two Confusions

Emotivists have been accused of *subjectivism* and *relativism,* but, as emotivists, they are not necessarily guilty of either.

I am using the expression *subjectivist* to mean a philosopher

[66] A. J. Ayer, *Logical Positivism* (Glencoe, Ill., 1959), p. 22.

[67] Cf. A. J. Ayer, "On the Analysis of Moral Judgments," *Horizon* XX.
117 (1949), reprinted in *Philosophical Essays* (1963), pp. 245–57.

[68] On Russell's views about ethics see his *Human Society in Ethics and
Politics* (1954).

who thinks that ethical terms convey psychological information about the speaker and nothing more. In brief, that "X is
good" means "I (We) like X." I touched on this above in my
subsection on *Disagreement in Attitude and Belief.* From the
very beginning, Stevenson was at pains to dissociate himself
from any such view. He began his earliest published paper
on emotivism by emphasizing the difference between it and
what he called "interest" theories; and he gave, as one example of the latter, Hobbes's view that "good" means "desired by me."[69] Though, on his first pattern of analysis, "I
approve of X" is included in the meaning of "X is good"; and,
on his second, may replace one of the variables, "X, Y,
Z . . . ," it must be remembered that this descriptive meaning
was, in both cases, *only part* of the meaning of "X is good."
The "major use" of moral judgments, he said, is "not to indicate facts but to create an influence. . . . They *recommend*
an interest in an object, rather than state that the interest
already exists. . . . The difference between the traditional interest theories and my view is like the difference between
describing a desert and irrigating it."[70]

Other emotivists have been more explicit even than Stevenson in dissociating their theory from all forms of subjectivism.
Ayer, for example, says that although his theory is subjectivist in the sense that it denies objective validity to moral judgments, it differs in an important way from the orthodox
subjectivist theory. "We reject the subjectivist view that to
call an action right, or a thing good, is to say that it is generally approved of, because it is not self-contradictory to assert
that some actions which are generally approved of are not
right, or that some things which are generally approved of are
not good. And we reject the alternative subjectivist view that
a man who asserts that a certain action is right, or that a
certain thing is good, is saying that he himself approves of
it, on the ground that a man who confessed that he sometimes
approved of what was bad or wrong would not be contradicting himself."[71] This is, in effect, Moore's argument against

[69] *Facts and Values,* p. 11.
[70] *Ibid.,* pp. 15–16.
[71] *Language, Truth and Logic,* p. 104.

"the naturalistic fallacy" applied explicitly to subjectivism. In a later paper, entitled "On the Analysis of Moral Judgments," Ayer seems to dislike the expression "subjectivist" even when it is used to mark the difference between his own theory and any theory which takes moral language to describe objective properties of actions or of states of affairs. Insisting that moral judgments are not in any sense at all concerned with the applicability of a description, he writes:

> The familiar subjective-objective antithesis is out of place in moral philosophy. The problem is not that the subjectivist denies that certain wild, or domesticated animals, "objective values," exist and the objectivist triumphantly produces them; or that the objectivist returns like an explorer with tales from the kingdom of values and the subjectivist says he is a liar. It does not matter what the explorer finds or does not find. For talking about values is not a matter of describing what may or may not be there, the problem being whether it really is there. There is no such problem. The moral problem is: What am I to do? What attitude am I to take? And moral judgments are directives in this sense.[72]

A *relativist* in ethics is, to take the view in its most extreme form, someone who thinks that whatever anyone approves of is good. Stevenson's first pattern of analysis, if not his second, might appear to reduce moral judgment to that absurdity, but Stevenson firmly and effectively rebutted the charge that it does so.[73] For any X and any speaker, "I approve of X" is, according to the first pattern, equivalent in descriptive meaning to "X is good"; but again remember that this is *only part* of the latter's meaning. If I say "Whatever anyone approves of is good," I am saying, according to the first pattern of analysis, "I approve of whatever anyone approves of; do so as well"; and according to the second pattern, I am supplying "whatever anyone approves of" as one possible value for the variables "X, Y, Z. . . ." According to both, I am commending something, namely whatever anyone approves of.

[72] "On the Analysis of Moral Judgments," p. 242.
[73] *EL*, pp. 102–8.

That is, then, my moral position. Whatever anyone approves of has my moral approval. This is a logically possible moral position, though it is doubtful whether anyone really holds it. However, the important point is that there is *no* reason at all to suppose that everyone, or anyone, who accepts Stevenson's emotivism is under a logical necessity to hold it.

Is Stevenson Self-Consistent?

Stevenson's exposition of both his patterns of analysis has been criticized as internally inconsistent. Was he guilty of this fault? Let us look at two points where, it is alleged, he was.

(i) Urmson has pointed out[74] that Stevenson speaks of "I approve of this . . ." throughout the first pattern of analysis as the *purely* descriptive meaning of "This is good." That is to say, it has to do only with belief, not at all with attitude. But, in the course of his account of the first pattern of analysis, Stevenson gives this example. A says, "This is good" and B replies, "I fully agree. It is indeed good." Stevenson analyzes A's remark as "I approve of this; do so as well" and B's as "I fully concur in approving of it; [continue] to do so as well." Then he comments, ". . . the *declarative* parts of these remarks, testifying to convergent *attitudes,* are sufficient to imply the agreement [in attitude]."[75] But this takes "I approve of this . . ." and "I fully concur in approving of it . . ." to be *not* purely descriptive, i.e., not attitude-free. Here, then, Stevenson seems to be plainly inconsistent.

(ii) Again, Urmson has pointed out,[76] with respect to Stevenson's second pattern of analysis, that at one point he put some limitation on what may be substituted for "X, Y, Z. . . ." He remarked that although "good" is vague, it is not so vague that any words whatever can be substituted for these variables.[77] But then he went on, according to Urmson, to introduce, not just vagueness, but a "double dose of ambiguity" into his account of "good." He gave, that is to say, no indication why what "good" means should not vary limitlessly

[74] Urmson, *op. cit.,* p. 54.
[75] *EL,* p. 22; italics mine.
[76] Urmson, *op. cit.,* pp. 78–79.
[77] Cf. above, p. 127.

(a) when used of different things in one person's vocabulary and (b) when used of the same thing by persons differing in attitude. Therefore, Stevenson seems to argue for an application of "good" which is both limited and limitless. Once more, then, he is apparently inconsistent.

Urmson said that Stevenson was confused in these ways because he failed to recognize certain features of the language which he was using.

In the case of the first inconsistency, (i) above, Stevenson was, in effect, recognizing the illocutionary force of "I approve of this." This utterance does not—or does not simply—report a fact, as "I have a feeling of liking for this" would normally do. It also registers a pro-attitude toward the object of the approval. In saying "I approve of this" I am commending this. The utterance has, in Stevenson's terminology, emotive meaning. That is the feature of it which Stevenson was recognizing when he spoke of "the *declarative* parts of these remarks, testifying to convergent *attitudes.* . . ." But the rest of his exposition of the first pattern of analysis allows no room for an emotive meaning of "I approve of this," and so Stevenson's present point is inconsistent with it.

It is perhaps of some interest to digress for a moment at this point and to notice that Moore raised the question why Stevenson required "I approve of this" in his analysis of "This is good" at all. Why should Stevenson not simply have said that "This is good" means "Do approve of this!"—an emotive utterance with no cognitive, or declarative, meaning whatever? On such an analysis, when you said "This is good," you would not be asserting anything which could be true or false except perhaps that this exists; though, Moore said, you would be "implying" that you approve of this. You would be doing the latter in a sense which Moore stated thus: "The fact that you *imply* that you approve of or have some such attitude to this . . . simply arises from the fact, which we have all learnt by experience, that a man who makes this kind of assertion does in the vast majority of cases approve of" this.[78]

---

[78] See "A reply to my critics" in *The Philosophy of G. E. Moore*, edited by L. A. Schilpp (Evanston, 1942), p. 543. Moore was, in fact, discussing "right" rather than "good," but his points can apply to both.

It is perhaps the more surprising that Stevenson did not in fact adopt some such first pattern of analysis as Moore suggested, when we bear in mind, (a) that Stevenson did have a second pattern which provided for the descriptive meaning of "good," and (b) that he evidently thought of the first pattern as logically prior to the second. The answer may well be that he considered it plausible to include "I approve of this . . ." in his first pattern because, as we have seen, he thought, however inconsistently, of this "declarative part" of the analysis as "testifying to . . . attitudes"—i.e., he realized subconsciously the attitude-expressing illocutionary force of the performative "I approve of this."

The second example of inconsistency, (ii) above, is attributed by Urmson to Stevenson's failure to differentiate clearly between the *meaning* of "good" and the *criteria* for its application. Stevenson, Urmson holds, failed to see that, though the criteria for the use of "good" may vary endlessly, it does not follow that the meaning of "good" does so. I am not convinced that he did fail to see this or that he really tried to have an application of "good" which was both limited and limitless. It was surely his whole point that the emotive meaning of "good" has a more or less constant characterization, although its application will vary according to what objects its users happen to approve of. Is not this the distinction between the meaning of "good" and the criteria for its application? Again, what he said about limitations on the possible criteria for the use of "good" is not really self-contradictory. He recognized (a) that all communities and all individuals who engage in talk of what is good will have ccrtain, to some degree, settled criteria, but also (b) that these criteria may differ very widely indeed from case to case. If we concentrate on (a), we shall be aware of restriction on the use of "good"; if on (b), of the seemingly infinite variety in its use. Stevenson was never in the position of holding that the application of "good" is, in the same *sense* and the same *respects,* both limited and unlimited. What he did hold to was that, by drawing a distinction between emotive and descriptive meaning, one could account for both the restriction and the infinite variety in its use.

I think, then, that Stevenson can be largely exonerated from the charge of internal inconsistency, at any rate so far as the putative examples of such inconsistency which we noted above are concerned. So far as the second of these, (ii) above, is concerned, there seem to be no grounds for saying that he was inconsistent. And as for the former, (i) above, while Stevenson does seem to have been inconsistent, it could perhaps be argued in extenuation of his misdemeanor that this was due to a creditable, if subconscious and momentary, recognition of the inadequacies of his own ethical theory.

Stevenson's Psychological Theory of Meaning

There is a difference between language (a) having, or not having, a natural power or disposition to produce, or be produced by, certain psychological processes and (b) being, or not being, in accordance with certain linguistic conventions or rules. Is the distinction between being meaningful and meaningless that noted in (a) or in (b)? I argued in the second chapter, when criticizing the psychological theory of meaning, that it is the latter. Stevenson made the mistake of supposing that it is the former.

He recognized that some place must be allowed for the operation of linguistic rules, but the only function which he took them to fulfill was, as we have seen, to make descriptive meaning more precise.[79] They are a part of the conditioning process whereby the power of language is built up, but this is to say no more than that they "render more fixed any rough meanings that may have developed in other ways."[80] The development of the power or disposition of language to produce, or be produced by, psychological processes is therefore logically prior to the rules which make it more precise. When linguistic rules do operate, and only then, Stevenson further recognized, can distinctions be drawn between meaning and suggestion, truth and falsity, validity and invalidity. Because he thought that emotive meaning is not susceptible of linguistic regulation, he held that these distinctions do not apply to it.

[79] See above, p. 123.
[80] *EL*, pp. 68–69.

Whether or not a piece of language produces, or is produced by, certain psychological processes is a matter of contingent fact. Stevenson seeks to reduce the question whether or not language is meaningful to this question. In other words, he seeks to reduce a normative question to one of contingent fact. Now, whether or not language has meaning, i.e., makes sense, logically depends upon some standard or criterion which prescribes what is sense and what is nonsense. Such a norm lays down, in effect, what language *ought* to be. But this "ought" cannot (logically) be reduced to an "is"; or at the least, it is clear that it cannot in the facile way in which Stevenson seeks so to reduce it. For, even if you say, as he chose to do, that the meaningfulness of language is its causal efficacy, you have, by implication, chosen the latter as your standard of meaning. In the last analysis, meaning is constituted by the conventional rules which govern the use of expressions, which determine whether they are appropriate or inappropriate to the occasions and circumstances of their use. This conclusion is reinforced by considering the characteristics which meanings share with rules but not with the dispositions to which Stevenson likened them. Meanings can be learned, remembered or forgotten, adhered to or departed from, as rules can. In learning one may certainly acquire a disposition, but one does not learn a disposition. Nor does one remember or forget, adhere to or depart from a disposition, even though to do any of these things with regard to a piece of language may be evidence that one has such-and-such a disposition.

If rules constitute meaning and *if* we admit emotive as well as descriptive meaning, then obviously we must depart from Stevenson's conclusion that rules do not apply to emotive meaning. Are there any good grounds for rejecting this conclusion? Undoubtedly, there are possibilities of precision in language which describes, that are not paralleled in language which expresses or evokes a range of emotions. But it does not follow that there are no rules governing the use of emotive language. Take the emotive expression "Oh!" for example. Given the right tone of voice, it is used to express

or evoke alarm; and it is appropriately used in certain kinds
of circumstances and on certain kinds of occasions, in a word,
unusual ones. There would be a failure in communication,
if anyone, for instance, said "Oh!" (in a surprised tone of
voice) every time he got on the bus to work, so that his
fellow passengers had come to expect it. His remark would
be nonsense. Take again the dependently emotive word "nigger" and suppose that the cultured and liberal-minded chairman at a learned society introduced a colored lecturer with
the words, "Our visitor, this nigger. . . ." The reaction would
not be one so much of outrage as of puzzlement. What on
earth did he mean? Conventional rules, admittedly much less
precise in their application, do provide a criterion for differentiating sense from nonsense in the case of emotive, as well
as descriptive, language.

The interesting question which therefore arises is: does it
follow that distinctions between meaning and suggestion, validity and invalidity, truth and falsehood, contrary to Stevenson's opinion, *can* be drawn in the case of emotive language?

Meaning and Suggestion

Stevenson said that, so far as emotive language is concerned, we cannot differentiate between what language means
and what it suggests, as we can, for instance, between the
precise definition of "pig" and what it suggests when applied
to a man. He thought that this lent support to his view that
linguistic rules do not apply to emotive meaning. He was
mistaken. There is certainly a distinction, within the descriptive meaning of a word like "pig," between its precise definition and what it suggests about a man if you call him a pig.
Linguistic rules apply in both cases, but they are, so to say,
tighter in the former case than in the latter. It is no doubt
true that one could not offer any similar examples of a
"tight" and a "loose" use of "Oh!" and to that extent Stevenson is correct. But it does not follow that there are no linguistic rules for the use of "Oh!" We have seen that there
are.

Dr. G. C. Kerner[81] thinks that Stevenson was deceived by his own idea that emotive language operates through "a flexible mechanism of suggestion."[82] "Suggestion" admits of two interpretations: (i) "to suggest" may be taken to mean "to induce or arouse a thought or feeling." In that sense, any utterance, descriptive, emotive, or whatever, may be suggestive and what it induces a hearer to think or feel will depend upon any of an infinite number of factors; but this is logically quite distinct from what the utterance means. This kind of suggestiveness is not the *differentia* of emotive meaning. (ii) Suggestion may be a linguistic performance comparable, say, to stating, promising, questioning. In this sense, emotive language does suggest as descriptive does not; and one could say that such suggestiveness is its meaning. But, in this latter sense, what makes any utterance a suggestion is conformity to the linguistic rules for suggesting. To succeed in suggesting, all I need to do is to keep these rules. In the former sense, on the other hand, I could succeed in suggesting only if my hearer had the thoughts or feelings which I was trying to induce him to have. The alternatives, therefore, where emotive language is concerned are: (i) to say that it can suggest apart from rules, which is true but does not differentiate it from any other sort of language; or (ii) to say that it suggests in accordance with rules, which contradicts Stevenson's view that linguistic rules do not apply to it.

Truth and Falsity

Stevenson contended that the distinction between truth and falsity does not apply to utterances with emotive meaning. A description may be true or false and in so far as moral judgments are descriptive, this distinction does apply to them. If I say "This is good," it may be true or false that "I approve of this . . ." or that this can replace the variables "X, Y, Z. . . ." But ". . . do so as well," and the laudatory

[81] G. C. Kerner, *The Revolution in Ethical Theory* (Oxford, 1966), pp. 45–52.
[82] *EL*, p. 33.

emotive meaning of "good" are neither true nor false. Stevenson concedes that someone who agreed with my "This is good" might express agreement by "That's true," but in such a case the remark would, in effect, be equivalent to an ethical judgment of the speaker's own.[83]

Urmson rejects[84] Stevenson's contention. He asks whether or not it would make sense to say, for instance, "Is it true that killing is wrong?" This question seems to him no less meaningful than, for instance, "Is it true that it is six o'clock?" It would, as a rule, be odd to say "Is it true that killing is wrong?"; but then it would be equally odd to ask "Is it true that it is six o'clock?" rather than "Is it six o'clock?" The conditions which have to be fulfilled to remove the oddness are in both cases: (i) it must have been put to us that such-and-such is the case and we are surprised or doubtful; and (ii) we must be addressing our question to someone whom we consider to be an authority. Admittedly, authorities on the time are easier to come by than on right and wrong; and we may not in fact believe that there are any of the latter sort at all, in which case we shall have no use for the question "Is it true that killing is wrong?" But whether such an authority exists or not is a separate issue from whether or not this latter question makes sense. "Is it true that it is six o'clock?" would make sense even if all the timepieces in the world had suddenly stopped. So, whether or not we believe it empirically possible to find the answer, the question "Is it true that killing is wrong?" makes just as much sense as "Is it true that it is six o'clock?" according to Urmson's view.

This seems plausible enough, but the fact remains that in asking some putative authority whether or not it is true that it is six o'clock, we are asking a question, his answer to which can in its turn be checked for truth or falsity in accordance with known and generally accepted tests. But what generally accepted tests are there for checking a moral authority's answer to "Is it true that killing is wrong?"

[83] *EL*, p. 169.
[84] Urmson, *op. cit.*, pp. 83–85.

Validity and Invalidity

Stevenson appears to have had two main arguments to offer in support of his view that moral judgments cannot be valid or invalid: (i) He held that an argument is valid, if, and only if, its premises being true, its conclusion is true; and therefore where there is no possibility of truth, there is none of validity either.[85] (ii) As we have seen,[86] he held that the connection between beliefs and attitudes is always factual, never logical, and this of course cuts out all talk of validity or invalidity concerning that connection.

Against the first of these Urmson puts the case well:

> The criterion of the validity of an argument may well be that if its premises are true its conclusion must be true; but this no more shows that the notion of validity has to be explained in terms of truth than the fact that a criterion of a valid marriage is that both parties must be without an existing spouse shows that the notion of validity has to be defined in terms of the concept of spinsterhood. It is indeed much more plausible to hold that the notion of argument is bound up with the notion of validity and invalidity; it might well be thought to be analytic that every argument is either valid or invalid, somewhat as it is analytic that every statement is true or false—in fact I am more certain of the former of these two than of the latter.[87]

What of Stevenson's second argument? He never denied that when a moral judgment has been delivered two questions can always be asked: (i) is the reason given for it true?; and (ii) does the person who has given this reason hold consistently to the moral commitment implicit within it? When he said that the connection between beliefs and attitudes is not logical, he was not, of course, going back on either of these points. He was simply making the further point that, in the last analysis, there is always an attitude (or attitudes) to which a moralist holds and which does not follow from any belief which he holds. This is the moralist's ultimate com-

[85] *EL,* pp. 151–55.
[86] Above, p. 118.
[87] Urmson, *op. cit.,* p. 86.

mitment and with regard to it questions of validity or invalidity cannot arise. At every stage of ethical reasoning, this
commitment is implicit and determines what moves the moralist makes; and so the whole process can only be called reasoning in a qualified sense of that word, according to
Stevenson.

There is, however, a distinction which needs to be drawn
in this connection. It is between: (i) questions about the
validity or invalidity of a whole system of reasoning, e.g., "Is
induction valid?" and (ii) questions about the validity or invalidity of particular moves within any system of reasoning.
Whether or not the axioms of the system are acceptable is
one thing; whether or not an inference is in accordance with
them is another. This latter question *can* certainly be raised
with reference to any particular piece of moral argument;
the latter's conclusion may not follow logically from its premises. Some commentators[88] seem to think that Stevenson was
unaware of this point but I do not think that they are right.
Nothing in Stevenson's ethical theory is necessarily at variance with it.

There is one point, however, where Stevenson does seem
to be overconfident about validity and moral argument. He
takes it for granted that *any* belief whatever could logically
serve as a reason for a moral attitude. In his view, it makes
perfectly good sense to say "X is good (or bad) because it
is Y," where Y is any putative fact whatever. Suppose, for
instance, I say that apartheid is morally wrong, and when
asked why, I reply, "Because it occurs in South Africa." I
back this up by saying that I am morally opposed to everything which happens in South Africa. Have I given what is
recognizable as a reason for a *moral* judgment? To say the
least, this question gives one pause. If the answer is no, then
my reason is invalid. It is not so because I refuse to work
with it consistently. I am, remember, opposed to *everything*
which occurs in South Africa. Rather, my reason is invalid
in the way that it would be invalid, if I said at a cricket match,
"The umpire ought to send that fielder off," and when asked

[88] Cf. Kerner, *op. cit.*, pp. 80–83, and Urmson, *op. cit.*, pp. 86–87.

why, replied, "He persistently handles the ball." This is invalid because it runs counter to the rules of cricket which
permit, indeed necessitate, that fielders persistently handle
the ball. Are there similar rules of "the moral language game"
so that not simply *anything* which I could choose to give as
a *moral* reason will serve as such? This is a question into
which we must go further below; but it certainly cannot be
answered with an obvious "No" as Stevenson appears to think.
What makes a move part of the moral language game is a
more complicated matter than he takes it to be.

Does Stevenson's Theory Fit the Facts?

Stevenson claimed to have formulated his theory by pay-
ing careful attention to the way in which moral language is
ordinarily used. How accurate was his observation? Most of
what has already been said by way of criticism bears upon
this question. To recall one instance, we saw reason to think
that he conceived of the attitudes which moral judgments express too much as though they were simply emotions. A more
accurate observation of moral discourse would have made
him alive to the logical differences, which we noted above,[89]
between what is ordinarily said of moral judgments and what
is said of emotions. We may deliberately choose or take up
our stand in morals, we are held responsible for it, said to
maintain it. We can be consistent or inconsistent in it, argued
into or out of it. If asked why we take it, we most naturally
reply in terms of reasons rather than causes. In all these respects, our talk of moral judgments differs logically from our
talk of emotions.

Is it any more in accordance with the facts to say, as Stevenson did, that the purpose for which moral language is used
is primarily "to create an influence"?[90] G. J. Warnock has
pointed out that, if one is setting out to create an influence
when one utters a moral judgment, then certain assumptions
are in order: (i) one takes one's hearer not to share one's
moral opinion; (ii) one wishes him to do so; (iii) one thinks

[89] Above, p. 124.
[90] *Facts and Values*, p. 16.

that by delivering the judgment, one will cause, or tend to cause, him to adopt it.[91] All these assumptions, however, may *not* apply and yet it be *not* absurd for me to issue my moral judgment. My hearer may already hold the same moral opinion as I; I may not care whether he does so or not; and I may not consider it likely that my giving my opinion will have any effect on his. But even so, it may make perfectly good sense to deliver my opinion. Frequently moral judgments are delivered where these latter conditions are fulfilled. It would be ridiculously dogmatic to say that all such cases of moral utterance are pointless or nonsensical. Absurdity lies rather in an analysis of their meaning from which such a conclusion follows.

Stevenson is very sensitive to the objection that his account of ethical argument reduces it to the level of propaganda or even blunt coercion.[92] If the point of ethical judgments is to exert an influence and if no question of validity arises concerning the connection between the attitudes recommended and the "reasons" given in their support, then it does seem to follow that the only test left for an argument in morals is whether or not it will be efficacious in producing the desired attitudes. Stevenson replies that "it would be a gross distortion of people's motivation to say this factor is always the decisive one"[93] and he protests that he is doing no such thing. He is right of course. Martin Luther King's advocacy of civil rights was not characterized by that complete indifference to all considerations of truth which marked Goebbels' Nazi propaganda; and no one supposes that Stevenson would have said that it was. But these are not the points at issue. What is at issue is whether or not Stevenson misrepresents the logical structure of moral argument, not the motives of those who participate in it.

He does not say that anything goes in moral discourse so long as it produces the desired attitudes. But the considerations which, in his opinion, determine what does, or does not, "go" are *moral* and *utilitarian* rather than *logical*. How

[91] Warnock, *op. cit.*, p. 25.
[92] *EL*, p. 157 and Chap. XI.
[93] *EL*, p. 157.

shall I treat my opponent in a moral argument? If he is a cold fish who has "let his reflective habits devitalise his emotional ones," then, says Stevenson, maybe "persuasion will assist, whereas rational methods will actually hinder, any quickening of his practical attitudes."[94] So I ought to weigh in with heavily emotive language. On the other hand, I myself may not be absolutely firm in my own attitudes and conceive of the possibility that, if I considered certain aspects of the relevant situation more carefully than I have hitherto done, I might change my attitudes. In that case, when commending my view to a hearer, or a fortiori an opponent, I must choose rational methods, says Stevenson, "to open the way to a counteruse of them."[95] This will be a useful move on my part because it gives me a chance of hearing the other side of the argument, and will help to confirm, or to correct, my attitude. Stevenson has, therefore, substituted for the distinction between an argument's being valid and its producing conviction, a distinction between an argument's being moral or useful and its producing conviction.

In this account of what is permissible or desirable, and what is not, in moral argument, is Stevenson telling us (a) how he thinks people ought *morally* to behave in moral argument or (b) that recognition of such moral or utilitarian considerations as he instances is part of the *logic* of moral discourse, i.e., part of what it means to say that an argument is moral? If the former, it doubtless does him credit but sheds no light on the nature of moral discourse as such. And why restrict the point to talk about morals? What is the difference between, say, scientific discourse and moral discourse which makes sensitivity to the effect of the moves which one makes upon the character of one's opponent or on the well-foundedness of one's own opinions applicable in the one instance but not the other? If, on the other hand, Stevenson is saying that it is a rule of the moral language game that these moral or utilitarian considerations must logically be taken into account when making a move within it, then he is simply mistaken. The

[94] *Ibid.*
[95] *Ibid.*

statement, "I am saying that you ought *morally* to do to X, *but* I am quite deliberately *not* putting my point in language calculated to quicken the emotions which you have devitalized through excessive ratiocination, nor supporting my point with arguments calculated to invoke a counteruse of argument by you which will correct or confirm my own uncertain attitude" —is *not* a self-contradictory statement. A *moral* judgment can (logically) be such quite apart from any considerations about the effect of the way in which it is expressed or supported upon the hearer or speaker.

Urmson accuses Stevenson—and says that this is the basic defect of his theory—of failing to distinguish clearly between setting up a standard and using it.[96] The distinction itself is obvious enough. I use "good" in deciding that my criteria for goodness in cars, students, or whatever shall be C; and then I proceed to use "good" in accordance with C when I say that X is a good car, student, or whatever. Notice that this is *not* simply the distinction between "good" and criteria for its use; it is a distinction between two uses, or meanings, of "good." According to Urmson, Stevenson failed to bring out two important points about the meaning of "good": (i) that "This is good" is *normally* a standard-using evaluation;[97] and (ii) that there is *no point* in setting up a standard unless it is a preliminary to using it.[98]

Because he failed to recognize the former, it is said, he spoke as though the remark "X is good" were always analyzable as setting up a standard. Most of the time, though, we are not doing that at all when we say that things are good. We are evaluating them in accordance with the *accepted* criteria. Did not Stevenson, however, recognize this in his second pattern of analysis? If, as I think, he did then, Urmson's criticism loses its force on this count.

On the second count: did Stevenson fail to see that the only point of setting up a standard is to use it? Here again I think that, although we might be inclined to say that he did, if we take account only of his first pattern of analysis, the thing to

[96] Urmson, *op. cit.*, pp. 64–71, 77–80.
[97] *Ibid.*, p. 68.
[98] *Ibid.*, p. 79.

notice is that his whole discussion of persuasive definition is about how people get, or try to get, certain standards *used*. What other purpose is he supposed to have thought that persuasive definition serves? None that one can think of.

Does Stevenson's theory fit the facts so far as our use of the word "moral" is concerned? What logical features of the moral use of "good" differentiate it from wider evaluative uses? Stevenson's answer, as we have already noted, is this: "We may recognise a sense where 'good' abbreviates 'morally good' and refers not to *any* kind of favour that the speaker has, but only to the kind that is marked by a special seriousness and urgency."[99] It would seem to follow from this that one could take *any* action or state of affairs and intelligibly predicate "morally good" of it (according to Stevenson's first pattern of analysis), or one could take the expression "morally good" and intelligibly define it in terms of *any* set of qualities or relations (according to his second pattern of analysis) *provided only* that one did so with "special seriousness and urgency." But is that how we normally use "moral" and its cognates? Suppose I announce that it seems good to me to spend my life taking one step forward and two steps backward and recommend this way of life to others as "good" with intense seriousness and urgency. Would my serious and urgent use of "good," in itself, make my point of view generally recognized as a "moral" one? Surely not. At first blush, then, it seems absurd to locate the difference, between the moral use of "good" and wider evaluative uses, where Stevenson does. But is what he says entirely absurd?

The question of what makes a moral judgment moral has aroused much controversy in the quarter-century since Stevenson published his *Ethics and Language*, as we shall see in the next two chapters. Some philosophers locate the defining characteristics of moral discourse in its form; others in its content; and others in a combination of form and content. There are some grounds for wondering whether any definition of moral judgment can be enunciated which will net *only* those judgments which we would normally call moral.

[99] *EL,* p. 90.

If, with the prescriptivist, we say that a moral judgment is
a commendation, or discommendation, for which a reason
must be given on demand and this reason must be consistently
adhered to in argument, counterexamples like that at the end
of the last subsection spring to mind. We supposed, it will be
remembered, that I condemn apartheid as morally wrong because it happens in South Africa and that I am prepared to see
this reason universalized and to maintain that everything
which happens in South Africa is morally wrong just because
it does so. Such a point of view, we noted, would not naturally be described by ordinary users of English as a *moral*
one.

If, with the descriptivist, we say that a moral judgment, as
such, is concerned with some specific content, e.g., what all
men want, then it immediately occurs to us that other sorts of
discourse besides moral have the same content. Advertising
consultants, for example, may discuss what all men want.

If we put form and content together and say that moral
judgments, as such, have the content which descriptivists
would attribute to them *and* the form which prescriptivists say
that they have, does such a definition net *only* moral judgments? Compare the judgments passed in our society upon
abortion with those passed on the scattering of litter. Both
these activities, it may be said, concern what all men want,
namely freedom from hazard to life, health, or beauty. Again,
it may be pointed out, those who deliver judgments upon
either abortion or litter-scattering are prepared to give reasons
for their judgments and to see these universalized in argument. So, in both cases, content and form are the same. Yet,
in our society, while almost everyone would say that abortion
is a moral issue, not everyone would agree—or, at any rate,
not so readily and naturally—that scattering litter is.

The appeal to content, or form, or a combination of the
two, therefore, does not seem to be sufficient to net only moral
judgments. Is "special seriousness and urgency" of any use in
supplying a criterion which will differentiate judgments which
we readily and naturally call moral from those which we do
not? It is true, of course, that advertising consultants can be

just as serious and urgent in their talk of what men want as moralists are. Again, it is true, to revert to the above example, that my condemnation of everything which happens in South Africa could be just as serious and urgent as it is consistent. We may be inclined, then, to say that seriousness and urgency do not come into it. So long as we think only of cases like the difference between advertising consultants and moralists, or of cases like the difference between my supposed view about everything which happens in South Africa and a moral point of view, we might be inclined to say that recognizing the difference between moral and nonmoral discourse is a matter of recognizing a differentiating moral *form*, where both are about what all men want, or a differentiating moral *content*, wherein both reasons are given and universalized. But the whole point of my example above of the difference in opinion about abortion and scattering litter lay in the fact that, in both these cases, there is a common form *and* a common content. Why, then, is the one more readily and naturally thought of as a moral issue rather than the other? It is hard to resist the conclusion that this is because in our society at the present time what we do about abortion is felt to be a more serious and urgent matter than what we do about the scattering of litter. I do not, of course, for a moment say that the whole difference between what is a moral judgment and what is not lies in this special seriousness and urgency. It is, at most, only one necessary condition of a judgment being a moral one. Other necessary conditions concerning form or content or both must be added to it before we have a sufficient condition. All I am saying is that *some* room must be left for seriousness and urgency. When writers of leading articles and others urge their publics that this, that, or the other *is* a moral issue, they may not be pointing out that it has such-and-such a form or such-and-such a content. Form and content may be well known. These guides of public opinion may simply be calling upon their hearers to regard the matter with greater seriousness and urgency than they are wont to do. Stevenson's criterion of the difference between "good" and "morally good," therefore, though it might with justice be said to have over-

simplified the matter to the point of naiveté, was not entirely
and absolutely wide of the mark. His error was to treat a necessary condition as a sufficient one, an error by no means rare
in philosophy.

CHAPTER 5. PRESCRIPTIVISM

We turn now to a second type of ethical theory which was developed under the influence of the view that the meaning of language is to be looked for in the use to which it is put. This is known as prescriptivism and its foremost exponent is Professor R. M. Hare. Hare's moral philosophy has some affinities with emotivism but differs from it in certain important respects. Like the emotivists, Hare rejects all forms of descriptivism, that is all theories of moral judgment which take it to be logically equivalent to factual statement, whether the fact concerned be natural, as in the case of those whom Moore accused of the naturalistic fallacy, or nonnatural, as in the case of Moore, Prichard, and Ross. Why then does Hare also reject emotivism? I think one could say, as a preliminary statement of his position, that he does so on two closely related grounds: (i) because emotivism confuses reasons for action with causes of action; and (ii) because it confuses the perlocutionary force of language with its meaning.

I. THE REJECTION OF EMOTIVISM

Reasons and Causes

Two points may be recalled from the discussion, in the last chapter, of the emotivists' account of the methodology of moral argument. First, we saw[1] that Stevenson allowed a place within that methodology to what he called "non-rational psychological" ways of getting people to change their feelings or attitudes. His examples of moral argument included the predication of moral terms (first pattern of analysis), supported by nothing more than the emotive force of a word such

[1] Above, p. 131.

as "dictator," and the persuasive definition of moral terms (second pattern of analysis), likewise supported by arguments which appeal to attitudes rather than beliefs. Since he thought that the aim of moral argument is to get people to change their attitudes, and since these irrational methods of argument are sometimes effective to that end, it seemed to Stevenson perfectly legitimate to regard them as part of the methodology of morals. The second point[2] which may be recalled is Stevenson's opinion that the "reasons" given for moral judgments never support them in the way that reasons support a scientific hypothesis or a mathematical theorem, and his consequent quest for a "different sort of proof" or some "substitute for proof" in ethics. This "proof" he claimed to have discovered. But his account of it was, to say the least, unfortunate. One can change one's hearer's beliefs about a situation, Stevenson said, and thereby swing "a preponderance of the hearer's desires" behind one's judgment that a given situation should be altered, or preserved, or brought into being, as the case might be. By this means, in his own phrase, one "removes the hesitations" which prompt people to ask for proof of a moral judgment. All that this amounts to, in other words, is that one "proves" one's moral judgments by calling attention to various considerations which will *cause* one's hearers to assent to these judgments. As Stevenson himself put it: "A reasoned agreement . . . is theoretically possible only to the extent that agreement in belief will *cause* people to agree in attitude."[3] As we have already remarked, this is indeed a substitute for proof or reasoned argument. To effect such psychological conditioning in order to secure assent to one's opinions is logically a quite different procedure from offering valid reasons for what one says.

It is hardly surprising, there being such elements as these in emotivism, that its critics have condemned it as rendering the rational justification of moral judgments impossible. From the point of view of these critics, it is not simply the case that emotivism offends their prejudice that morality is a solemn

2 Above, p. 120.
3 *EL*, p. 31; italics mine.

and serious matter. They are of the opinion that a little reflection upon moral discourse as it actually occurs will show quite clearly that it is far from being irrationalist in character. In it reasons are given for what is said; and distinctions are drawn between good reasons and bad ones, between conclusions which follow and ones which do not. A theory which appears to put morality beyond reason flies in the face of these facts. Thus it was that prescriptivism took shape. Hare has remarked that this was why he entered the lists. After the war, when he began to do moral philosophy, emotivism was the height of fashion. He found its rejection of ethical naturalism entirely convincing. But he could not bring himself to accept its denial that reasoned argument in ethics is possible. He therefore set himself to work out—as he himself has called it—"a rationalist kind of non-descriptivism."[4]

There is undoubtedly a good deal in emotivism to give ground for the conclusion that it takes moral thinking to be irrationalist. At the conclusion of his early paper, "The Emotive Meaning of Ethical Terms," for example, Stevenson included in a summary of his position, the regrettable remark that "to ask whether [a thing] is good is to ask for *influence*."[5] This seems patently false. Even someone who knows all about the "hidden persuaders" of the advertising world does not page through magazine advertisements or watch television commercials in search of influence. If he has any conscious purpose in mind at all, it is to discover what is worth buying. Albeit warily, he takes the advertisements and commercials to be answering that question. A fortiori when it comes to moral questions, no one who asks "Is this good?" or "What ought I to do?" is looking for influence. He is looking for guidance.[6] He wants to be told what is good or what he ought to do. And if he has doubts about the guidance which he receives, it will not be because he wonders whether or not it will *cause* him to choose, or act, accordingly. It will be be-

---

[4] In unpublished introductory lectures on moral philosophy.
[5] *M* XLVI (1937), reprinted in *Fact and Value*, p. 30.
[6] Cf. R. M. Hare's paper, "The Freedom of the Will," *PAS*, Supp. Vol. XXIX (1955).

cause he wonders whether or not there is good *reason* why he should do so. At many points in the literature of emotivism, there is this failure to differentiate clearly between causes and reasons.

However, something can be said on the other side. Stevenson found a place in his methodology for other elements besides the "non-rational psychological." And, when we take account of all he had to say in his mature writings the question does arise: is prescriptivism's methodology of moral argument radically different from his?

Two methods which Stevenson named, besides the "non-rational psychological," were, as we saw above, respectively the "logical" and the "rational psychological."[7] By the former, we may call in question the *consistency* with which "good," or any other moral expression, is predicated or defined; by the latter, the *comprehensiveness* of the reasons which are given for any such predication or definition, and the *truth* of the beliefs which these reasons express. What Stevenson had in mind in the case of the former is obvious enough: I can shake an opponent by showing him that he is using the same words in different senses at different points in his argument. What he had in mind in the case of the latter method is the fact that one may not have taken into account (comprehensiveness), or be mistaken about (truth), such matters as the nature and consequences of an act, the motive from which it is done, and so on, all of which are relevant when assessing its morality. His fundamental position was that both the "logical" and the "rational psychological" ways of supporting moral judgments presuppose logically anterior attitudes to which the last appeal is always made. He recognized, of course, that the nature and consequences of an act or the motive from which it is done are matters of belief, but he thought that they are only relevant because of underlying attitudes. And so a rational man who applies either the "logical" or the "rational psychological" method in moral discussion is really asking such questions as: Are the relevant attitudes being consistently expressed? Are these attitudes

[7] Cf. above, p. 130.

narrow-minded? Is the belief that such-and-such a case falls under them true? The final determinant of what is right or wrong, good or evil, is always the attitude, or attitudes, which have been adopted.

Now, how far removed is all this from what a prescriptivist, such as Hare, would say about rational procedure in moral thinking? We are not yet in a position to answer that question; but, anticipating, one can indicate some of the points at which it may well come into focus. Hare, we shall find, speaks of morality as grounded logically in decisions of principle—we are entitled to ask whether these differ radically from Stevenson's logically fundamental attitudes. Hare recognizes that one way of rationally defeating an opponent in moral discussion is to show that the reason which he offers for his judgment is in fact untrue; and he considered that rational moral thinking would range over all morally relevant aspects of an act or state of affairs before pronouncing judgment upon it. Are not these the very points which Stevenson was making when, in explaining his "rational psychological" method, he dwelt upon the necessity for comprehensiveness and truth in the reasons with which attitudes are supported? Again, Hare, as we shall see, considered that it is constitutive of moral argument, as moral, that the reasons given within it shall be universalizable. At this point perhaps we have come to the parting of the ways. Stevenson's "logical" method of supporting a moral judgment was by consistency in the attitude expressed or in the reasons given for it. He thought, however, that this is simply *one* method, among others, of moral argument or deliberation. Hare, on the other hand, thought of the universalizability of the reasons offered within it as a *sine qua non* of moral argument, or deliberation, as moral.

We shall return below to the matters upon which I have just touched. But first I must outline a second ground—closely related to the charge of confusing reasons with causes—upon which Hare rejected emotivism. There is a difference between him and the emotivists more radical than that which lies in what respectively they take the methodology of morals to be. It lies in what they take meaning to be.

Meaning and Perlocutionary Force

We have seen in the last two chapters that Stevenson's emotivism was based on a general theory of meaning. I will recapitulate briefly. The psychological theory of meaning is to the effect that the meaning of a sign is its dispositional property to cause, or to be caused by, certain psychological processes in the hearer or the speaker respectively. To this Stevenson subscribed. If this theory were true, then we should have explained the meaning of any given piece of language when we had shown either what psychological process in the speaker had caused it, or what psychological processes it itself had caused in the hearer, or possibly both. We noted the basic defect in this conception of meaning. There is a logical distinction between empirical generalizations to the effect that such-and-such psychological processes cause, or are caused by, the utterance of such-and-such language, on the one hand, and normative rules or conventions, which lay down when it is appropriate or inappropriate to use such-and-such language, on the other. Whether or not language is meaningful is determined, not by whether or not it has such-and-such a cause or effect, but by whether it is or is not in accordance with certain conventions or rules for its use.

We see that what causes a *speaker* to say something is clearly a different matter from the meaning of whatever it is that the speaker says, when we recognize that what he says can have the same meaning, though conceivably quite different causes. Suppose two colleagues of Smith, Jones and Brown, are members of an academic committee which is considering Smith for promotion. Both say "Smith is a poor scholar. Don't promote him." Jones says these things because he feels malice toward Smith and wants to prevent the latter's advancement. Brown says them because he sincerely believes that Smith does not deserve promotion and feels bound to express his opinion honestly to the committee. In this example, the psychological processes which caused Jones and Brown respectively to speak about Smith as they did were radically different, but even so the *meaning* of what each of them said was precisely the same.

If we turn now to the view that the meaning of language is its dispositional property to cause certain psychological processes in the *hearer,* then a similar logical distinction has to be drawn. The meaning of an utterance cannot (logically) be identified with its effects, or even with what it is intended to effect. Depending on the circumstances and on the hearers concerned, the remark "Smith is a poor scholar. Don't promote him" could cause a wide variety of psychological processes to occur: surprise, resentment, contempt, amusement—the list is endless. But the meaning of "Smith is a poor scholar. Don't promote him" would remain the same whatever the effect which it produced. Hare has pointed out[8] that what a speaker *gets* his hearers to do by saying something is logically distinct from what he *tells* them to do in saying it. Jones or Brown would have *succeeded* in telling their committee that Smith is a poor scholar simply when they had uttered the words "Smith is a poor scholar," and in telling it not to promote Smith when they had simply said "Don't promote him." But they might *not* have succeeded thereby in getting the committee to believe the former or act upon the latter. A speaker may—indeed if he is sincere, usually will—intend to effect something by whatever it is that he says. If you tell people that Smith is a poor scholar, you normally intend thereby to get them to believe it; and if you say, "Don't promote him," you normally intend thereby to stop them from promoting him. But—and this is the important point—in neither case is what is said meaningless if it does *not* have the intended effect. The difference which must be recognized here is that between the *perlocutionary force* of an utterance—what the speaker intends to do by making it—and the *meaning* of the utterance.[9] Hare, with full justification, maintained that a basic defect in emotivism is the failure of its exponents to draw this distinction clearly—or indeed at all—in their theory of ethics.

Notice that they could (logically) have done so. Within

[8] Cf. Hare, *op. cit.,*
[9] Cf. above, pp. 54–63.

their own conception of emotive meaning, the distinction just referred to could have been drawn. Suppose moral utterances are logically comparable to *ejaculations,* as some early emotivists thought. There are rules by reference to which expressions such as "Boo" or "Hurrah" make sense or nonsense on any given occasion.[10] "Boo" and "Hurrah" are *words* and, as such, should be distinguished clearly from expressions of emotion such as tears or giggles, sighs or screams, grunts or groans, etc. Frequently these latter expressions of emotion are involuntary. If, in such a case, one asked what, for instance, a groan "meant," one would really be looking for some causal explanation of the groan—such as, for instance, "He's groaning because he's lost all his money." This would explain it because there is a common connection in our experience between losing all one's money and involuntary groaning. It is important to differentiate such a use of the verb "to mean" from the sense in which I have been using it in this section so far.[11] Perhaps Stevenson's mistakes about meaning are due to a failure on his part to mark this difference and all that it implies. In the sense in which I have been using "to mean," an involuntary groan does not mean anything. There are no rules or conventions for its appropriate use. And so there is no point in the question "Does this groan make sense or nonsense?" In so far as a groan, or similar expression of emotion, is voluntary, there will be rules or conventions which determine whether it is meaningless. But this is to say no more than that, in such a case, a groan functions as a word (or words), not a mere exhalation of breath. Where *words,* i.e., conventional signs of one sort or another, are concerned, their meaning consists in rules for their correct use. And so, if we say that moral judgments are logically similar to ejaculations such as "Boo" or "Hurrah," we must still recognize that there is a distinction which can be drawn between: (i) what they mean; and (ii) each of the following—(ii.a) what causes anyone to utter them, (ii.b) what effect they have on those who hear them, (ii.c) what effect they are intended to have by the speaker on those who hear them.

[10] Cf. above, pp. 141–42.
[11] Cf. above, p. 40.

If we suppose, as some other early emotivists taught, that moral judgments are logically comparable, not so much to ejaculations as to *imperatives,* exactly the same distinctions can be drawn. What an imperative, and any utterance comparable in logical character, means is determined by rules or conventions for its use. Its meaning is distinct from what causes anyone to utter it, from whatever effect its utterance may have, and from whatever effect it may be intended to have. We have seen that the imperative, "Don't promote Smith!" could be caused by malice or conscientiousness on the part of the speaker; and that it could produce varying reactions—surprise, resentment, etc.—in those who hear it. It is true that if we ask what effect an imperative is intended to have the normal answer will be: the doing of whatever it is that we are telling our hearers to do. But this need not be the invariable answer. To revert to our example, it is conceivable that Jones and Brown should not have been motivated by malice and a sense of duty respectively as we supposed, but have been both of them eager to see Smith promoted, and yet still said precisely what we supposed them to say. On the committee with them, let us imagine, are three other colleagues. Jones and Brown do not feel sure of carrying any one of these with them in support of Smith by expatiating upon the latter's good qualities. But they do know that all the other three members of the committee dislike them and lose no opportunity to disagree with them. They therefore decide to say "Don't promote Smith," confident that this will unite the other three in saying "Let us promote him" and thereby secure a majority in favor of Smith. A fantastic example, perhaps, though stranger things have happened on academic committees. The point is that in such an example the meaning of "Don't promote Smith" would be exactly the same as if, by uttering that imperative, Jones and Brown were trying to get the committee *not* to promote him. The perlocutionary force of their imperative is different in the two instances, but its meaning is the same.

So, the emotivists *could* have drawn—on either an "ejaculatory" or an "imperative" interpretation of the emotive meaning of moral judgments—the distinction between perlocution-

ary force and meaning, which Hare rightly accuses them of
overlooking.

II. HARE'S ACCOUNT OF PRESCRIPTIVISM

Hare lists the following as the "three most important truths
about moral judgments":[12] (i) They are a kind of prescriptive judgment. (ii) They are distinguished from other prescriptive judgments by being universalizable. (iii) There can
be rational procedure in moral thinking and argument because logical relations between prescriptive judgments are possible. I will attempt an exposition of Hare's moral philosophy
under three corresponding heads.

(I) PRESCRIPTIVITY

Supervenience

Value-words, i.e., words such as "good," "right," and
"ought," have, according to Hare, a "supervenient character." He arrived at this conclusion by reflecting upon certain
features of their ordinary use. It is, for instance, *always* logically legitimate to ask for a reason when value judgments
have been delivered.[13] Take these examples: "This is a good
book," "This is the right road," "You ought to pay your
tailor's bill." In every case it would be in order for the person
so addressed to ask "Why?" And the answer to the question
typically would be some naturalistic description of the thing
concerned, e.g., "The characters in this book are very funny,"
"This road will take us to our destination," "Your tailor made
you a suit on the understanding that you would pay for it."
The justification, or ground, of goodness, rightness, or oughtness respectively lies in certain non-evaluative characteristics
of the thing or action being judged. To take another, closely
related, feature of the ordinary use of "good," "right," and
"ought," there is something which it is *never* logically legitimate to say.[14] You would puzzle your hearers if you said
that two things, A and B, are alike in every respect except

[12] *FR*, pp. 4–5.
[13] *LM*, p. 176; *FR*, pp. 36–37.
[14] *LM*, pp. 81, 153.

that A is good and B is not; or if you said that two actions, C and D, were exactly the same except that C was right, or obligatory, and D was not. They would insist that there must be some other difference to account for this one. But if you said, for instance, "This book is exactly like that one except that this has a red cover," no such insistence would be forthcoming. Differences in value have to be accounted for by differences of another kind as other sorts of difference do not.

Why then do value words have this supervenient character? Hare rejected two ways of explaining it: those of the ethical naturalist and the ethical intuitionist respectively. According to the naturalist, there are certain natural properties—call them P—which acts or states of affairs may have, such that the statement "X has P" entails "X is good" (or "right," or "obligatory"). This is so because "having P" is what "being good" means. We have already discussed[15] Moore's famous refutation of any such naturalistic theory. It is a mistake to suppose that "good" *means* "producing happiness," or whatever, because, in ordinary use, "Is what produces happiness (etc.) good?" is always an open question and "What produces happiness (etc.) is good" is never an insignificant tautology. Hare thinks that this argument of Moore's "rests, albeit insecurely, upon a secure foundation."[16] We shall see where the insecurity lies in a moment. But note first that Hare goes along with Moore in the view that the relationship between value judgments and the naturalistic descriptions upon which they are supervenient is not one of entailment due to equivalence of meaning.

Neither—and here we come to the insecurity in Moore's view and the second account of supervenience which Hare rejects—is it an entailment apprehended by intuition. According to Moore, and more explicitly to Ross, the relationship between, for example, "giving aesthetic enjoyment" and "being good," or between "fulfilling a promise" and "being right," respectively, is a self-evident one of which all rational beings, as such, are aware. The natural properties are, to be

[15] Pp. 69–74.
[16] *LM*, p. 83.

sure, logically distinct from the nonnatural. The former statement in each of the pairs just quoted does not mean the
same as the latter. Nevertheless, the former in each case entails the latter in the sense that if anything is describable as
"giving aesthetic enjoyment" all rational beings as such will
see that it is also describable as "being good," or if as "fulfilling a promise," also as "being right." This view—that words
like "good" and "right" describe nonnatural properties intuitively perceived to be entailed by natural ones—Hare finds just
as unacceptable as the naturalists' view that value judgments
have the same meaning as certain naturalistic descriptions.
The "insecurity" which he detects in Moore's view is Moore's
failure to perceive that value words, in their typical primary
use, *do not describe at all.*

Whereas Moore and Ross had asked to what value-words
refer, Hare asked what job they are used to do. Reflection
upon their ordinary use convinced him that they "are used
primarily for giving advice or instruction, or in general for
guiding choices."[17] In a word, their use is *prescriptive.* Hare
recognizes that prescribing is a many-sided activity: it includes
such diverse uses of language as, for example, commending
pictures, instructing pupils, or deciding questions of duty. His
main point against both the naturalist and the intuitionist explanations of supervenience was that, if you take value words
to be descriptive, you put them out of work; it is then logically
impossible for them to do any of the jobs which they are primarily used to do. Says Hare: "Let us generalise. If 'P is a
good picture' is held to mean the same as 'P is a picture and
P is C,' then it will become impossible to commend pictures
for being C; it will be possible only to say that they are C. It
is important to realize that this difficulty has nothing to do
with the particular example that I have chosen. It is not because we have chosen the wrong defining characteristics; it
is because, whatever defining characteristics we choose, this
objection arises, that we can no longer commend an object
for possessing those characteristics."[18]

[17] *LM*, p. 155.
[18] *LM*, p. 85.

Given, then, the primarily prescriptive character of value words, how does Hare account for their supervenience? He says that the reason for the latter is that value words are used in order to teach, or affirm, or otherwise draw attention to, standards, rules, or principles for choosing between actions or states of affairs.[19] In order to see how this explains it, we must anticipate the next section so far as to notice one further feature of the ordinary use of words like "good," "right," and "ought." We have already noted the logical legitimacy of asking why, for instance, a certain book is said to be good. Suppose the answer is "Because the characters in it are very funny." Anyone who then wished to refute the judgment that the book is good could—and typically would—challenge this reason for thinking it good by taking either of two steps. He might dispute the factual claim that the characters in the book are amusing. Alternatively, he might call attention to another book which also has amusing characters but which he hopes those with whom he is arguing would not consider a good book. In making this latter move, he would be universalizing the reason which had been given. He would treat it as setting up a standard of goodness and challenge it accordingly. This shows us what constitutes the relationship of supervenience between "This is a good book" and "The characters in this book are very funny." When we give the latter as a reason for the former, we are invoking or applying a general criterion—a standard, rule, or principle. It is our subscription to that general criterion, not any equivalence in meaning or mysterious intuition, which logically constitutes the supervenience. To this subject I shall return below.[20]

Value-Judgments and Imperatives

We must now look a little more closely at the notion of prescriptivity to see precisely what Hare meant by it. He makes it true by definition that value judgments entail imperatives: "I propose to say that the test, whether someone is using the judgment 'I ought to do X' as a value-judgment or

[19] *LM*, p. 159.
[20] See pp. 182–84.

not is, 'Does he or does he not recognize that if he assents
to the judgment, he must also assent to the command 'Let
me do X'?"[21] With particular reference to moral value judgments he writes as follows in *The Language of Morals.*

> All the words discussed . . . [i.e. "good," "right," and
> "ought"] have it as their distinctive function either to com-
> mend or in some other way to guide choices or actions; and
> it is this essential feature which defies any analysis in purely
> factual terms. But to guide choices or actions, a moral judg-
> ment has to be such that if a person assents to it, he must
> assent to some imperative sentence derivable from it; in
> other words, if a person does not assent to some imperative
> sentence, that is knock-down evidence that he does not as-
> sent to the moral judgment in an evaluative sense—though
> of course he may assent to it in some other sense. . . .
> This is true by my definition of the word evaluative. But to
> say this is to say that if he professes to assent to the moral
> judgment, but does not assent to the imperative, he must
> have misunderstood the moral judgment (by taking it to be
> non-evaluative, though the speaker intended it to be evalu-
> ative). We are therefore clearly entitled to say that the
> moral judgment entails the imperative; for to say that one
> judgment entails another is simply to say that you cannot
> assent to the first and dissent from the second unless you
> have misunderstood one or the other; and this "cannot" is
> a logical "cannot"—if someone assents to the first and not
> to the second, this is in itself a sufficient criterion for say-
> ing that he has misunderstood the meaning of one or the
> other. Thus to say that moral judgments guide actions, and
> to say that they entail imperatives, comes to much the same
> thing.[22]

A number of questions arise here, in answering which we
shall, I hope, get the notion of prescriptivity into clearer
focus.

(i) Is Hare's definition of a value judgment arbitrary?
While admitting that he has carried his point by definition,
Hare claims that this definition is in accordance with ordinary

[21] *LM,* pp. 168–69.
[22] *LM,* pp. 171–72.

usage. Value-judgments in general, and moral ones in particular, are used to guide choices, i.e., to tell people to select one thing rather than another or to do one thing rather than another. They prescribe action. We shall see shortly that as Hare recognized, this statement requires some qualification, but it undoubtedly represents *one* typical use to which value judgments are put. When people get into arguments about what is good, right, or obligatory, it would be absurd to say that these are normally arguments the conclusion of which has no direct bearing on what anybody is to do.[23] Hare's definition is therefore not arbitrary.

(ii) How precisely did Hare conceive of the connection between value judgments and action? He recognized that someone might assent to the value judgment "I ought to do X" but dissent from the command "Let me do X." But he held that there are only two possible explanations of this occurrence: either the speaker does not understand the meaning of the words which he is using or he is insincere. Hare's claim is that, where these two conditions *are* fulfilled—that the speaker understands what he is saying and is sincere—a speaker who is using "I ought to do X" as a value judgment will assent to the command "Let me do X."

Given the sincerity of the value judgment, what constitutes sincere assent to the entailed command? Hare's answer is: "It is a tautology to say that we cannot sincerely assent to a command addressed to ourselves, and *at the same time* not perform it, if now is the occasion for performing it, and it is in our (physical and psychological) power to do so."[24] One common objection to Hare's prescriptivism, which he thinks so important that he devotes a whole chapter of *Freedom and Reason* to its rebuttal, is as follows. If value judgments implied sincere assent to an imperative, as such assent has just been defined, then it would be logically impossible to assent sincerely to any such judgment and yet act contrary to it. But manifestly this is *not* logically impossible. Sincere people can be morally weak. It makes perfectly good sense to say that someone thinks he ought to do X but is failing to do it. Hare's

[23] Cf. *FR*, p. 90.
[24] *LM*, p. 20; cf. *FR*, p. 79.

reply is that it is to meet just such an objection that he has included in his above defini on of sincere assent to a command the condition, "if . . . it is in our (physical and psychological) power to do so [i.e., to perform the command]"; and he drives his point home: "Nobody in his senses would maintain that a person who assents to an imperative must (analytically) act on it even when he is unable to do so."[25] This of course is so; it is logically possible to conceive of the following train of events, for example. I think that I ought to pay my tailor's bill. I assent to the entailed imperative "Let me pay it." I draw a check and then *either* (a) find that I have no money with which to honor the check *or* (b) put it in my pocket and forget to post it. In this example, I am supposing that it is not in my power (a) to avoid bankruptcy or (b) to avoid such lapses of memory as that supposed. To deny, with such cases in mind, that I can sincerely assent to a value judgment and yet act contrary to it would be absurd. Hare maintains (a) that he does not deny this and (b) that it is precisely what he would have to be denying if the sort of counterexamples which his critics quote against him served their purpose.

Hare refers to two such counterexamples commonly used. One is Medea's case—*video meliora proboque deteriora sequor;*[26] the other St. Paul's—"The good that I would I do not; but the evil which I would not, that I do."[27] Both Medea and St. Paul were patently sincere in their judgments of what is morally good but lamentably contrary to these in their actions. However, they would only serve as counterexamples to Hare's prescriptivism, if we wished to say that (a) Medea and St. Paul failed to act in accordance with their moral judgments *though able to do so* and (b) were nevertheless sincere. But no one does wish to say this. It is common ground between Hare and his critics that (a) Medea and St. Paul were not merely pretending to be unable to do what was good; and (b) if they had been, they could properly have been called insincere. The very common metaphorical interpreta-

[25] *FR*, p. 79.
[26] Ovid, *Metamorph.* vii. 30.
[27] *Romans* 7:19.

tion—divided personality—of conditions such as that of Medea and St. Paul, Hare maintains, witnesses to the truth of his prescriptivism. St. Paul, for instance, speaks as if there were two selves within him, one which gives orders to the other, the latter being too weak to obey. Notice that it is the self which makes moral judgments that gives the orders; but it is the other self, i.e., *not* the one which makes these judgments, which fails to obey them. So it is perfectly consistent with this divided-personality account of St. Paul's condition to say that (a) value judgments entail commands and (b) they are insincere if the one who delivers them does not act upon them.[28] These are the very points which Hare is intent upon making.

(iii) Is there a legitimate use of value judgments in which they do *not* entail imperatives? I have spoken so far as though Hare thought that the *only* meaning which value judgments have is prescriptive, and the time has come to put this right. In *Freedom and Reason* Hare differentiates three kinds of meaning. "An expression which, in a certain context, has descriptive meaning and no other, I call a *descriptive* term, word, or expression, as used in that context; one which has prescriptive meaning (whether or not it also has descriptive meaning) I call a *prescriptive* term; and one which has both kinds of meaning I call an *evaluative* term."[29] This, as Hare notes, is rather different from the terminology of *The Language of Morals*, where he uses "evaluative meaning" for the prescriptive meaning of evaluative expressions.

In what sense do all value judgments have descriptive meaning? We noted above the essentially supervenient character of value words and that this is to be explained, according to Hare, by the fact that they are invariably used in accordance with standards or principles. It follows on this view that when you call anything good, for instance, you are, in effect, saying that it conforms to some standard; and thereby you are describing it for those who know what your standard is. "This is a good book" tells anyone who knows that your standard of goodness in books is that they have funny char-

[28] *FR*, pp. 77–82.
[29] *FR*, pp. 26–27; italics mine.

acters that the characters in this book are, in your opinion,
funny. Of course, he needs to know that this is your standard
before your remark has any such descriptive meaning for
him, since not everyone assesses the goodness of books by
that criterion. However, sometimes the standards or principles
invoked when a value judgment is expressed are so firmly
fixed and well known that one does not need to ask what
they are. For instance, if, in academic circles, anyone says
that Jones is a good scholar, we can safely assume that they
are thereby describing him as one who has read a great
deal, who backs up his judgments with relevant facts, who
carefully checks references, and so on. Or, to take an example which Hare borrows from Stevenson, if a clergyman
says that a girl is a good girl, we can safely assume that she
is devout and chaste.[30] True, it is not as safe as it once was
to make assumptions of this kind, especially where moral
value judgments are concerned; standards are much less fixed
than they used to be, even among clergymen. But, with that
proviso, there are certainly some value judgments which have
a firmly fixed and well-known descriptive meaning.

It is important not to lose sight of the fact that the parallel between the descriptive meaning of value judgments and
that of other sorts of utterance is not exact. Compare the
descriptive meanings of the expressions "good" and "motor
car." If the defining characteristics of a motor car are a, b,
and c, then "X is a, b, and c" is equivalent in meaning to
"X is a motor car." But if the standard of goodness for some
kind of thing is G, and even if this standard has become so
fixed that to call anything of that kind good is tantamount to
calling it an instance of G, nevertheless a distinction between
the meaning of "good" and the criteria for its application can
—and must—still be drawn. From the fact that value words
have descriptive meaning it does not follow that the naturalists were right after all. The descriptive meaning of value
words, as we shall see in a moment, is subject to another
kind of meaning, namely prescriptive, as the descriptive meaning of other sorts of expression is not.

[30] See *EL*, p. 85.

(iv) We turn then to the question: in what relationship does the descriptive meaning of evaluative terms stand to their prescriptive meaning? We are concerned here with what Hare calls "primarily evaluative" words. In passing, however, we must note his distinction between "primarily" and "secondarily" evaluative words. "Industrious" is an example of a secondarily evaluative word. It is so called because its descriptive meaning is more firmly attached to it than its prescriptive, according to Hare. By "industrious" we describe certain qualities and express our approval of them. If, through some change of social circumstances, we came to disapprove of these qualities, we could hardly retain the commendatory force of "industrious" while altering its descriptive meaning so that it referred to the qualities which we now call dilatoriness, carelessness, or whatever. Its descriptive meaning is too firmly attached to it for that. With a primarily evaluative word like "good" the case is different. We can, usually at any rate, detach from the word "good" the criteria for its application and substitute others. Here the prescriptive meaning of the word is logically prior to its descriptive. This, as Hare points out, can be seen from the following two considerations.[31] (a) The prescriptive meaning is constant for every class of object of which a value word may be used. This meaning of "good," for example, is identical in "a good book," "a good road," and "a good act." And it is identical whatever may be the standards of goodness invoked; "good" in "a good road" means the same prescriptively, whether the person using that expression judges roads by their surface or the surrounding scenery. Hare says that we learn the prescriptive meaning of "good" in our earliest years and it remains the same; but we have constantly to be learning, or devising, its descriptive meaning. Sometimes we get the latter from others by accepting their standards of goodness; sometimes we make it up for ourselves by creating our own standards. But amid all this change and variation in descriptive meaning, the prescriptive meaning remains constant.

[31] See *FR*, pp. 24, 27, 189; also *LM*, Chap. 7, where Hare uses "evaluative" for "prescriptive."

(b) Changes in a value word's descriptive meaning are effected by using it with its prescriptive meaning. To recall Moore's point against the naturalists, whatever reason is given why something is good (i.e., whatever descriptive meaning the word may have) it is always open to a reformer to propose a new standard of goodness (i.e., a new descriptive meaning). There is no standard, S, such that "Whatever is an instance of S is good" is tautologous. "Is whatever is an instance of S good?" always makes sense. Notice, this is so not only where changes in descriptive meaning are being effected. Prescriptive meaning is *always* logically prior to descriptive. Any standard must (logically) be accepted before it is invoked; and its acceptance is (logically) an instance of the prescriptive use of the value word concerned. If I say that books are good if they have funny characters, it must (logically) be because I have accepted that books with funny characters are good.

(v) Has Hare, by defining value judgments as entailing imperatives, reduced them to the status of mere universal commands? It should be clear by now that he has not. The universal imperative "No smoking," for example, entails "Do not smoke!" just as, according to Hare, the value judgment "You ought not to smoke" does. But these utterances do not amount to the same thing. Hare is perfectly explicit as to why they do not. Value judgments, remember, are supervenient. They are so, as we saw, because it is always legitimate to ask "Why?" when one has been delivered; and because it is never legitimate to deliver a different value-judgment on something which, in the respects indicated by the answer to "Why?" is exactly like the thing already judged. Now, would it not be absurd if some traveler, pointing out to the railroad officials that the carriages to which "No Smoking" signs are attached do not differ in any noticeable respect from those to which they are not, claimed that it was unreasonable therefore to have put these signs on the said carriages? But it would not be in the least absurd if this traveler accused you of being unreasonable when you had said that he *ought* not to smoke in a given compartment and, when he asked you why, been unable to point to anything which made the given compartment different from those in which you would consider him at liberty to smoke.[32] It might be, of course, that the difference to which you pointed in reply to his question was the fact that the given carriage had a "No Smoking" sign on the window; you could say that he ought not to smoke because of that. But this does not affect the point. The point is that "No smoking," as a universal command, does not have to be supervenient, as "You ought not to smoke" does.

Hare says that value judgments are "proper universals" but universal commands are not. "No smoking" is short for "Do not ever smoke in *this* compartment" and refers implicitly to an individual. True, "You ought not to smoke in this compartment" also contains references to individuals (you and this compartment). But a reason can always be asked for the value judgment. This reason, as we have seen, invokes a standard or principle. And, as we shall see in the next section, Hare believed that where ought judgments, and in particular moral ones, were concerned this standard or principle must be completely universal. "Thus," he writes, "the particular moral judgment 'You ought not to smoke in this compartment' depends on a proper universal, even though it is not itself one. But this is not true of the imperative 'Do not ever smoke in this compartment.' This invokes no more general principle, it is itself as general as it requires to be, and this is not general enough to make it a proper universal."[33]

(vi) What account does Hare give of the difference between intrinsic and instrumental goodness, or between the hypothetical and categorical uses of "ought"? Compare:

	(1) He is a good poisoner. (instrumental)
with:	(2) He is a good man. (instrinsic)
And:	
	(3) You ought to give a second dose. (said to a would-be poisoner) (hypothetical)
with:	(4) You ought to tell the truth. (categorical)

[32] Cf. *LM*, pp. 175–79.
[33] *LM*, p. 176.

A poisoner is, so to say, *for* poisoning; a good poisoner is therefore one who fulfills this function well. But a man is *not* for anything; his goodness, if he is good, makes him good in himself, not as a means to something beyond himself. Again: one ought to give a second dose (in certain supposed circumstances) *if* one wants to kill one's victim. But one ought to tell the truth *without* condition.

Is there, therefore, some difference in the meanings of "good" in (1) and (2) and of "ought" in (3) and (4)? Hare says not. The primary—or evaluative—meaning of "good" is the same in (1) and (2): in both it commends. The primary meaning of "ought" is the same in (3) and (4): in both it prescribes. The secondary—or descriptive—meaning of "good" in (1) and (2), and of "ought" in (3) and (4) respectively is, of course, different. But this is not relevant to the difference between instrumental and intrinsic uses of "good" or hypothetical and categorical uses of "ought," because descriptive meaning differs *within* each of these uses and not simply between them. The standard applied by "He is a good poisoner" differs from that by "He is a good watchmaker"; the principle invoked by "You ought to give a double dose," from that by "You ought to fasten your safety belt." There is certainly one very important difference between (1) and (2) and between (3) and (4). It has to do with the extent of the class of comparison. As Hare points out, we commend or prescribe "within a class of comparison." (1) commends one man ("he") within the class of poisoners; (3) prescribes one act (giving a double dose) within the class of acts which would-be poisoners as such perform. But notice the *universality* of the class of comparison in (2) and (4). (2) commends one man ("he") as a man; and though we are not all poisoners we are all men. (4) prescribes one act (telling the truth) within the class of actions which we all perform; and, though we do not all poison, we all communicate with others.

The nature of this difference must not be mistaken. Notice that (1), (2), (3), and (4) are all *universalizable*. The difference between (1) or (3) on the one hand, and (2) or (4) on the other, is not a difference in logic. They are all value judgments and share the logical characteristics of value judgments. If we utter any of them, we can legitimately be asked why, and our reason be universalized. If we utter (3), for instance, we are committed thereby to saying that, if we ourselves were would-be poisoners in the given circumstances, we ought to give a double dose. But the point is that we have an option as to whether or not we ever will be in that position. On the other hand, as Hare puts it, "We cannot get out being men."[34] He goes on: ". . . and therefore moral principles, which are principles for the conduct of men as men—and not as poisoners or architects or batsmen—cannot be accepted without having a potential bearing upon the way that we conduct ourselves. If I say to a certain person 'You ought to tell the truth,' I signify my acceptance of a principle to tell the truth in the sort of circumstances in which he is; and *I may find myself placed unavoidably in similar circumstances.* But I can always choose whether or not to take up poisoning or cricketing as a profession. This is bound to make the *spirit* in which we consider moral questions very different from that in which we consider how we ought to poison Jones, or build him a house; but the logic of the word 'ought' is not markedly different in the two cases."[35]

(vii) Does Hare's prescriptivist theory apply to all value-words? There are, of course, differences in meaning between value words. "Right" does not mean, in ordinary use, the same as "good," nor either the same as "ought." A right act might not be good, at any rate if "right" is defined as "in accordance with such-and-such a rule or principle" and "good" as "done from such-and-such a motive"; and these words are in fact frequently so defined in ordinary use. For example, a schoolmaster might inflict statutory punishment on a pupil and there be no doubt that his act was morally right, but if he derives pleasure from it, it would not be morally good. Again, a good act may not be right; a philan-
thropist's act, for instance, may well be good in the sense of being done from the motive of kindness, but wrong in the sense that it is the kind of thing which encourages shiftless-

[34] *LM*, pp. 142, 162.
[35] *LM*, p. 162.

ness. "Ought" is distinct from both "right" and "good." The philanthropist's act, for all its goodness, and the schoolmaster's, for all its rightness, were not, in either case, what they ought to have done. However, Hare concentrates on "ought." Much of his moral philosophy, as readers will see in what follows, is derived from the analysis of ought judgments. So we have to ask whether his conclusions with regard to "ought" apply equally to value-judgments in terms of "right" or "good." In the concluding chapter of *The Language of Morals,* Hare argues that "artificial" words *right* and *good* (italicized to indicate their artificial character) can be invented, which are definable in terms of "ought," as that word is used in natural language; and that so defined, these artificial words will do *most* of the jobs done by "right" and "good" respectively in natural language. Undoubtedly, there are many instances in which judgments in terms of "right" and "good," as naturally used, can be translated without loss of meaning into ought judgments. "It is right (or not right) to do X" means the same as "one ought (or ought not) to do X"; and "The right X" can be rendered "The X which ought to be chosen." Again, "A is a better X that B," Hare claims, means the same as "If one is choosing an X, then, if one chooses B, one ought to choose A." These judgments in terms of "right" or "better than" guide choices in the same way as ought judgments. Hare's argument, that this sort of translation can be made from "right" and (at least in the comparative degree) "good" into "ought," is complicated and to some degree tentative. If it fails, then presumably Hare will have to say that his conclusions concerning the logical character of ought judgments apply to judgments in terms of "right" and "good" *only in so far as the latter* (i.e., judgments in terms of "right" and "good") can be translated into terms of the former (i.e., ought judgments). Although in his later writings Hare has been interested almost exclusively in "ought," I think that he takes his prescriptivist account of value judgments to apply to every such judgment, whether in terms of "ought," "right," or "good." I do not say here that he is not entitled to do so; only that, even if he were not, that would not necessarily diminish the illumination which his theory might cast over part of the field. If Hare is correct in his analysis of "ought," then he is correct also about many uses of "right" and "good."

So much, then, for the prescriptivity of value judgments, as Hare conceived of it. I have once or twice already used the words "universalizable" or "universalizability." The latter is the second of those "three most important truths about moral judgments" which Hare lists. We must turn now to consider it more carefully.

(II) UNIVERSALIZABILITY

How and Why Are Value Judgments Universalizable?

What Hare meant by universalizability is grounded fundamentally in the very notion of meaning itself. For language to be meaningful it must be used in accordance with rules. And if its use is to be intelligible, i.e., if language is not to lose whatever meaning it has, then that use must be consistent. Of course, this is not to deny that meanings may change, or that the same piece of language may have a number of different meanings, or that the rules for the use of language may be very complex. Allowing for all such qualifications, however, the fact remains that if there were no meaning-rules, there would be no meaning; and if there were no meaning, there would be no language. Words with descriptive meaning are universalizable in the sense that, if they refer to one thing, then they refer to everything else which is like it in the respects specified by their descriptive meaning-rule.

However, what Hare means by the universalizability of value judgments goes beyond that. To make clear what he does mean, he compares and contrasts evaluative and descriptive terms with regard to their universalizability. True, he says, ". . . the feature of value-judgments which I call universalisability is simply that which they share with descriptive judgments; namely the fact that they both carry descriptive meaning."[36] But he soon makes it clear that there are differences as well as similarities between the two sorts of

[36] *FR*, p. 15.

judgment with regard to their universalizability. As far as I understand him, I will try to say what Hare thinks these differences and similarities are.

First the similarities. Hare writes, "If I call a thing red, I am committed to calling anything else like it red. And if I call a thing a good X, I am committed to calling any X like it good."[37] I may define a descriptive expression ostensively or verbally. If, for example, I say "X is red" and, when asked what "red" means, define it by pointing to a patch of color (C), then I must also call anything else red which resembles C as closely as X does. Or again if I say "X is a postbox," then, whatever the verbal definition (V) of "postbox" might be, I am committed to calling anything else which conforms to V a postbox as well. Evaluative language is similar in that, if you call anything, for example, good, then you must so speak of anything else which is identical with it in those respects on account of which you call it good. Universalizability is thus a common characteristic of evaluative and descriptive language.

But it is when you ask what precisely we are doing if, for example, we call something good, as contrasted with what we are doing if we call something red or a postbox, that the differences begin to appear. Immediately after the remark quoted a moment ago, Hare adds, "But whereas the reason in the former case is that I must be using the word 'red' in accordance with some *meaning*-rule, the reason in the latter case is much more complicated."[38] How and why? Succinctly, the answer to both questions, which Hare gives, is: in the case of evaluative language "the descriptive meaning-rule becomes more than a mere meaning-rule."[39] How is the universalizability of value judgments more complicated than that of descriptive ones? By the fact that questions of value cannot—to recall Moore's open-question argument and Hare's restatement of it—be settled merely by reference to the meanings of the words used. And why not? Because a value judg-

[37] *Ibid.*
[38] *FR*, pp. 15–16.
[39] *FR*, p. 23.

ment always applies, or invokes, something more than a meaning-rule, namely a synthetic standard or principle.

Contrast these two cases. (i) An American says, "These are suspenders." "Oh no," says an Englishman, "they're braces." (ii) A Powellite says, "We ought to encourage immigrants to go back where they came from" and a left-wing socialist replies, "Oh no, we ought not." In the former case the disagreement is entirely verbal. It can be settled simply by pointing out that Americans use the word "suspenders" to mean what the English mean, not by that word, but by "braces." No sane person will then ask· "Who is right?" They are both right. But would anyone suggest that the Powellite and the socialist are both right? Following Hare, we may say that in case (i) an analytic point is at issue, in case (ii), a synthetic one. The *ground* of the universalizability of "These are suspenders" is a meaning-rule; that of "We ought to encourage immigrants to go back where they came from," a principle of action. It doubtless makes sense to say that a Powellite and a socialist can agree to differ about this point at issue between them. But what would that mean? It might mean that they agree to suspend further argument until certain questions of fact (e.g., facts about the effect on a locality of a large influx of immigrants) have been settled; or perhaps that they agree not to badger one another on the point but to talk about something else; or whatever. But one thing which "agree to differ" could not mean in such a case is the kind of thing that the phrase would mean if anyone said that Americans and Englishmen "agree to differ" about the use of the word "suspenders." If *per impossibile* Enoch Powell and Lord Constantine announced that they had agreed to differ as to what ought to be done about immigration, then, whatever they might mean, they could not conceivably mean simply that they had recognized the fact that they subscribed to different meaning-rules for the word "ought." Their disagreement is not about that; it is about standards or principles for the treatment of human beings in situations like that of immigrants. They could therefore not, in any sense, resolve it simply by an agreement as to meaning-rules.

What is the connection between the supervenience of value judgments, which was noted in the last section, and their universalizability? We took Hare, it will be remembered, to be saying that value judgments are supervenient in the sense that when one has been delivered, e.g., "X is good," it is: (a) always logically legitimate to ask why X is good; and (b) never logically legitimate, when the answer is given, to deny that anything else like X in the relevant respects is also good. In other words, we can always ask a reason for a value judgment and then always universalize that reason. But it may now be objected that a rational being, as such, will give reasons for many things which he says besides value judgments, and that reasons, by their very nature, are universalizable, whether given for value judgments or for anything else. If you said to me "Go to the station" and I asked "Why?" I should not expect the reply "Just do." Even if that were your reply, I should assume that you had a reason for the command which, for some other reason, you were concealing from me. Suppose your reply was, "Then you can collect my luggage." Since this was your reason for sending me to the station on the present occasion, I should be entitled to assume that *ceteris paribus,* on any other occasion, if you wanted your luggage from the station and I could collect it, you would instruct me to do so.[40] Now, it may seem to follow from all this that, given Hare's account of the matter, (a) it is not only value judgments which are supervenient, and (b) the universalizability of value judgments amounts to no more than their supervenience. But these conclusions would be mistaken.

[40] The distinction between ought judgments and singular imperatives is not, therefore, that the former require reasons while the latter do not. However, there are *some* singular imperatives which, unlike ought sentences and other singular imperatives, do not require reasons, e.g., orders in the Forces. D. H. Monro, noting this in *Empiricism and Ethics* (Cambridge, 1967), p. 173, writes: "In the order-giving situation it is the man who gives the order who takes the responsibility for the action. That is why the reason for the action need not concern the agent. But if you accept advice, the responsibility for the action is still yours, and the principle behind it does concern you. To accept advice, then, is to accept the principle behind the advice; but to carry out an order is not *necessarily* to accept the principle behind it."

(a) According to Hare, value judgments alone are supervenient. What he meant by supervenience has, perhaps, been slightly misrepresented in my account of it this far. The point which he notes about, e.g., "X is good," is not simply that one may ask a reason why and universalize the answer. It is rather that one can always ask "What is good about it?" and that the answer can *never* be "Just its goodness." This is where "X is good" differs from e.g., "X is yellow." To "What is yellow about it?" the answer may, though it need not, be "Just its yellowness." Goodness (and, equally, rightness or oughtness) is always necessarily supervenient upon other characteristics, as yellowness (or any other non-evaluative characteristic) is not.

(b) Universalizability is a characteristic distinct from supervenience. We shall see in the next subsection that Hare recognized only a certain type of reason as valid for a moral judgment and, eventually, for any ought judgment. This was a reason which did not contain any reference to particular individuals—or, as we shall see that he calls it, a "U-type" reason. If someone says, "The Chancellor's action was right because it will help Britain's balance of payments," the rightness here is supervenient. But the judgment is not, as it stands, a moral one. And why? Because the reason given is not, in the required sense, universalizable. It refers to a particular individual country, "Britain." The speaker gives a reason; if he is a rational being, he will *ceteris paribus* consistently commend as right any action in other situations which would help Britain's balance of payments; but his judgment could, nevertheless, be one of expediency rather than of moral rightness. Notice that there is a difference between supervenience and universalizability. The necessary and sufficient conditions of supervenience are here fulfilled; but not those of universalizability. For these latter to be fulfilled, the speaker would have to agree that for the Chancellor of another country, or anyone similarly placed, to act in like manner to help the balance of payments of that *other* country, when it was situated as Britain is, would also be right. This the speaker may not be willing to admit. In which case it could not, according to Hare, be moral rightness of which he was speaking. Universalizability is more than supervenience, though Hare does not bring this out.

Hare notes a difference between value judgments in terms of "ought" or "right" and those in terms of "good." Because "good" has a comparative "better than" whereas "ought" and "right" have none, there is a difference in the way in which they are universalizable. Hare says, ". . . whereas the judgment that I ought in a certain situation *to do* a certain thing commits me to the view that no similar person in a precisely similar situation ought to *fail to do* the same thing, this is not the case with a judgment framed in terms of 'good.' "[41] To say, for example, that we ought to encourage immigrants to return to their countries of origin is to say that no one, placed as we are, ought to fail to encourage them to do so. But to say that Enoch Powell is a good politician is to imply only that, if anyone acted on the political scene as he does, that man would be a good politician also. It is not to say that anyone who fails to act on that scene as he does must be a bad politician. One could say that both Mr. Powell and Lord Constantine are good politicians.[42] In the light of this distinction—between "ought" and "right" on the one hand and "good" on the other—Hare acknowledges the persuasiveness of Professor P. F. Strawson's view that morality should be divided into two parts: one aimed at producing uniformity of practice (what ought to be done), the other, diversity of kinds of life (what is good).[43]

What Makes a Value Judgment Moral?

The time has now come to face the question: how, if at all in Hare's opinion, do moral value judgments differ from those of other kinds? In his paper "Universalizability,"[44] he represents the difference as entirely a matter of differing degrees of universality in the reasons given for moral judg-

[41] *FR*, p. 153; italics mine.
[42] Cf. *FR*, pp. 153–54.
[43] *FR*, pp. 151–55; cf. P. F. Strawson, "Social Morality and Individual Ideal," *P* XXXVI (1961).
[44] *PAS* LV (1954–55).

ments, and in those given for value judgments of other kinds, respectively. Compare the following:

(a) "The Chancellor's squeeze was right."
    "Why?"
    "It resulted in an improvement in Britain's balance of payments."

Following Professor E. A. Gellner,[45] Hare calls this an E-type valuation.

(b) "You ought to write to him."
    "Why?"
    "You promised to do so."

Following Gellner, Hare calls this a U-type valuation.

Implicit in each reason is a standard or principle: "Whatever results in an improvement of Britain's balance of payments is right" and "One ought always to keep one's promises," respectively. Hare recognizes that people might give the reason in (a) who only consider it a reason for the rightness of the Chancellor's squeeze because it refers to Britain's balance of payments; they would not necessarily consider the Chancellor of another country right to institute a squeeze if by so doing he improved that country's balance of payments. By contrast, the reason in (b) does not contain any reference to a particular individual and so could not be regarded in a similar light. This is the difference between E-type and U-type valuations: it lies in the degree of universality possessed by the reasons given for them. The thesis which Hare is arguing in his paper is that moral judgments are U-type valuations. He points out that he cannot be accused of making this analytic in virtue of the meaning of the word "reason," for he is ready to admit that reasons such as that given in (a) are reasons. Nevertheless, he insists that his thesis is analytic. It is true by definition of the word "moral."[46] Hare's point, it should be noted, is a logical one. It is true, as he recognizes,

[45] See "Ethics and Logic," *ibid.*
[46] Hare, *op. cit.,* p. 302.

that any reason which is given for A to do X is, in some sense, universalizable. If it is a reason for A to do X, it is a reason for anyone like A in the relevant respects to do something like X in similar circumstances. But notice carefully what this means. It does not mean that, if X's being, for example, in Britain's interest is a reason for Britain's Chancellor to do X, then Y's being in some other country's interest is a reason for that country's Chancellor to do Y. It simply means that, if X's being in Britain's interest is a reason for Britain's Chancellor to do it, it is a reason for anyone else in his position to do it. That is, anyone who is Britain's Chancellor. The reference to an individual in the reason can be as particular as you like and the reason still be universalizable in this sense. To distinguish between two things on the basis of a particular relational characteristic—e.g., being in the interest of one's country—is not to be irrational. That is to say, it is a distinction to which one can consistently adhere in thought and practice. But it is certainly to be partial, to be biased in a certain direction. Inconsistency is a logical fault; partiality, a moral defect. Hare has been accused of confusing the two in his account of universalizability. In saying that it is a logical characteristic of moral judgments that U-type reasons are required for them, it is contended, Hare has smuggled in his own moral commitment to the principle of impartiality. I think this contention misses Hare's point. I take the latter to be that in any judgment, which according to the normal use of "moral" we should call a *moral* judgment, there will be some recognition of the principle of impartiality. That is a logical point pure and simple. It is about the defining characteristics of morality.

In a footnote to his article,[47] Hare raises, only to dismiss as not his present concern, the question whether or not E-type valuations can properly be called valuations. By the time he wrote *Freedom and Reason* (1963), he appears to have decided that all ought judgments, not simply moral ones, are U-type valuations. He writes: "The word 'moral' plays here a far smaller role than I was at one time tempted to assign to

[47] P. 295, note 2.

it. It is the logic of the word 'ought' in its typical uses that requires universalisability, not that of the word 'moral'; the word moral' needs to be brought in only in order to identify one class of the typical uses, and that with which as moral philosophers we are most concerned."[48] I have found some difficulty in harmonizing Hare's views at this point. In the words just quoted, he is claiming universalizability for *all* ought judgments. At the end of the last section, I noted his view that what characterizes moral judgments, and indeed all ought judgments, as distinct from all other value judgments, is that the former are necessarily universalizable (that U-type reasons are required for them) and not merely supervenient. In this respect, they differ, for instance, from a value judgment such as "The Chancellor's action is right because it will help Britain's balance of payments." But at the end of the section on *Prescriptivity,* we noted Hare's contention that his prescriptivism holds for *all* value judgments because those in terms of "right" and "good" can be translated into judgments in terms of "ought." So, presumably, we could rewrite the above judgment ("The Chancellor's action is *right* because it will help Britain's balance of payments") thus: "The Chancellor is doing what he *ought* to do because his action will help Britain's balance of payments."

But then: (a) If Hare thinks that these two sentences *are* equivalent in meaning, he is landed with an ought judgment which is not, in the required sense, universalizable (i.e., not U-type). (b) If he thinks that the two sentences are not equivalent in meaning, he is landed with an evaluative use of "right" which cannot be translated into terms of "ought," and so which may fall outside the prescriptivist theory of value judgments which Hare derives from his analysis of ought judgments. It does seem that Hare must forego either (a) the view that all ought judgments, not just moral ones, are universalizable, or (b) the view that all evaluations in terms of "right" could conceivably be translated into terms of "ought" without loss or change of meaning.

What then constitutes a typically *moral* piece of thinking? Hare says that there are four "necessary ingredients" of moral

[48] *FR*, p. 37.

argument, "four factors . . . whose combination governs a man's moral opinion on a given matter."[49] They do not appear to be exactly necessary conditions of moral reasoning, for Hare is able to conceive of an argument's being moral where one of them is unfulfilled: he says that ". . . the absence of even one of these ingredients may render the rest ineffective."[50] Note: "may," not "will." However, it is clear that he thinks all four ingredients will normally be present in any example of moral reasoning. The four are: (i) a logical framework provided by prescriptivity and universalizability; (ii) an appeal to fact; (iii) an appeal to inclination or interest; (iv) an appeal to imagination. The first factor—the logical framework—is said to be common to all ought judgments. I will deal briefly with the other three in turn.

(i) *Appeal to Fact*

In moral reasoning there is invariably some appeal to the facts of the case. Take this example:

The sale of pornographic literature ought to be prohibited. Why?
Because the sale of such literature leads to an increase of sex crimes.

The reason given here is a statement of fact which may be true or false. The first thing to notice is that this putative fact is stated only because it instantiates a universal principle. The above piece of moral reasoning, set out in the form of a syllogism, would read:

A: Whatever literature leads to an increase in sex crimes ought not to be sold.
B: Pornographic literature leads to an increase in sex crimes.
C: Therefore pornographic literature ought not to be sold.

A, the major premises, is a universal ought principle; B, the minor premises, is a statement of fact; C, a particular ought

[49] *FR*, pp. 92, 97.
[50] *FR*, p. 94.

judgment, is the conclusion. Now, there are, after all, an indefinite number of factual statements which could be made about pornographic literature, e.g., who writes, prints, sells, reads it, how many such works exist, what prices are charged for them, etc. When, in the above argument, one putative fact—that it leads to an increase in sex crime—was selected as a reason for condemning it, this was because the speaker who selected that fact subscribed to a principle which made it, rather than any of the other facts about pornographic literature, relevant. If those with whom he is arguing do not subscribe to the same principle, they will of course reject his reason out of hand. But if they do subscribe to it then they might call in question the truth of the reason which he has given. *Does* pornographic literature in fact lead to an increase in sex crime? That is certainly debatable. In June 1967 the Danish Parliament largely repealed the law under which purveyors of pornographic literature were liable to prosecution. If newspaper reports[51] can be believed, the incidence of sex crime in Copenhagen fell last year (1968) by 25 per cent. This fact, if it is a fact, certainly impugns the reason given for the judgment that the sale of pornographic literature ought to be prohibited.

Appeal to fact is undoubtedly a feature of moral reasoning, but it is not of course the *differentia* of that kind of argument. To the reason given in such an example as:

This wine is good.
Why?
It has an unusual aftertaste.

Everything which was said of the reason in the pornographic literature example could *mutatis mutandis* be applied. The appeal to fact in the two cases is of exactly the same kind.

(ii) *Appeal to Inclination and Interest*

To what extent do moral valuations involve an *appeal to inclination or interest*? By "inclination or interest" is meant

[51] E.g., B. Norman, "The Total Truth about Sex," *Daily Mail*, Nov. 27, 1968.

here any wants or desires which those involved have, or may
have,[52] and feel it important to gratify. It is true that if we
had none, if it made no difference to us what happened, we
should have no use for moral argument.[53] The universalizability of value judgments, according to Hare, has two logical
consequences so far as inclinations or interests are concerned.[54] First, we can—and in moral argument frequently
do—universalize a prescription in order to test it against the
inclinations of those with whom we are arguing. Hare uses
the illustration of a man who is owed money by another man
(call the latter X). If the first man says that he ought to
prosecute X because X owes him money, he implies, this
judgment being universalizable, that if he owed money himself, he ought to be dealt with similarly. But this would be
against his inclination; he would not want to be prosecuted.[55]
So from appeal to inclination, within the logical framework
of universalizability, it seems to follow that the creditor in
such a case ought not to prosecute. Universalizability, together with appeal to inclination, is the logical basis of "golden
rule" morality.[56] Hare uses another illustration to bring out
the second logical consequence of universalizability in this
connection. A judge has to deal with a criminal. What the
judge does he will, in effect, do to many people; not just to
the criminal but also to those whom the latter may rob, etc.[57]
In such a case, Hare says, it follows from the universalizability
of ought judgments that "everyone is entitled to equal consideration"; "the principle often accepted by utilitarians,
'Everybody to count for one, nobody for more than one' can
. . . be justified by the appeal to the demand for universal-

---

[52] Inclination and interest are not identical. A subject may have interests but no inclinations. In an unpublished paper on abortion, Hare
notes this distinction. He says that, when deciding what ought to be
done about a fetus and its mother, one matter which may have to be
taken into consideration is the interests of the children yet unborn (e.g.,
the probability of their not existing if this present pregnancy is not
terminated). The unborn, however, cannot have inclinations.

[53] *FR*, pp. 92–93.

[54] Cf. *FR*, p. 195.

[55] *FR*, pp. 90–91.

[56] *FR*, p. 108.

[57] *FR*, pp. 115–17.

isability. . . ."[58] From the appeal to inclination, within the framework or universalizability, it follows that the judge in such a case ought to impose a penalty on the criminal. Universalizability together with appeal to inclination, is the logical basis of utilitarian morality.[59]

I have been trying to show how Hare thought that appeal to inclination or interest gives a value judgment a moral character. It must be noted, however, that he recognized the possibility of a person rejecting any such appeal and still insisting with justification that his reasoning is moral. Such a person may, so to speak, refuse to let certain of his *own* inclinations count; he may be what Hare calls a *fanatic*. Take the case of a Nazi who thinks that Jews ought to be exterminated. Suppose we trick this Nazi into believing that his own parents were in fact Jews. Then we show him that it was just a trick. Hare thinks it not at all likely that, while this Nazi believes himself of Jewish birth, he will say, "All right. Let me and my family be exterminated"; and that it is very likely, once the Nazi has thus faced the question "What ought to be done with me if I were a Jew?" he will no longer think that Jews ought to be exterminated. Perhaps Hare is right on both counts. But nevertheless he sees that it *is logically possible* for the Nazi to accept the implication, "Let me be exterminated if I am a Jew," contrary as that may be to his inclination to go on living, and *still* persist in his view that Jews ought to be exterminated. If he does so, his view will be a *moral* view.[60]

Again, a man may refuse to let the inclinations of *others* count. He may be concerned with what Hare calls an ideal, rather than anyone's inclination. Hare's example is a person who thinks it wrong for girls to undress themselves in strip clubs for the pleasure of middle-aged men. He remarks: ". . . those who call such exhibitions immoral do not do so because of their effect on other people's interests; for, since

[58] *FR*, p. 118.
[59] *FR*, p. 123.
[60] *FR*, pp. 171–72. G. J. Warnock in *Contemporary Moral Philosophy* (1967), p. 59, says that "moral" would not be applicable in such cases. Cf. below, pp. 227–30.

everybody gets what he or she wants, nobody's interests are harmed. They are likely, rather, to use such words as 'degrading.' This gives us a clue to the sort of moral question with which we are dealing. It is a question not of interests but of *ideals*. Such conduct offends against an ideal of human excellence held by many people; that is why they condemn it."[61] We referred above[62] to the view of Strawson, and Hare, that morality should perhaps be divided into two parts, one aiming at uniformity of practice (the realm of "ought" and "right"), the other at diversity of ideal (the realm of "good"); but notice that our anti-strip-club "idealist" would not simply say that strip clubs are not good but that they ought to be closed. And he would mean that no one who has the opportunity ought to fail to close them. He would regard the issue as a moral one in that sense and it is surely impossible to claim that he would be opting out of the ordinary use of the word "ought" in its moral sense. *Ex hypothesi* he firmly refuses to take the interests of others into account; but he does not thereby render his judgment nonmoral.[63]

(iii) *Appeal to Imagination*

In some of the above examples—those of the creditor, the judge, the fanatical Nazi—an effort had to be made by the person judging morally to put himself in the place of someone else. An *appeal to imagination* was involved. Such an appeal is the third of Hare's necessary ingredients of moral argument.

At this point Hare draws a parallel between his account of moral thinking and the hypothetico-deductive account of scientific thinking. Both reveal the exploratory character of the thinking with which they are concerned. According to the hypothetico-deductive theory, of which Professor K. R. Popper is the foremost exponent, the logic of scientific discovery is as follows. From a hypothesis, together with certain initial conditions, an empirically testable predication is deduced and if this prediction is fulfilled, the original hypothesis

---

[61] *FR*, p. 147.
[62] P. 184.
[63] Warnock, *op. cit.*, would not agree here either.

is, to that extent, corroborated.[64] To take a very familiar example, the logic of the discovery of the planet Neptune was as follows: (i) hypothesis: the theory of gravitation; (ii) initial conditions: the orbit of the planet Uranus, which could not be accounted for by this theory, given simply the gravitational pull of the hitherto observed planets; (iii) empirically testable prediction deduced: if a telescope of sufficient strength is used, it will be seen that there is a planet of the size and orbit of Neptune exerting a gravitational pull on Uranus. Powerful telescopes were used and, at the appropriate time, the planet we now call Neptune was observed. Hare's claim is that the logic of moral discovery follows a similar pattern. For example:

"Hypothesis": All debtors ought to be prosecuted.
"Initial conditions": I am a debtor.
"Prediction": I ought to be prosecuted.

The creditor in our example rejected this "prediction" and so he rejected the "hypothesis" also—i.e., he rejected the reason "Because he is a debtor" which he had originally given for "He ought to be prosecuted."

There is, of course, an important difference between scientific and moral reasoning as thus conceived. The initial conditions in the scientific example (i.e., the movement of Uranus) are matter of *fact*. Those in the moral example (the thought of himself as a debtor) are matter of *supposition* only. This is where the appeal to imagination comes into moral argument and this is the sense in which Hare speaks of moral thinking as exploratory.[65] He writes: "Just as science, seriously pursued, is the search for hypotheses and the testing of them by the attempt to falsify their particular consequences, so morals, as a serious endeavour, consists in the search for principles and the testing of them against particular cases. Any rational activity has its discipline, and this is the discipline of moral thought: to test the moral principles that suggest themselves

[64] K. R. Popper, *The Logic of Scientific Discovery* (1959), Chap. X.
[65] *FR*, p. 88.

to us by following out their consequences and *seeing whether we can accept them.*[66] The sphere within which the exploration goes on is the imagination. The reasons given for moral judgments are universalized in the imagination and accepted or rejected there.

Two comments are called for on the phrase "seeing whether we can accept them." (i) The fact that the exploration is conducted in the realm of supposition, not of fact, does not destroy the analogy with scientific reasoning. Hare writes:

> If we enter imaginatively into a hypothetical situation, and think about it *as if* it were going really to happen to us, we logically cannot have desires about it which are different from those which we would have if it *were* going to be real. This is because, whenever we desire anything, we desire it because of something about it; and, since being hypothetical and being actual are not, in the required sense, "things about" objects or events (a hypothetical toothache, exactly like this actual one, *would* hurt as much as this actual one *does* hurt), it is impossible for there to be anything about the hypothetical similar situation which makes us desire something different concerning it. A hypothetical similar situation *is* similar.[67]

(ii) However, it is important to recognize that the "can" in "seeing whether we can accept them" is *not* logical. On his theme of moral argument as a kind of exploration, Hare says:

> We are to go about looking for moral judgments which we can both accept for our own conduct and universalise to cover the conduct of other actual or hypothetical people. What prevents us from accepting certain moral judgments which are perfectly formulable in the language is not logic alone, but the fact that they have certain logical consequences which we cannot accept—namely certain singular prescriptions to other people in hypothetical situations. And *the "cannot" here is not a logical "cannot."* It would not be self-contradictory to accept these prescriptions; but all the same we cannot accept them except on one condition which

[66] *FR*, p. 92; italics mine.
[67] *FR*, p. 197.

is most unlikely to be fulfilled—namely that we should become what I have called "fanatics."[68]

The "other people in hypothetical situations" here may of
course include the person who delivers the judgment himself;
the creditor, the judge, and the Nazi, in Hare's examples, all
put themselves in the position of someone else to see if they
could accept the singular prescriptions, "Let me be prosecuted," "Let me be robbed," "Let me be exterminated," respectively, when they did so. But the important point is that
the discovery which the moral explorer has to make is not, in
the last analysis, concerned with what is or is not logically
possible. It is simply whether or not he can stomach what his
moral judgments, when universalized, require him to stomach. "Our argument [*sc.* against 'fanatics' and 'idealists'] . . .
will rest, not upon logic by itself—though without logic [*sc.*
i.e., universalizability and prescriptivity] we should never
have got to this point—but upon the fortunate contingent fact
that people who would take this logically possible view [i.e.,
of the fanatic or idealist], after they had really imagined
themselves in the other man's position, are extremely rare."[69]

(III) LOGICAL RELATIONS

The third of the "three most important truths" about moral
judgments which Hare enumerated was that there can be rational procedure in moral thinking because logical relations
between prescriptive judgments are possible. We have already
remarked that it was the conviction that this "truth" needed
safeguarding which first brought him into the arena of moral
philosophy.[70]

In an article called "Imperative Sentences" (*Mind,* 1949),
Hare sets out to refute a view which he attributes to most
logicians, namely that the proper subject matter of deductive
logic is, exclusively, indicative sentences (i.e., sentences which
tell us that something is, or is not, the case). He argues that
exactly the same logical relations hold between imperative

[68] *FR,* p. 193. (italics mine)
[69] *FR,* p. 172.
[70] Above, p. 157.

sentences (i.e., sentences which tell us to make, or not to make, something the case) as hold between indicative ones. He regards all moral reasoning as deductive. Imperatives certainly seem able to entail and to contradict one another, just like indicatives. The imperative "All vehicles turn left" entails, in the appropriate circumstances, the imperative "This vehicle turn left" just as surely as "All vehicles will turn left" entails "This vehicle will turn left." And the imperative "Halt" contradicts the imperative "Proceed with caution" just as surely as "You will halt" contradicts "You will proceed with caution."[71] In "Imperative Sentences," Hare was content to claim simply that imperative sentences may be the subject matter of deductive reasoning and, when they are, can have the same logical relations with one another as indicative sentences. In *The Language of Morals*, he goes further and claims that imperative conclusions may follow from premises, one of which is imperative and the other indicative. I shall return to this "mixed" or "practical" syllogism shortly, but first it is important to notice: (i) how Hare conceives of logical relations in general; and (ii) why it seemed to him to follow from this conception of them that they can subsist between imperative sentences, and between an imperative conclusion and premises respectively indicative and imperative in the mixed syllogism.

How does Hare conceive of logical relations? He holds that "all deductive inference is analytic in character."[72] That is to say, it depends solely upon the meanings of the words being used, and particularly that of the logical words such as the sign of negation, "not," the connectives, "if," "and," "or," and the quantifiers, "all" and "some." Failure to recognize an entailment or a contradiction is failure to understand the meanings of the words, particularly the logical ones, being used. "Thus, if someone professed to admit that all men were mortal and that Socrates was a man, but refused to admit that Socrates was mortal, the correct thing to do would be not, as

[71] See "Imperative sentences," *M* LVIII (1949), 34.
[72] *LM*, p. 32.

has sometimes been suggested, to accuse him of some kind of logical purblindness, but to say 'You evidently don't know the meaning of the word "all"; for if you did you would *eo ipso* know how to make inferences of this sort.' "[73]

Why does it follow from this that logical relations may hold between imperatives as well as indicatives? In brief, Hare's answer in *The Language of Morals* is: because the logical words "are best treated as part of the phrastics of sentences" and "this means that they are common ground between indicatives and imperatives."[74] We need to understand what "phrastics" are and why they are said to be common ground between indicatives and imperatives.

Hare compared the following two sentences:

(1) Mary, please show Mrs. Prendergast her room.

(2) Mary will show you your room, Mrs. Prendergast.

Common to both, he argues, is a description of a series of events, namely:

(3) Showing of her room to Mrs. Prendergast by Mary at time *t*.

Sentence (1) is logically equivalent to (3) plus:

(4) please.

Sentence (2) is logically equivalent to (3) plus:

(5) yes.

So (1) may be rewritten:

Showing of her room to Mrs. Prendergast by Mary at time *t*, please.

And (2) may be rewritten:

Showing of her room to Mrs. Prendergast by Mary at time *t*, yes.

In "Imperative Sentences," Hare calls (3) the common "descriptor," and (4) and (5) the respectively imperative and indicative "dictors" of (1) and (2). In *The Language of Morals,* he revised his terminology, substituting for "descriptor," the expression *phrastic* (from a Greek word meaning "to point out or indicate"); and for "dictor," the expression *neustic* (from a Greek word meaning "to nod assent").[75]

[73] *LM*, p. 33.
[74] *LM*, p. 21.
[75] *LM*, p. 18.

Sentence (1) above is in the imperative mood; sentence (2), in the indicative. Their moods are shown by differing neustics: "please" for the imperative, "yes" for the indicative. Anyone who actually uses or asserts a sentence, as distinct from merely mentioning or quoting it, so to speak, "nods" the sentence. Hare thus compares his neustic to the assertion symbol in the logical systems of Frege and of Russell and Whitehead. According to Hare,[76] affirming a statement is different from affirming a command. (It strains the ordinary use of "affirm" a little to speak of affirming commands but Hare recognizes this.) One way of seeing the difference which he has in mind is to ask what is understood where the respective meanings of an indicative and imperative are communicated. To understand an indicative sentence is to understand that assent to it consists in thinking or believing that something is, or is not, the case. Understanding an imperative sentence is understanding that assent to it consists in having a disposition to do, or refrain from doing, something. The rules and conventions of our language, in respect of the expression of mood, implicitly constitute this difference of meaning between indicatives and imperatives. It is our reliance upon these conventions to which Hare is referring when he speaks of neustics. All sentences have a neustic, which is here conceived as the sign both of assertion *and* of mood.[77]

It is, however, according to the Hare of *The Language of Morals,* in the other particle, the phrastic, that all the logical words, which determine any piece of deduction, are to be found. To take the word "not" as an example, if, instead of telling somebody to make something the case (imperative) or telling them that something is the case (indicative), we wished to tell them *not* to make it the case or that it is *not* the case, we should do this, not by any change in the mood of the sentence, for that would remain the same, but in that part of the sentence which does not indicate mood. In terms of the above example, we should have to say:

No showing of her room to Mrs. Prendergast by Mary at time *t*.

[76] *Ibid.*
[77] But cf. below, pp. 232.

and then add either "please" to make an imperative, or "yes" to make an indicative. But we have made a negation irrespective of which we add; and indeed of whether or not we add either. The phrastic is common ground to indicatives and imperatives.

"All vehicles turn left" entails "This vehicle turn left" just as surely as "All vehicles will turn left" entails "This vehicle will turn left" because the deduction is the same in both cases: from the phrastic, "Turning left by all vehicles" to the phrastic, "Turning left by this vehicle." Again, "Halt" contradicts "Proceed" as surely as "You will halt" contradicts "You will proceed" because the contradiction is the same in both cases: between the phrastics "Halting by you" and "Proceeding by you." Hare remarks:

> If we had to find out whether someone knew the meaning of the word "all" in "Take all the boxes to the station," we should have to find out whether he realized that a person who assented to this command, and also to the statement "This is one of the boxes" and yet refused to assent to the command "Take this to the station" could only do so if he had misunderstood one of these three sentences. If this sort of test were inapplicable, the word "all" (in imperatives as in indicatives) would be entirely meaningless. We may therefore say that the existence in our language of universal sentences in the imperative mood is in itself sufficient proof that our language admits of entailments of which at least one term is a command.[78]

He goes on to suggest that, since logical words appear in the phrastics, it should be possible "to reconstruct the ordinary sentential calculus in terms of phrastics only, and then apply it to indicatives and imperatives alike simply by adding the appropriate neustics."[79]

He recognizes that certain difficulties might be encountered in doing so. For example, it might be found that in ordinary speech there are a number of different rules for the uses of

[78] *LM*, pp. 25–26.
[79] *LM*, p. 26.

words like "all," "if," etc., in different contexts; in particular, for their use in imperative, as opposed to indicative, contexts. But it is still tautologously true that "so long as we continue to use our words in the same sense their entailment-relations will remain the same":[80] as, for example, the words "all" and "not" were used in the same senses in the imperative and indicative sentences instanced above. Another difficulty which Hare notes is the question: how are we to know, given two premises in different moods, in what mood the conclusion is to be? This brings us to his "mixed" or "practical" syllogism, one illustration of which was quoted at the beginning of this paragraph.

> Take all the boxes to the station (imperative).
> This is one of the boxes (indicative).
> *Therefore* Take this to the station (imperative).

Or:
> Taking of all the boxes by you to the station, *please.*
> This being one of the boxes, *yes.*
> *Therefore* Taking of this by you to the station, *please.*

The question is: why not:

> Take all the boxes to the station.
> This is one of the boxes.
> *Therefore* You will take this to the station

Or:
> Taking of all boxes by you to the station, *please.*
> This being one of the boxes, *yes.*
> *Therefore* Taking of this by you to the station, *yes.*

The latter would not be valid syllogisms; but why not? In reply, Hare states "two of the rules that seem to govern this matter." (i) "No indicative conclusion can be validly drawn from a set of premises which cannot be validly drawn from the indicatives among them alone"; and (ii) "No imperative conclusion can be validly drawn from a set of premises which

[80] *LM*, p. 27.

does not contain at least one imperative."[81] The justification
for these rules he takes to lie in the general logical consideration that nothing may be said in the conclusion of a valid
deductive inference which is not said explicitly or implicitly
in the conjunction of the premises—except what can be added
solely on the strength of the definitions of terms.[82] The conclusion "You will take this to the station" (or: "Taking of
this by you to the station, yes") *is not* said explicitly or implicitly either by "Take all these boxes to the station" ("Taking
of all the boxes by you to the station, please") or by "This is
one of the boxes" ("This being one of the boxes, yes") or
by their conjunction. Whereas there *is* implicit in the major
(imperative) premise, "Take all the boxes to the station,"
the singular imperative, "Take this to the station," "this" having been defined by the minor premise as one of the boxes.
To deny that this conclusion is implicit in such a conjunction
of premises would be to misunderstand the word "all." It
should be noted, however, that Hare would not, I think, now
hold to the first of his two rules. More will be said about this
below in the subsection of criticism entitled *Hare's Rules*
(pp. 234–37).

III. CRITICISM

(I) CRITICISM: PRESCRIPTIVITY

Hare himself has recently said that the perlocution-
illocution distinction "makes the main difference between
emotivism and prescriptivism."[83] As we have seen, he attacks the emotivist view that the major use of moral judgments is to create an influence. The emotivists thought that
they could get at the meaning of moral discourse by asking
what we do *by* engaging in it. It is true that the answer to
this question may be that we influence people. I may get
someone to switch on the "News at Ten" by saying "We
ought to hear the news." But then again I may do so by say-

[81] *LM*, p. 28.
[82] *LM*, pp. 32–33.
[83] Review of Warnock's *Contemporary Moral Philosophy* in *M*
LXXVII (1968), 437.

ing, according to circumstances, "It's ten o'clock" (factual statement), or "Switch on" (command), or "If only someone would turn on the news" (expression of a wish), or "Am I going to be allowed to hear the news or not?" (question), etc. It is not a *differentia* of moral judgments that they create an influence. Any speech-act may do so. It seemed clear to Hare that, if you want to get at the meaning of moral discourse, the question to ask does not concern its perlocutionary, but its illocutionary,[84] force. The effect which we intend to produce *by* an utterance may not be realized, and yet that utterance be perfectly meaningful. For example, none of the above remarks would lose any of its meaning if, though uttered with the intention of getting the news switched on, it failed to have that effect. The real clue to any utterance's meaning, or so it seems to Hare, is what are we doing *in* saying it. This question, or rather the relative answers to it, *would* differentiate the above speech-acts from one another. *In* saying one we are stating a fact; *in* saying the others, giving a command, expressing a wish, asking a question. And if we were not doing what we are doing *in* saying any one of them, then they *would* be meaningless. If you said "Switch on" and I said "Is that a command?" and you said "No," then I, and anyone else who overheard, would be at a loss to know what you meant. (Of course, we may have misjudged what you purport to be doing, e.g., this may be a request; but my argument assumes that we have got what you purport to be doing right.) If you do not succeed in doing what you purport to be doing *in* saying anything, then what you say is meaningless. So when we come to moral judgment the question which gets us to its meaning is: what are we doing *in* making it? I think Hare's most severe critics would concede that he has made a valuable contribution to metaethics by thus applying the perlocution-illocution distinction to moral discourse.

There is, of course, nothing like the same measure of agreement that Hare has got the right answer as there is that he is asking the right question. Briefly, his answer comes to this.

[84] On this distinction see above, pp. 54–63.

What we are doing centrally and importantly[85] in making moral judgments is prescribing. This speech-act of prescribing takes place within a logical framework which has the further feature of universalizability; and in contexts where there are normally appeals to fact, to inclination or interest, and to imagination, respectively. To say that moral, and indeed all ought judgments are prescriptive is to say, not that they are imperatives, but that they entail imperatives. In saying sincerely "Capital punishment ought to be abolished," for example, I commit myself to abolishing it in so far as this possibility is open to me; and in sincerely accepting this judgment, any of my hearers will commit himself similarly.

I shall consider two questions concerning this prescriptivism. (i) Is its account of what we are doing in uttering moral judgments plausible? (ii) How far does it really go beyond emotivism? Hare's prescriptivism has in fact been widely criticized. In the next chapter, I shall be concerned with a school of thought which has recently arisen largely in reaction against his views; and what I have to say in the rest of this section should be supplemented by what is said there.

Is Prescriptivism Plausible?

There is undoubtedly some intimate connection between moral judgments and action. Most, if not all, of Hare's critics would agree with his contention that the surest way to find out what a man's moral principles are is to discover what he does.[86] Nevertheless, they dispute two things. One is Hare's belief that, as a matter of fact, the most central and important use of moral language is prescriptive; and the other, the view, which they take Hare to hold, that the close connection between moral judgment and action can only be explained by this putative fact.

Against the former it is urged that a man may judge morally by one set of principles and conduct his life, or advise others to conduct theirs by another set. In this sense his judgment may not be prescriptive. Professor A. C. MacIntyre, for

[85] Cf. *FR*, p. 84.
[86] *LM*, p. 1; cf. Warnock, *op. cit.*, p. 37.

example, writes: "A man might commit himself to a certain moral appraisal but not use it as a guide for action—'This in the light of morality is how your action would be appraised: but don't follow the guidance of morality.'"[87] He expressly excludes, as the only possible explanation of such a remark, Hare's distinction between evaluative and descriptive meaning. Of course, "in the light of morality" might mean "by the generally accepted standards of this community"; but MacIntyre's point is that it might *not*. What if the morality concerned is the speaker's own? If prescriptivism were true, it would not make sense to say that a man could morally appraise actions by one standard and guide his own conduct by another. But MacIntyre claims that this does make sense. Notice that he is not thinking of weakness of will for which, as he recognizes, Hare provides.[88] He does not simply mean that a man can (logically) fail to live up to his moral principles; but rather that he can (logically) be said to have moral principles which he sincerely holds but does not put into practice, even when physically and psychologically able to do so.

Well, can he? I am assuming that MacIntyre would not object to the use of "sincerely" in my penultimate sentence. (There is nothing to indicate that he would. And if he would, then in effect he concedes the point which I am about to make against him and his case collapses.) Would we, in fact, call such a man as MacIntyre speaks of sincere? We saw that, according to Hare,[89] sincerity is one of the necessary conditions of its being true that a speaker who is using "I ought to do X" as a value judgment will assent to the command "Let me do X" So, for MacIntyre to carry his point against Hare, it is necessary that his man should be sincere. But I do not think it can (logically) be said that a man sincerely adheres to moral principles which he does not put into practice if he can.

MacIntyre charges Hare with building his own *moral* commitment, to the principle that one ought to be sincere, into

[87] A. C. MacIntyre, "What Morality Is Not," *P* XXXII (1957), 330.
[88] See above, p. 169.
[89] Above, p. 169.

his account of the logic of moral discourse;[90] but I do not think that there is anything in this. It is one thing to be committed to the principle that one ought to practice what one preaches, quite another to believe that one cannot (logically) hold sincerely to a moral principle and not, given the physical and psychological opportunity, act upon it. It may well be the case that Hare, as a liberal moralist, subscribes to the former opinion; but what makes him a prescriptivist is something quite different, namely the fact that he holds the logical belief just stated.

Against Hare's prescriptivism it is also said that he restricts far too narrowly what a man may be doing in making moral judgments. He may indeed be prescribing; but he may be doing a variety of other things. G. J. Warnock writes: ". . . there are . . . dozens of things which those who employ moral words may therein be doing. They may be prescribing, certainly; but also they may be advising, exhorting, imploring; commanding, condemning, deploring; resolving, confessing, undertaking; and so on, and so on."[91] Hare's reply is to the effect that he has never denied this variety. All the speech-acts listed by Warnock are, according to Hare, species of the genus, prescribing; that is to say, all, in their primary use, entail imperatives.[92] This reply seems to me to be justified. It does not, of course, show that Hare is right. But it does show that simply to present such a list as Warnock's will not in itself dispose of prescriptivism. It is as plausible to argue that all the "alternatives" to prescribing which Warnock lists entail imperatives as that prescribing does.

What of the view, attributed to Hare, that the undoubted connection between moral judgment and action is explicable only in terms of his prescriptivism? Warnock thinks he finds this view in Hare and he rejects it. He says:

From the fact, if it be a fact, that a man's moral principles are revealed most decisively in his behaviour, it does not follow in the least that those principles have to be con-

[90] MacIntyre, *op. cit.*, 332–33.
[91] Warnock, *op. cit.*, p. 35.
[92] *M* LXXVII (1968), 438.

ceived as, or as implying, *prescriptions*. They might, so far
as that point goes, equally well be conceived as expressions
of taste or of approval, as avowals of wants or aims, as
views about values or ideals, as resolutions, as beliefs about
interests, and in many other ways too. On this score at any
rate, "Eating people is wrong" is no more closely akin to
"Don't eat people" than it is to "I don't want people to be
eaten": for in each of these cases the eating of people, or
looking on complacently while people are eaten, would be
in some sort of conflict with, even in a sense would contradict, what is said.[93]

But need Hare dissent from any of this? I should not expect
him to deny that *if* moral judgments were expressions of taste,
avowals of wants, or beliefs about interests, the connection
between them and action would be explained by appeal to the
logical fact that part, at least, of what we would be saying in
saying that we have a taste for something, or want it, or think
it in our interest, is that, given the chance to attain it, we
would seize that chance. Hare does not say that the prescriptivity of moral judgments is the only *conceivable* account of
the connection between them and action. He would, I think,
accuse Warnock of a *petitio principii* at this point. All he
wishes to claim is that if *moral* judgments are prescriptive,
this will explain the fact that they have the intimate connection which they do have with actions.[94]

How Far Does Hare's Prescriptivism Go beyond Emotivism?
   The second of the two questions which I said that I would
discuss is: how far does Hare's prescriptivism really go beyond
emotivism? Without question, it goes some distance. For one
thing, it differentiates what Stevenson called the "non-rational
psychological" from what he called the "logical" and the "rational psychological" methods of moral argument[95] by refusing to recognize the first as a method of moral argument
at all. Then again, Hare shows, as Stevenson scarcely began
to do, the use to which the consistency, or universalizability,

[93] Warnock, *op. cit.*, p. 39.
[94] Cf. *M* LXXVII (1968), 439–40.
[95] Cf. above, pp. 130–31.

test can be put in moral argument. Within this logical framework, rational argument can go on, by the adducing of
counter-examples, and by the appeal to inclination or interest
and imagination, at least up to a point where those who opt
out of it can only do so at the cost of becoming what Hare
calls "fanatics." And it is an empirical fact, as he realizes, that
most people are reluctant to end up in that position. We remarked above that Hare's early ambition was to show the
possibility of rational argument in morals. He certainly shows
the possibility of a good deal of such argument.

Some have denied this. They have said that prescriptivism,
like emotivism, "cannot find much place for argument."[96]
The telling point which they have to make is that both emotivism and prescriptivism do not simply consider it possible on
moral issues for us to make up our own mind *on* the evidence,
but no less possible for us to make up our own minds what
shall count *as* evidence. To quote Warnock again: "I do not,
it seems, decide that flogging is wrong because I *am* against
cruelty; rather, I decide that flogging is wrong because I *decide to be* against cruelty. And what, if I did make that decision, would be my ground for making it? That I am opposed
to the deliberate infliction of pain? No—rather that I *decide
to be* opposed to it. And so on."[97] There are people, he goes
on, who make up not only their own minds, but also their
own evidence; but such people are a menace, not a model, not
exemplars of, but abstainers from, reasoning. It is not enough,
for such critics, to say simply, as Hare seems to do, that
moral argument provides us with an instrument whereby we
can test the self-consistency of our opponents. Are not mad-
men and knaves often completely self-consistent? Surely moral
argument should be able to defeat them.

Two things at least need to be said about this, I think. (i)
An instrument which enables you to bring home to your opponents the fact that they are on a course which, followed
to its conclusion, leads to what Hare calls "fanaticism" should
not be despised. Most men would wish to avoid that terminus

[96] Warnock, *op. cit.*, p. 42.
[97] *Ibid.*, p. 47.

and so, if you can show them that they are heading for it, this will seem to them sufficient reason for a change of direction. (ii) Warnock calls people who want to decide for themselves what counts as evidence, a menace. And so they are in many contexts. One such context would be a moral argument in which a person said, for example, that X was wrong because it was the breaking of a promise and then refused to count the fact that Y was also the breaking of a promise as evidence of Y's wrongness. Once what counts as evidence is decided, one is a menace if one goes back on that decision. But, of course, the precise content of that decision may vary. If you decide to do mathematics you are, in effect, deciding to count a different kind of thing as evidence than you would be if you had decided to do natural science. The content of your decision differs from both of these if you decide to think morally. Why, then, should there not be a universe of discourse in which what counts as evidence is any reason which a speaker chooses to give for something being good or obligatory, the point of the discourse being to see how consistently he can adhere to that choice under cross-questioning? And why should not morality be such a universe of discourse? Warnock seems to think that, simply by representing it as such a universe of discourse, prescriptivism has represented morality as irrationalist and so discredited itself, since moral discourse is manifestly not irrationalist. But anyone who engaged in a universe of discourse such as we have just supposed would not thereby become a menace to reasoning or an abstainer from it; he would only become such if, having given his reason for a moral judgment, he refused to let himself be tested for consistency in holding it. And it is expressly no part of prescriptivism to permit such refusal.

The real issue, of course, is whether or not moral discourse *is* of this kind. There is nothing inherently absurd in the conception of such a universe of discourse, but it may be absurd so to conceive of morality. If morality *is* that kind of discourse, then it seems to follow that it would make perfectly good sense to say that *anything* whatever was good or that *any* conceivable course of action ought to be taken. I could (logically) offer *anything whatever* as a reason for a moral judgment: for instance, that a certain action ought to be performed because it will effect the greatest misery of the greatest number, or injure the health of my children, or constitute the breaking of a promise, or whatever. The same question arises here as arose when we were considering Stevenson's emotivism.[98] Would such remarks make sense? Or is there some logical limitation on what may intelligibly be offered as a reason for a *moral* judgment which would exclude them? Some think that there is and that it is a defect in Hare's philosophy that he fails to see this. I shall return to this question below.[99]

(II) CRITICISM: UNIVERSALIZABILITY

Hare's view, that universalizability is a defining characteristic of ought judgments in general and moral ones in particular, has also come in for much criticism. In his article "Universalisability," Hare speaks of U-type valuations, i.e., applications of a "rule wholly devoid of any personal reference containing merely predicates (descriptions) and logical terms."[100] His central thesis in the article is "that all *moral* valuations are of type U—or, which comes to the same thing, that whenever moral reasons are given for actions, the maxims involved are of type U."[101] In *Freedom and Reason* (particularly pp. 35–37), Hare claims that *all* uses of "ought," not only moral ones, involve a U-type maxim. He finds corroboration of this in the impossibility, which he claims, of using "ought" to make a legal judgment. A statement of law always contains an implicit reference to a particular jurisdiction: "It is illegal to marry one's sister" means "It is illegal (e.g.) in England to marry one's sister." Here "England," a singular term, prevents the maxim from being U-type. "It is illegal to marry one's sister" does not mean "One ought not to marry one's sister" for it is always open to us to ask, "Ought we to do what it is illegal to do?" What Hare says

[98] Above, p. 151.

[99] See Chap. 7.

[100] R. M. Hare, "Universalisability," *PAS* LV (1954–55), 295. Hare takes this definition from Gellner, *ibid.*, p. 163.

[101] Hare, *op. cit.*, 304.

about the universalizability of ought judgments is intended to apply equally to moral and nonmoral ones. The wider thesis (all ought judgments are universalizable) is impugned as well as the narrower one (moral ought judgments are universalizable) if the latter cannot be sustained.

Some Misunderstandings

Hare's theory, that ought judgments apply U-type principles, has often been misunderstood and we must follow him in sweeping away some superficial misunderstandings first of all. To begin with, about principles. Sometimes, when men say that something is a matter of principle with them, they mean that they take a hard and fast line about it and do not waste time any longer wondering whether they are justified in doing so. In some degree no doubt we all have—and need to have, if we are to avoid spending so much time in reflection that we have none left over for action—some such principles. But, be that as it may, Hare most certainly does not mean that all moral reasoning is, or ought to be, of that kind. When he maintains that the grounds of moral judgment must always imply universal principles, he is simply saying that these grounds are reasons which necessarily invoke and apply universal rules; and that is quite different. Again, Hare nowhere says that to be moral is necessarily to be a busybody, always poking one's nose into other people's ethical concerns. Nor is it to be intolerant with those who disagree with one on moral issues. His point is simply that, in saying "X is wrong because it is Y," I must, if I have really given the complete reason for what I say, be saying that anything else which is Y is also to that extent wrong. The point is logical. It does not in the least imply that I must go around looking for things which are Y in order to denounce them.

A more common misunderstanding is the widespread belief that anyone who subscribes to the universalizability thesis is insensitive to the extremely complicated character of most of the situations in which moral issues arise. Hare's very careful distinction between universality and generality[102] is fre-

---

[102] *Ibid.*, 311; *FR*, pp. 38–39.

quently overlooked. "Specific" is the opposite of "general," *but not* of "universal." A moral judgment can be universalizable and at the same time very specific.

We may note, in passing, that the question has been raised: how specific, given the universalizability thesis, can a moral judgment be? It has been claimed that the universalizability thesis cannot be formulated simply thus: "A judgment is a moral judgment, if and only if the person who makes it accepts some universal moral principle which, together with some true statement *about the nonmoral characteristics* of the situation originally judged, entails the original judgment." This formulation, it is said, must be revised to read: ". . . together with some true statement about *some but not all of the nonmoral characteristics* of the situation originally judged." Two assumptions seem to lie behind the proposal that the universalizability thesis should be thus reformulated: (a) that it is logically possible to offer a description of the nonmoral characteristics of a situation, such that only that particular situation answers to it; and (b) that every item in such a description could (logically) be morally relevant—i.e., could conceivably figure in some "true statement" about nonmoral characteristics which, together with a universal moral principle, entails a moral judgment. It will be seen that, if both these assumptions held good, a judgment could be moral and not universalizable. The universalizability thesis is designed to obviate that contingency and must be formulated accordingly. If moral judgments can (logically) be moral and not universalizable, then of course the universalizability thesis is mistaken. Are the above assumptions well founded? (a) I am inclined to think that the former is. It seems clear to me that, if the description in question included an exhaustive account of the spatial and temporal relations of the given situation, then it could (logically) be so complete as to apply to that situation and no other. Even if the universe within which the given situation occurs were repetitive or symmetrical, so that situations whose description would be in many respects identical with that of the given situation, could occur, a complete description of the spatial and temporal relations of the given situation could be offered, which would differentiate it from any other similar situation. This assumption raises the whole complicated problem of the identity of indiscernibles and it lies beyond the scope of this book to go any further into it. (b) The second assumption is not well founded. Suppose part of your description of a given situation were a description of its spatial and temporal relations, such that this part of the description referred to the particular location in space and time of that situation. Then this part of your description would be irrelevant to the morality of the given situation. The reason why an act is, say, wrong cannot *simply* be that it was done in such-and-such a place at such-and-such a time. You might, of course, say, for example, that Enoch Powell did wrong to make his so-called racialist speeches where and when he did. But if you do, you will not be saying that it was the place or time *in themselves* which made his speeches wrong, but the conditions obtaining at or in them. An act cannot be wrong solely because it occurred in Birmingham at one particular time.

The point which I want to bring out here is that it is not necessary to build into your formulation of the universalizability thesis some safeguard against the possibility that the reason given for your *moral* judgment will be such that it could (logically) apply *only* to something done in a certain place at a certain time, thereby rendering the moral judgment grounded in it non-universalizable. That possibility does not exist. The·only reasons which would be recognizable as *moral* reasons are such as render the judgment grounded in them universalizable. So, the "true statement" referred to above in the formulation, and the reformulation of the universalizability thesis, could be about *all* the nonmoral characteristics of the situation—all, that is, which could conceivably be morally relevant. The original formulation, as given above, viz. ". . . some true statement about the nonmoral characteristics . . . ," appears to recognize that this is so. The suggested reformulation, viz. ". . . true statement about *some but not all* of the nonmoral characteristics . . . ," seems to fail to recognize that it is. The latter appears to assume falsely that there could conceivably be morally relevant nonmoral characteristics which would render a judgment based upon them non-universalizable, and therefore we need to formulate the universalizability thesis in such a way as to cut out such cases. There is no need to do that because such cases are inconceivable.[103]

Situation Ethics

If moral judgments are universalizable, it does not follow that they will be sweeping generalizations which take no account of the extremely complicated character of most situations in which moral issues arise. A recent attack on the notion of moral principles has come from a type of ethical theory which purports to show that moral judgments are "situational." It exists in both religious and secular versions. Professor Joseph Fletcher amusingly gives some indication of this viewpoint at the beginning of his *Situation Ethics:* "A friend of mine arrived in St. Louis just as a presidential campaign was ending, and the cab driver, not being above the battle, volunteered his testimony. 'I and my father and grandfather before me, and their fathers, have always been straight-ticket Republicans.' 'Ah,' said my friend, who is himself a Republican, 'I take it that means you will vote for Senator So-and-So.' 'No,' said the driver, 'there are times when a man has to push his principles aside and do the right thing.' That St. Louis cabbie is this book's hero."[104] However, it transpires in the sequel that Fletcher, a religious moralist, has, or says he has, nothing against principles provided they do not harden into rules or laws.[105] But he seems curiously unaware of the distinction between (a) hard-and-fast principles, appeal to which is made a substitute for thinking by the morally insensitive, and (b) reasons which must be given where moral thinking is rational and which are reasons only because they

---

[103] For the suggested reformulation see J. Bennett, "Moral Argument," *M* LXIX (1960), 544. For a recent discussion of the problem of the identity of indiscernibles see P. F. Strawson, *Individuals* (1959), especially pp. 120–30.

[104] Joseph Fletcher, *Situation Ethics* (London, 1966), p. 13.

[105] *Ibid.*, pp. 31 ff.

invoke principles or rules. The former it is empirically possible to forego; but with the latter we cannot (logically) dispense.

Avant-garde religious moralists of late have launched a fierce and sustained attack upon the rigid application of moral principles. The Cambridge theologian, H. A. Williams, for example, wrote a few years ago about the English film *The Mark:*

> It tells of the rehabilitation into normality of a man strongly attracted to small girls. His abnormality, which can do nothing but untold harm to everybody, is due to his fear of commitment to an adult woman. However, in time, a woman of his own age inspires him with enough confidence for them to go away for the week-end together. They have separate rooms at the hotel. But it is clear that until he sleeps with her he will not have established enough confidence in himself to deliver him from his utterly destructive abnormality which tends to exploitation to the *n*th degree. Will he be able to summon up the necessary courage or not? When he does, and they sleep together, he has been made whole. And where there is healing, there is Christ, whatever the Church may say about fornication. And the appropriate response is—Glory to God in the Highest.[106]

I am not concerned here to discuss the value of these opinions or their consistency with the Christian ethic. All I wish to argue is that, if you favor some such loosening up of traditional Christian morality, it does not follow that you are putting principles aside, in the sense of reasons which embody rules. Consider what another advocate of situation ethics, Bishop John Robinson, says in a section of his *Honest to God* entitled "Nothing Prescribed—Except Love": ". . . nothing can of itself always be labelled as wrong."[107] But he goes on to say that "because it is an act of love" states a good reason why an act ought to be done. He seems to think that we can look at situations, ask "What would love do

[106] H. A. Williams, *Soundings* (Cambridge, 1962), edited by A. R. Vidler, p. 82.
[107] J. A. Robinson, *Honest to God* (London, 1963), p. 118.

here?" and perceive the answer. But, unless he is advocating some extreme form of intuitionism or emotivism, he will have to say that there is always a statable reason why the act in question is, or would be, an act of love. For instance, he would have to say presumably, if he agreed with Williams about the film, that, in so far as an action helps another human being to overcome sexual perversion or inadequacy, it is an act of love. That is what "love" means in this situation and therefore that is the reason why the act embodying it is right. To say that this is the reason why this act is right, however, is to say that in so far as *any* act would help another human being to overcome sexual perversion it would be *to that extent* always right, and its omission always wrong. To deny this is to deny that one has offered a reason why the given act is right. There are really only two alternatives open to a moralist who wants to take the Bishop's line that nothing is prescribed except love: either (i) he means that no statable reason can be given why an act is an act of love; and what this would come to is that neither he nor anyone else knows what "love" means. It is then singularly unhelpful to tell anyone to do what love would do. Or (ii) he means simply that, while love is the overriding moral principle, the statement of what "love" means is a highly complex business and our minds must always be open to the possibility that we have got it wrong. Hare's form of universal prescriptivism can accommodate this latter view perfectly comfortably. It simply amounts to what, as we saw, Hare himself says about conceiving of moral reasoning as a kind of exploration.[108]

Act- and Rule-Utilitarianism

In secular ethics there has been a more or less parallel development to this so-called "new morality" of the radical Christians. It is the contention that utilitarianism should be act-, not rule-, utilitarianism. The principle of utility, that is, should be invoked directly to determine the morality of individual acts, and not simply to justify universal rules such as "Promises ought to be kept," which may then be instantiated

[108] Above, pp. 192–95.

in particular acts. Hare argues that, given the universalizability of moral judgments, act-utilitarianism and rule-
utilitarianism "collapse into each other."[109] He claims first
that "there cannot be a case which is consistent with *act*-
utilitarianism but inconsistent with *rule*-utilitarianism"[110] and
says, in support of this, substantially what I said a moment or
two ago against the situationalists: "If it were possible to apply
the principle of utility directly to actions without the inter-
mediacy of any subordinate principle, then we should have
such a case. But it can be shown that this is impossible. For
how could it be the case that an action could be known to
be such as to maximise satisfactions without it being known
that it did so *because* of the sort of action that it was?"[111]
The individual act is right because it instantiates a rule to the
effect that that sort of action maximizes satisfactions. Conversely, Hare claims that neither can there be "a case consistent with *rule*-utilitarianism but inconsistent with *act*-
utilitarianism."[112] Here there would have to be a rule which
we believed it right to observe, even though the individual act
which we performed in consequence was not right, e.g., keeping a promise because keeping promises effects the greatest
happiness of the greatest number, even though our promise
was made to a man now dead and many more people would
be happy if we broke it than if we kept it. It does not seem to
me that this argument need worry a rule-utilitarian. Would
any rule-utilitarian who was able to think clearly, ever have
to find himself in the position of holding to a rule, but except-
ing an individual act from it? Would he ever have to say—
would it, indeed, ever make sense if he did say—"This act instantiates the rule and is in that respect right, but in itself it is
wrong"? Would not his rule, if *that* particular act *as right*
came under it, always be such as stated the rightness of *all*
acts *of the kind*—e.g., "It is always right to keep promises
even where this causes the present degree of privation of happiness because in the end this produces the greatest happiness

[109] *FR*, p. 135.
[110] *FR*, p. 132.
[111] *FR*, p. 131.
[112] *FR*, p. 132.

of the greatest number." Unless it would, he would not be a utilitarian at all.[113]

MacIntyre's Criticism

Hare, in putting forward his view that ought judgments apply U-type principles, said that this will become clearly apparent, if we consider the following conversation between an existentialist and a Kantian.

E: "You oughtn't to do that."

K: "So you think that one oughtn't to do that kind of thing?"

E: "I think nothing of the kind; I say only that *you* oughtn't to do *that*."

K: "Don't you even imply that a person like me in circumstances of this kind oughtn't to do that kind of thing when the other people involved are the sort of people that they are?"

E: "No; I say only that *you* oughtn't to do *that*."

K: "Are you making a moral judgment?"

E: "Yes."

K: "In that case I fail to understand your use of the word 'moral.'"

Says Hare:

Most of us would be as baffled as the "Kantian"; and indeed we should be hard put to it to think of any use of the word "ought," moral or non-moral, in which the "Existentialist's" remarks would be comprehensible. Had the "Existentialist" said "Don't do that," instead of "You oughtn't to do that," the objections of the "Kantian" could not have been made; this illustrates one of the main differences between "ought" and ordinary imperatives. Indeed, the fault of the "Existentialists" might be characterised thus: because moral judgments are like ordinary

[113] I think that Hare's argument here is substantially correct, but I realize that the issues raised are complicated and a satisfactory discussion of the act-rule controversy would require a much more detailed, and perhaps sympathetic, treatment than that which I give it here, if justice were to be done to it. Hare, I imagine, would agree with this.

imperatives in some respects, they conclude that they are like in all respects.[114]

Criticism of Hare has taken the form of a defense of the existentialist's use of the word "moral" in this imaginary conversation. The by now famous example given by Sartre in his essay *L'Existentialisme est un humanisme* (Paris, 1946) is quoted against Hare. One of Sartre's pupils during the war lived alone with his mother. She was estranged from his father who was something of a collaborator; and her elder son had been killed fighting the Germans in 1940. She was deeply affected by the semi-treason of the one and the loss of the other. Sartre's pupil realized that his presence with his mother was her only consolation; but he was also eager to avenge his brother's death. He had the choice of going to England to join the Free French Forces or of staying with his mother and making her life tolerable. What could help him to choose? asks Sartre. Not Christianity, for it says "Love your neighbor," and he cannot say who is his neighbor, his mother or those whom he would benefit by fighting for France. Again, not the Kantian ethic, for it says "Treat persons as ends, never means"; but the problem is, which persons, his mother or those others? In a dilemma such as his, says Sartre, all we can do is "trust in our instincts," follow our "affections." But this does not mean that we can find some guidance before the action as to what it should be. "I can only estimate the strength of [an] affection," says Sartre, "if I have performed an action by which it is defined and ratified. But if I then appeal to this affection to justify my action, I find myself drawn into a vicious circle."[115]

MacIntyre, who uses this example against Hare, comments on it thus:

> Part of the force of his [Sartre's] argument is this. Someone faced with such a decision might choose either to stay or to go without attempting to legislate for anyone else in a

[114] Hare, "Universalisability," *op. cit.*, 304–5.
[115] English version, J. P. Sartre, *Existentialism and Humanism* (1948), trans. by P. Mairet, p. 37.

similar position. He might decide what to do without being willing to allow that anyone else who chose differently was blameworthy. He might legitimately announce his choice by saying, "I have decided that I ought to stay with my mother." If he did so, his use of "ought" would not express any appeal to a universalisable principle. It would not be a U-type valuation, but it would be a moral valuation.[116]

I think first of all that Hare is entitled to reply, as in fact he does,[117] that it is by no means certain that Sartre would recognize this as "part of the force of his argument." One central theme of the essay is, to be sure, the importance of making one's own moral choices and not taking them, in bad faith, second-hand from other people; but another is the responsibility and consequent anguish which, according to Sartre, lie in the very fact that, in making moral choices, we have to choose not only for ourselves but for all mankind. Sartre says, for example, "I am thus responsible for myself and for all men, and I am creating a certain image of man as I would have him to be. In fashioning myself I fashion man. . . . We are left alone, without excuse. That is what I mean when I say that man is condemned to be free. . . . Every man, without any support or help whatever, is condemned at every instant to invent man."[118] It is to illuminate remarks such as this that Sartre goes on to use the illustration of his pupil. These remarks themselves, and others like them, do seem to lend support to Hare's claim that the Sartre of *L'Existentialisme est un humanisme* is "as much of a universalist as I am, in the sense in which I am."[119]

Be that as it may, the important point is how well-founded the criticism which MacIntyre levels at the universalizability thesis is. I will take its main points in turn.

(i) "Someone faced with such a decision [as Sartre's pupil] might choose either to stay or to go *without attempting to legislate for anyone else in a similar position*" (italics mine).

[116] MacIntyre, *op. cit.*, 326.
[117] *FR*, p. 38.
[118] Sartre, *op. cit.*, pp. 30–34.
[119] *FR*, p. 38.

Notice that MacIntyre says "to stay," and makes no mention of *"ought* to stay." This makes his remark seem the more plausible. He adds, a little later in his article: "The fact that a man might on moral grounds refuse to legislate for anyone other than himself (perhaps on the grounds that to do so would be moral arrogance) would by itself be enough to show that not all moral valuation is universalisable."[120] But I do not think that it is logically possible to pass a moral judgment without legislating for anyone else in a similar position. Notice first MacIntyre's parenthesis. His man is saying, in effect, "I ought not to legislate for (i.e., to pass moral judgments upon) anyone other than myself." And, confronted with "Why?" he is replying, "Because to do so is morally arrogant." It is perfectly in order to say that his judgment instantiates the universal principle "No one in a position similar to mine ought to do what is morally arrogant." His reason does, in this sense—and it is the sense of the universalizability thesis—legislate for other people. There is nothing inconceivable in the thought of someone making a moral decision not to make any *more* moral judgments after this one. And it is in no sense self-contradictory to say that, in so far as that decision was moral, one would be entitled to ask a reason for it. Any reason given would invoke a universal principle.

(ii) "He might decide what to do *without being willing to allow that anyone else who chose differently was blameworthy*" (italics mine). MacIntyre refers, in this connection, to the "works of supererogation" attributed to saints or heroes.[121] He evidently thinks that the language which saints and heroes use about themselves, or which we use about them, is inconsistent with the universalizability thesis. The story of Captain Oates is often told to exemplify heroism. He was a member of Scott's ill-fated expedition to the Antarctic. Being disabled to a degree which was delaying his companions' return to safety, Oates, having said simply, "I am going outside for a moment," left the tent and walked away into the blizzard to certain death. On the universalizability thesis, if

120 MacIntyre, *op. cit.,* 328.
121 *Ibid.*

Captain Oates had said to himself, "I ought to walk away," or if we said of him that he did what he ought to have done, he would have meant, and we would mean, that anyone else so placed also ought to have done it. There are two questions: (a) would Oates naturally have spoken, or would we naturally speak, in terms of "ought" about his case? and (b) if he, or we, would do so, what would he have meant, or we mean? We have already noted the distinction which Hare draws between "ought" and "good": "ought" commits to the view that no similar person in a similar situation ought to fail to do the same thing; "good" only to the view that whatever is the same in relevant respects is good.[122] Now, we should certainly say that what Oates did was good. But should we say that he *ought* to have done it? Prima facie it seems clear that we would not. We should not have blamed Oates, or anyone else in his position, if they had failed to walk away. That is what is meant by calling this heroic act supererogatory. But Oates himself doubtless thought, "I ought to walk away." By the universalizability thesis, this commits him to the view that no one else similarly placed ought to fail to do so. Would Oates have rejected that implication? I doubt it. Surely a man in his position, acting as he did, we presume from a sense of duty, would think that anyone in the same position who failed so to act would be blameworthy. Admittedly, we can conceive of him imagining some acquaintance, X, in his position, and saying to himself, "If X were in my shoes, I wouldn't think less of him if he didn't do what I'm doing." But, if he asked himself why, the answer would reveal some relevant respect—e.g., "I have a duty to set others an example," "I've had a good life," "I shouldn't be able to live with myself afterward if I didn't"—in which he took his own situation to *differ* from X's. There may even be, as I think Hare suggests,[123] a sense in which, not only Oates himself, but we also are perfectly entitled to say that he ought to have done what he did. We would naturally say that a man ought to live up to his own ideals, even though we were not prepared

[122] *FR*, p. 153; above, p. 184.
[123] *FR*, p. 154.

to say that everyone ought to have the same ideals. If we can
say of any ideal only that it is *good,* not that it ought to be
embraced, we can still say that, whatever a man's ideal may
be, he *ought* to live up to it. And in this sense we could say
that Oates did what he ought to have done, implying thereby
that anyone who failed to do the same (i.e., live up to his
own ideals) would be blameworthy.

(iii) "He might legitimately announce his choice by saying,
'I have decided that *I ought* to stay with my mother'" (italics
mine). MacIntyre is illuminating the point he makes here,
when a moment later he adds that the use of "I ought" to announce a decision "is a performatory use . . . in that its use
makes one responsible for performing a particular action
where before saying 'I ought' one could not have been held
responsible for performing that action rather than some alternative one." In this sense, MacIntyre goes on, one could
never say "You oughtn't" but only "I oughtn't."[124] It is undoubtedly true that we cannot (logically) make other people's
moral decisions for them; and if "I ought" (or "oughtn't")
is used as MacIntyre says, then there is no corresponding
"You ought" (or "oughtn't"). But would it be true to say of
such a use of "I ought," as MacIntyre does, that "it would
be a moral *valuation"?* The "I ought" of which MacIntyre
speaks *commits* one to the performance of a certain action.
This can be differentiated from the making of a judgment
about an action. "I ought to do X"—in what I hope I shall not
be accused of begging any questions, if I call the normal
universalizable sense of that expression—entails an imperative.
To *say* "I ought" is to say by implication "Let me." If I have
said the former in the full realization of what I am doing,
then I have *said* the latter also. This is different from actively
committing myself to the fulfillment of that imperative in saying "I ought." When I am merely making a judgment, "ought"
in "I ought" means the same as in "You ought." But there is
a speech-act logically distinct from this. When I am committing myself, taking on responsibility to *do* the act—not just to
say "Let me do it"—I mean by "ought" something which I

[124] MacIntyre, *op. cit.,* 326–27.

never can mean if I use the verb in the second or third persons. It does not seem to me that there is anything here which constitutes a denial, much less a refutation, of universal prescriptivism. Perhaps there is not, even if you call the speech-act of commitment a valuation, as MacIntyre does. A man may say "Two shillings" in answer to either the question "What is this worth?" or to "What am I bid?" He commits himself in the latter case as not in the former. Both are, if you like, valuations. But both are not the same speech-act. MacIntyre's point—that there is a special responsibility-incurring use of "I ought"—may be sound. But this does not show that Hare is mistaken in what he says about a *different* use: namely that in which "I ought" simply makes a moral judgment.

Is the Universalizability Thesis True but Trivial?

The universalizability thesis is sometimes criticized on the ground that it is true but trivial. To see what is at issue here, consider the following imaginary conversation.

A: Capital punishment ought to be discontinued.

B: Why?

A: It requires one man to take another's life.

B: So you think that whatever requires one man to take another's life ought to be discontinued?

A: Yes.

B: But do you think that doctors ought not to sacrifice the baby's life, when they know that it is probable the mother will die in childbirth if they don't?

A: No. I think they ought to sacrifice the baby's life in such circumstances.

B: Why? This is a case of one person being required to take another's life just like capital punishment.

A: The cases differ. In the doctor's case, he is saving a life thereby.

B: So you think that whatever requires one person to take another's life, if he does not save another life thereby, ought to be discontinued?

A: Yes.

B: Well now, suppose the West was faced with a choice between war and submission to, say, Russia or China.

If the West chose war it would be choosing a course which led to death on a vast scale. Far *more* people would suffer that fate than would if the West simply submitted. But do you think the West would do wrong if it chose war?

A: No. Even at that cost, I would say that the West ought to fight.

B: So you do *not* really think that whatever requires one man to take another's life, if he does not save another life thereby, is wrong?

A: All right, I don't.

B: Then you have no reason for saying that capital punishment ought to be discontinued.

The point of B's moves in such a conversation is to convince A that he (A) does not consistently adhere to the reason which he gives for saying that capital punishment ought to be discontinued. He elicits this reason from A and then, by adducing counter-examples (surgery, war), tries to get A to renounce it. Notice that A is allowed to qualify his original reason in order to cope with these counter-examples. It is quite legitimate in moral—as perhaps in any other form of argument—to restate one's meaning more precisely or carefully in the face of objections. B's aim, however, is to produce a counter-example with which A cannot cope. A's reason, modified to cope with previous counter-examples, for condemning capital punishment would apply equally to war in the supposed circumstances, but A does not think that such a war ought not to be fought. He is therefore inconsistent in disapproving of capital punishment and not of war. As a rational being, he has to abandon his reason and with it the original judgment. With this paradigm of a moral argument in mind, I turn again to the charge that the universalizability thesis is true but trivial.

This charge may assume either of two forms:[125] (i) It may turn on the purely logical point that it makes no sense to call anything a criterion of the difference between genuine and non-genuine X's, if it lets through any X whatever, the charge

[125] Cf. Bennett, *op. cit.*, 547–48.

being that this is what the universalizability thesis does. A could conceivably go on accepting the modifications to his original principle in order to escape the charge of inconsistency in face of B's counter-examples, until his principle referred to *nothing but* capital punishment. In the end his argument would be:

> Whatever is a, b, c, etc., ought to be discontinued.
> Capital punishment is a, b, c, etc.
> *Therefore*   Capital punishment ought to be discontinued.

where "a, b, c, etc." was a *complete* description of the nonmoral properties of, and so could (logically) not refer to anything but, capital punishment. His judgment "Capital punishment ought to be discontinued" would then be entirely particular—in the sense that it could (logically) apply only to capital punishment—*and yet pass the universalizability test.* That it would permit such a state of affairs to arise—so the charge runs—shows that the universalizability test is no test. (ii) Alternatively the charge of triviality may turn simply on the *practical* point that, whatever its logical status, the universalizability test does not provide us with a useful frame for moral argument because someone in A's position can, as a matter of fact, always find some difference in principle between his own example and counter-examples which he does not wish to accept. So, a moral argument, conducted in accordance with the universalizability criterion can (empirically) just go on forever.

In attempting a defense of the universalizability thesis against the first of these charges, everything will turn on whether or not it is logically possible to give a description of the situation being morally judged, such that it applies only to that situation. If it is, then the universalizability thesis will need to be reformulated in the way suggested above.[126] If it is not, then the logical point being made here against the

[126] Above, p. 211.

universalizability thesis is groundless. I tried to show above[127] that, while it is conceivable that a description of the nonmoral characteristics of a situation should apply to that situation alone, such a description could not be given as the reason for a *moral* judgment. If this argument was sound, then the universalizability thesis serves as a criterion of moral judgment and is not trivial.

In reply to the second charge—that the universalizability thesis is of no practical use—Bennett[128] concedes that a moral argument can never be lost by a moralist who has the requisite degree of perseverance and pigheadedness—that is, by one who goes on forever refusing to acknowledge defeat and modifies his major premise to cope with all counter-examples. However, pigheadedness of this extreme kind is fortunately not all that common. Within the frame of universalizability, one can constantly present one's opponents with a challenge to their own consistency. It is usually the case that they are not prepared to narrow their principles down beyond a certain point—as A in the above discussion of capital punishment was not. So the charge of practical triviality is not well founded. Moral argument does sometimes effect changes of opinion. It is true that prejudice plays no small part in much of it. Nevertheless, it is the convention that any specifically moral judgment must be, to use Bennett's phrase, "rationalisable on demand."[129] That is to say, one who makes such a judgment must, when required to do so, be prepared to see counter-examples adduced. If he is to retain whatever reputation he has for rationality, he must stand upon the principle(s) implicit in his reason(s) consistently. The point of moral argument is to put that consistency on trial. To recall Hare,[130] moral argument, whether carried on by an individual as a dialogue with himself or between more than one participant, is a form of exploration—exploration into what we find ourselves able as a matter of empirical fact to believe.

[127] See above, pp. 211–13.
[128] Bennett, *op. cit.*, 547.
[129] *Ibid.*, 546.
[130] See above, pp. 192–95.

The question remains, however, as to whether or not rationality in morals is *simply* a maker of such consistency. It is one to which I shall return.[131]

The Universalizability Thesis and Utilitarianism

Hare wishes to establish "a point of contact" between his universal prescriptivism and utilitarianism.[132] He claims that universal prescriptivism provides "a formal foundation" for utilitarianism.[133] If I understand him rightly, his argument goes as follows. Because moral judgments are *universalizable*, anyone who passes such a judgment on another person must accept that, were he himself in the other's place, the judgment would apply equally to him. And because moral judgments are *prescriptive*, anyone who assents to a moral judgment must assent to the imperative implicit within it. If, for instance, I say to someone "Because you are a Jew you ought to be exterminated," I must: (i) recognize that the same judgment would apply to me, if I were a Jew; and (ii) assent to the imperative "If I am a Jew, let me be exterminated." The *universalizability* of moral judgments requires me, in making such judgments, to go "the round of all the affected parties . . . giving equal weight to the interests of all," as Hare puts it.[134] The *prescriptivity* of moral judgments requires me, in making such judgments, to ask the question, as Hare has it, "How much (as I imagine myself in the place of each man in turn) do I want to have this, or avoid that?"[135] Here "this" and "that" refer to the content of the relevant imperative entailed by the judgment; for I think Hare would say that for someone to want to have (or to do) something is for him to be willing to assent to the imperative, "Let me do it (or have it)."[136] Bringing such universalizability and prescriptivity together, then we have the argument in Hare's own words thus: "It is in the endeavour to find lines of conduct which we can

---

[131] See Chap. 7.
[132] *FR*, p. 122.
[133] *FR*, p. 123.
[134] *Ibid.*
[135] *Ibid.*
[136] See Chap. 8.

prescribe universally in a given situation that we find ourselves bound to give equal weight to the desires of all parties . . . and this, in turn, *leads* to such views as that we should seek to maximise satisfactions."[137] Hare, I think, is here saying that universal prescriptivism *leads* to utilitarianism in the following sense. Universalizability, in our moral judgments, requires us to take account of *all* the affected parties. Prescriptivity requires us, in our moral judgments, to take account of the *wants* of all the affected parties. To be a universal prescriptivist is, therefore, to be a utilitarian: it is to approve morally of that which maximizes satisfactions. I raise two questions: (i) Where does this place those whom Hare calls "fanatics"? (ii) Where does it leave minorities?

To deal with the former, let us take the example of the man who thinks that all Jews ought to be exterminated. If this man is a universal prescriptivist, he will have to do two things. He will have to assent to the imperative "Let all Jews be exterminated"; and he will have to put himself imaginatively in the place of each Jew in the world and, having done so, decline assent to the imperative "Let me not be exterminated." It is logically possible for him to do both of these things. But it is arguable that it would be empirically impossible. This fanatic would have to find a satisfaction in the thought of the extermination of all Jews which was greater than that which he found in the thought of the survival of all the Jews in the world after putting himself imaginatively in the place of each. No human being, it might be argued, could in fact experience such a degree of satisfaction as this fanatic would have to experience in the thought of the extermination of the Jews. On such grounds, I think Hare would wish to say that what he means by fanaticism is logically possible but does not, and indeed cannot, empirically, occur. But what if we suppose that our fanatic is not alone in his fanaticism? Suppose others in his society want all Jews to be exterminated. Then, as a universal prescriptivist, our fanatic, in considering what ought to be done with Jews, will put himself in the place of these fellow fanatics and take the satisfaction which they would derive from the extermination of the Jews into account. It is not beyond the bounds of empirical possibility that the satisfaction which one group of people derived from the extermination of another should outweigh the satisfaction which that other group would derive from avoiding extermination.

This brings me to the second question: where does Hare's universal prescriptivist utilitarianism leave minorities? The utilitarian principle of equity, to which Hare likens the universalizability thesis, requires that everybody count for one and nobody for more than one in the felicific calculation. But it provides no safeguard, once that calculation has been made, against discounting the minority completely in the interests of the majority. Hare, for example, thinks that murderers ought to be punished and says that his reasons "are utilitarian ones."[138] If you count everybody as one and nobody as more than one, you arrive at the conclusion that more people will get what they want if you punish murderers than if you do not. But would Hare be prepared to uphold a color bar on the same grounds? Evidently not, for he says, "reasons of this [utilitarian] sort are not available to racialists."[139] Why not? There is, Hare would presumably have to say, no logical difference between the "ought" in "Murderers ought not to be punished" and that in "Negroes ought not to be given civil rights." The difference is simply that, as a matter of fact, the majority get what they want if murderers are punished, but not if Negroes are denied civil rights. The wrongness of denying Negroes civil rights, then, lies in this contingent fact. But it follows from this that if it were not a fact—if the majority would get what they wanted by keeping colored people in subjection—then, that is what ought to be done. We know that, in some restricted communities, the majority would in fact get what they wanted if there were a color bar. Suppose this were true of the community formed by mankind as a whole. Would a color bar, then, be morally

[138] *FR*, p. 222.
[139] *Ibid.*

right? I can hardly think that Hare would give an affirmative answer. But to such an answer his universal prescriptivist utilitarianism seems to commit him.

Is the Universalizability Thesis a Moral Principle?

It is sometimes said, against Hare, that he deceives himself, and would deceive his readers, into thinking that he is elucidating the logic of moral discourse, when all he is really doing is commending a particular morality. I dismissed this criticism above[140] with respect to Hare's view that moral judgments are essentially prescriptive. There are no better grounds for it with regard to his universalizability thesis.

The criticism brought against him is that he only thinks moral discourse to be universalizable, as a matter of *logical* fact, because he subscribes to the liberal Protestant *moral* principle that one ought to apply to oneself the standards which one applies to others and *vice versa*.[141] Now, of course, it is possible that, as a matter of psychological fact, the universalizability thesis only took shape in Hare's mind because he was brought up a liberal Protestant. I do not know whether or not such is the case, but presumably there are psychological techniques which could establish whether it is or not. But whatever the answer to that question, it is entirely beside the point so far as any critique of Hare's moral philosophy is concerned. Hare's opinions about the *logic* of moral discourse are one thing. The *moral* principles to which he holds, or in which he was trained, are another. The universalizability thesis is one of the former (logical) opinions and purports to give an account of how moral language works. It should be discussed on its merits, logical and philosophical. To attempt to discredit it by playing the amateur psychologist and discussing its genesis within Hare's mind is ridiculous. How Hare came by it psychologically, if that can be discovered, would be of interest to his biographer, no doubt. It is of no interest whatever to those who are attempt-

[140] Above, p. 205.
[141] See note 90 and above, pp. 204–5.

ing to assess the correctness or otherwise of his moral philosophy.

(III) CRITICISM: LOGICAL RELATIONS

Neustics and Phrastics

In hitherto unpublished papers, Hare has pointed out inadequacies in the account of neustics and phrastics which he offered in *The Language of Morals* and which was outlined above.[142] He has recalled that, in his T. H. Green Prize Essay, which he abridged to form the first part of *The Language of Morals,* he had drawn a threefold distinction between signs of mood, completeness, and subscription. Thinking this rather pedantic and irrelevant to his argument, when he wrote the book he used the single word "neustic" to cover at least the sign of subscription; and the word "phrastic" to cover the element, common to imperatives and indicatives, which contained all the logical properties of a sentence. He has said that he now thinks this was a mistake. It is to be hoped that Hare will soon publish his further thoughts on this subject. In the light of the unpublished work which he has been kind enough to let me see, though without, of course, claiming authoritatively to represent his opinions, I suggest that his reasons for thinking his account of neustics and phrastics in *The Language of Morals* mistaken might include arguments somewhat on the following lines.

(i) Contradiction or entailment cannot be known to hold between sentences irrespective of mood, as would have to be the case if all logical properties were in the phrastic and the neustic was the sign of mood.

(1) "Take these boxes to the station"

and

(2) "You will not take these boxes to the station"

do not contradict one another, though, on Hare's earlier analysis, they have contradictory phrastics: "Taking of these boxes by you to the station" and "No taking of these boxes by you to the station," respectively.

(3) "Take all these boxes to the station"

and

[142] Pp. 195–201.

(4) "You will take all these boxes to the station"
have on the earlier analysis, the same phrastic: "Taking of all these boxes by you to the station." But we can validly infer

(5) "Take this to the station,"
where "this" is known to refer to a box, from (3), though we cannot validly infer it from (4). We know that (1) and (2) do not contradict each other, and that (5) follows from (3) but not from (4), *only* when we know the mood signs of these sentences. That is, on Hare's earlier analysis, only when we know their neustics. So, contrary to what he then thought, not all logical properties reside in the phrastic; some must reside in what he then called the neustic.

(ii) The sign of subscription or assertion, which shows that a sentence is actually being used and not merely mentioned or quoted, cannot be identified with the mood sign, as Hare appeared to identify them in *The Language of Morals*. We know that "p" and "not p" contradict one another *before* we know whether they are being used or only mentioned; but as we have just seen, we may *not* know this before we know in what mood they are. Hare has now invented a term, *tropic* (from the Greek word for mood), for the mood sign and restricts the meaning of "neustic" to subscription sign.

(iii) The third sign which Hare distinguished in his prize essay he called the sign of completeness. It is necessary to differentiate this from the neustic and the tropic in a sentence and to recognize that some logical properties of the sentence depend upon it. Hare now calls it the *clistic* (from the Greek word meaning "to close or shut"). It serves to enclose a sentence: to show the beginning and the end of what is being said, so that we know that nothing has been overlooked or is still to come. It is logically necessary to know this. An illustration (framed along the same lines as one which on occasion Hare himself has used) will make this clear. If I say to a pupil, "You've got that wrong. Oh no, you haven't," that is not a contradiction, but a correction. Had I said, "You've got that wrong and you haven't," I should have been contradicting myself. The full stop—the clistic—

makes the difference. It ends one thing which I have to say and shows that what comes next is a new beginning. So some logical properties of a sentence depend upon its clistic. The clistic is obviously distinct from the signs of subscription and mood. A sentence which is merely mentioned, not used, may nevertheless be complete. Restricting "neustic" to the meaning "sign of subscription or assertion," as Hare now seems to do, you could therefore say that two sentences both have a clistic but one lacks a neustic. Again, you might also say that an utterance possessed a tropic but lacked a clistic: for example, "Take all these boxes to . . ." is in the imperative mood, but it is incomplete. Neustics, tropics, and clistics are therefore logically distinct from one another and severally from phrastics; and the logical properties of a sentence are not all contained in the latter.

It lies beyond the scope of this book to discuss any further the intricacies of these sentential particles. How they are in fact constituted by the rules and conventions of our language; whether there are other such particles besides those named here; whether or not neustics, like tropics and clistics, con- tribute to the logical properties of sentences or not; and so on—these are all matters now exciting the interest of logi- cians. But the most important question for anyone attempting an evaluation of Hare's prescriptivism, seems to me to be whether or not, in any of this, Hare is going back—or ought to be—on his contention that mixed, or practical, syllogisms are possible. I think the answer is that he is not and ought not.

In the example:

> Take all the boxes to the station
> This is a box
> *Therefore* Take this to the station

the imperative conclusion follows from the conjunction of the two premises because (a) the minor premise shows the reference of "this" and (b) "this" having that reference, the conclusion is implicit in the major premise. To deny this

would be to fail to understand the meaning of the word
"all." The defects of the earlier analysis in terms of neustics
and phrastics alone do not impugn the two rules which Hare
gave in *The Language of Morals* as governing the practical
syllogism or the general logical considerations upon which
he based them.[143]

Hare's Rules

This is not to say that there are no other objections to
Hare's rules.

The two rules to which reference has just been made are as
follows:

    (i)   No indicative conclusion can be validly drawn from a
            set of premises which cannot be validly drawn from
            the indicatives among them alone.
    (ii) No imperative conclusion can be validly drawn from
            a set of premises which does not contain at least one
            imperative.

In enunciating these rules, Hare was contributing to a discussion which has gone on for some time among logicians and
still continues. Can there be "mixed syllogisms," i.e., syllogisms in which a conclusion in either the indicative or imperative mood is drawn from premises which are either respectively in the indicative and imperative moods, or both
in that one of these two moods in which their conclusion is
not. The logical issues arising in connection with Hare's two
rules are complicated and technical and it lies beyond the
scope of this book to deal with them in any great detail. A
useful introduction to the whole subject of imperative inference, together with a valuable bibliography of the relevant
literature, is provided in Professor N. Rescher's monograph
The Logic of Commands.

As for the *first* of Hare's two rules, plausible counter-
examples have been adduced against it and I do not think
that Hare would wish any longer to defend it as it stands.
Consider these examples, which I borrow from Rescher.

[143] *LM*, p. 28.

From:
> John, drive your car home (imperative)

we can validly infer:
> John owns a car (indicative).

And from:
> Never do anything illegal (imperative)

together with:
> Do A (imperative)

we can validly infer:
> Doing A is legal (indicative)

Such instances seem to dispose of Hare's first rule. True, it can be argued plausibly that the indicative conclusion is, in some cases, concealed within an imperative premise. For instance:

> John, drive your car home

could plausibly be analyzed thus:
> John, you have a car (indicative)
> Drive it home (imperative).

But it is not possible to claim that "Do A", in the second of the above examples, is correctly analyzed thus:

> Doing A is legal (indicative)
> Do A (imperative).

Hare's *second* rule is the logical mainstay of his moral philosophy. He is careful to say that he is not the first to have formulated it. Henri Poincaré proposed it in "La morale et la science," *Dernières Pensées* (Paris, 1913), as did Professor K. R. Popper in "What Can Logic Do for Philosophy?," *Proceedings of the Aristotelian Society,* supplementary volume XXII (1948). I think that this second rule holds good. There are a number of logical problems which arise in connection with it, but they are problems of precise definition and correct formulation rather than doubts about the "viability" of the rule itself.

One such problem concerns hypothetical imperatives. Consider an example which Hare gives:

If you want to go to the largest grocer in Oxford, go to Grimbly Hughes.

Prima facie this seems to follow from and amount to nothing more than:

Grimbly Hughes is the largest grocer in Oxford.

However, we cannot say that it is really an indicative because, as Hare points out, someone who had learned the meaning of indicative verb-forms, but not imperative verb-forms, would not understand it. Hare thinks that there is an imperative neustic concealed in the word "want" and suggests this analysis:

Going by you to the largest grocer in Oxford, please
Grimbly Hughes being the largest grocer in Oxford, yes

Going by you to Grimbly Hughes, please.

Such an analysis would bring this hypothetical imperative under his second rule. However, Hare does not claim that he has settled the matter. That his analysis of the hypothetical imperative is correct remains to be proved.

Another problem which arises in connection with Hare's second rule concerns how validity, in the case of a mixed syllogism, should be characterized. We might say perhaps that a necessary condition of valid inference in such cases is as follows. An imperative conclusion is valid, only if this imperative must (logically) be obeyed, when the imperative premise(s) is (are) obeyed and the indicative premise(s) is (are) true. But this condition, though necessary, would not be sufficient. The following syllogism fulfills the condition just referred to, but its conclusion is *not* valid.

John, do A whenever you do B
John does in fact do C whenever B

John, do A and C whenever B

The question of what would constitute a sufficient condition remains to be answered.[144]

Value-Words and Speech-Acts

Hare wishes to explain the meanings of value words like "good," in terms of the speech-act—commending, prescribing, or whatever you call it—which these words are normally used to perform. Some critics have maintained that this cannot be done. They make two points among others: (i) if it tells us the literal meaning of "good," for example, to say that it is used to perform the speech-act of commendation, then wherever "good" has literal meaning it will be used to commend; *but* (ii) there are numerous examples of "good" being used with its literal meaning, though it is not being used to commend. Examples of such latter uses are:

X is not good (negation)
Is X good? (interrogation)
If X is good, then Y (hypothesis).

It seems to follow from these considerations that Hare's explanation of the meaning of words like "good" must be mistaken.

Hare may be right in thinking that to call something good is to commend it; but an analysis of calling something good is not the same as an analysis of "good." This is how the argument against Hare goes. Any analysis of "good" must allow for the fact that the word is used in different speech-acts, such as those listed above. And "good" must mean the same in all of these, otherwise there will be the absurd consequences that "X is good" may not be denied by "X is not good"; may not be an answer to the question "Is X good?"; may not validate, along with the further premise "If X is good, then Y," the conclusion, "Y." "Good" must mean the same, in each of the three examples listed above, as it means in "X is good," if the latter answers the interrogation, contra-

[144] See *LM*, pp. 33–38, and N. Rescher, *The Logic of Commands* (London, 1966), Chaps. 7 and 8, in particular pp. 99–100.

dicts the negation, and together with the hypothesis, entails the conclusion "Y." But in none of the former three sentences (interrogation, negation, hypothesis) is "good" being used to commend, as it is in the categorical statement "X is good."[145] It seems to follow from considerations such as these that Hare's explanation of the meaning of words like "good" must be mistaken. Can that explanation be defended? Again with due acknowledgment to hitherto unpublished work which he has kindly shown me, but without any claim whatever adequately to be representing his opinions, I venture to think that Hare's position might be defended along some such lines as the following. Words like "good" must, of course, be considered as they come incorporated in appropriate sentences, uttered on appropriate occasions, before they can be understood; but, so considered, they give the utterances in which they occur a certain illocutionary force. In the case of "good," this may be called commendatory, interpreting the word in a wide sense. That this illocutionary force is retained even in interrogatives, negatives, and hypotheticals can perhaps be shown by an analysis of these various sentence-forms in the light of neustics and tropics, as Hare now uses those terms.

The *interrogative* sentence-form can be explained as an invitation, or an order, to make one of a number of assertions: to add a neustic (a sign of subscription or assertion) to, for instance, either "X is good" or "X is not good." If we added the assertion sign to the former we should be using "good" to commend. What if we added it to the latter?

Anyone who utters the *negation* "X is not good" would be performing a commendatory speech-act whose content is the negation of the content of the commendation "X is good." In doing so, he would have to rely upon the rules for the use of "not" in conjunction with the logical fact that "good" is used to commend.

The *hypothetical*, "If X is good, then Y" is more difficult. Here "X is good" is clearly not being used to commend. But

[145] Cf. J. R. Searle, "Meaning and Speech-Acts," *PR* LXXI (1962).

why? Simply because it is not asserted. What is asserted is not "X is good" but the whole sentence in which this occurs as part of one clause. However, the presence or absence of a neustic does not alter what Hare now calls the tropic of a sentence. He uses this word for the sign which, in accordance with the rules and conventions of our language, indicates not simply grammatical mood but to which sort of speech-act a sentence must be assigned. Its tropic shows its illocutionary force. When a categorical sentence such as "X is good" becomes part of a clause in a hypothetical sentence, there is no reason to say that it must have changed its tropic. But it does now lack a neustic. So "X is good" in "If X is good, then Y" may not be said to commend because it lacks a neustic. However, it may still be said to have commendatory force, for it retains the tropic which it has as a categorical sentence. To whatever extent this tropic is an element in the meaning of "good" in the one case, it is equally so in the other.

Kinds and Levels of Meaning

Dr. G. C. Kerner in *The Revolution in Ethical Theory* brings two criticisms, among others, to bear on Hare's moral philosophy: (i) that Hare was mistaken in the view that moral judgments may have two kinds of meaning, descriptive and evaluative; and (ii) that he failed to recognize the *total* difference in meaning between imperatives and ought judgments. Kerner thinks that if only Hare had made better use of his own distinction between phrastics and neustics in *The Language of Morals,* he might have avoided both these errors. Any speech-act, Kerner argues, has, so to say, two "levels" of meaning: (i) certain criteria of application (the phrastic element: what has traditionally been known as sense and reference); and (ii) a performative, or illocutionary, force (the neustic element). To apply words is simply to correlate them with something in the world, says Kerner. The rules or conventions of sense and reference effect this. They are logically prior to the rules or conventions which constitute illocutionary force, i.e., in the phraseology of *The Language*

of Morals the neustics of description, interrogation, impera-
tion, or whatever.[146] A speech-act involves reliance upon
both sorts of rule or convention. That is, I have not said
anything, if I have merely applied words to things in the
world. I have not described, commanded, questioned, recommended, etc. But neither have I said anything unless I have
said something specific.[147] I have not described, etc., unless
I have singled some thing(s) out for description, etc. Against
this background, Kerner criticizes Hare on the two counts
noted above. I will try to make clear what Kerner's criticisms
are and then to say whether or not they prevail against Hare.
First, I will outline more fully the two criticisms, noted above,
in reverse order.

(i) Kerner charges Hare with failing to recognize the
"total difference" in meaning between imperatives and ought
judgments.[148] Hare said that ought judgments entail imperatives; this implies that there is some similarity of meaning
between them. Of course, Hare recognized that there are also
differences, two in particular: (a) imperatives cannot occur
in the past tense and are predominantly in the second person,
whereas ought judgments come naturally in any tense or
person; (b) ought judgments are universalizable. It is, as I
have already suggested, arguable that a reasonable man will
have reasons for the commands which he utters no less than
for his moral judgments; but even if that is so, these reasons
need not be in the former case, as according to Hare they
need to be in the latter, U-type.[149] If I said "Form fours"
and, when asked "Why?" replied "Because I say so," this
would not offend against, so to say, the rules of the commanding game. But if, when asked why I had said that capital punishment ought to be abolished, I replied "Because I
say so," that, to someone of Hare's persuasion at least,
would seem bizarre.

[146] G. C. Kerner, *The Revolution in Ethical Theory* (Oxford, 1966),
pp. 148–49, 167.
[147] *Ibid.*, pp. 154, 158.
[148] *Ibid.*, p. 163.
[149] See above, p. 185.

To eliminate these differences, Hare in *The Language of Morals* suggests modifying and "enriching" the imperative mood in such a way that it is universalizable and can occur in any tense or person.[150] Analysis in terms of phrastics and neustics will, he thinks, effect this. The phrastic of an indicative sentence can be universal and in any tense or person; and it is possible to take the phrastic of any such indicative and make it into an imperative sentence simply by adding the imperative neustic. Thus, says Hare, we may take the indicative sentence "All mules are barren" and write it thus:

All mules being barren, yes.

The proper universal imperative sentence will then be written:

All mules being barren, please.

This differs in meaning from the imperative of ordinary language "Let all mules be barren" in that the latter can refer only to future mules, whereas the former is a fiat directed to all mules, past and present as well as future. Thus, if a mule in 23 B.C. produced offspring, this would not be a breach of the command "Let all mules be barren" said in 1970 A.D., but it would be a breach of a proper universal command uttered at any time.[151] In this enriched or modified imperative mood we can frame imperatives which are equivalent in meaning to ought judgments. "Instead, therefore, of the cumbrous terminology of phrastics and neustics, let us adopt the artificial word 'ought,'" says Hare. "This is to be defined as follows: if we take a proper universal indicative sentence 'All P's are Q' and split it into phrastic and neustic, 'All P's being Q, yes,' and then substitute for the indicative neustic an imperative one 'All P's being Q, please,' we may, instead of the latter sentence, write 'All P's *"ought"* to be Q.'"[152] The *"ought"* here is italicized and put in quotation marks to point the fact that Hare is not saying that this is how "ought" is used in ordinary language, but is simply seeing what modifications need to be made to imperatives before they can do the jobs ordinarily done by "ought."[153]

[150] *LM*, pp. 187–88.
[151] *LM*, pp. 189–90.
[152] *LM*, pp. 190–91.
[153] *LM*, p. 180.

Kerner's objection to all this is that whereas general ought judgments can be satisfactorily translated into Hare's modified and enriched imperative mood, *singular* ones cannot. The judgment (1) "One ought always to speak the truth" is equivalent to (2) "All things that are being said being true, please." But (1a) "You ought to tell him the truth" is not equivalent to (2a) "The thing you are about to tell him being true, please." According to Kerner, (2) is universalizable in the way that (1) is: both refer to all things that are being said. The singular (1a), being an ought judgment, is conceivably universalizable. But (2a), with which it is said to be equivalent, is in fact logically indistinguishable from a singular imperative "Tell him the truth." Therefore (2a) is not equivalent to (1a). Kerner says that, in order to make it equivalent, Hare had to rewrite it thus: (2b) "If you do not tell him the truth, you will be breaking the principle 'All things that are said being true, please' and I hereby subscribe to that principle."[154] He points out that (2b) is "not by any stretch of imagination an imperative of any kind or even like one, artificial or not." It is in the indicative mood. And so, he concludes, Hare's attempt to make out the logical similarity between ought judgments and imperatives, which is necessary if the former are to entail the latter, fails. The neustics of ought judgments, he maintains, must be quite different from those of imperatives. If this criticism can be sustained it appears to call in question Hare's basic belief that ought judgments are essentially prescriptive.

I do not feel convinced that it can be sustained. It strikes me as misconceived in at least two respects.

(i) If (2a) is no more than a singular imperative, then surely (2) is no more than a universal one, equivalent to "No lying." In that case the distinction which Kerner wishes to draw between (2) and (2a) in respect of universalizability does not hold. For universal imperatives are not universalizable any more than singular ones in the way that ought judgments are. The request for a U-type reason for them can be refused.

154 Kerner, *op. cit.*, p. 164; cf. *LM*, p. 191. My numbering of the sentences here is different from Kerner's.

(ii) (2b) is Kerner's version of the following (2c) in Hare: "If you do not tell him the truth, you will be breaking a general *'ought'*-principle to which I hereby subscribe."[155] Kerner, it will be remembered, renders the general "ought" principle thus: "All things that are said being true, please," and no doubt he is entitled to do so in the light of Hare's remark that for "All P's being Q, please" we may write "All P's *'ought'* to be Q."[156] But has Kerner really taken Hare's point here? Was Hare substituting for (2a) something which was really not by any stretch of imagination an imperative as Kerner says? Hare goes on immediately after (2c) above to give a more formal version of his point. "More formally," he says, "we might write 'There is at least one value for P and one for Q such that (1) all P's *ought* to be Q and (2) your not telling him the truth would be (or was) a case of a P not being Q.' "[157] His intention seems to be to show that "You ought to tell him the truth" can be represented as the conclusion of a practical syllogism of which the major premise is "All that is said ought to be true," and the minor premise is "What you are telling him is something that is said." This analysis stands in contrast to that suggested by Kerner's contention that Hare had to substitute (2b) for (2a) above. If "You ought to tell him the truth" is analyzed in terms of (2c), i.e., of Hare's own analysis, then "You ought to tell him the truth" does not *state* that if you do not, you will be breaking a principle; nor does it *state* that the speaker subscribes to this principle. It invokes or applies a principle as the standard of judgment. In so far, then, as Kerner's criticism of Hare is to the effect that, in order to make (2a) equivalent in meaning to (1a), Hare had to rewrite (2a) as (2b), and (2b) is not, by any stretch of imagination, in the imperative mood, but is a straightforward indicative, that criticism fails. For it rests on a misinterpretation of Hare. Hare rewrites (2a) as (2c), *not* as (2b); and *furthermore* he gives a "more formal" rendering of (2c) which makes it quite clear that,

[155] *LM*, p. 191.
[156] Kerner, *op. cit.*, p. 164; *LM*, p. 191.
[157] *LM*, p. 191.

to his way of thinking, the latter is *not* simply a statement in the indicative mood.

I suspect that Hare would say that there is a more radical defect in Kerner's criticism. For Kerner takes it that, in modifying and "enriching" the imperative mood, Hare was attempting to show that ought judgments are equivalent in meaning to imperatives. But Hare has always insisted that they are *not* equivalent in meaning. His point has always been that ought judgments *entail* imperatives, *not* that they can be equated with them. I think he would say that his attempt to modify and enrich the imperative mood was intended simply to make it possible for entailments in any person or tense to be stated. So that, for instance, "He ought to have told the truth" can be said to entail a statable imperative in the third person singular and the past tense. However, it must be admitted that some of Hare's remarks in Chapter 12 of *The Language of Morals,* where he proposes this modified and enriched imperative mood, do read as if he is attempting to equate statements in that mood with ought judgments. For instance, in the first sentence of the chapter, he writes: ". . . let us imagine that our language does not contain any value-words; and let us then ask, to what extent a new artificial terminology, defined in terms of the imperative mood and of the ordinary logical words, could fill the gap which this would leave."[158] But, even if such remarks can be said to entitle Kerner to take Hare to be equating the meanings of ought judgments with imperatives, his criticisms of Hare are open to the objections which I have set out above.

(ii) Kerner's more radical criticism of Hare was that in conceiving of moral judgments as having two kinds of meaning, evaluative and descriptive, Hare misconceived both of these kinds of meaning. According to Kerner, Hare thought that, whereas the evaluative meaning of value words, like "good," is logically distinct from the appropriate criteria of application, the descriptive meaning of words like "red" is identical with their criteria of application. But Kerner argues in the first place that there is more to descriptive meaning

[158] *LM,* p. 180.

than sense and reference; descriptions, as such, have an illocutionary force which distinguishes them from other sorts of speech-act. And, in the second place, there is more to evaluative meaning than commendation (or whatever term you choose to use for it). The commendation must be given application; something specific must be commended, otherwise nothing is being said. In Hare's terms, as used by Kerner, descriptions would be meaningless without their neustics; as would evaluations without their phrastics.[159]

Kerner suggests that Hare confused two *levels* of meaning (neustic and phrastic) with two *kinds* of meaning (evaluative and descriptive) because he concentrated on single terms, such as "good" or "ought," instead of full sentences. There may be one-word sentences of course, but it is the sentence which constitutes a unit of communication and "has meaning in the primary sense,"[160] the meaning of single words being an abstraction from this. Some words or expressions (e.g., "I promise," "I command," "Do," "I will"), considered in isolation, have no criteria of application. But we do not say that they lend a special kind of meaning to the discourse or speech-acts in which they figure. We look on them as being like Hare's neustics. Kerner thinks that moral terms, like "good" and "ought," are very similar. They do not lend moral judgments a separate kind of meaning, only a peculiar illocutionary force. So, Kerner thinks, Hare's analysis of moral judgments is unnecessarily complicated. Hare analyzed words like "good" into two kinds of meaning; and meaningful sentences into two elements, phrastics and neustics. He was therefore operating with four factors, whereas, according to Kerner, he could have got on very well with two: phrastics (sense and reference) and neustics (illocutionary force). And if he had restricted himself to these two, he would have avoided the absurd position in which, says Kerner, he lands himself, of maintaining that it is possible "to perform two full speech-acts at once, to say two complete and separable things in the same breath."[161] Kerner concedes that it would

---

[159] Kerner, *op. cit.*, pp. 150 ff.
[160] *Ibid.*, pp. 158–59.
[161] *Ibid.*, p. 147.

make sense to say that someone had described and persuaded in the same breath, as the emotivists were wont to say. But if one asks of a speech-act "Is this a description or a prescription?" "the proper answer seems never to be 'I am doing both.'" Yet "in Hare's theory this would have to be the only proper answer."[162]

Kerner notes that Hare regards the criteria of application for words like "good" as identical with their descriptive meaning. This raises two questions: (a) what is the relation between the descriptive and evaluative meanings of these words? and (b) what constitutes a reason for a value judgment? Kerner thinks Hare's belief in two kinds of meaning: (a) renders the former problem insoluble; and (b) necessarily reduces reasons for evaluation to mere indications of contingent fact, namely of how the relevant evaluative terms are used by individuals or communities.

In defense of Hare's position against these criticisms, I think that at least three points can be made.

(i) It is no part of Hare's position that a *single* speech-act may be both descriptive and evaluative (or prescriptive), at least not in the way Kerner takes Hare to have thought that it could. Hare seems to me to be clear that there are two quite distinct things which you might be doing in saying "X is a good person." You might be *describing* X: that is, informing someone who knows what criteria of goodness you are invoking that X has certain qualities corresponding to these. In this respect, you could, for example, intentionally inform the members of a Conservative Association that X was not a thief in saying that he was a good man, even though you yourself did not consider respect for the institution of private property a criterion of goodness. On the other hand, in saying that X is a good man, you could be *evaluating* X; that is, grading him by criteria to which you yourself do subscribe. In this respect, in saying that X was good because honest, you would imply your own approval of honesty. But these two sorts of remark are not one speech-act. The circumstances and the intention of the speaker determine, on any given occasion, *which* of them

[162] *Ibid.*, p. 148.

is taking place. Hare never said that they can both occur at once.

(ii) It is characteristic of value words like "good" that they can be used to revise their own criteria of application. Someone who hitherto has thought, for example, that a good man, as such, is one who never appropriates other people's property, may come to ask himself whether there may not be circumstances in which a good man, as such, might undertake what is called stealing. Now, could this logical characteristic of "good" and other value words be covered simply by saying that sentences containing such words have neustics of commendation? Surely, *within* the class of speech-acts with neustics of commendation there must be two subclasses: one in which value words are used in accordance with generally accepted criteria, and the other in which they are used to question these criteria. Hare's *way* of differentiating them, as having descriptive and evaluative meaning respectively, may of course be open to question; but that there is a difference which needs to be accounted for seems indisputable. It is not clear that Kerner recognizes the necessity for this difference or how he would account for it.

(iii) Kerner finds in Hare what he considers the absurd view that "we can give no reasons for our evaluations" and he thinks this due to Hare's mistaken theory about two kinds of meaning.[163] Whatever its source, Hare's view of evaluative reasoning does seem to resolve itself, in the last analysis, into consistency and nothing more. I form a value judgment. I can be asked a reason for it. Having given my reason, I am required, in order to qualify as a reasonable moralist, only to adhere to it consistently. Kerner, like others, finds this unsatisfactory because fanatics can be consistent. As I have already said,[164] it seems to me perfectly conceivable that there should be a form of discourse, quite properly called reasonable, in which being reasonable would amount to no more than being consistent. And it is conceivable that this is what moral discourse amounts to. As Hare has shown in his discussion of universalizability, if it is this and no more, many

[163] *Ibid.,* p. 159.
[164] Above, p. 208.

of the moves which we recognize as natural moves in moral argument are explained. However, the question can be asked: is there any logical limitation on what may be offered as a reason for a moral judgment? This is the question which, in one form or another, has cropped up repeatedly in our consideration of emotivism and prescriptivism. In the final section of the next chapter I will attempt to answer it.

CHAPTER 6. THE DERIVATION OF "OUGHT" FROM "IS"

The three types of ethical theory which we have so far considered had at least one thing in common. They all maintained that there is a logical gap between statements of natural, or supernatural, fact, on the one hand, and judgments of moral value on the other. This divide is commonly called "the is-ought gap", where "is" stands for any statement of fact and "ought" for any moral judgment. The ground, which all three types of theory took for their view that this gap exists, was the "open question argument", as it is often called. Whatever factual description is offered of an action or state of affairs, they argued, it is always logically open to us to ask whether that act is right or wrong, that state of affairs good or evil.

The intuitionists, we saw in Chapter 3, thought of this is-ought gap in terms of *properties*. There are "natural" properties, which can be described in statements of fact such as "It produces happiness", etc., and "nonnatural" ones, which are described in moral judgments such as "It is right", etc. The two kinds of properties are logically distinct from one another; what is said in terms of the one can never be translated, without loss or change of meaning, into terms of the other.

The emotivists and prescriptivists, by contrast, thought of the is-ought gap as a matter of the different kinds of *use* to which language may be put. Factual statements describe; but moral judgments evaluate. The two jobs, so to speak, are different and logical confusion arises if the lines of demarcation between them are not observed. The emotivists and prescriptivists, as we saw in Chapters 4 and 5, had rather different ideas from each other about what is involved in the job of evaluation, which moral judgments perform. The emotivists took it to be simply a matter of expressing attitudes of approval or disapproval; but the prescriptivists thought it more than that. To their way of thinking, moral judgments do not only express pro- or con-attitudes but also guide choices and actions; they do this by entailing imperatives and by being consistently applied.

Besides the difference between an interpretation of the is-ought gap in terms of properties and one in terms of the varying jobs words can do, there was a further difference between intuitionists, on the one hand, and emotivists and prescriptivists, on the other. The intuitionists saw the is-ought gap simply as a difference in *meaning*. No conceivable factual statement means exactly the same as any conceivable moral judgment. This view did not prevent the intuitionists from thinking that there is a logical connection between certain factual statements and certain moral judgments. If Smith, in fact, promises to do act *A*, it follows that Smith is under a moral obligation to do *A*. This necessary connection is perceived by ethical intuition, which is one exercise of reason. Moral judgments are, therefore, *consequential* upon factual statements; and to think *morally* is to intuit this connection. The emotivists and prescriptivists, by contrast, did not only hold that "is" and "ought" differ from one another in meaning, but also that the latter *cannot be deduced* from the former. They recognized, of course, that it is normal to offer factual statements as reasons for moral judgments; but they held that, when this is done, it is not a case of discerning moral necessities, which belong to the nature of things, but of invoking moral standards, which the speaker, or the members of his society, have set up. The emotivists and prescriptivists did not consider moral judgments to be consequential upon factual statements in the same way that the intuitionists did.

I have recapitulated these matters in order to set the scene for a new group of modern moral philosophers, whom we must now consider. They are sometimes called collectively the descriptivists. That name is not altogether inappropriate, because they all take the view, in one way or another, that moral evaluations are logically grounded in factual descriptions; but the differences between them are so considerable that it would be misleading to give the impression that they form a single school of thought. To avoid giving that impression, I shall divide them into groups. But, even so, one thing which could be said, without hesitation, to characterize *all* these groups equally is a strong aversion to prescriptivism; and in the remaining chapters of this book, I will show how, in their different ways, they have reacted against it.

In the present chapter, I will begin by referring to a famous passage from Hume's *Treatise*, which has often been said to be a classic exposure of the unbridgeable gap between "is" and "ought". Some philosophers now contend that it is nothing of the kind. So far from intending to show that this gap is unbridgeable, they argue, Hume was in fact trying to indicate how it can, and should, be bridged. It will be instructive, as an introduction to descriptivism, to compare the grounds on which some philosophers argue to this effect with those on which others defend the more traditional interpretation of Hume's famous passage.

In the second part of the present chapter, I shall discuss two attempts, that have been made by contemporary moral philosophers, formally to deduce "ought" from "is". The several stages of the derivation will be set out, in each case, and the validity of the deductions assessed.

In the next chapter we shall consider some rather less formal attempts to show that moral evaluations are logically grounded in descriptive statements. The question, which all the philosophers to whom I shall there refer attempt to answer, is: what counts as a reason for a moral judgment? It is natural to give reasons for such judgments, but what kind of reason is it appropriate to give? Three sorts of answer, which have been offered to that question, will be considered. Firstly, the view that appropriate reasons for moral judgments are logically grounded in human wants of one kind or another; secondly, that they are grounded in some conception of man's true end or function; and thirdly, that they invoke the moral traditions of the society within which the judgments are voiced. Each of these views has found eloquent and persuasive exponents in recent years.

I will try to show what is involved in each, how it constitutes an attack on prescriptivism, and what there is to be said for, and against, it.

In the final chapter, I will introduce a point of view that I venture to call neo-intuitionism. It is, in important respects, very different from the intuitionism we were dealing with in Chapter 3, but there are some similarities. In particular, both the earlier intuitionism and this later neo-intuitionism proceed on the assumption that there are certain kinds of conduct which we just apprehend to be right, or wrong, irrespective of their consequences. From the description of an act as the judicial execution of an innocent man, for instance, it follows that the act is wrong, however expedient or advantageous his death might be from some points of view. This version of descriptivism obviously brings those who hold it into conflict with utilitarianism and we will consider precisely how it does so.

In the latter part of the final chapter we shall consider the recent attempts of R. M. Hare to develop a "two-level" theory of moral thinking, in which what he takes to be the elements of truth in neo-intuitionism can be reconciled with his own prescriptivist utilitarianism.

I have called all the anti-prescriptivist views, to which I have been referring, versions of descriptivism. This may seem a little odd in the case of the neo-intuitionists and the philosophers who think that moral judgments must be grounded in traditional concepts of virtue or vice. In both these cases, the reasons it is appropriate to invoke for a moral judgment are thought to consist, in the last analysis, of moral evaluations—either those furnished by one's own conscience or those generally accepted within one's society. And this is obviously a different idea of their grounding from the idea that moral obligation is grounded in such purely, or putatively, natural facts as that there are certain wants which all men have, or a certain end for which we all exist. But I have called all the anti-prescriptivist views versions of descriptivism because they all take moral judgments to be logically grounded in certain descriptions of fact, or supposed fact—such as, for example, "He said 'I promise' ", "All men want to be free from physical injury", "This will enable us to attain our true end, or fulfil our proper function as human beings", "This would be a courageous thing to do." From all these points of view, not just anything can be spoken of as right or wrong, good or evil, in the moral sense; but only that which can be described in a certain way.

I. HUME ON "IS" AND "OUGHT"

Hume's famous is-ought passage, to which I referred just now, is as follows:

> I cannot forbear adding to these reasonings an observation which may, perhaps, be found of some importance. In every system of morality, which I have hitherto met with, I have always remarked that the author proceeds for some time in the ordinary way of reasoning, and establishes the being of a God, or makes observations concerning human affairs; when of a sudden I am surprised to find that, instead of the usual copulations of propositions *is* and *is not*, I meet with no proposition that is not connected with an *ought* or an *ought not*. This change is imperceptible; but is, however, of the last consequence. For as this *ought* or *ought not* expresses some new relation or affirmation, it is necessary that it should be observed and explained; and at the same time that a reason should be given for what seems altogether inconceivable, how this new relation can be a deduction from others, which are entirely different from it. But as authors do not commonly use this precaution I shall presume to recommend it to the readers; and am persuaded, that this small attention would subvert all the vulgar systems of morality, and let us see that the distinction of vice and virtue is not founded merely on the relations of objects, nor is perceived by reason. (*Treatise* III.i.1)

Those who think that Hume is here intent on exposing an unbridgeable logical gap between "is" and "ought" interpret these words in the following way. Hume speaks of

a "deduction" and says that it "seems altogether inconceivable" how it can be made. They take his word "deduction" to mean logical entailment and his phrase "seems
altogether inconceivable" to be a typically ironical under-
statement for "*is* altogether inconceivable." So they assume
his point to be that, from the premises (i) "ought" cannot
be entailed by "is" and (ii) arguments are either deductive
or defective, the conclusion follows that there is an impas-
sable logical gulf between moral judgments and statements
of natural, or supernatural, fact. This logical gulf, they say,
is that to which Moore was referring when he spoke of the
indefinability of "good," that which Stevenson had in mind
when he differentiated beliefs from attitudes, and that which
Hare claimed to be exposing when he contended that no
description can be used to prescribe. They assume Hume to
have been contending that some additional premise—viz. a
moral principle such as "Whatever is in the common interest
ought to be done"—is needed to bridge the gap between a
statement of fact such as "X is in the common interest"
and a judgment of moral value such as "X ought to be done."

Those who now reject this "accepted" interpretation, as
I shall call it, maintain the very opposite. Hume, they say,
was arguing that there *is* a logical connection between
"ought" and "is" and claiming that, whereas other moral
philosophers had failed to explain it correctly, he was able
to do so. For convenience, I will call this "a new interpretation" of Hume's famous passage. While there is agreement
among those who offer a new interpretation that Hume
believed himself able to resolve the is-ought problem, there
is some divergence of opinion among them as to precisely
how he thought himself able to do so.

In passing, the possibility should at least be recognized
that the differences of opinion between exponents of the
accepted interpretation and of a new interpretation respectively, and between those who offer one new interpretation
and those who offer another, may be due to inconsistencies
within Hume's moral philosophy itself. These conflicting
interpretations may simply have fastened onto different
elements in that philosophy which cannot in fact be reconciled. In support of this possibility, it could be said that

anyone who, so to speak, reads Hume through modern analytical spectacles will detect seeming ambiguities in those passages which are usually referred to in an attempt to settle this controversy and to which we shall turn below. It can hardly be denied that a good deal has to be conceded, to the effect that we cannot expect in Hume the clear distinction between psychological and logical considerations which we should look for in a modern philosopher, if Hume is to be saved from all charge of ambiguity. However, when dealing with a philosopher of Hume's stature, there is always a presumption that we have failed to understand him rather than that he is confused. So, to begin with, we must assume that he had a self-consistent point to make about the connection between "is" and "ought" and ask whether the accepted interpretation or one of the new interpretations most faithfully represents this. We have seen what exponents of the accepted interpretation took his point to be. Now we turn to the question: how, according to his new interpreters, did Hume get from "is" to "ought"? (The papers which I shall refer to by MacIntyre, Atkinson, Hunter, Flew and myself are all reprinted in my *The Is-Ought Question*, London, 1969; and my page references will be to that collection.)

New Interpretation No. 1

I will call the first of the two new interpretations to which I shall refer N.I.(1). It is to be found, for instance, in G. Hunter's paper, "Hume on *Is* and *Ought*" (first published in *P* XXXVIII, 1963). Hunter does not reject the assumptions of the accepted interpretation that Hume (i) thought that "ought" (at least as used in those systems of morality which he was attacking) cannot be entailed by "is"; and (ii) believed that arguments are either deductive or defective. He simply claims that Hume eliminated the is-ought gap altogether by *identifying* ought-propositions with certain is-propositions. If this interpretation is correct, Hume's point was that it only "seems altogether inconceivable" how moral judgments can be deduced from statements of fact when you assume that such a move *needs* to be made. In fact it does *not*. For moral judgments *are* statements of

fact. Such passages from Hume as the following are quoted
in support of N.I.(1).

   (i) From the paragraph immediately preceding the
       is-ought passage:

       . . . when you pronounce any action or character to
       be vicious, *you mean nothing, but* that from the
       constitution of your nature you have a feeling or
       sentiment of blame from the contemplation of it
       (italics mine). (*Treatise* III.i.1)

   (ii) From the section immediately following that which
        the is-ought passage concludes:

        We *do not infer* a character to be virtuous, because
        it pleases: but in feeling that it pleases after such a
        particular manner, we in effect feel that it is virtuous
        (italics mine). (*Treatise* III.i.2)

Such passages have been taken to show that, in Hume's
opinion, there is no need to account for an inference from
"is' to "ought" because what ought-propositions *mean* can
be adequately *defined* in terms of "is". Ought-propositions
simply state that certain objects cause the speaker, or the
spectator, to have certain sorts of feelings. This interpretation makes Hume a subjectivist, i.e. one who takes moral
judgments to *report* the occurrence of certain emotions.

    Against it, some admirers of Hume claim that it is more
appropriate to think of him as an emotivist than a subjectivist. Quite properly, they say that Hume's famous passage
should be set in its eighteenth-century context. Hume, they
then contend, was intent on denying: (i) the belief of the
rational intuitionists that moral judgments, such as "Promises ought to be kept", state necessary truths self-evident to
all reasonable men; and (ii) the conviction of his religious
contemporaries that to call anything wrong is to say that it
is against God's will. In opposition to these systems of
morality, they maintain, Hume was insisting that moral
judgments are ultimately grounded in human sentiment.
But of course the crucial question is: how so grounded?
A. G. N. Flew in his paper "On the Interpretation of Hume"

(first published in *P* XXXVIII, 1963), contends that we "get the emphasis wrong" if we think Hume's answer would have been that moral judgments *report* human sentiments. It is "so much better to say" that his "central insight" was that moral judgments *express* feelings of praise or blame. Hume said, for instance, in an Appendix to his *Enquiry Concerning the Principles of Morals*: "And when we *express* that detestation against him (Nero) . . . it is not that we see any relations of which he was ignorant, but that . . . we *feel* sentiments against which he was hardened . . . " One may take the grounding in feeling to lie in the fact that our judgment expresses our detestation. Flew does not pin his whole case to this one quotation, of course; nor does he claim for a moment that Hume was as clear and explicit in his emotivism as Stevenson or Ayer. He is fully alive to the point already made, that Hume did not differentiate psychological description from logical analysis in the way that a modern philosopher would. But Flew says in effect that, just because of this, we ought not to take Hume too literally when he says that "X is vicious" means "I have a sentiment of blame from the contemplation of X," or that "is virtuous" in "X is virtuous" is to be defined as "causes the speaker, or spectator, to have a feeling of approbation for X." All Flew claims is that Hume is closer to emotivism than to any other modern ethical theory. There seem to me to be much better grounds for Flew's account of what Hume meant than for Hunter's. If Hume thought that ought-judgments are expressions of emotion (not statements to the effect that it has been experienced) then we can see why it seemed to him "inconceivable" that they can be deduced from statements of fact. The point of Flew's argument that Hume was an emotivist, not a subjectivist, is to defend the accepted interpretation.

New Interpretation No. 2

I turn now to a second new interpretation of the is-ought passage, which I shall speak of as N.I.(2). It is to be found in A. C. MacIntyre's "Hume on 'Is' and 'Ought' " (first published in *PR* LXVIII, 1959). We saw that N.I.(1) could allow the assumptions of the accepted interpretation that Hume (i) thought that "ought" (as used in the systems of morality to which he was referring) cannot be entailed by "is", and (ii) believed arguments to be deductive or defective. However, N.I.(2) rejects the second of these assumptions. On what grounds? We will begin with two exegetical points and then go on to wider considerations.

The accepted interpretation, it will be recalled, took Hume's word "deduction" in the is-ought passage to mean logical entailment, and his 'seems altogether inconceivable" to be ironical. The second new interpretation challenges that exegesis on both counts. It takes Hume's "deduction" to mean simply inference. In the eighteenth century the word "deduction" appears to have been used of all discursive, as opposed to intuitive, reasoning. In his other writings Hume himself sometimes speaks of what we call induction as deduction, referring to what we call deduction as "demonstrative argument." This is the ground on which N.I.(2) takes "deduction" to mean simply inference. But that interpretation does not go unchallenged. It is pointed out that Reid, Hume's contemporary, took the latter's "deduction" in the is-ought passage to mean entailment (see R. F. Atkinson, *I–OQ*, p. 55). However, if there is any plausibility in N.I.(2)'s interpretation of "deduction", it means that one main support of the accepted interpretation is that much less secure. It may then be possible that Hume was not discussing entailment, but some other form of inference.

N.I.(2) also rejects the accepted interpretation of Hume's "seems altogether inconceivable." Ironic this expression certainly is, if it means "is altogether inconceivable." But does it mean that? Because Hume is often ironic it does not follow that he is invariably so or that, whenever his words could be so taken, they must be. If there is, as we shall see that N.I.(2) suggests, a possible nonironic interpretation of Hume's remark just quoted, we need not conclude that it is mistaken just because it is nonironic.

Freed, then, from the necessity to read "deduction" as "entailment" and "seems inconceivable" as ironic, N.I.(2) has taken Hume to be saying in the is-ought passage that there is an explanation of the connection between "is" and "ought" which corrects the misconceptions of other moral philosophers on the point. So far from pronouncing the gap between "is" and "ought" to be unbridgeable, Hume was saying that it can be bridged. Put summarily, the way in which N.I.(2) thinks that Hume purported to bridge this gap is: by showing the reasonableness of inferring what ought to be done from a consideration of what is in the common interest. N.I.(2) draws a comparison between this move and induction. The point is not, of course, that this inference is an instance of induction, but simply that it is like induction in a certain respect which I will now indicate. By induction we predict, for example, that the sun will rise tomorrow. But we cannot demonstrate that it will. All we have to go on is the fact that it has risen on every morrow within our experience; and it does not necessarily follow from this fact that it will do so again tomorrow. Therefore the principle of induction—that conformities within our past experience can, under certain conditions, provide a rational basis for predicting their repetition within future experience—admits of no logical demonstration. Is it therefore logically disreputable? Hume, it will be remembered, gave classic expression to the feeling that it is (*Treatise* I.ii.6). But his doubts about induction are rejected by many modern philosophers for the very reason that these doubts take arguments to be defective unless they are deductive. Modern philosophers contend that deduction is one method of argument and induction is another; each is appropriate to its own purpose and subject matter—deduction, to the demonstration of necessary conclusions; induction to the prediction of contingent events (cf. P. F. Strawson, *Introduction to Logical Theory*, London, 1960, pp. 248–63). According to N.I.(2), there is just the same sort of objection to regarding inferences from "is" to "ought" as either deductive or defective. Why should there not be a non-deductive method of argument, as appropriate for settling moral questions as induction is for settling questions about what the empirical facts are, or will be? We are assured that Hume, despite his doubts about induction, saw nothing against the idea of some such nondeductive inference of "ought" from "is." N.I.(2) takes him to be saying, in the is-ought passage, that his moral philosophy indicates the appropriate nondeductive way of passing from the one to the other.

There is obviously an initial implausibility about N.I.(2).

If Hume assumed, in the case of induction, that arguments are either deductive or defective, it seems hardly plausible to suppose that he rejected that assumption when he came to think about arguments from "is" to "ought." MacIntyre, in his presentation of N.I.(2), considers it curious that modern philosophers, whilst thinking Hume wrong to make the assumption referred to with regard to induction, have (in subscribing to the accepted interpretation) so generally thought him right to have made it with regard to the inference from "is" to "ought." But if that is curious, is it not just as curious to suppose that Hume would have made the said assumption when thinking about induction but not when thinking about the gap between "is" and "ought"?

Undisturbed by any such reflections, however, MacIntyre proceeds to put forward his own account of how Hume thought "ought" is to be inferred from "is." In a passage where he is firmly rejecting the view that Hume thought that the inference from "is" to "ought" requires some general moral principle to make it possible, MacIntyre has this to say:

> . . . the notion of "ought" is for Hume only explicable in terms of the notion of a consensus of interest. To say that we ought to do something is to affirm that there is a commonly accepted rule; and the existence of such a rule presupposes a consensus of opinion as to where our common interests lie. An obligation is constituted in part by such a consensus and the concept of "ought" is logically dependent on the concept of a common interest and can only be explained in terms of it. (*I–OQ*, pp. 40–41)

What ground is there for this view that "the notion of 'ought' is for Hume only explicable in terms of the notion of a consensus of interest"? Well, he certainly did say things like the following:

> When therefore men have had experience enough to observe that, whatever may be the consequences of any single act of justice performed by a single person, yet the whole system of actions, concurred in by the whole

society, is infinitely advantageous to the whole, and to every part; it is not long before justice and property take place. (*Treatise* III.ii.2)

But at least three observations are apposite. (i) To say this is perhaps to say that, *because* there are common interests, rules of justice and property get made and observed. But it is not necessarily to say that the "ought' in such rules amounts to nothing more than the fact that their general observance is in the common interest. (ii) MacIntyre may have been taking this point when he said: "The existence of such a rule *presupposes* a consensus of opinion as to where our common interests lie" (italics mine). But is even this interpretation of Hume's point in the passage just quoted, indisputable? When he speaks of justice "taking place" does he mean that as a matter of logical *fact* its rules cannot *exist* unless it is observed that they will be in the common interest, or simply that as a matter of *psychological* fact they will not be *accepted* until that observation has been made? The answer may indeed be hard to determine but it does affect the sense in which the notion of a common interest *explains* the notion of "ought." (iii) MacIntyre was evidently taking Hume to be making the logical, rather than the psychological, point, for he went on: "An obligation is constituted in part by such a consensus and the concept of 'ought' is *logically dependent* on the concept of a common interest and can only be explained in terms of it" (italics mine). But this simply raises, and does not answer, the question: in what part?

Against MacIntyre's view that Hume did not think a moral principle necessary to get from "is" to "ought", some defenders of the accepted interpretation (e.g. Atkinson, *I–OQ*, p. 57) have invoked Hume's criticism of Wollaston. Wollaston believed that all immorality is, in the last analysis, lying—i.e. the denial of what is. For instance, that the wrongness of an ungrateful act to one's benefactor lies in the fact that such an act denies the truth that he is one's benefactor. On this, Hume trenchantly commented that, in Wollaston's "whimsical system" the immorality of denying what is the case is simply presupposed (*Treatise* III.i.1n).

What this seems to mean is that you cannot get from "X is a lie" to "X is wrong" without the premise "All lies are wrong."

But does it follow that Hume would similarly have said that you cannot get from "X is in the common interest" to "X ought to be done" apart from the premise "Whatever is in the common interest ought to be done"? I think not. In the criticism of Wollaston, Hume's point was not simply that a major premise is presupposed, but that the question of its justification remains. He wrote: "I shall allow, if you please, that all immorality is derived from this supposed falsehood in action, provided you can give me any plausible reason why such a falsehood is immoral" (*ibid.*). If Hume would have said that this "reason why" has to show that such falsehood is against the common interest, we cannot argue that because, in his opinion, the move from "X is a lie" to "X is wrong" requires the premise "All lies are wrong," then the move from "All lies are against the common interest" to "All lies are wrong" must, in his opinion, require the premise, "Whatever is against the common interest is wrong." His opinion *could* have been that some such notion as that of "interest" *itself* effects the logical transition here from "is" to "ought."

That is precisely the opinion which MacIntyre attributes to him. He contends that, in the is-ought passage, Hume was summing up his view that apart from some such notion as that of interest, need, or want, no justification can be given for moral judgments. When any such judgment has been delivered, Hume, according to MacIntyre, is saying the question, "Why do you say that?" can (logically) be answered by an appeal to human interests, needs, or wants, with a finality which no appeal to a moral principle, perceived by rational intuition or laid down by God, can supply. MacIntyre writes to that effect as follows:

> The transition from "is" to "ought" is made . . . by the notion of "wanting". . . . Aristotle's examples of practical syllogisms typically have a premise which includes some such terms as "suits" or "pleases". We could give a long list of the concepts which can form such bridge notions between "is" and "ought": wanting,

needing, desiring, pleasure, happiness, health—and these are only a few. I think there is a strong case for saying that moral notions are unintelligible apart from concepts such as these . . .

The interpretation of the "is" and "ought" passage which I am offering can now be stated compendiously. Hume is not in this passage asserting the autonomy of morals—for he did not believe in it; and he is not making a point about entailment—for he does not mention it. He is asserting that the question of how the factual basis of morality is related to morality is a crucial logical issue, reflection on which will enable one to realise how there are ways in which this transition can be made and ways in which it cannot. One has to go beyond the passage itself to see what these are; but if one does so it is plain that we can connect the facts of the situation with what we ought to do only by means of one of those concepts which Hume treats under the heading of the passions and which I have indicated by examples such as wanting, needing and the like. (*I–OQ*, pp. 46–48)

Which Interpretation is Correct?

Summing up, there seem to be three possibilities concerning the role which some such proposition as "We ought to do what is in the common interest" plays in the moral philosophy of Hume. They are: (a) that it states a *general moral principle*; (b) that it states a *definition* of "ought"; (c) that it states *a rule of inference* by reference to which we can logically derive "ought" from "is". Exponents of the "accepted interpretation" come down in favour of the first of these. Advocates of N.I.(1) prefer the second. And those of N.I.(2) are for the third possibility. What conclusions must we come to in the light of these varying interpretations concerning Hume's is-ought passage? I think the following.

First, Hume seems to have affinities with both subjectivists and emotivists but cannot be said to belong unambiguously to either school. For reasons given above, it is unsatisfactory to say that he simply regarded ought-propositions as a special kind of is-propositions, but, equally clearly, he did not draw the sharp logical distinction between "is" and "ought" which a modern emotivist would draw.

Secondly, Hume believed that it is the passions, not reason, which invariably move to action. Moral judgments, in so far as they are action-guiding, must be grounded in the passions. He wrote: "Upon the whole, it is impossible that the distinction betwixt moral good and evil can be made by reason; since that distinction has an influence upon our actions, of which reason alone is incapable" (*Treatise* III.i.1). He believed that moral judgments are in fact grounded in men's desire for that which is in their common interest. But it is very difficult to say what he took the nature of this grounding to be. Did he hold that it is only because they are in the common interest that the rules of justice, in fact, induce men to obey them; or that the fact that they are in the common interest logically constitutes the rules of justice? I can find no unequivocal answer to this.

Thirdly, such understanding of Hume's is-ought passage as we can attain will be gained only by setting it firmly in its eighteenth-century context. The section of the *Treatise*, at the end of which it occurs, is entitled "Moral distinctions not derived from reason" and that which immediately follows, "Moral distinctions derived from a moral sense." One thing seems certain. In the great eighteenth-century debate about the nature of conscience, Hume intended to refute the rational intuitionists and to side with the moral sense philosophers. But he seems to have had a further intention: to refute those religious moralists, which ever side they were on, who wanted to ground morality in God's will. Hume rejected (he professes reluctantly) any such grounding. He wrote to Hutcheson in 1740: "I wish from my heart I could avoid concluding that since morality, according to your opinion as well as mine, is determined merely by sentiment, it regards only human nature and life. This has often been urged against you, and the consequences are very momentous" (*Letters*, edited J. Y. T. Grieg, vol. i. No. 16., p. 40, quoted by Flew *I–OQ*). Some think that the derogatory reference in the is-ought passage to "vulgar systems of morality" which he is "subverting" is intended by Hume to apply only to religious moral codes (e.g.

MacIntyre, *I–OQ*, p. 46). But whether that is the case or not, it is certain that Hume believed morality to be grounded in human sentiments or interests and not in reason or the will of God.

Fourthly, I think we have to say, in the end, that Hume simply raised the question as to the precise nature of this grounding, but provided no clear answer to it. Morality, as such, he clearly took to have an intimate logical connection with human wants or needs. But was he saying merely that if we had no wants—if it made no difference to us what happened—then we should have no use for evaluative language, moral or otherwise? This is a view with which any emotivist or prescriptivist would agree. Is that what Hume was saying or more? And if more, what more? Was he saying that "ought" must be *defined* as "is wanted;" or that "ought" can be *inferred* from "is wanted"? Or what? The answer to these questions is not certain. We must conclude, I think, that to expect Hume to have come out clearly for one position or another is to treat him as though he were a philosopher of our own age and not of his own. I think that Hume did not take "We ought to do whatever is in the common interest" as exclusively a moral principle, a definition, or a rule of inference, but as some amalgam of all three. Expositors, as we have seen, can find quotations which seem to support the view that Hume took it as each of them respectively; and I think that there is no very clear preponderance in favor of one as against the others. That is why I say that, for us, Hume's famous is-ought passage, when set within the context of his moral philosophy as a whole, simply raises, but does not answer, the question of how wants and interests are related to obligations. We shall come back to this question in the next chapter.

II. CONTEMPORARY ATTEMPTS TO DEDUCE "OUGHT" FROM "IS"

I come now to two contemporary philosophers, who claim that they can formally deduce "ought" from "is". They are J. R. Searle and Alan Gewirth.

(I) SEARLE'S DERIVATION OF "OUGHT" FROM "IS"

J. R. Searle published an article in 1964 called "How to Derive 'Ought' from 'Is' " (*PR* LXXIII), which has been the occasion of much discussion. In it he says that the distinction between description and evaluation, fact and value, drawn by moral philosophers such as Moore, Stevenson and Hare, is really a conflation of at least two distinctions: viz. (i) that between different kinds of illocutionary force; and (ii) that between utterances which involve claims objectively decidable as true or false, on the one hand, and utterances which do not involve such claims because they are matters of decision or opinion, on the other. It has been assumed, he says, that the former distinction is a special case of the latter—that if something has the illocutionary force of an evaluation, it cannot be entailed by factual premises. Searle sets himself to show that this assumption is false: that factual premises can entail evaluative conclusions. He does so by expanding an idea found in embryo in Miss Anscombe's writings (see "Modern Moral Philosophy", *P* XXXIII, 1958 and "Brute Facts", *A* 18, 1957—8), namely that of an "institutional fact". (Searle's article and others by Anscombe, Flew, McClellan and Komisar, Hare and myself, mentioned below, are contained in my *The Is-Ought Question* and the page references will be to that collection.)

There are, Searle claims, different types of fact. Some facts presuppose institutions, others do not. They may be differentiated as "institutional" and "brute" facts respectively. Institutional facts are facts which exist only within our institutions; that is to say, within a system of constitutive rules. Constitutive (as distinct from simply regulative) rules create or define (and also regulate) new forms of behaviour, as distinct from regulating antecedently existing forms of behaviour. Eating is an antecedently existing form of behaviour regulated by rules of politeness. Chess is a new form of behaviour constituted by the rules of the game. Eating exists apart from etiquette; but checkmating does not exist apart from chess. "Brute" facts are, so to say, the factual raw materials out of which institutional facts are made. To each institutional fact certain other facts are "brute relative."

The movement of certain pieces on a board is brute relative to checkmating; the utterance of "I promise" is brute relative to promising; and so on.

Searle contends that "many forms of obligations, commitments, rights, and responsibilities are similarly institutionalized" (*I–OQ*, p. 131). He takes, for his example, one such institutionalized form of obligation, namely promising. It is his intention to show that we can start with the "brute" fact that a man uttered certain words; then invoke the institution of promising in such a way as to generate institutional facts; then appeal to the constitutive rule of the institution; and so arrive at an evaluative conclusion. In this way, Searle purports to deduce "ought" from "is." The stages of his derivation are:

(1) Jones uttered the words "I hereby promise to pay you, Smith, five dollars."
(2) Jones promised to pay Smith five dollars.
(3) Jones placed himself under (undertook) an obligation to pay Smith five dollars.
(4) Jones is under an obligation to pay Smith five dollars.
(5) Jones ought to pay Smith five dollars.

Searle says of this list, "the relation between any statement and its successor, while not in every case one of 'entailment', is nonetheless not just a contingent relation; and the additional statements necessary to make the relationship one of entailment *do not need to involve any evaluative statements, moral principles, or anything of the sort*" (*I–OQ*, p. 121, italics mine).

What are these "additional statements" to which he refers? Searle says that they consist of "empirical assumptions, tautologies, and descriptions of word usage" (*I–OQ*, p. 125) and nothing more. The requisite additional premises are as follows:

Between (1) and (2):
    (1a) Under certain conditions, C, anyone who utters the words (sentence) "I hereby promise to pay

you, Smith, five dollars" promises to pay Smith five dollars.

(1b) Conditions, C, obtain.

Between (2) and (3):

(2a) The tautological premise: All promises are acts of placing oneself under (undertaking) an obligation to do the thing promised.

Between (3) and (4):

(3a) Other things are equal.

(3b) The tautological premise: All those who place themselves under an obligation are, other things being equal, under an obligation.

Between (4) and (5):

(4a) Other things are equal.

(4b) The tautological premise: Other things being equal, one ought to do what one is under an obligation to do.

Some explanatory comments on these additional premises may be useful.

Premise (1a) starts with "brute" fact and invokes the institution of promising to generate institutional fact. The brute fact that some one utters the words "I promise," "in a proper context," as Miss Anscombe would say, "ordinarily amounts to" the institutional fact that he promises (*A* 19, p. 71). Premise (1b) simply says that this is such a "proper" context. As examples of the conditions fulfilled to make it proper Searle offers: "that the speaker is in the presence of the hearer Smith, they are both conscious, both speakers of English, speaking seriously. The speaker knows what he is doing, is not under the influence of drugs, not hypnotized or acting in a play, not telling a joke or reporting an event, and so forth" (*I–OQ*, pp. 121–22).

Premise (2a) embodies the constitutive rule of the institution of promising, that to make a promise is to undertake an obligation. Just as, by undertaking to play chess or any other game, one commits oneself to the observation of certain constitutive rules, so if one promises, one commits oneself thereby to certain obligations. *Within* the game of chess I cannot question or reject the rules; similarly, *within* the institution of promising I cannot reject the obligation.

Premises (3b) and (4b) are simply tautologies, explicating the ordinary usage of the words "obligation" and "ought."

The *ceteris paribus* clauses, premises (3a) and (4a), exclude the possibility that there is some reason for supposing that the obligation is void—step (4)—or that the agent ought not to keep the promise—step (5). What such reason could there be? Searle answers this question in a footnote (*I–OQ*, p. 123). The clause "other things being equal" between (3) and (4) excludes, for example, the promisee saying to the promiser, "I release you from your obligation," which would cancel the obligation. Between (4) and (5) "other things being equal" excludes the overriding of the present obligation by some other obligation, for example, by Jones's obligation to spend the five dollars on his children, who will starve if he does not.

Criticism of Searle

Searle's derivation of "ought" from "is" has been challenged in at least two ways. (i) It has been pointed out that there is a distinction between using the word "promise" as a detached reporter of verbal usage and as an engaged participant in the language of which it forms a part. If one changes from being a detached reporter to being an engaged participant, as Antony Flew points out (*I–OQ*, p. 141), this can only be by "commitment to the incapsulated values which alone warrants us to draw the normative conclusions." That is to say, by bridging the gap between "is" and "ought." But, against this, I have elsewhere (*I–OQ*, p. 169) raised the question: when one refuses to use a word like "promise" as an engaged participant, what precisely is one doing? Surely, not just retaining a descriptive, or factual, element in the word's meaning, while rejecting an evaluative. One is rejecting a whole way of speaking; one is stopping using a word with all that word's implications. Flew seems to think that, by exposing the difference between a reporter of verbal usage and a participant in that usage, he is exposing a gap between "is" and "ought." But exposers of the naturalistic fallacy were not concerned to show what Flew has shown, viz., that where descriptions entail evaluations we can decide whether or not to use them as engaged participants. They were showing, or trying to show, that there is no description such that it validly entails an evaluation.

A possible refinement on the distinction which I have just been considering between "a detached reporter of verbal usage" and "an engaged participant" is the distinction between: (a) someone who uses "promise" to mean simply uttering certain words (sense 1) and (b) someone who uses "promise" to mean undertaking an obligation (sense 2). It might then be said that, if Searle's premise (1a) above is really descriptive, all his move from his premises (1) to (2) proves is that Jones made a promise in sense 1. But in order to get from his (2) to (3), Searle has to prove that Jones made a promise in sense 2. In addition to (2a) above, therefore, he needs another extra premise between (2) and (3). And this has to be an evaluative one.

Searle himself takes account of this possible objection in his later book *Speech Acts* (Cambridge, 1969). He puts these words into the mouths of his critics against himself: "You prove that Jones made a promise in sense 1 and then assume that you have proved that he made a promise in sense 2 by assuming incorrectly that these two senses are the same. The difference between sense 2 and sense 1 is the difference between a committed participant and a neutral observer . . . for it is only the neutral observer who is making genuine factual or descriptive statements" (*Speech Acts*, p. 265). Searle's reply to this is, I think, quite effective. He denies the charge of equivocating on senses 1 and 2 of "promise" by contending that sense 1 *does not exist*. He says, "There is no literal meaning of 'promise' in which all it means is uttering certain words . . . . A sentence of the form 'X made a promise' is not lexically ambiguous as between 'X said some words' and 'X really promised.' 'Promise' is not thus homonymous" (*ibid.*, p. 266).

(ii) The other criticism of Searle to which I shall refer fastens on his *ceteris paribus* clauses, i.e. (3a) and (4a). As we saw, they are intended to secure that (to use Searle's own words) "no reason to the contrary can in fact be given" why we should not move from (3) to (4) and from (4) to (5) (*I–OQ*, p. 124). We gave examples of what such reasons might be. That which is supposed to be excluded by these "other things being equal" clauses is the necessity for any evaluation, particularly between (4) and (5). Searle obviously has to exclude that necessity in order to carry through his attempt to get an "ought" in (5) from exclusively nonevaluative premises. He acknowledges, of course, that an evaluation may have to be made between (4) and (5), if there is a clash of obligations in any situation; but his point is that this does not need to be made in all cases and so it is possible to have counter-examples to the thesis that "ought" cannot be derived from "is." That is, if there is no obligation in conflict with that of promise-keeping in a given situation, we can move from (4) to (5) without an evaluation. Against Searle, the point may be made that his "no reason to the contrary can in fact be given" is either a statement of fact or a judgment. If it simply means that at this moment someone cannot, in fact, offer a reason why he does not have an obligation—perhaps because his mouth is stuffed with food—it is ridiculous to think that this makes an act obligatory which otherwise would not be. But, if we take the other alternative—that the quoted words are a judgment—is not that judgment necessarily evaluative? If it is, Searle has not got from (1) to (5) without an evaluative premise. Perhaps with this sort of objection in mind, Searle says that he could, if need be, put the "other things being equal" into (5) which would then read: "Other things being equal, Jones ought to pay Smith five dollars." It would not then matter, from his point of view, if this *ceteris paribus* was evaluative. For he would have got from (1) to (5), i.e. to the evaluative conclusion, without any evaluative premises en route. However, (5) would not then be categorical, but hypothetical: "If other things are equal, then Jones ought to pay Smith five dollars." Searle cannot call the "ought" in (5) categorical, as he does (*I–OQ*, p. 125), and include the *ceteris paribus* clause in (5).

While admitting the force of such criticisms, I myself have tried (*I–OQ*, pp. 170–72) to defend Searle against them by arguing that his position can be held without any "other things being equal" clauses at all. "Other things being equal" between (3) and (4) purports to exclude possibilities such as that the promisee has released the promiser from his obligation. Why should not the exclusion of this possibility be included in the conditions, C, referred to in Searle's premises (1a) and (1b)? Above I quoted a sample list of such conditions. There does not seem any reason why something like "the promisee has not released the promiser from the implications of what the latter has said" should not be included among them.

What of the *ceteris paribus* clause between (4) and (5)? This, we saw, is intended to exclude possibilities such as a conflict of obligations. But it is only necessary to exclude such possibilities, if their realization would inhibit the move from (4) to (5). Would it do so? Whatever difficulties there may be in deriving (5) from (4), the mere fact that Jones was involved in some other obligation, besides that to pay Smith five dollars, does not seem to me to constitute such a difficulty. Suppose Jones has children who will starve if he pays Smith the five dollars. Why cannot we say that he ought to pay Smith and he ought to feed his children? True, "ought" implies "can." Jones can pay Smith. And he can feed his children. What he cannot do is both. But that is beside the present point. How one ought to resolve the position when there are two things one ought to do, not one, is a familiar problem in moral philosophy. It has exercised thinkers as different as W. D. Ross and J. P. Sartre; the former talked about "weighing" prima facie obligations against one another, and the latter said that all one can do is choose between them. But the fact that there is this problem does nothing to show that it is contrary to the ordinary uses of the words "obligation" and "ought' to say that, if we are under an obligation to do X, then we ought to do X.

It is interesting to notice that, in his 1969 book, *Speech Acts*, Searle restates his derivation of "ought" from "is" in substantially the same form as he gave it in the 1964 article, except that he dispenses now with the *ceteris paribus* clauses. They were, he says, "a standing invitation to various kinds of irrelevant objections" (cf. *Speech Acts*, pp. 259–60).

Take the first such clause between (3) and (4) in the 1964 version. In the 1969 book Searle says, "in order to get a straight-forward entailment between 3 and 4 we need only construe 4 in such a way as to *exclude any time gap*

between the point of the completion of the act in which
the obligation is undertaken, 3, and the point at which it is
claimed the agent is under an obligation, 4. So construed
3 entails 4 straight off" (*ibid.*, italics mine). So, in his 1969
version, Searle rewrites the 1964 tautological premise, (3b)
above, thus:

All those who place themselves under an obligation are
(*at the time when they so place themselves*) under an
obligation.

This tautology, he now thinks, is enough to take us from
(3) to (4).

What of the other *ceteris paribus* clause between (4) and
(5) in the 1964 version? Searle says in his 1969 book,
pp. 180–81, "Analogous to the tautology which explicates
the relation between 3 and 4 there is here the tautology
that if one is under an obligation to do something, then *as
regards that obligation*, one ought to do what one is under
an obligation to do" (italics mine). So, Searle rewrites the
tautological premise (4b) thus:

If one is under an obligation to do something, then *as
regards that obligation* one ought to do what one is
under an obligation to do.

Searle sets out two possible senses in which (5) above—
i.e. "Jones ought to pay Smith five dollars"—may be taken:

(5′) *As regards his obligation* to pay Smith five dollars,
Jones ought to pay Smith five dollars.
(5″) *All things considered*, Jones ought to pay Smith
five dollars.

Given the tautological premise (4b), he now thinks "if we
interpret 5 as 5″ we cannot derive it from 4 without additional premises. But equally clearly if we interpret it as
equivalent to 5′ . . . we can derive it from 4. And regardless
of whether we wish to interpret 5 as 5′ we can simply derive

5′ from 4, which is quite sufficient for our present purposes"
—i.e. to show that "ought" can be derived from "is".

We noted above the criticism that Searle could not include
his *ceteris paribus* clause in (5) and get a categorical "ought."
With that criticism no doubt in mind, Searle now adds:
"even with 5 interpreted as 5′ the 'ought' is in Kant's sense
a 'categorical' not a 'hypothetical' ought. 5′ does not say
that Jones ought to pay up *if he wants such and such*. It
says he ought, as regards his obligation, to pay up" (*ibid*).

All told, Searle's conclusion is, I think, in line with what
I have said concerning his *ceteris paribus* clauses above and
elsewhere in my attempt to defend him against criticism
which turned on these clauses. Searle draws his 1969 version
of how to derive "ought" from "is" to an end with the
words: "We rely on definitional connexions between
'promise', 'obligate', and 'ought' and the only problems
which arise are that obligations can be overridden or removed
in a variety of ways and we need to take account of that
fact. We solve our difficulty by specifying that the existence
of the obligation is at the time of the undertaking of the
obligation, and the 'ought' is relative to the existence of
the obligation" (*Speech Acts*, p. 182).

Is Searle Successful?

Does this attempt to derive "ought" from "is" succeed?
The nub of the problem is a question which is crucial
between prescriptivists and descriptivists. It is: can one
logically separate, within the notion of promising, a factual,
or descriptive, element from a normative, or evaluative,
element? The prescriptivist would say that one can: the
word "promise", as we ordinarily use it, encapsulates a
general decision of principle, to the effect that promises
ought to be kept. Descriptivists like Searle deny this. They
ask the rhetorical question: when did I, when did anyone,
decide that promises ought to be kept?

In support of the latter position, it could be pointed out
that there does not seem to be any "engaged participant"
use of the word "promise" where it is not taken for granted
that an obligation is involved. However, the case is different
with some other "institutional obligations." Consider this

conversation:

> *A* : You ought to help X.
> *B* : Why?
> *A* : He's your father and he's in need.
> *B* : What has that to do with it?

This last sentence sounds bizarre. Surely we all know what that has to do with it *B* ought to help X, if X is his father and is in need. Agreed. But, obligations to fathers are a matter about which there has been a considerable development and change of opinion over the years. One might say, therefore, that these obligations *have* been decided upon, or discovered. It is not, therefore, implausible, to suggest, as a prescriptivist might, that the word "father" (a) describes certain facts, such as that X contributed the male element in the procreation of *B*; and (b) encapsulates a general moral principle to which we in our society have come to subscribe, namely that we ought to help the man who contributed the male element in our procreation, if he is in need.

However, those descriptivists who rest their case on institutionalized obligations will not have this. They insist that it manifestly will not do simply to hold that a statement of institutional fact "adds something nonfactual" to the statement of the relevant "brute relative" facts, (cf. Anscombe, "On Brute Facts", *I–OQ*, p. 70). Against this, the prescriptivist asseverates, that which is added can *only* be nonfactual. Hare, for example, in a paper called "The Promising Game" writes of Searle's derivation: "It may seem as if the 'brute fact' that a person has uttered a certain phonetic sequence entails the 'institutional fact' that he has promised, and that this in turn entails that he ought to do a certain thing. But this conclusion can be drawn only by one who accepts, in addition, the nontautologous principle that one ought to keep one's promises. For unless one accepts this principle, one is not a subscribing member of the institution which it constitutes, and therefore cannot be compelled logically to accept the institutional facts which it generates in such a sense that they entail the conclusion . . . " (*I–OQ*, p. 155).

There seems to be a difference of opinion here which it is impossible to resolve. Recall the conversation instanced a moment ago. Suppose *B* asks *A* what he means by saying that X is *B*'s father, and *A* replies, "I mean he begat you," "I mean he brought you up," "I mean apart from him you wouldn't be here," etc. All these are brute relative facts. But now suppose that *B* asks, with reference to each, "But ought I to help the man who begat me (brought me up, without whom I wouldn't be here, etc.)?" These are open questions, all of which make quite good sense. Descriptivists would not deny it. But they would insist that "He is your father" is a statement of institutional fact and that "Ought I to help my father?" is *not* an open question. There is more in the statement "He is your father" than in the sum total of the above statements of brute relative fact. What more? Quite simply, the more which renders "Ought I to help my father?" *not* an open question. The prescriptivists, for their part, would agree with that. They too would say that there is more in "He is your father" than in any of the other statements of fact and that it follows from this "more" that one ought to help one's father. But, while descriptivists insist upon calling this "more" an element of institutional fact, the prescriptivists insist upon calling it an encapsulated general moral principle.

Does it matter which we call it? It does not seem to me that either side, at the end *of this particular dispute*, has shown that their way of describing the "more" is the right one. Of course, if in the light of wider considerations there is on the whole a better case for prescriptivism than for descriptivism, or vice versa, then these wider considerations will weigh in favour of deciding here for one way of putting it rather than the other.

Which is the more acceptable view? Against the descriptivist view, I think it can be said that it retreats into mystery. The element of fact, which is said to entail moral obligation, is explained only as something factual over and above all brute relative facts. But, in effect, that is not to explain why it entails obligation but only to repeat that it does. The prescriptivist solution, on the other hand, has at least the merit of nonmysteriousness. If the rules for the normal use of "to promise" are such that to use this word as an engaged participant is to commit oneself to an encapsulated moral principle, then the entailment of "ought" is thereby made unproblematic.

(II) GEWIRTH'S DERIVATION OF "OUGHT" FROM "IS"

Another attempt to deduce "ought" from "is" can be found in Alan Gewirth's *Reason and Morality* (Chicago and London, 1978); and, more succinctly stated, in his 1974 presidential address to the American Philosophical Association, which was published under the title *The Is-Ought Problem Resolved.* (Unless I say to the contrary my quotations and page references will be from *Reason and Morality*.)

The "is" from which Gewirth starts is the performance of an action and the "ought" which he deduces from it is, of course, the "ought" of morality. He defines action as "human voluntary and purposive behaviour" and explains these adjectives as follows:

> By an action's being *voluntary* or free I mean that its performance is under the agent's control in that he unforcedly chooses to act as he does, knowing the relevant proximate circumstances of his action. By an action's being *purposive* or intentional I mean that the agent acts for some end or purpose that constitutes his reason for acting; this purpose may consist in the action itself or in something to be achieved by the action (*RM*, pp. 22, 27, italics mine)

Since voluntariness and purposiveness are necessary conditions of action, Gewirth calls them its "generic features." In essence, he conceives of morality as respect for these features. His argument is intended to show that our obligation to respect the generic features of agency can be deduced from the fact that we are agents. The rational analysis of the concept of action, he affirms, will provide answers to the three central questions of moral philosophy; namely, the *substantive* one ("What ought we to do?"), the *distribu-*

tive one ("To whom ought we to do it?") and the *justificatory* (or authoritative) one ("Why ought we to do it?") (*RM*, p. 3). Being capable of voluntary, purposive action Gewirth calls "well-being". This capability necessitates such goods as life, health, peace of mind, etc. (*RM*, pp. 53—63). As we shall see, in his deduction of "ought" from "is", he refers comprehensively to the necessary conditions of human action as "freedom and well being."

In his presidential address (pages 35—36) Gewirth lists the five defining characteristics which in his view an "ought" must have in order to be a moral one. It must be (i) *other-regarding* in that it takes "positive account of the interests of other persons as well as the agent or speaker;" (ii) *prescriptive* in that its "users advocate or seek to guide or influence actions;" (iii) *egalitarian* in that it requires that "at least basic well-being be distributed equally as between the agent addressed and his potential recipients;" (iv) *determinate* in that the actions it prescribes "have definite contents such that the opposite contents cannot be obtained by the same mode of derivation;" and (v) *categorical* in that its "bindingness cannot be removed by, and hence is not contingent on or determined by, variable, escapable features either of the persons addressed or of their social relations."

Gewirth's attempt to deduce "ought" from "is" is nothing if not thorough-going. Each of these five defining characteristics of "ought" he grounds firmly in the generic features of action. The moral "ought" is other-regarding and egalitarian because all agents possess these features; prescriptive because one of them is purposiveness, or conativeness; determinate, because we know what these generic features are; and categorical, because no agent can deny that he has these features without self-contradiction. He claims to be able to prove each of these points and thereby show that the generic features of action "constitute the logical justificatory basis of the supreme principle of morality" (*ibid*, p. 27). So much for claims and intentions, then. But what of execution?

Gewirth's Reason and Method
    Before considering Gewirth's proposed derivation of

"ought" from "is" in detail, a word or two should be said concerning his reason for attempting it and the method by which he hopes to achieve it.

His reason is that he thinks the only final justification which moral judgments can have—if justifiable they be—lies in the fact that they are true, or are implied by something which is true. His theory of truth is the correspondence theory. It follows, therefore, that from his point of view there must be some matter of fact (he calls it the "correspondence-correlate") which entails the practical demand that a justified moral judgment makes upon those to whom it is addressed (*RM*, pp. 5–6, 26). The generic features of agency constitute this matter of fact to Gewirth's way of thinking. He affirms that, unless moral value judgments can be grounded in some such objective factual truth as that agents possess these features, they will necessarily lack the categoricalness which is one of their defining characteristics. I shall come back to the question of whether or not this is so.

Gewirth's method of deriving "ought" from "is" he describes as a "dialectically necessary" one. Let me explain this expression. Gewirth draws two distinctions (*RM*, pp. 42–47). The first is between what a free and purposive agent would say contingently and what he would say necessarily. By the latter, Gewirth means what he would say as a matter of conceptual necessity, i.e. because he is an agent. Since the concept of an agent is that of a being who behaves voluntarily and purposively, what an agent would say necessarily will express his freedom and purposiveness. Gewirth's second distinction is that between "assertoric" and "dialectical" judgments or statements. One may say assertorically, for instance, that X ought to be done; or dialectically, that *from within the standpoint of some person* it ought to be done. The standpoint that Gewirth has in mind is that of an agent *qua* agent. Putting what he means by "necessary" and by "dialectical" together, then, a "dialectically necessary method" of deriving "ought" from "is" will be one in terms of statements or judgments which all agents would necessarily make, solely in virtue of the fact that they are agents. As Gewirth has it: "the statements the method attributes to the agent are set forth as necessary ones in that they reflect what is conceptually necessary to being an agent who voluntarily or freely acts for purposes he wants to attain" (*RM*, p. 44). All the moves by which Gewirth proposes to get from "is" to "ought" must be conceived as moves from within the standpoint of an agent *qua* agent.

To prepare us for what is to come, Gewirth bids us also bear in mind that agents are both rational and conative. It will not be surprising, therefore, to find that "within the standpoint of the rational agent" certain inferences are drawn. Not every conceivable inference, of course, but certain simple and direct ones. Gewirth will be saying in effect that, given *p*, any normal human agent would *see* that it entails *q*, where *p* entails *q* in an *obvious* manner. Again, since agents are not only rational but also conative, or purposive, it will not be surprising to find that from "within the standpoint of the conative agent" certain demands will be made. Demands, that is, which express self-interest (cf. *RM*, p. 90). The agent will be "opposed to whatever interferes with his having freedom and well-being" and will advocate "his having these features." In consequence, some of the inferences drawn within the standpoint of the agent will be "prescriptive and not only descriptive" (*RM*, p. 79).

Gewirth proposes to adopt this "dialectically necessary method" because he considers that it will get him out of some of the problems which have bedevilled attempts to deduce "ought" from "is" by a more traditional method. Confidently, he asserts that "the dialectically necessary method is able to avoid certain difficulties that confront naturalistic approaches to ethics, including relativism and the justification of value judgments on the basis of empirical facts" (*RM*, p. 45). What these difficulties amount to, in a nutshell, is having, at any stage of your derivation, more in your conclusion than you have in your premises. We must now see if Gewirth does manage to avoid them. I will first set out as clearly as I can what the stages of his derivation are and how he conceives of the logical connexions between them. Then I will attempt a critical assessment of the moves he makes.

Gewirth's derivation

The stages of Gewirth's derivation are not listed as clearly as Searle listed those of his; but I think it is true to say that there are seven of them and that they can be listed as follows:

(I) "I do X for purpose E" (*RM*, p. 49).

(II) "E is good" (*ibid*).

(III) "My freedom and well-being are good as the necessary conditions of all my actions" (*RM*, p. 61).

(IV) "I have a right to freedom and well-being" (*RM*, p. 64).

(V) "All other agents ought to refrain from interfering with my freedom and well-being" (*RM*, p. 66).

(VI) "All prospective purposive agents have a right to freedom and well-being" (*RM*, pp. 104ff).

(VII) "I ought to refrain from interfering with the freedom and well-being of all prospective, purposive agents" (*ibid*).

Let us consider them one by one.

(I) *"I do X for purpose E"*. The speaker is an agent who is free and purposive. In effect, therefore, he is stating that he does a certain act X from unforced choice and with the intention of achieving thereby a certain end E. Since the speaker is a conative, as well as a rational, being this speech act will, according to Gewirth, have evaluative as well as descriptive illocutionary force. As he has it:

> From this (*sc*. the speaker's) conativeness it follows that the purposes for which he acts seem to him to be good. Hence he implicitly makes a value judgment about this goodness. Suppose the fact of the agent's performing a purposive action is expressed by him in such a descriptive statement as 'I do X for purpose E'. Because of the presence of purposiveness in action, from the standpoint of the agent this statement entails 'E is good'. (*RM*, p. 49)

Eventually, we shall have to consider whether, by saying

this, Gewirth has begged the whole question at issue; but
for the time being, let us proceed as he would have us do.

(II) *"E is good"*. The words just quoted under (I) indicate
that Gewirth thinks it is the agent's conativeness which
accounts for the fact that, if he said (I) he would, from
within his own standpoint, necessarily go on to say "E is
good." Now, if E is his purpose, it certainly cannot fail to
seem to him to be good. But is he entitled to say that it *is*
good? Gewirth's reply is that, within the standpoint of the
agent, no distinction can be drawn between what *seems*, or
is thought, good and what *really is* good (*RM*, p. 51). Here
we begin to see why the "dialectically necessary method"
of deriving "ought" from "is" commends itself to Gewirth.

(III) *"My freedom and well-being are good as the necessary
conditions of all my actions"*. This follows from (II), according to Gewirth, because if an agent thought E good, then he
would think his own capability of attaining E good. Freedom
and well-being are the necessary conditions of action and
action is the necessary means of attaining E. So, considered
in isolation from any other effects which the agent's freedom
and well-being may have, they must appear to him to be
good in so far as they are essential to the attainment of E.

(IV) *"I have a right to freedom and well-being"*. It must be
borne in mind throughout this derivation that we are considering what an agent *qua* agent would say from within his
own standpoint. Gewirth's ground for the deduction of (IV)
from (III) is the agent's awareness that his own freedom
and well-being are the necessary conditions of any good he
might attain by his own actions. The point is not that,
because he has said freedom and well-being are good, the
agent must go on to say that he has a right to them. That is
not necessarily so. The point is rather that, since these
capabilities are obviously essential to his existence as an
agent, he must as a rational being be aware of that fact, and
as a conative one, seek to secure these necessary conditions
of his own agency (*RM*, p. 90). His rationality and conativeness both find expression in this claim, "I have a right to

freedom and well-being." Its illocutionary force is therefore both constative and prescriptive (*RM*, p. 66). His rationality would be satisfied by *stating* that, if he is to be an agent, he must have freedom and well-being. But his conativeness is only satisfied by *insisting* that he be accorded these capabilities.

This seems to ground the claim expressed in (IV) entirely in the speaker's conativeness; and that, of course, raises the question of how the idea of "having a right" gets into it. It is one thing to say that one *insists* upon having something; another, to say that one is *justified* in doing so. Just as Gewirth claimed that, within the standpoint of the agent, there is no distinction between what seems good and what is good, so now he appears to be claiming that, within that same standpoint, there is none between insisting upon having the necessary conditions of one's own existence and being entitled to do so. But whether or not this is so is a question to which we shall return.

(V) *"All other agents ought to refrain from interfering with my freedom and well-being"*. A right implies a correlative "ought" (*RM*, p. 66). That is Gewirth's ground for deducing (V) from (IV). The argument is as follows. From within his own standpoint, an agent who had said that he has a right to something, would go on to say, when he came to speak of others, that they ought not to prevent him having that to which he has a right. As Gewirth has it: "Since he here proceeds solely from within this standpoint (i.e. that which he has as an *agent*), its necessary conditions provide the basis for his addressing to other persons the requirement that they at least not interfere with his having these conditions" (*RM*, p. 73, parenthesis mine).

However, Gewirth recognizes that the "right" in (IV) and the "ought" in (V) are "prudential" (not moral) ones:

. . . it is directly because freedom and well-being are necessary goods for his own purposive actions that the agent holds that he has rights to them, regardless of what may be the specific contents of his purposes and actions. In holding that all other persons ought at least to refrain

from interfering with his having freedom and well-being,
the agent likewise appeals not to moral criteria but to
prudential ones. This 'ought' judgment is made from
within the agent's own standpoint in purposive action:
what grounds his judgment is his own agency-needs, not
those of the persons about whom he makes the judgment.
(*RM*, p. 71)

The question which Gewirth now has to face is how to
get from prudential considerations to moral ones. Moral
judgments are "other-regarding", not simply in the sense
that they require others to respect one's own self-interest,
but, as Gewirth himself pointed out, that they require one
to respect the interests of others. How then does he get
from a prudential "ought" to a moral one?

(VI) *"All prospective, purposive agents have a right to freedom and well-being"*. In so far as a claim is justified, there
has to be a sufficient reason for it. In (IV) the agent claimed,
in effect, that there was a sufficient reason for his being
accorded freedom and well-being. What was this sufficient
reason? The only thing it could be, is Gewirth's reply;
namely, a description of the claimant (*RM*, p. 104). There
could, in his opinion (*RM*, p. 72) be no more sufficient
reason for a claim than a description of the claimant which
shows that he needs what is claimed in order to be what he
is. In the case of (IV) above, it is, as we noted, the awareness
of the agent that he is an agent in which the claim to freedom and well-being is grounded. Or, as Gewirth now spells
it out, in the agent's awareness of himself as a "prospective,
purposive agent."

We need not linger here on the new word "prospective."
I will come back to its significance below. The point to
fasten on at the moment is the rule of sufficient reason,
which Gewirth now invokes and enunciates as follows:
"if some predicate P belongs to some subject S because S
has the property Q (where the 'because' is that of sufficient
reason or condition) then P must also belong to all other
subjects $S_1 S_2 \ldots S_n$ that have Q" (*RM*, p. 105). Given this

rule,[1] if being a prospective, purposive agent is a sufficient reason why an agent can claim his own freedom and well-being, it is a sufficient reason why anyone else of whom this is a correct description can claim theirs. If I have this right, others who conform to the relevant description have it too. This is the bridge, according to Gewirth, which takes an agent within his own standpoint across the divide between moral considerations and merely prudential ones. Having said (IV), an agent must necessarily go on to say (VI).

(VII) *"I ought to refrain from interfering with the freedom and well-being of all prospective, purposive agents"*. If the "ought" in (V) is the correlative of the "right" in (IV) then there is now no escaping the conclusion that the "ought" in (VII) is the correlative of the "right" in (VI). Gewirth embodies this latter "ought" in what he calls "the supreme principle of morality, viz. in the Principle of Generic Consistency: 'Act in accord with the generic rights of your recipients as well as of yourself' " (*RM*, p. 135). The obligation to do so is presented as the fulfilment of all the five defining characteristics of the moral "ought". It is obviously other-regarding and prescriptive. It is egalitarian in so far as its sole and sufficient reason is the fact that all one's recipient's like onself, are prospective, purposive agents. It is determinate in so far as its specific content is respect for freedom and well-being. And it is categorical in so far as no change in an agent's own inclinations, interests or ideals, or in the conventions of his society, can provide a way of escape from it (*ibid*).

---

[1] There is something wrong with this rule. The "because" may be either logical or empirical. If the former, then the rule would be:

$$Ga \rightarrow Fa$$

$$\therefore (x) \, Gx \rightarrow Fx$$

which is invalid. If, on the other hand, the "because" is empirical, any example will initially admit of exceptions; but, if tightened up to exclude these, will become analytic and be subject to the logical objection.

Criticisms of Gewirth

How convincing, then, is this attempt to deduce "ought" from "is"? In assessing it, I think the important critical questions that arise are as follows:

(i) The first of them concerns Stage (I) of the derivation, "I do X for purpose E." I suggested above that Gewirth may have begged the whole question at issue by saying that this first stage of his derivation "implicitly makes a value-judgment." I had some doubt as to whether it could do so and still remain the kind of statement which it would need to be, if the derivation is a genuine one. Can "ought" be deduced from "is"?—surely, that question is begged if one starts from an "is" which is also an "ought", from a putative statement of fact which also "makes a value-judgment"!

The same sort of doubt arose, it will be remembered, with regard to Searle's attempt to deduce an ought-judgment from a statement of institutional fact. "I promise to do X" does imply "I ought to do X," but the question remains as to how this is to be correctly explained. We noted two alternative opinions about that. Descriptivists think the "ought" follows from some factual element in promising, over and above the facts (e.g. saying "I promise") which are "brute relative" to it. Prescriptivists, on the other hand, think that "to promise" has both descriptive and evaluative meaning and that the "ought" follows from a general moral principle (such as "Everyone ought to do that of which he has said 'I promise to do it' ") subscription to which is involved in the normal use of "to promise" (and its cognates). If we agree with the descriptivists, then we may say that Searle has deduced "ought" from "is", but only at the price of postulating a mysterious factual element in the concept of promising, which stands apart from all the brute relative facts, and, unlike any of them, is supposed, in some unexplained way, to entail value-judgments. If, on the other hand, we agree with the prescriptivists, we must deny that Searle has deduced "ought" from "is". All he has done is beg the question from the start by his notion of an institutional fact.

Now, much the same thing, I think, can be said about Gewirth's derivation. He gets his (II) "E is good" from (I)

"I do X for purpose E." But how? When he says that his (I) "implicitly makes a value-judgment," all he can mean is either that it states a sort of fact which mysteriously entails value-judgments; or it has evaluative as well as descriptive meaning and therefore is not the unadulterated "is" it needs to be, if the derivation is genuine. The fact that Gewirth speaks so explicitly of (I) expressing the speaker's conativeness, as well as simply describing his performance of an action, reinforces the impression that he has simply begged the question.

It is rather surprising to find that he considers his own derivation superior to Searle's; and his reasons for doing so are yet more surprising. If I have understood him correctly, one of them is that, whilst promising is attached to rights and oughts by means of rules that need justifying, acting is not; and another is that, whilst we can choose whether to make promises or not, and so conceivably evade the entailed "ought", we cannot choose whether or not to be agents and so cannot refuse to make the moral judgments which are logically implied in all purposive action. But, as to the former, I do not see how "I do X for purpose E," in conjunction with other entailed premises, can entail the Principle of Generic Consistency apart from rules for the use of the words in the premises. And, as to the latter, I do not see how the fact that we cannot avoid making certain deductions (if it is a fact) constitutes proof that the premise from which they all start must be an unadulterated statement of fact.

Whatever may be this superiority, which Gewirth's derivation is supposed to have over Searle's, I do not think that any sort of case can be made out to the effect that Gewirth has managed to avoid the dilemma of either begging the question or retreating into mystery, on the horns of which Searle landed.

(ii) My second line of criticism concerns stages (II) and (III) of Gewirth's derivation.

We saw above that Moore accused those who commit the naturalistic fallacy of two mistakes, namely: (i) of treating an open question as if it were closed and (ii) of reducing a significant moral judgment to a trivial tautology.

If "good" were correctly defined as "satisfying desire", for example, then the question, "Is what satisfies desire good?" would be a closed one, which answers itself in the affirmative. But that is not what it is. Then again, the judgment, "What satisfies desire is good" would be a trivial tautology. But again that is not what it is. Now, Gewirth does *not* say that stages (II) and (III) of his derivation represent what stage (I) *means*; so he is not a naturalist in quite the same sense as those Moore was attacking. But he does say that (II) and (III) are what (I) *entails*. The point I wish to make about Gewirth is similar to the one Moore made about those who define moral terms naturalistically. Gewirth, I think, must be mistaken because his derivation, in effect, (a) treats an open question as if it were closed, at stage (II); and (b) trivializes morality, at stage (III). It does not do either of these things, I repeat, in exactly the same way as Moore's ethical naturalists; but it does them in a way that springs from the same sort of failure to recognize how deep and wide is the gap between "is" and "ought".

As to stage II, let two points be granted to Gewirth. The first, that if E is the speaker's purpose, then he will think it good. The second, that from within the speaker's own standpoint there is no difference between him thinking it good and it being good. But now the additional point to take is this. *From within his own standpoint*, the speaker can *evaluate his own evaluation* and that in either of two ways. He can say, "Is it good that I do X for purpose E?", and thereby be wondering whether the end justifies the means. That is to say he may approve of a purpose E and not approve of the act X by means of which he is seeking to attain it. But, more radically, when he asks this question, "Is it good that I do X for purpose E?", he may thereby be wondering whether it is good that he should be the sort of person who thinks E good. He may have a certain purpose but wish that he were the sort of man who had a better one. The prayer that we might "love the thing which Thou commandest and desire that which Thou dost promise" was, presumably, composed for just such a man.

When I say, then, that Gewirth's move from (I) to (II) treats an open question as if it were closed, I mean that he takes this move to settle the question of what is good, at least within the standpoint of the agent, whereas in reality that question is still open. Normally, when facts are said to entail values, or "ought" to be deducible from "is", this is taken to mean that the question of value has been settled. But if, within the context of the move itself, so to speak (that is, within the standpoint of the agent himself in the present case) the value question is still open, as we have seen it to be, what has been settled? Surely, nothing as to value.

Coming now to Stage (III), viz. "My freedom and well-being are good as the necessary conditions of all my actions," notice in passing that this does not say that the necessary conditions of the particular action X are good, but those "of *all* my actions." This could be interpreted as deliberately leaving room for the possibility, just noted, of the speaker not approving of X as the means to E. However, the main point seems to be that an agent would, from within his own standpoint, necessarily regard his own freedom and well-being as good. Gewirth comments: "For him not to evince such an evaluation (*sc.* of freedom and well-being) . . . would be for him not to value his generic ability for purposive fulfilment at all, and hence to cease being even a prospective, rational agent" (*RM*, p. 60). The argument, then, appears to be as follows. If an agent would say, "My freedom and well-being are *not* good," he would say "My agency is *not* good." This is what the first part of the sentence just quoted states, in effect. But what do its closing words, "and hence cease being even a prospective, rational agent" state, in effect? Quite clearly, that, if an agent would say, "My agency is *not* good," then he would say, "I am *not* an agent." From which it follows that, if he would say "I am an agent," then he would say, "My freedom and well-being are good." The logical grounding of that respect for freedom and well-being, in which Gewirth sees the central principle of morality, is, within the standpoint of the agent, ultimately the fact of his own agency. Gewirth spells it out that for a speaker to say "I am an agent" and then to say "My freedom and well-being are not good" would be "contradictory" (*ibid*).

Why do I say that this trivializes morality? Because it sees the latter in the last analysis as my obligation to be what I am. There is a German proverb, "Become what you are" and, in so far as this aphoristically reminds us of our moral potentialities, one can see some point in it. But what is the point of a morality which *in the most literal sense* is simply to *be* what one *is*? Is not this a repudiation of the whole idea of morality; of the idea, that is, that we should look, not only on what is, but on what ought to be?

(iii) The third line of criticism concerns Stage (IV), viz. "I have a right to freedom and well-being." Gewirth is, of course, aware that, even within the standpoint of the agent, there will have to be some progress from the thought of being an agent, and the necessary conditions thereof, if we are ever to get to a moral "ought". So, at Stage (IV), he brings in the idea of a "right"—"I have a right to freedom and well-being."

One initial objection which some might raise to this move is as follows. Stage (IV) claims a right to freedom and well-being. Now, making such a claim is an action. Therefore, it requires the necessary conditions of action, viz., freedom and well-being, to be fulfilled. What then, is the point of this claim? What is the point of claiming something, when as a matter of logical necessity, one must have what is claimed before one can make the claim? To this Gewirth has a reply and it explains why he uses "prospective" in his description of the claimant as "a prospective, purposive agent" (cf. above). He points out that we do not only act in the present; we also hope to act in the future. For the sake of our future actions, then, we must make sure that we shall have the capability of acting when the time comes. Freedom and well-being constitute that capability, and so there is a great deal of point in insisting now upon our right to them. I think this reply of Gewirth's is effective as far as it goes.

The mention of "insisting", however, raises another, and I think more serious, doubt concerning Stage IV. Gewirth grounds the right to freedom and well-being in the speaker's conativeness. Because the speaker is conative as well as rational he will not only see that he needs freedom and well-being in order to continue in existence as an agent, but

will insist upon having them. It is this insistence which finds
expression in Stage IV. But why does the fact of the agent's
conativeness—i.e. his insistence upon having freedom and
well-being—enable him to say that he has a *right* to them?
I think Gewirth's reply to this is that it does so within the
agent's standpoint. Just as there is no distinction within
that standpoint between "E is good" and "I think E is good"
at Stage (II), so there is none between "I insist on my
freedom and well-being" and "I have a right to them" at
Stage (IV). But this leaves open at Stage (IV) the same sort
of question which, as I pointed out, is open at Stage (II). It
may be true that from within his own standpoint, if our
agent thinks his freedom and well-being good as necessary
conditions of being an agent, he will say he has a right to
them. But he may ask himself if it is right for him to insist
on his right. Even within his own standpoint he could thus
reopen the question of value. Since the rights claim is simply
the expression of his own conativeness, he can wonder
whether it is right to make it.

(iv) A fourth line of criticism concerns the fact that
Gewirth has no time for the idea that moral judgments are
justified by the fact that they have been arrived at in accordance with the canons of the moral way of thinking. He
rejects this idea as "circular or superfluous" (*RM*, p. 16),
quoting Wittgenstein to the effect that "justification consists in something independent" (*RM*, p. 15 and *Philosophical Investigations*, I, 265). Evidently he thinks that
"something independent" of the whole moral way of thinking is needed in order to justify the moral "ought". As we
saw his view is that this "something independent" can only
be what he calls a "correspondence-correlate", or matter of
objective fact. His main ground for this view was that,
without such a grounding, the moral "ought" would lack
categoricalness. But I have two doubts about all this.

First, there are notorious difficulties about the very idea
of justifying a whole way of thinking by "something independent" of it, be that way of thinking morality, science,
religion, or whatever. Each such discipline, or universe of
discourse, can appropriately be regarded as constituted by a
constitutive concept—moral obligation, physical objectivity,

divine consciousness and agency, or whatever. Everything said within any such universe of discourse is said in terms of its constitutive concept. By this I mean that questions and answers are not moral unless they are about moral obligation; nor scientific, unless about physical objects; nor religious, unless about divine consciousness and agency; and so on. Now, if we ask "But does moral obligation (or physical objectivity, or divine consciousness and agency, etc.) really exist?", the difficulty is knowing where to go with this question. If we take such a question into its own universe of discourse, it is begged from the start, since the answer is inevitably "Yes". Everything said in morality, for instance, presupposes the real existence of moral obligation. But, if on the other hand, we take such a question into a universe of discourse other than that constituted by the concept to which it refers, it can only be answered by regarding the constitutive concept implicit in the question as an instance of the constitutive concept of the universe of discourse into which we take it. For instance, to say, "What scientific proof is there that moral obligation really exists?", is to presuppose that moral obligation is some kind of physical object; and surely that is absurd! No one, I think, has done more than Wittgenstein himself to raise doubts about this idea of providing "something independent" which will justify a whole universe of discourse, such as morality undoubtedly is.

Then, secondly, I do not see why the categoricalness of moral obligation must collapse if it is not rooted in some "supreme principle of morality," which in its turn is grounded in the fact that action has certain generic features, as Gewirth would have us believe. He is very sure that "the content as well as the form . . . of the justificatory argument will have to be necessary and not merely contingent . . . " (*RM*, p. 24). That is to say that morality has to be grounded in a supreme principle such as that of generic consistency, which is deduced from fact, and not merely in a method of reasoning, if it is to be categorical and not at the mercy of the "variable, escapable features" of those on whom it is supposed to be binding. But why? Why should not the justification of the answers that are given to the substantive ("What ought we to do?") and distributive ("To whom ought we to do it?") moral questions be justified by the fact that they have been arrived at by reasoning that is appropriate to such questions? Gewirth evidently thinks that they can only be justified in so far as they are in accordance with a supreme principle of morality—respect for the generic features of action—which it would be self-contradictory for a human agent to disobey. His point is presumably that in disobeying it, the agent would be denying that he is an agent. But even if that were true, would it not, in effect, reduce the moral obligation to a logical one and thereby eliminate it? What makes a moral judgment binding is not its logical necessity but its moral obligatoriness. And what makes it morally obligatory is the fact that it has been arrived at by reasoning that is appropriate to establishing moral obligation and definitive of what the latter means.

Gewirth himself says at one point that the "ultimate justificans" of morality is reason (*RM*, p. 25). His argument is that the supreme principle of morality is justified by the generic features of action; but that these in turn "are ascertained by deductive rationality, so that the ultimate justificans of the supreme principle consists in reason" (*ibid*). His point is evidently that it is by reflection upon what is meant by action that morality is justified. But why not, by reflection on what is meant by morality? Surely "reason", when it comes to morality, means the moral way of thinking. If a justification of the latter is demanded, is not this to require a reason for reason itself? Gewirth, for his part, said that if answers to the substantive and distributive moral questions are justified simply by appeal to the fact that they have been arrived at by the moral way of thinking, that renders their justification "circular or superfluous" (*RM*, p. 16). I think that to require a justification for moral reasoning as a whole is both circular *and* superfluous. There just is no answer to: What reason is there for reason? One may, of course, be able to opt out of the moral way of thinking; there could presumably be considerations of a prudential kind for and against doing so. For example, that one will avoid a lot of inconvenience if one does opt out (for); or that one will cease to be trusted by one's friends, if one does so (against). But this is a different matter. It is not the logical justification for moral thinking which would then be in question, but the advisability of anyone engaging in it.

CHAPTER 7. SOME FURTHER FORMS OF DESCRIPTIVISM

I. TWO ASSUMPTIONS OF PRESCRIPTIVISM REJECTED

I think a descriptivist would say that, in my criticisms of Searle and Gewirth (Chapter 6), I made two closely related assumptions, which are false. One is the assumption that we can always hold apart the descriptive and evaluative meanings of a moral judgment. And the other, that we can always reject the criteria of moral value, in accordance with which any moral judgment has been made. As to the former assumption, I think he would say that I was guilty of it in my criticism of Searle. I pointed out that none of the facts which are "brute relative" to promising entails an ought. Then I accused Searle of retreating into mystery by his insistence that even so, whatever does entail the ought must still be factual. This, I suggested, rejects the more intelligible explanation that a moral principle is encapsulated in the meaning of "to promise." But our descriptivist might ask me in reply why I am so sure that my alternative explanation is the more intelligible; and then go on to argue that, on the contrary, the real mystery lies in conceiving of how a single speech-act can have two different sorts of meaning at the same time.

Coming now to the second false assumption, of which I said our descriptivist might accuse me, I think he would say that I was guilty of it in my criticism of Gewirth. I accepted the latter's contention that an agent, from within his own standpoint, would see no difference between "I think E is good" and "E is good" and conceded that, because of his conativeness, an agent would also see none between "I insist on having my freedom and well-being" and "I have a right to freedom and well-being." Having agreed to these points, I went on to argue that the agent—still from within his own standpoint—could nevertheless raise the questions "Is it good that E seems to me to be good?", or "Is it right for me to insist upon my right to freedom and well-being?" In each case, I claimed that the value question would still be open if, so to speak, the agent took one step further back. Here again, our descriptivist would ask me why I am so sure that it is open; and perhaps go on to claim that, if we can always re-evaluate our own evaluations—i.e. always step back from the criteria by which we have made our judgments and question them as I am assuming—then we can never arrive at what we really think is right or good.

The two assumptions, of which I have just been supposing a descriptivist would accuse me, are ones which he would say are typical of prescriptivism. It almost amounts to a definition of descriptivism to say that those who subscribe to it reject these two prescriptivist assumptions. They deny, first that it is always logically possible to separate the descriptive and evaluative meanings of a moral judgment; and secondly, that it is always logically possible for us to choose whether we will accept or reject the criteria of moral value applied in a judgment. The descriptivists whom I talked about in the last chapter would certainly repudiate both these assumptions and so, I think, would those of whom I am going to speak in the present one. Before going on to do so, however, let me give some account of why descriptivists take such a poor view of what they regard as these two false assumptions. Why are they, for their part, so sure: (i) that we cannot always hold apart the descriptive and evaluative meanings of a moral judgment; and (ii) that we are not always free to choose our own criteria of moral value? (The papers by Mrs. Foot and Hare, to which I shall refer, are reprinted in my *The Is-Ought Question* and my page references will be to it.)

Description and Evaluation

To see why descriptivists think that the descriptive and evaluative meanings of a moral judgment cannot always be separated, let us take as our example, the judgment, "Smith is courageous."

To start with, what would a prescriptivist say about it? Here is the kind of thing Hare says in his 1963 paper "Descriptivism":

> There are certain ways of behaving, describable in perfectly neutral terms, which make us commend people as, for example, courageous. Citations for medals do not simply say that the recipient behaved courageously; they give descriptive details; and though these, for reasons of brevity, often themselves contain evaluative terms, this need not be the case, and in a good citation it is the neutral descriptions which impress. They impress us because we already have the standards of values according to which to do *that* sort of thing is to display outstanding merit. (*I–OQ*, p. 246)

This comment assumes that a clear distinction can be drawn between: (a) the facts described by "Smith is courageous;" and (b) the speaker's commendation of Smith on account of these facts.

Why do descriptivists deny this? Mrs. Philippa Foot, one of the earliest of Hare's opponents to enter the lists against him, had written with his prescriptivist analysis of words like "courageous" in mind, as follows in her 1958 paper "Moral Beliefs".

> What is this extra element which is supposed to be present or absent after the facts have been settled? It is not a matter of liking the man who has courage, or of thinking him altogether good, but of "commending him for his courage." How are we supposed to do that? The answer that will be given is that we only commend someone else in speaking of him as courageous if we accept the imperative "let me be courageous" for ourselves. But this is quite unnecessary. I can speak of someone else as having the virtue of courage, and of course recognise it as a virtue in the proper sense, while knowing that I am a complete coward, and making no resolution to reform. (*I–OQ*, pp. 208–9)

Her contention is evidently that she can *sincerely* form the moral judgment that someone did well to be courageous, yet not assent to the entailed imperative "Let me be courageous."

Well, can she? Hare, it will be recalled (see above, p.169) built two conditions into his contention that moral judgments entail imperatives: (i) that the speaker will assent to the entailed imperative if, and only if, he is *sincere* in his judgment; and (ii) his assent to the imperative will be sincere if, and only if, where he is physically and psychologically *able* to do so, he acts accordingly. Hare recognized weakness of will as a possible form of inability. Is Mrs. Foot simply saying, when she speaks as she does at the end of the last quotation, that she may suffer from such weakness of will and so not carry out the imperative "Let me be courageous"? If so, there is nothing at issue between her and Hare. Or is she saying that she can be *sincere* in commending someone for the virtue of courage and, though *able* to practise that virtue herself, *not* assent to the entailed imperative "Let me be courageous"? If so, then here again there *may* not be anything at issue between her and Hare. For Hare (*FR*, p.155) allows that I may say that another man is a better man than I am in a certain respect, yet be under no obligation to try to be more like him in that respect because I am trying to be good in a different way from him. An example would be a scholar who commends a businessman's determination to get things done without seeking to emulate it because the life he leads calls for virtues of another kind, such as perpetual self-criticism, which might well be inhibited by too much determination to get things done. However, in the case of courage, it is arguable that "all goes if courage goes" and so perhaps this is a virtue which good men of any kind need. In that case Mrs. Foot is mistaken if she is forthrightly saying that, when we commend someone for a virtue such as courage, we need not imply our assent to the imperative "Let me be courageous" (or whatever). If I commend Smith as courageous while I turn to run from a dangerous duty I invite the comment 'How about you?" It would not be natural for me to answer with "What do you mean—how about me?" I know very well what they mean. If I am (a) sincere and (b) able, it is to be expected that, having commended Smith for being courageous, I shall be, or at least try to be, courageous myself. If I make no such effort, it will be assumed either that I cannot help being a coward or that I do not sincerely rate courage a virtue. *Ex hypothesi* the former alternative is excluded. We are left with the latter.

Now, if descriptivists are mistaken about the logical relationship between descriptive and evaluative meanings in cases such as that which we have been considering, in precisely what way are they mistaken? Why do they think that, when anyone calls a man courageous (or by any other such apparently descriptive-cum-evaluative expression, e.g. dangerous, cowardly, etc.), we cannot (logically) separate the descriptive element in what is said from the evaluative? Hare's account of why they are mistaken is along these lines.

He points out that there are two ways in which evaluation and description can be conceived to be connected: (i) the evaluation of a *thing* may be *supervenient* upon a description of it; (ii) description and evaluation may be *tied together* within the meaning of a *word*. To indicate the former kind of connection, one would point to some property, which *a thing has*, as the reason why one thinks it has such-and-such a value. To indicate the latter kind of connection, one would call attention to something which it would be *odd to say*. In the former case, for example, one might say, "He is a good man because he gives a lot of his money to the poor." In the latter case, one might say, "It is odd to call a man generous and then to say that you do not admire him." Now, Hare maintains that descriptivists are guilty of two fallacies: (i) they equivocate on these two different ways in which description and evaluation can be connected (viz. supervenience and what I call being tied together); and (ii) they assume that what is true of words must also be true of things. They argue in the following way:

Evaluation is connected with description *either* by supervenience *or* by being tied together (as these two expressions have been explained above).

In some *words*, e.g. "courageous", evaluation and description are tied together.

Therefore, in some *things* they are also tied together—that is to say, we cannot e.g. indicate what it is about a man which we are describing when we call him courageous without at the same time evaluating (commending) him.

Hare does not deny that within certain *words* description and evaluation are logically so closely tied together that, if you use one of these words as an engaged participant then you are thereby committed to the evaluation as well as the description. It *is* odd to *say*, "He promised to do X but he ought not to," or 'He is your father but you have no duty to help him," or "Smith is courageous but I do not approve of him," and so on. The oddness of such remarks, upon which descriptivists insist, as they are entitled to do, is not in Hare's view what is at issue. Hence his reminder about the difference between words and things. What is at issue is whether or not we can always differentiate with regard to the *thing* we call a promise, a father, courageous conduct, or whatever, between the factual statements we are thereby making about it and the value judgments under which we are thereby bringing it. Hare thinks we can. But all descriptivists find this distinction artificial. They insist, in their different ways, that one cannot hold facts and values apart like that.

It may be of some interest to refer at this point to one of the most remarkable recent arguments to this effect. It is to be found in Morton White's *What Is and What Ought to be Done* (New York and Oxford, 1981). He starts from a view, taken by W. V. Quine about scientific thinking, which is called corporatism. According to this view, whenever we test any of our individual beliefs, we are in effect always testing the whole corpus of them. The body of our beliefs purports to organize and predict our sensory experience. If it fails to do so, all the beliefs within it are thereby put in jeopardy, whether they be logical, practical, empirical, metaphysical, or whatever. That is to say, any one of them could conceivably be mistaken and call for revision in order to dispose of the experiential falsification which we have encountered. Now, White extends this idea to moral thinking. When we form a moral judgment, we have in effect derived it from a number of premises. If we subsequently begin to have doubts about it, that puts *all* these premises in jeopardy. Some of them will have been factual beliefs, some moral value judgments. But no matter. It is conceivable that any one of them should need revision because the moral judgment, to which they led us, now no longer commends itself to our moral feelings. The remarkable conclusion to which this line of argument leads is expressed by White in the closing sentences of his book as follows:

> . . . what corporatism implies (is) . . . that we have a right to reject a descriptive premise upon rejecting a moral conclusion while reorganizing our experiences and feelings. This shows that our moral feelings may legitimately influence our description of the world and that we must harmonize our experiences and those feelings while justifying any action we contemplate. (*What Is and What Ought to be Done*, p.124)

The words to fasten on are "our moral feelings may legitimately influence our description of the world." What White is doing here is eliminating a difference between facts and values which has been widely taken for granted. It is to the effect that, while facts are given, values are chosen; while we are free to decide what *ought* to be done, we are not free in the same way to decide what *is* the case. As the famous newspaperman put it: "Comment is free, facts are sacred." Against all that, White is putting forward the thesis that it is as open to us to decide what the facts are as to choose what our values will be. And not simply that. In the same way that factual discoveries may affect our moral judgments, so, White is saying, our moral judgments may "legitimately" affect our factual descriptions. He offers, by way of illustration, the case of abortion and argues thus. (I am foreshortening his argument but not, I hope, misrepresenting it.) Suppose, first, that someone comes to the conclusion that abortion is morally wrong by the following piece of reasoning:

(1) Anyone who destroys a human being does what ought not to be done.
(2) Acts of abortion destroy living foetuses.
(3) Every living foetus is a human being.
(4) Therefore, acts of abortion destroy human beings.
(5) Therefore, acts of abortion ought not to be done.

Now, suppose that his moral feelings begin to change. No one thing in particular makes them do so but gradually he loses his abhorrence of that which once seemed wicked to him. This is a very common experience. It occurs not only in consciences that are becoming more benighted, but also in those that are becoming more enlightened. According to White, such change puts in jeopardy all the premises from which the man in whom it has taken place argued to his one-time belief in the wickedness of abortion. So, in "harmonizing" his experience and his moral feelings, as White would have him do, this man can "legitimately" reject any of his premises. The one he may well reject is number (3) above: "Every living foetus is a human being." That is indeed what very many people cease to believe when they cease to think abortion wrong. But (3) is a putative statement of fact. So here is a case where "our moral feelings may legitimately influence our description of the world."

There is undoubtedly some truth in this view. The moral evaluations we make may affect our descriptions of objective reality. Compare, for example, the different ways in which two people, with different moral feelings about abortion, might describe it. Judith J. Thomson in her paper "A Defence of Abortion" (*Philosophy and Public Affairs*, 1., No. 1., 1971) takes a morally permissive view of it. In consequence, she can contemplate with equanimity descriptions of an act of abortion, which conceive of it as similar to unplugging oneself from a kidney machine, by means of which one's own kidneys are being used to cleanse someone else's blood and to which one has been attached without one's consent after being kidnapped. By contrast,

Mother Teresa, who regards abortion with unqualified moral disapproval, describes it in these terms: "Abortion is the greatest destroyer of peace because it is pure murder. If a mother can kill her own child, what is left for others but to kill each other?" Murder of one's defenceless child is a very different kind of action from getting out of a situation into which one has been shanghaied, even though compassion could conceivably inhibit one from performing the latter as well as the former. These differing descriptions of what is happening, when an abortion occurs, are certainly consequential upon differing value judgments.

However, this is not what is at issue. No one denies that there are words which combine descriptive and evaluative meaning; and that, if one approves of something, one may choose to describe it by words which have positive evaluative force. Look again at the premise (3) above: "All living foetuses are human beings." "Human" is a description with positive evaluative force. It is understandable that, whilst disapproving of abortion, the man in Morton White's illustration should have so described foetuses; and that, when he came to disapprove of abortion, he should have denied premise (3). There is certainly a sense in which he changed his beliefs about the facts—now he thought some foetuses, at least, are *not* human.

But are we entitled to say that, in such a case "ought" has entailed "is"? Does such a case prove that matters of fact are at the mercy of value judgments? The man's denial of premise (3) can be explained as due to his rejection of the *value* judgments implicit in "human". That is to say, "ought" simply entailed "ought", not "is".

Contrast his case with that of someone who thinks an abortion is wrong because he believes (i) 'All killing of foetuses over three months old is wrong" and (ii) "This foetus is over three months old." Suppose he then comes to think it would be right to perform the abortion. Would he, in any conceivable circumstances, be entitled to say *solely on the ground of the change in his value judgment about abortion* that the foetus concerned was *not* three months old? Surely not! It seems clear that there are some descriptive premises which are not at the mercy of changes in our evaluative conclusions as Morton White maintains *all* descriptive premises are.

Criteria and Choice

The second assumption that I said it is definitive of a descriptivist to deny is that we can always choose our own criteria of moral value. Here again it was Philippa Foot who most cogently took up the cudgels against prescriptivism. In her 1961 article "Goodness and Choice", she claims that a connection with the speaker's choice is neither a sufficient nor a necessary condition for the use of terms such as "good". It would be a *sufficient* condition if all that were required to make my use of "good" in "a good X" appropriate were the fact that I am ready to choose the kind of X which I have called good. It would be a *necessary* condition if, whenever I call an X a good X, one thing required to make my use of "good". appropriate were that I am ready to choose Xs of the kind to which I refer. Mrs. Foot's contention is that in neither case is the if-clause fulfilled. Is this contention correct? Consider these examples:

    I. A: Smith is a good father.
       B: But he neglects his children.
       A: I know.
       B: Then why do you call him good?
       A: If I could choose, I would always choose for myself,
          or others, a father who neglects his children.
       B: Oh, I see.

Does B's last remark make sense? Does he "see"? Can A, that is to say, *intelligibly* call fathers good because they neglect their children, provided only that this is a reason which he chooses to have for doing so? He could, if the readiness of the speaker to choose in accordance with the criteria invoked were a sufficient condition for the use of "good".

    II. A: Smith's son is a good lad.
       B: What do you mean?
       A: I mean that I would choose Smith's lad as a son
          any day.

Is that what A is saying? It is manifestly not all that he is saying, of course. But is it even *part* of what he is saying? It would be, if the speaker's readiness to choose in accordance with the criteria invoked were a necessary condition for the use of "good".

The answer to the questions which I pose after each of these conversations seems to be *no*. So, such examples as these appear to constitute *reductiones ad absurdum* of the views which Mrs. Foot is attacking. She attributes such views to Hare. In reply he contends that either: (i) Mrs. Foot is attributing to him views which he has never held, and there is really no difference of opinion between him and her; or (ii) she is maintaining a highly implausible position.

To support this contention he calls attention to an ambiguity in the expression "conditions for the use of a word" (*I–OQ*, p. 252). This latter expression, he says, may mean: (i) "conditions for a word being said to be used correctly to express what the speaker who calls a thing 'good' (for example) wishes to convey;" or (ii) "Conditions for a thing's being said to be 'good'." I take the relevance of this distinction to the point at issue to be, in Hare's intention, as follows:

The rules for the use of "good" are such that:

(i) Suppose that a man said "X is good," we asked him "Why?" and he replied "I am ready to choose X (or things like X)." This reply (to use an expression of Mrs. Foot's) does not "legitimatize" his words. His being ready to choose X is *not* a sufficient, nor a necessary condition of X's *being* good. He could be ready to choose X, and X not be good; X could be good, and he not be ready to choose it.

(ii) Now suppose that a man says "I *think* X good," we ask him "Do you really?" and he replies "Yes. I am ready to choose X." This reply does "legitimatize" his words. His being ready to choose X *is* a sufficient, and necessary, condition for saying that he thinks X good. If he is ready to choose it, we may safely say that he thinks it good; and if he thinks it good, we may safely say that he is ready to choose it.

If Mrs. Foot is simply saying that a speaker's being ready to choose X is neither a sufficient, nor a necessary, condition of X's being correctly said *to be* good, Hare has no quarrel with her. He claims that he has insisted upon this himself (*I–OQ*, p.253). If, on the other hand, Mrs. Foot is saying that the speaker's being ready to choose X is not a sufficient, or necessary , condition of his being correctly said to *think* X good, then Hare considers her contention "not very plausible" (*I–OQ*, p.254).

Hare's opponents, I think, would respond that all this is a missing of the point. Even if a distinction such as this can be drawn between what is thought good and what is good, the question remains: is it open to anyone to choose what the criteria for determining goodness shall be? Whether the goodness in question is moral or not does not affect the point at issue. I have referred earlier in this book (see above, p.207) to Warnock's insistence, against what he takes to be Hare's position, that we must not confuse: (i) being free to decide for ourselves in moral questions *on the evidence*; and (ii) being free to decide *what evidence is*. He represents Hare's position thus: "I do not, it seems, decide that flogging is wrong because I *am* against cruelty; rather, I decide that flogging is wrong because I *decide to be* against cruelty. And what, if I did make that decision, would be my ground for making it? That I am opposed to the deliberate infliction of pain? No—rather that I *decide to be* opposed to it. And so on." It seems to Warnock that if you allow this sort of thing—people making up, not only their own minds, but also their own evidence—all reasoning must necessarily be at an end. I argued above, against Warnock's view, that moral discourse is not essentially irrationalist if it amounts to no more than choosing reasons why things are good, etc., and being tested for consistency in one's choice. But I said that the question remained as to whether moral reasoning really does amount to no more than that. According to Mrs. Foot it amounts to more. One does not simply choose the criteria of goodness, moral or otherwise. Rather, in her words, "Criteria for the goodness of each and every kind of thing . . . are always determined, and not a matter for decision" (*I–OQ*, p.216). She admits what she calls "competition examples" as an exception; judges or examiners can, of course, decide quite arbitrarily what shall constitute criteria of goodness for the purpose of some competition. But, these apart, is her thesis supportable? The kind of example with which she endeavours to substantiate it is "a good knife," "a good rider," "a good father," etc. A good knife, she thinks, is one which fulfils the purposes for which knives are normally used, i.e. cutting; a good rider, one who achieves the characteristic purposes of the rider, e.g. pleasure, exercise, locomotion. We cannot say that a good knife is one which rusts quickly and justify this use of "good" simply by saying that that is the sort of knife which we choose for our own use. Nor can we say that a good rider is one who, like a clown in a circus, rides in such a way as to make people laugh, and justify this use of "good' simply by saying that that is what we want riders to achieve by riding. Such is not, says Mrs. Foot, "the language of mankind." Of fathers she writes:

> Being a good *father* must have something to do with bringing up children, and more specifically caring for them. While opinions may differ as to what is best for children, and while more or less of the children's care may be assigned to parents in different communities, it is only within such limits that the criteria of a good father will differ from place to place. If, in a certain community, a man were said to be a good A in so far as he offered his children up for sacrifice, 'A' could not be translated by our word 'father'. (*I—OQ*, p.219)

In none of these cases, according to Mrs. Foot, can a man simply choose what shall constitute the criteria of goodness. Something is taken for granted—the purposes to which things like knives are put, the point of an activity like riding, the conduct we look for in fathers. These impose a limit upon what the relevant criteria of goodness can be. If a speaker did not adhere to these in commending knives, riding, fathers—or whatever—we could not understand him.

In reply to all this, Hare points out that when some

things are called good an explanation seems called for; but
not when some other things are called good (*I–OQ*, p.254).
To take the sort of example around which this point in the
discussion has revolved, suppose a man persistently clasps
and unclasps his hands as he sits idly in his chair and tells us
that he thinks it a duty to do so. We shall be puzzled. Why?
Not, Hare would say, because it is a "logical absurdity" for
anyone to think this; but because it is a "contingent improb-
ability" that anyone should. Now suppose that someone
explains that our handclasping man is a sculptor who fends
off rheumatism by this exercise and does this so persistently
because he thinks that he has a duty to finish certain works
of art so that they will not be lost to posterity. We are
puzzled no longer. There is nothing contingently improbable
in a man thinking it his duty to bequeath as much pleasure
to posterity as he can. Though apart from some such "background" explanation, it is odd for anyone to speak of
clasping and unclasping his hands as a duty. But, Hare insists, odd, not because logically illegitimate, only because
contingently improbable.

> . . . The reason is that very few of us, if any, have the
> necessary "pro-attitude" to people who clasp and un-
> clasp their hands; and the reason for this is that the pro-
> attitudes which we have do not just occur at random,
> but have explanations, albeit not (as the descriptivists
> whom I am discussing seem to think) explanations which
> logic alone could provide . . . We do not have, most of us,
> any disposition to choose, or to choose to be, men who
> clasp and unclasp their hands. We do not, accordingly,
> think that men who do this are good.
>
> The explanation of our not thinking this is that such
> choices would hardly contribute to our survival, growth,
> procreation, &c; if there have been any races of men or
> animals who have made the clasping and unclasping of
> hands a prime object of their pro-attitudes, to the ex-
> clusion of other more survival-promoting activities, they
> have gone under in the struggle for existence. I am I
> know, being rather crude; but in general, to cut the mat-
> ter short, we have the pro-attitudes that we have, and

therefore call the things good which we do call good, because of their relevance to certain ends which are sometimes called "fundamental human needs". (*I–OQ*, pp. 225–26)

Once we have called something a "need", however, there *is* a logical connection between calling it that and saying that a good man, as such, must (logically) possess it. Hare does not, of course, deny this. He simply insists that the point to take is that this connection is between the *words* "need" and "good". He thinks that failure to take this point is the descriptivists' root error. In denying that we can always choose our own criteria of goodness—just as in denying that the descriptive and evaluative meanings of moral judgments can always be separated—they take truths about *words* for truths about things. From the fact that anything which is called a need must logically be called good, it does not follow that anything in particular must be called a need. One thing can (logically), just as much as another, be taken for a "fundamental human need"—to recall Hare's list above, nonsurvival, nongrowth, nonprocreation, just as much as their opposites.

The group of descriptivists to whom we shall now turn our attention all, in their different ways, find this conclusion of Hare's absurd. We must consider one by one the kinds of reason they find for doing so.

II. MORALITY GROUNDED IN HUMAN WANTS

In this section, I shall consider the view that moral value judgments are logically grounded in the fact that human agents have certain wants. According to this view, moral "oughts" are intelligible only in so far as they are about the satisfaction (or dissatisfaction) of certain wants that the agents to whom they refer have. But there are two rather different versions of this view. To put things very crudely, one is that "ought" *means* "wants"; the other, that "wants" provides a *conclusive reason* for "ought". I will take them in turn.

(I) "OUGHT" TAKEN TO MEAN "WANTS"

Is it true *by definition* of "ought" that we ought to do what, in some sense or other, we want to do? The opinion has recently been canvassed by some philosophers that we can (logically) say in terms of "want" everything which, in the normal course of events, we would ever wish to say in terms of "ought" (e.g. M. Zimmerman, "The 'Is-Ought': An Unnecessary Dualism", *M* LXX1, 1962, reprinted in my *The Is-Ought Question*, and D. H. Munro, *Empiricism and Ethics*, Cambridge, 1967).

This opinion should, first of all, be quite clearly differentiated from others with which it seems easily to be confused. It is emphatically an opinion on a point of logic, not of psychology. That is to say, it has nothing to do with whether or not people will strive for X as strenuously if they think of it only as what they want, as they would if they thought of it as something which they ought to attain. Our concern is simply with the question: can we *say* in terms of "want" everything which we now say in terms of "ought"?

The precise meaning of the "want" in question may, of course, be open to much discussion. Someone who believes in the universalizability of moral judgments, for instance, may wish to say that "I ought to do X" means, not simply "I want to do X," but "I want to do X and I want others to do X;" and again, someone who thinks that the important feature of moral judgments is that they are overriding may wish to say that "I ought to do X" means "X is what I most want to do." For the moment, however, I shall leave all such refinements aside and simply consider the question: are there any patent differences between the ordinary uses of the words "want" and "ought" respectively, which discredit the view that their meanings can be equated?

It has sometimes been held that the use of "ought" has to be supported by reasons, whereas that of "want" does not. But against this it can be pointed out that, in many contexts, it is as natural to expect a reason for what is said to be wanted as for what it is said ought to be done. It is true that one feature which differentiates moral judgments from expressions of taste or descriptions of likes and dislikes is the fact that reasons are normally expected in the former case, as perhaps not in the latter. If I said "I ought to go on strike," and when asked "Why?" replied, "What do you mean 'Why?' I just ought," I should put my reputation as a reasonable man in jeopardy, as I should not if I said "I want to go on strike"—whether this was taken as an expression of, or description of, my feelings—and when asked "Why?" replied that I just did. But such cases may not be indicative of any very significant difference between "want" and "ought." For one thing, there are occasions on which it would be perfectly natural to turn aside the demand for a reason when one has used "ought." If I said, for example, "I ought to pay my debts" and to the question "Why?" replied, "What do you mean 'Why?' I just ought," that would be a natural thing to say. Moreover, not only are there some such occasions, but on all occasions when moral judgments have been voiced, they seem to be constituted, in the last analysis, by an appeal to something which just is, or is said to be, the case. If, for example, having judged that capital punishment is wrong because it contributes nothing to the general happiness, I were asked, "But why does that make it wrong?" I would, if I were a utilitarian, have to reply "It just does." If there is a logical gap between "want" and "ought," then, whatever else may constitute it, it can hardly be the fact that the justification of one as against the other rests upon that for which no further reason can be given. For, in the last analysis, they both do.

Another ground which has been offered for rejecting the definition of "ought" in terms of "want" is the fact that it makes perfectly good sense to say that I doubt whether I ought to do what I want to do. This, we are told, cannot mean that I doubt whether I want to do what I want to do, because that does not make sense. But does it not? Would it, for example, necessarily be meaningless if I said to my wife, "I don't know whether I want to do what I want to do or what you want to do"? It might prove me an infuriatingly indecisive spouse, but it would not be gibberish (cf. Munro, *Empiricism and Ethics*, pp. 208ff). "Want", of course, is being used in two different senses here. I am saying something like "I don't know whether I want (in the sense of 'most want' or 'want after reflection'—*sense 1*) to do what I want (in the sense of 'feel a strong desire at the moment'—*sense 2*) to do or what you want (in either of the two senses) to do." If "ought" were defined in terms of "want" (sense 1), then the statement "I doubt whether I ought to do what I want to do" could mean "I doubt whether I want (sense 1) to do what I want (sense 2) to do." It could, therefore, make sense to say that I doubt whether I want to do what I want to do, and so the simple contention that it could not, is not sufficient to dispose of the view that "ought" means "wants."

But can we simply say that "ought" means "wants" in either of the senses differentiated as 1 and 2? I do not think so. I think that there is a further distinction (cf. K. Hanly, "Zimmerman's Is—Is: Schizophrenic Monism", *M* LXXIII, 1964, reprinted in my *The Is-Ought Question*) which can, and must, be drawn, if there is to be any hope of equating the meanings of "ought" and "want." An illustration will help to make this distincion clear. Smith belongs to a religious sect which forbids members to marry unbelievers, i.e. people who do not belong to the sect. Now consider this conversation:

Smith: I do not want to marry Mary Jones.
Questioner: Why?
Smith: Because she is an unbeliever.

The questioner's "Why?" may be taken in two senses. He may be asking what *causes* Smith not to want to marry Mary Jones. If that is the question, Smith's reply explains his not wanting to marry Mary Jones by bringing the latter occurrence under some such causal generalization as: whenever Smith finds that a girl is an unbeliever he loses all desire to marry her. But the questioner may be asking what *reason* Smith has for not wanting to marry Mary Jones. Then Smith's reply will explain his first remark by bringing it under some such general principle of selection, or classification, as "Never marry an unbeliever." Smith's "want" in "I don't want to marry Mary Jones" thus has two possible senses, corresponding to these possible interpretations of his questioner's "Why?" In one, "want" is used simply to describe Smith's psychological condition, a sense to which causal explanations are appropriate (call it the descriptive sense). In the other sense, Smith's "want" is being used to evaluate, or classify, Mary Jones; this is the sense to which principles of selection are appropriate (call it the classificatory sense).

If "ought" could be defined in terms of "want," it would have to be in terms of this latter (classificatory) sense, for "ought" is never used simply to describe a psychological condition, as "want" sometimes is. We noted above that it is as natural in many contexts to ask a reason for what is said to be wanted as for what it is said ought to be done. But we see now that these must all be contexts in which "want" is being used in what I have called its classificatory sense.

Remember that the whole point of the attempt to define "ought" in terms of "want" which we are considering in this section is to bridge, or rather eliminate, the logical gap between "is" and "ought." But if what I have been saying is correct, the only sense of "want" in which it might conceivably be used to define "ought" is one which leaves the gap as wide open as ever. Smith's move from the statement of fact "Mary Jones is an unbeliever" to the "classificatory" utterance "I do not want to marry her" is not a straightforward move from "is" to "want." "I do not want to marry her" is not a factual description of his psychological condition but, in some sense, an *evaluation* of Mary Jones. The logical gap between description and evaluation is still there, and can be bridged only by the principle of evaluation "Never marry an unbeliever." All the logical objections to defining "ought" in terms of "is" apply to defining "want" (the evaluative, or classificatory, sense) in purely descriptive terms.

To summarize then: (i) "Want," if it is to define "ought," will have to be used in its evaluative, classificatory, or selective, sense—call it what you will—as distinct from its

purely descriptive sense. That is to say, it will have to be
used in the sense for which reasons, as distinct from causes,
can be given. (ii) When it is so used, a principle of evaluation or selection is always logically necessary to bridge the
gap between any statement of fact and any expression of
wanting or not wanting. (iii) Such principles of selection are
not analytic and so, however they bridge the gap, it is not
by definition. Though I have attempted to defend it against
some criticisms, I find myself unable, therefore, to accept
this view that "ought" means "wants."

(II) "WANTS" AS PROVIDING A CONCLUSIVE REASON FOR "OUGHT"

I turn then to the alternative version of the view that
"ought" is logically grounded in "wants," namely that
"wants" provides a conclusive reason for "ought." The first
thing to notice is that, if a man has a reason for doing anything, he surely has a reason for doing what he wants. There
is a certain finality about "Because I want to," when given
as an answer to "Why are you doing that?" What is the
point of reasoning about action at all, if not to get what
one wants? As Professor Kurt Baier remarks: "Our very
purpose in 'playing the reasoning game' is to maximize
satisfactions and minimize frustrations. Deliberately to
frustrate ourselves and to minimize satisfaction would
certainly be to go counter to the very purpose for which
we deliberate and weigh the pros and cons. These criteria
are, therefore, necessarily linked with the very purpose of
the activity of reasoning. In so far as we enter on that 'game'
at all, we are therefore bound to accept these criteria" (see
his *The Moral Point of View* (New York, 1958), pp. 301–3).
We can (logically) think of any such reason as "Because
doing X will be the keeping of a promise" as a reason which
I have *chosen* to adopt. We can think that I might *not* have
done so. It is not taken for granted that I would be mad
(insane), if I had not. But with "Because I want to . . . " the
case is different. To quote Baier again: "There is a correct
use of the word 'mad' and . . . people who prefer whatever
they do not enjoy doing to whatever they do differ from

normal people in just such fundamental and undesirable respects as would make the word 'mad' correctly applicable to them" (*ibid.*, p. 303).

It seems to follow from what I have just been saying that moral judgments, in so far as they give us reasons for action, must be grounded in wants. This is the view that Mrs. Philippa Foot has propounded and defended in a number of papers, including "Moral Beliefs" (1958–9), "Morality as a System of Hypothetical Imperatives" (1972), "Reasons for Actions and Desires" (1977) and "Are Moral Considerations Overriding?" (1978). They are bound up together in her collection, *Virtues and Vices* (Oxford, 1978) and my page references to those papers will be to that book. It has an Introduction in which she outlines the development of her ideas. There is a significant development, as we shall see, from the conception of "wants" as "interests" in her earlier writings to that of them as "desires" in her later work.

Mrs. Foot's Earlier View

She starts, in effect, from the point we were considering a moment ago, that if a man has a reason for doing anything, he has a reason for doing what he wants. As she puts it in "Moral Beliefs": "anyone is given a reason for action when he is shown the way to something he wants (*VV*, p. 127). Either the doing of the action itself, or its consequences, could conceivably be what the agent wants. but, either way, it is the fact that there is something he wants which gives him a reason for acting.

However, as Mrs. Foot immediately goes on to say, there are two sorts of want: "for some wants the question 'Why do you want that?' will make sense and for others it will not." Most of the wants to which we give voice are of the former kind. Where do we want to live; what do we want to wear; which job do we want to do; whom do we want to marry; and so on. When we have decided such matters, the question, "Why do you want that?" will make perfectly good sense. But, according to Mrs. Foot, there are wants of the other kind, for which this question does not make sense. What are they? She lists them as wanting to be free from "boredom, loneliness, pain, discomfort, or certain kinds of incapacity." Suppose someone said "Why do you want not to be bored, or lonely, or in pain, or uncomfortable, or lame or mad?" This is a question to which the answer a normal man would give, in each case, is something like, "I just do." That, however, is not really an answer but merely a reiteration of what is in question, namely the want for which a reason is asked. It is nevertheless an appropriate reply because the question admits of no other answer.

Wants of this second kind are both ultimate and universal. They are ultimate, in the sense that.in satisfying them action finds its final justification. If you ask a man, for instance, why he wants to go on living in his home town, he may well answer "Because I shan't be lonely there"; or why he wants to leave it, "Because it bores me stiff." These are good reasons for staying or going, as the case may be. None better could be conceived. Moreover, the wants in which they are grounded—for freedom from loneliness, boredom—are wants that everyone—outside an asylum as Mrs. Foot would say (cf. *VV*, p. 122)—will have. They are as universal as they are ultimate.

Moral judgments, in so far as they are intended to direct what is done, purport to give us reasons for action. If they are such as a reasonable human being can accept, then they must, on Mrs. Foot's basic presupposition, "show us the way to something we want." And if moral judgments are to be as *binding* and *universal* as moral philosophers have conceived them to be, then this "something we want" must, in the last analysis, be a want of her second kind, i.e. a want which all men have and for which it does not make sense to ask why they want it.

Mrs. Foot recognized that these early conclusions left her with a problem, where justice is concerned. In the case of the other three cardinal virtues, it is fairly easy to show that they satisfy wants of her second kind. A courageous man will the better defend himself against injury; a prudent man, the better avoid incapacity; a temperate man, be less likely to incur various sorts of pain; and so on. But what of justice? Here is Mrs. Foot on her problem:

But what, it will be asked, of justice? For while prudence,

courage and temperance are qualities which benefit the man who has them, justice seems rather to benefit others, and to work to the disadvantage of the just man himself. Justice . . . covers all those things owed to other people; it is under injustice that murder, theft and lying come, as well as the withholding of what is owed for instance by parents to children and by children to parents, as well as the dealings which would be called unjust in everyday speech. So the man who avoids injustice will find himself in need of things he has returned to their owner, unable to obtain an advantage by cheating and lying; involved in all those difficulties painted by Thrasymachus in the first book of the Republic, in order to show that injustice is more profitable than justice to a man of strength and wit. We will be asked how, on our theory, justice can be a virtue and injustice a vice, since it will surely be difficult to show that any man whatsoever must need to be just as he needs the use of his hands and eyes, or needs prudence, courage and temperance. (*VV*, p. 125)

Unless we can find a solution to this problem, which shows that justice repays the just man in terms of the satisfaction of his ultimate wants, says Mrs. Foot, "then justice can no longer be recommended as a virtue." She expresses some surprise that modern moral philosophers seem so reluctant to countenance this possibility and advises them to consider it. Plato in the *Republic* took it for granted that if justice is not a good to the just man, then moralists who recommend it as a virtue are guilty of fraud. But contemporary moralists seem content to accept Thrasymachus' premise—that injustice is more profitable than justice—and yet to go on insisting that justice is nonetheless a virtue. For her own part, Mrs. Foot was sure, at this early stage in her reflections, that justice is profitable and therefore a virtue. Here she is on the solution of her problem:

Is it true . . . to say that justice is not something a man needs in his dealings with his fellow, supposing only that he is strong? Those who think that he can get on perfectly

well without being just should be asked to say exactly
how such a man is supposed to live. We know that he is
to practise injustice whenever the unjust act would bring
him advantage; but what is he to say? Does he admit
that he does not recognise the rights of other people, or
does he pretend? In the first case even those who combine with him will know that on a change of fortune, or
a shift of affection, he may turn to plunder them, and he
must be as wary of their treachery as they are of his.
Presumably the happy unjust man is supposed . . . to be
a very cunning liar and actor, combining complete
injustice with the appearance of justice . . . Philosophers
often speak as if a man could thus hide himself even
from those around him, but the supposition is doubtful,
and in any case the price in vigilance would be colossal.
If he lets even a few people see his true attitude he must
guard himself against them; if he lets no one into the
secret he must always be careful in case the least spont-
aneity betray him. Such facts are important because the
need a man has for justice in dealings with other men
depends on the fact that they are men and not inanimate
objects or animals. If a man only needed other men as he
needs household objects, and if men could be manipu-
lated like household objects, or beaten into a reliable
submission like donkeys, the case would be different.
As things are, the supposition that injustice is more
profitable than justice is very dubious, although like
cowardice and intemperance it might turn out incidently
to be profitable. (*VV*, pp. 128–29)

So, in Mrs. Foot's estimation, there are two main counter-
considerations to set against the possibility that justice is
not a virtue. (i) If a man is to be unjust successfully, he will
have to deceive people into thinking he is really a just man;
it will be hard to do that all the time and cause him no small
inconvenience. (ii) Many of his relationships with other
people will be depersonalized in the process; he will have
to treat people as things, "thou's" as "it's", and this will
impoverish his own life. In a word, then, injustice does not
pay. It is in a man's own interest to avoid it. Justice is
profitable and therefore a virtue after all!

Perhaps some seeds of doubt about all this were germinating in Mrs. Foot's mind as she came to the end of her early paper called "Moral Beliefs", for she concluded it thus:

> The reason why it seems to some people so impossibly difficult to show that justice is more profitable than injustice is that they consider in isolation particular just acts. It is perfectly true that if a man is just it follows that he will be prepared, in the event of very evil circumstances, even to face death rather than to act unjustly— for instance, in getting an innocent man convicted of a crime of which he has been accused. For him it turns out that his justice brings disaster on him, and yet like anyone else he had good reason to be a just and not an unjust man. He could not have it both ways and while possessing the virtue of justice hold himself ready to be unjust should any great advantage accrue. The man who has the virtue of justice is not ready to do certain things, and if he is too easily tempted we shall say that he was ready after all (*VV*, pp. 129–30)

Well no, he certainly could not have it both ways: he could not have the virtue of justice and be ready to do unjust things. There is no doubt about that. But, if a just man may have to die in order to remain just, room is left for doubt about some other things. In particular, about two: namely whether justice pays on the one hand; and whether it is a virtue, on the other. Common sense raises doubt of the first kind. Conceivably, it could pay a man, in terms of freedom from boredom, loneliness and the rest of his ultimate wants to *live* justly, but how can it pay him *in those terms* to *die* justly? That is the first doubt. Mrs. Foot's insistence that a virtue must be profitable raises doubt of the second kind. If justice could require a man to die and thereby put an end to all possible satisfactions, how can it be a virtue in the sense that it pays?

Criticism of Mrs. Foot's Early View

On at least four counts this attempt to ground morality in wants that are ultimate and universal has been subject to criticism from other philosophers, notably D. Z. Phillips (see his "Does it Pay to be Good?", *PAS*, LXIV, 1964–5; and, with H. O. Mounce, "On Morality's Having a Point", *P*, XL 1965. The latter is reprinted in my *The Is-Ought Question*, to which the page numbers below refer).

The first two criticisms have to do with matters of empirical fact. For one, it is by no means as obvious as Mrs. Foot makes out that there are wants which are ultimate and universal. If we go through her list of such wants—viz. for freedom from boredom, loneliness, pain, discomfort, incapacity—we can think in each case of people who appear to have wanted other things more than these. Perhaps the most convincing item in her list is freedom from incapacity. She says of physical capacity, "the proper use of his limbs is something a man has reason to want if he wants anything" (*VV*, p. 122) and adds that only a lunatic would think otherwise. But against this, Phillips and Mounce (*I–OQ*, p. 237) invoke the counter-examples of St. Paul, who thanked God that his "thorn in the flesh" kept him mindful of his own insufficiency; and Brentano, who was grateful for his blindness in old age because it enabled him to philosophize without distraction. I suppose the reply from Mrs. Foot's side to such counter-examples would be that they only make sense because St. Paul and Brentano wanted freedom from another kind of incapacity—viz. spiritual pride or wandering thoughts—which their physical incapacities enabled them to have. So, perhaps there is not much in this first criticism.

The second one, I think, is more cogent. It calls in question Mrs. Foot's confident belief that the unjust man's personal relationships are inevitably impoverished by his injustice. She seems to assume that, once people catch him lying or cheating, they will regard him with suspicion for ever; and, consequently, that he will have to go in for more and more lying and cheating once he has started. But is this so? Two facts at least should be taken into account. One, that people are prepared to tolerate a certain amount of injustice in others because they know that they are not innocent of it themselves; and the other, that a certain amount of lying and cheating is sometimes necessary to keep personal relationships harmonious. (Moralists may not feel that it is very edifying to call attention to this fact, but fact I think it is.) To say the least, matters are more complicated than Mrs. Foot takes them to be. True, if a man lies and cheats at every turn, he will probably end up with no friends left. But it is false to suppose that any degree of injustice whatsoever will make one's personal relationships less secure or rewarding than they would otherwise be. Mrs. Foot eventually came to think, as we shall see, that people feel there is "an element of deception in the official line" about the autonomous authority of the moral law. But have they not even more reason to think this about her own early line that justice pays?

A third criticism is that this grounding of "ought" in "wants" gets things the wrong way round. Recall what was said a few moments ago about St. Paul and Brentano. I suggested that they lacked aversion to their physical incapacities because these protected them from incapacities of another kind. But why did St. Paul want to be protected from spiritual pride or Brentano from distracting thoughts? The answers lie in how they thought they ought to live— St. Paul, in dependence upon God, Brentano in dedicated intellectual inquiry. These moral value judgments determined what they wanted, not the other way round. Phillips and Mounce further illustrate this point from a typical disagreement between a Roman Catholic housewife and a scientific rationalist about the morality of birth control. Are we to say that such people disagree only about the means which will most completely satisfy wants which they both have? Is the issue between them one which can be settled by appeal to the facts about what will most effectively satisfy wants they share? The authors I refer to think not. The rationalist and the housewife, they say, want different things; and that because they have different ideas of how we ought to live:

> How would the scientific rationalist and the housewife reach the agreement which some philosophers seem to think inevitable if all the facts were known? It is hard to see how they could without renouncing what they believe in. Certainly, one cannot regard their respective

moral opinions as hypotheses which the facts will either
confirm or refute, for what would the evidence be? For
the rationalist, the possibility of the mother's death or
injury, the economic situation of the family, the provision
of good facilities for the children, and so on, would be
extremely important. The housewife too agrees about
providing the good things of life for children, but believes
that one ought to begin by allowing them to enter the
world. For her, submission to the will of God, the honour
of motherhood, the creation of a new life, and so on,
are of the greatest importance. But there is no settling of
the issue in terms of some supposed common evidence
called human good and harm, since what they differ
over is precisely the question of what constitutes human
good and harm. The same is true of all fundamental
moral disagreements, for example, the disagreement
between a pacifist and a militarist. The argument is unlikely to proceed very far before deadlock is reached.
(*I–OQ*, pp. 238–39)

What does all this come to? So far from accepting Mrs.
Foot's view that all moral "oughts" are grounded in wants,
Phillips and Mounce contend that things are seen the right
way round only when it is recognized that moral judgments
determine what those who make them want and not, or not
always, *vice versa*.

A fourth criticism of Mrs. Foot's early view of the
grounding of moral obligation is that it attempts the logically
impossible. An obligation may be autonomous or heteronomous; that is to say its justification may be conceived to lie
in itself or in some purpose beyond itself. Mrs. Foot attempts
a heteronomous justification of the moral "ought:" men
ought to act justly because it will pay them in terms of
freedom from boredom, loneliness, etc., to do so. But how
can justice be conceived to have any justification other
than itself? How can the moral "ought" be moral and not
autonomous? To give a heteronomous account of it, as
Mrs. Foot does, is to attempt to justify justice from something other than its justice. And that is logically impossible.

Phillips in his paper "Does It Pay to be Good?" takes

this line uncomprisingly. Mrs. Foot's idea that justice pays, he insists "has nothing to do with morality" (p. 55). The just man does not need any reason for action other than that what he is doing is just. That is "the way to something he wants" since all he wants *qua* just man is to be just. In so far as he is looking for something else, such as freedom from boredom or loneliness, he is simply a bored or lonely man and not necessarily a just one. If he is frustrated in his search for interesting occupations or congenial company, that will be a disaster to him from some points of view, but not from that of his justice. As a just man the only disaster he can suffer is to be unjust. As Phillips puts it, "for anyone concerned about justice, death for the sake of justice is not a disaster" (*ibid.*, p. 50). Phillips takes this point as far as it will go. He rejects altogether the Aristotelian view that the justice of an act can lie in the purpose it serves and takes the Stoic line that it can only lie in the act itself. He quotes Kirkegaard to the effect that "to will the good is to will one thing;" and J. C. Stocks, that "morality may call on a man at any moment to surrender the most promising avenue to this own perfection." The point of both quotations Phillips takes to be that an act, if just, must be just at the moment of its performance, not in virtue of any end to which it is the means, however lofty that end may be. In Stocks' words, "the act must first be shown to be right now before it can be relied upon to build up righteousness in the future" (*ibid.*, p. 59). The ground Phillips gives for all this is that "if the reason for moral actions is said to be beyond the actions themselves, it follows that actions are morally indifferent for anyone who follows this rule . . . it no longer matters to him whether he does one thing rather than another" (*ibid.*, p. 53). All that matters is finding some means to the end. Hence, even if that end is his own moral perfection, your just man must be ready to surrender it for the sake of the justice of an act.

I am more than a little inclined to think that Phillips has overstated his case. What is meant by "moral perfection" if not a disposition to act justly? And if that is what it is, then there is surely something contradictory, and not just para-doxical, in the idea that one may have to abandon the quest for moral perfection in order to act justly. How could one pursue that end except by acting justly? If the answer is "in no other way," then how could the pursuit of that end be morally incompatible with the performance of a just act?

However, there can be no doubt that this fourth criticism, stated more soberly, has much force. Something essential to the concept of morality is violated, when the just man is thought of as someone who expects his morality to pay him in heteronomous terms and sees no point in it unless it does. Mrs. Foot herself came to see that, in so far as her early views leave us there, they will not do.

Mrs. Foot's Later Views

In the Introduction to her 1978 book, *Virtues and Vices*, Mrs. Foot looks back on her earlier views and acknowledges that she "came to grief over justice" (*VV*, p. xiii). Whilst retaining her opinion that moral judgments are logically grounded in human wants, she was led by this acknowledgment to change her views about the nature of these wants. She ceased to think of them as wants which express an interest in one's own well-being and came to think of them as ones that are inspired by a desire for the well-being of others. The way in which this change came about can, I think, be accurately described as follows.

At the time of the early views, which we considered a moment or two ago, Mrs. Foot had accepted uncritically what she now describes as "the oft-repeated dictum that moral judgments necessarily give reasons for acting to each and every man" (*ibid.*). She shared in the widely-held, kantian-type of opinion that the moral "ought" constitutes a reason for acting that is both *conclusive* and *universal*. She did not consider that the reason must be categorical; from the first, she thought of it as grounded in certain ultimate wants that all men have, i.e. as hypothetical. Nevertheless, the fact that these wants are ultimate, makes the "ought" grounded in them conclusive, as a reason for acting, just as the fact that all men have them makes it a universal one. Now, the only wants which are ultimate and universal, it seemed to Mrs. Foot, are those of self-interest. It followed that moral obligations must satisfy self-interest.

Mrs. Foot found it comparatively easy to show that the virtues of courage, temperance, and prudence, do so. But what of justice? We saw above how she insisted that it too must serve the ends of self-interest. For a long time she refused to concede the point her opponents made against her, viz. that sometimes justice does *not* do so. But in the Introduction to her 1978 book, she finds she can no longer deny it—"it seems obvious that a man who acts justly must on occasion be ready to go against his own interests . . . " (*ibid*.). It is this obvious fact, she now concedes, which brings her early views to grief.

There were but two steps she could take from here. Either she must abandon the opinion that justice is a virtue— a step, it will be remembered, which she had once invited her opponents, who called her attention to the obvious facts about justice, to take. Or alternatively, she must find some logical ground for virtue and moral obligation, other than that of self-interest. It was this latter step Mrs. Foot took. She turned her attention away from wants inspired by self-interest to those which spring from the desire for others' good.

> A moral man must be ready to go against his interests in the particular case, and if he has reason to act morally the reason will lie rather in what he wants than in what is to his advantage. On this basis reasons will exist for many kind and upright men. We readily accept private affection as giving reasons for actions without the least hint of self-interest; why should a more extended fellow-feeling not do the same? If a man has that basic sense of identification with others that makes him care whether or not they live wretched lives, has he not the best possible reason for charitable action? And would it not be misrepresentation to speak of this as a charity dependent on the feelings and inclinations of the moment, since both public and private affections endure through periods of coldness, and lack of inclination never destroys the reason to act . . .

> We should also take into account, here and elsewhere, the desires that people have to live a certain kind of life.

Of course these desires vary greatly from person to person. One man likes to be useful; another demands a part in some great and noble cause. Perhaps it will be said that such people choose the life they choose because they think they *ought* to do so—because this is how a man ought to live. But perhaps no such thought, with its problematic reason-giving force, enters into the matter at all. Without any moral imperatives a man may have such desires. (*VV*, pp. 154–55)

At a single stride, she here leaves behind her erstwhile kantian obsession with "oughts" that are conclusive and universal, together with all the trouble it had caused her.

As for the putative universability of moral "oughts," she makes no attempt to argue that everyone has the "sense of identification with others, that makes him care," in which she now sees morality as grounded. Those who have it have it in varying degrees, and some do not have it at all. Moreover, in so far as it is basically a matter of "public and private affections," it is not something we can will ourselves to have. We cannot control our feelings as we can our actions. There is, therefore, no point in telling a man who lacks these feelings of concern for others, that he ought to have them. As Mrs. Foot spells it out, her present theory of the logical grounding of moral judgment "disallows the possibility of saying that a man ought . . . to have ends other than those he does have, e.g. that the uncaring amoral man ought to care about the relief of suffering or the protection of the weak" (*VV*, p. 170). Moral reasons for action, on this account of them, will weigh with some people, but not with others. And this, not simply for the psychological reason that the others have weak wills and so fail to do what they ought to do; but for the *logical* reason that there is no point in telling an uncaring man that he ought to do X, if the "ought" is a hypothetical one, as Mrs. Foot says it is, presupposing ends which the man addressed does not have. So far from being universal in their scope, then, moral judgments, on this view of their logical basis, only apply to those who have "wants," "affections," "feelings," "inclinations," "desires"—as Mrs. Foot variously calls them—"to

live a certain kind of life." The abandonment of the universality of moral obligation could scarcely be more complete.

What next, of its conclusive, or categorical, nature? Mrs.
Foot as we noted above had never believed that moral
judgments are categorical in the strictly kantian sense. Her
analysis of "You ought to do X" was "You ought to do X,
if you have certain wants." But in her early writings she had
spoken of these wants as (a) ones that all men have, and (b)
ones for which the question "Why do you want that?" does
not arise. These two considerations brought her conception
of moral obligation close enough to Kant's for her to think
of it as having what she later referred to as a special binding-
force, or an automatic reason-giving force. In her later
writings, however, she repudiated this view as entirely as
she rejected the view that moral judgments are universal.

In a paper called "Morality as a System of Hypothetical
Imperatives," (first published in 1972) she described as a
"fugitive thought" (*VV*, p. 163) the idea that the moral
"ought" has—to recall some of her descriptions of its supposed categoricalness—"a special dignity and neccessity," a
"binding force," an "inescapability," a "magic" force. Why
"fugitive"? Her point was that, when you try to find some
logical ground for this idea, you never can. Is it grounded in
physical or mental compulsion? No, for it is only in the
absence of such conditions that moral "oughts" apply. Is it
then grounded in the penalty we shall incur, if we disobey
the "ought"? No again, for the necessity of acting morally
is not supposed to depend on rewards and punishments.
Does it then take its binding-force from the demands of
rational consistency? Mrs. Foot will not have that; it would
land her in Hare's camp. Where then? The question seems
unanswerable. But why should we suppose that there *must*
be an answer? Says Mrs. Foot: "Suppose that what we take
for a puzzling thought were really no thought at all but
only a reflection of our *feelings* about morality. Perhaps it
makes no sense to say that we 'have to' submit to the moral
law, or that 'morality' is inescapable in some special way"
(*ibid.*).

She does not, of course, deny that the moral "ought" is
spoken of as if it were categorical, especially by those who

are instructing the young. We do not say to our children, "You ought to keep your promises, *if* you feel like it" or "You ought not to steal anything unless you want to." This, it seems to Mrs. Foot, is the clue to where the supposed inescapable binding-force of the moral "ought" is *really* grounded. It is simply in "the way morality is taught" (*VV*, p. 162). The thought of morality's categoricalness is only "fugitive" until we run it to earth in the instruction given by parents and teachers. But, of course, the mere fact that such instruction is designed to make us *feel* that the moral "ought" is inescapable does not prove that it is.

Comparison of Morality and Etiquette

Are we not taught in a similar way to regard the rules of good manners as unconditional? Our parents did not say "You must not interrupt unless you feel like it" or "You must not keep all the sweets for yourself unless you want to" any more than they said that truth-telling and respect for other people's property are conditional obligations. True, good manners are not commonly taken to have the same binding-force as good morals; and that, momentarily, gives Mrs. Foot pause. But again she looks to the way things are taught for an explanation. In her essay "Are Moral Considerations Overriding?", she says that good manners are taught "as a rigid set of rules that are on occasion to be broken" (*VV*, p. 186). That is to say, we are given to understand that there are times when we must cast aside entirely considerations of what it is polite to do. If, for instance, a building is burning down, we are not required to knock on people's doors and wait to be given permission to enter, before we dash in to rescue them. But now, mark the contrast with what we are taught about good morals.

> Moral rules are not taught as rigid rules that it is some-
> times right to ignore; rather we teach that it is sometimes
> *morally permissible* to tell lies (social lies), break prom-
> ises (as e.g. when ill on the day of an appointment) and
> refuse help (when the cost of giving it would be as we
> say disproportionate). So we tend, in our teaching, to
> accommodate the exceptions *within* morality, and with

> this flexibility it is not surprising that morality can seem "unconditional" and "absolute". In the official code of behaviour morality appears as strong because it takes care never to be on the losing side. (*VV*, pp. 186—87)

That is to say, we are taught that we must never cast aside moral considerations altogether, as we may sometimes cast aside good manners. We are brought up to regard morality as ultimate in a sense in which etiquette is not. Mrs. Foot's point is that, whereas we have been *psychologically* conditioned to regard moral considerations as more important than those of other kinds, it is not *logically* necessary that we should do so.

D. Z. Phillips in his paper, "In Search of the Moral Must" (*PQ*, 27, No. 107, 1977) challenges this attempt to reduce the binding-force of moral obligation to the level of that which etiquette has; and insists that it is part of the *concept* of morality that moral considerations are overriding. Accepting for the purposes of the argument Mrs. Foot's contention that moral obligation is grounded in desire, or caring, for the welfare of others, which only some people have, Phillips contends that, in so far as such caring is what we would normally mean by moral concern, those who have it will necessarily regard it as "unconditional," in the sense that it does not yield to considerations of any other kind. He illustrates his point from the case of a great, but gracious, man, who, if some ignoramus offers to shake hands with him instead of bowing to him as protocol requires, will accept the outstretched hand rather than cause the ignoramus embarrassment. The great man will feel that he ought to set the moral consideration, that one should not hurt other people's feelings, above the rules of etiquette.

To this Mrs. Foot replies that this is only so when the inconvenience caused is not too great. Then she offers a counter-example of her own. Suppose a man giving a party observes that some of his guests, who will have to drive home, have already had rather too much to drink. If he goes on filling their glasses, they will be drunk when they drive home and may kill or injure someone. It is time they stopped drinking. But will this host, if he is a man who cares about morality, necessarily feel that he ought to put the drink away? Not in "circles familiar to many of us," thinks Mrs. Foot. Good manners would forbid it. But, she adds, "to say that no one in these circles 'cares about' morality would be a bit stiff." It does not seem to her that, if a person fails to put a certain concern above all others, it cannot be a moral concern. Phillips, who thinks it cannot, will—she contends—have to say of the host in her example *either* (i) that he does not really care about morality *or* (ii) that, should an accident occur, involving one of his drunken guests, he will inevitably feel remorse. The former point is about the meaning of "care." Mrs. Foot dismisses it as trivial, presumably on the ground that all it amounts to is giving a certain definition to "care" and then insisting it be used in that sense. But this is only trivial, if the said definition is stipulative. If it is lexical, Phillips surely has the right to ask whether we would say the host in Mrs. Foot's illustration cared about the moral obligation to prevent death and suffering. She thinks that the second supposition above— that the host, if he cares about morality, will feel remorse should an accident occur, is simply not true. She writes with reference to Phillips: "Has he not noticed that it is quite common for people who do care about morality to admit that some of the things they do are morally indefensible and never lose a wink of sleep over it? Only a philosopher could say the kinds of things that Professor Phillips says; and if the Martians take the writings of moral philosophers as a guide to what goes on on this planet they will get a shock when they arrive" (*VV*, p. 186). To this I think Phillips has some right to reply, as he does, that if they come armed with testimonials from Mrs. Foot, they will be even more surprised to see what some people, whom she has said do care about morality, actually get up to.

Divested, then of the universality and categoricality that have so generally been thought to give the moral "ought" its *magisterium*, what will become of it? Mrs. Foot is aware that her later views will seem to many dangerous and subversive of morality. If it is logically grounded only in the things that certain people happen to care about, what will happen if they cease caring or their numbers diminish drastically? Presumably, to Mrs. Foot's way of thinking, it is that possibility which moral educators have in mind when they perpetrate the illusion that morality has "an automatic reason-giving force." For her own part she is undismayed and concludes her "Morality as a System of Hypothetical Imperatives" with these words:

> Perhaps we should be less troubled than we are by fear of defection from the moral cause; perhaps we should have even less reason to fear it if people thought of themselves as volunteers banded together to fight for liberty and justice and against inhumanity and oppression. It is often felt, even if obscurely, that there is an element of deception in the official line about morality. And while some have been persuaded by talk about the authority of the moral law, others have turned away with a sense of distrust. (*VV*, p. 167)

Criticism of Mrs. Foot's Later Views

The first thought which strikes one about the views we have just been considering is: why have the educators, whom Mrs. Foot accuses of perpetuating the myth of an "automatic reason-giving force," been guilty of so doing? If the reason is, as I have just suggested it might be, that they fear morality would otherwise die out, then the question becomes: why are they so afraid of that? Is it because they know in their bones that the things a moral man cares about hold society together and so they are instinctively concerned to make this hold as secure as possible? That may be the reason, but then again the answer may be that they have no ulterior motive at all. Having themselves grown up believing in the "automatic reason-giving force" of moral judgments, they may simply be perpetrating that way of talking and thinking in those who come after them, because they know no better. But if Mrs. Foot's analysis of moral judgment is correct, is it not something of a mystery why they should?

That raises a second critical thought. Does what she is offering purport to be an analysis of moral discourse or a proposal for its reformation? A good deal of the time she writes as if it were the former. In reply to Phillips, for instance, she appeals to what people other than philosophers would say; and this quite clearly is an appeal to the ordinary use of moral language. In the ordinary meaning of "ought," it would, to her mind, make perfectly good sense for someone to say that he had done what he "ought" in a moral sense, even though he had put other considerations before moral ones. The absence of any "automatic reason-giving force" in the moral "ought" is thereby something which she endeavours to establish from the latter's ordinary use.

But, on the other hand, a good deal of what Mrs. Foot has to say sounds more like reformation than analysis. We undoubtedly use the moral "ought" as if it had a "special dignity and necessity;" but Mrs. Foot is concerned to show that, when we try to run this "fugitive thought" down to its logical base, to find a coherent reason why it should be entertained, we never can. And her obvious intention is to recommend that we should discontinue regarding the moral "ought" as if it had this "magic" binding-force we take it to have.

Now, there is no reason, of course, why a philosopher should not go in for both analysis and reformation. But the two activities need, I think, to be a little more clearly distinguished from one another than they are here. Is there not something anomalous about contending that the fundamental idea in ordinary moral discourse is mistaken and, at the same time, taking ordinary moral discourse as one's authority for its proposed alternative?

Two further, related criticisms concern the words I quoted above about, respectively (i) the impossibility of the uncaring, amoral man being told he ought to care and (ii) volunteering for the moral cause. I agree that, if morality is rooted in the desires to which Mrs. Foot refers, it is pointless to tell a man that he ought to be feeling them when he is not. However, it is not pointless to tell him that he ought to cultivate them. We cannot feel desires at will but we can put ourselves in the way of them. A man who does not care about the poor and needy might well do so, if he acquainted himself more fully with their circumstances. Surely, in the ordinary use of "ought", we would be entitled to tell him that he ought to acquaint himself with their condition. But now consider what this would mean, if Mrs. Foot's analysis of moral language—or her proposal for its reformation, as the case may be—is accepted. "Ought" has significance, in her account, only for those who have certain desires. Therefore, if we say to anyone that he ought to try to have these desires, what we say will be significant only if he already has them. In which case, it is otiose. What is the point of telling someone he ought to have what he must already have, if he is to see any force in what you say?

Then again, Mrs. Foot hopes people will think of themselves as "volunteers banded together to fight for liberty, etc." and come into "the moral cause" that way. Perhaps she would add that, just as you have to have a certain degree of physical fitness before you can join an army, or even certain kinds of inclination before you can be conceived as trying to join it, so you have to be a "kind and upright" man before you can be thought of as a volunteer for the moral cause. But the question remains: what is it to volunteer for the moral cause (as distinct from to be in it)? Surely, it is to feel that moral "oughts" are important. But you can feel that only if you have certain kinds of desire. But, if you have the latter, you will already be in the moral cause, for these are desires in which moral "oughts" are logically grounded. The notion of "volunteering," then, also seems to be otiose. People are either in the moral army or they are not, on Mrs. Foot's premises. The only sense that can be made of the idea of "volunteering" presupposes that some room is left for that of cultivating the relevant desires. But as I have tried to show, Mrs. Foot's theory has made that otiose already.

III. MORALITY GROUNDED IN MAN'S *TELOS*

I turn now to the view—to put it in its plainest terms— that men are *for* something and that the point of morality is to show them how to attain this *telos* or end. It is a view which found classical expression in Aristotle's *Nichomachean Ethics* and has recently been revived by some modern moral philosophers, who are commonly called Neo-aristotelians.

Aristotle explained things in terms of their causes, just

as we often do, but he had a richer conception of cause
than we have. There are, in his opinion, four kinds of cause.
First, there is the "material" cause of a thing, i.e. the stuff
of which it is composed. Secondly, there is its "formal"
cause, i.e. the essence, or definition, to which the material
of which it is composed conforms. Thirdly, there is its
"efficient" cause, i.e. whatever fashions its material cause in
accordance with its formal cause. Then, fourthly, there is
its "final" cause, i.e. the purpose or function for which it is
conceived to exist. To borrow an illustration of Aristotle's
own, the material cause of a statue is the marble from
which it is made; its formal cause is whatever shape the
sculptor intends the marble to assume; its efficient cause is
the impact of the sculptor's chisel on the marble; and its
final cause is whatever purpose it is being made to serve.
Aristotle took it that human nature can be explained in the
same way; so he thought it appropriate to speak of men as
existing for some purpose, function, or end; or, as he sometimes put it, for some good at which they aim.

What, then, is this good or end? Aristotle's answer was
that it is *eudaimonia*, a word commonly translated "happiness." But he acknowledged that this is a vague reply,
admitting of many different meanings. To the question
"How can we give it a clearer meaning?" his reply would
have been:

> This might perhaps be given, if we could first ascertain
> the function of man. For just as for a flute-player, a
> sculptor, or any artist, and, in general for all things that
> have a function or activity, the good and the 'well' is
> thought to reside in the function, so would it seem to be
> for man, if he has a function. Have the carpenter, then,
> and the tanner certain functions or activities, and has
> man none? Is he born without a function? Or as eye,
> hand, foot, and in general each of the parts evidently has
> a function, may one lay it down that man similarly has a
> function apart from all these? What then can this be?
> (*Nichomachean Ethics*, 1097b)

Aristotle thinks one can indeed so lay it down and his

answer to the final question in the above quotation is that the "function of man is an activity of the soul."

The soul has two parts, a rational and an irrational, according to Aristotle. Virtue, therefore, as the means whereby a man fulfils his function, is of two kinds, viz. intellectual and moral. The intellectual virtues are exercised in contemplation and concern the rational part of the soul; the moral virtues control the irrational part (or parts) of the soul by habituating it (them) to behaviour in accordance with a rational principle. Virtue is thus "concerned with means" (*ibid.*, 1113a). It enables us to fulfil our proper function as rational beings. But it is also concerned with the end as well as the means; for it is part of that *telos* itself. In Aristotle's terminology, the practice of the virtues, both intellectual and moral, is part of that activity of the soul, called happiness, which is the good for man.

It has seemed to some modern philosophers that, despite the obvious difficulties in this type of ethical theory—most notably, that of defining what the function or *telos* of man is—it gives an account of moral thinking which is superior to that given by any alternative type of theory. I shall take, as examples of this point of view, P. T. Geach, Stuart Hampshire, A. C. MacIntyre and Basil Mitchell.

(I) P. T. GEACH ON THE MEANING OF "A GOOD MAN"

P. T. Geach, in his paper "Good and Evil" (*A* 17, 1956, reprinted in P. Foot, *Theories of Morals*, 1967) argues for certain opinions that are fundamental to an Aristotelian type of ethic. Put summarily, these are the opinions that, (a) the word "good" is a logically attributive adjective and (b) the word "man" is a functional noun. I will explain as clearly as I can what is at issue here and show how Geach makes these two opinions the bases of his descriptivism.

"Good" as an Attributive Adjective

Logically attributive adjectives are contrasted by Geach with logically predicative ones. He takes, amongst others, the two examples "This is a red car" and "This is a big flea."

The adjective "red" in the former example is *predicative*, but "big" in the latter is *attributive*. The difference lies here. The sentence "This is a red car" can be split into two sentences, "This is a car" and "This is red," each of which is meaningful, independently of the other. But "This is a big flea" does not split up in the same way into "This is a flea" and "This is big" because "big" is a relative term, whereas "red" is not. That is to say, one could know what "red" meant without knowing what "car" meant in the former example, as one could not know what "big" meant without knowing what "flea" meant in the latter. The point is simply that a lot of things, such as cars, flags, corners of boxing rings, etc., etc., could all be red in an absolute sense; but bigness in fleas is not the same thing as bigness in elephants. From "This is a red car" one could infer "This is a red thing;" but it would be a sizeable mistake to deduce "This is a big animal" from "This is a big flea." The meaning of "big" depends on that of the noun to which it is attributed, as the meaning of "red" does not depend on the meaning of that of which it is predicated.

Coming, then, to the adjective "good," Geach declares uncompromisingly his opinion that " 'good' and 'bad' are *always* attributive, not predicative adjectives . . . there is no such thing as being just good or bad, there is only being a good or bad so-and-so" (*GE*, pp. 64—65, italics mine). He recognizes, of course, that "good" and "bad" can be grammatically (as distinct from logically) predicative. We could say, for instance, "This is good' or "Seggie is good," where "this" is a demonstrative pronoun and "Seggie" a proper noun. But, says Geach, in such cases, the continued use of the pronoun or proper noun "always presupposes a continued reference to an individual as being the same X, where 'X' is some common noun" (*GE*, p. 65). His point is that "good" and "bad" are always logically attributive in the sense that we need to know, what "this" refers to (a car?, a book?, etc.,) and who or what "Seggie" is (a town?, a dog?, a man?) before we can know what it means to say that this is good or Seggie is bad.

Now, on the basis of this distinction between the attributive and predicative uses of "good," Geach thinks he can demolish all those who deny that "good" and "bad" are primarily descriptive in meaning, and in particular the prescriptivists. He says that he "totally rejects" their view (*GE*, pp. 67–68) and he directs his attack at two false assumptions, on which he considers it to be based.

The first is the assumption that, if the primary meaning of a word is descriptive, then that word must describe some property that is common to all the things to which the word can be correctly applied. Prescriptivists, such as Hare, inherited this initial assumption from intuitionists. The latter, of course, took the view that there is no *natural* property common to everything correctly called "good" but they claimed that there must therefore be a common *nonnatural* one. The prescriptivists saw the flaws in this intuitionist manoeuvre but they did not abandon the initial assumption. They simply came to the conclusion that, since there is no one description, natural or nonnatural, to which all good things answer, the primary meaning of "good" cannot be descriptive.

Geach believes that the falsity of the initial assumption in this line of argument can be shown by a simple comparison. Take the expression "square of." It describes the number obtained when a number is multiplied by itself. If we ask what is common to all numbers so described, can we say they are all doubled, trebled, etc.? No. What we say will vary in each case—2 is doubled, 3 is trebled, and so on. But does it follow that "square of" lacks descriptive meaning? Geach says not: "There is no one number by which you can always multiply a number to get its square; but it does not follow either that 'square of' is an ambiguous expression meaning sometimes 'double of', sometimes 'treble of', etc., or that you have to do something other than multiplying to find the square of a number. . . " The light which he takes this comparison to shed on the falsity of the initial assumption under consideration, Geach spells out as follows: "Similarly there is no one description to which all things called 'good so-and-so's' answer, but it does not follow either that 'good' is a very ambiguous expression or that calling a thing good is something different from describing it" (*GE*. p.69). So "good" could have descriptive meaning even though there is no property common to all things that are good.

The second false assumption of which Geach accuses prescriptivists is the assumption that, since all things called good do not answer to one description, what they have in common must be that they are all commended by those who call them "good." That is to say, the primary function of "good" must be, not to describe anything, but to commend things and thereby guide choices and actions. But it seems clear to Geach that this is *not* the primary meaning of "good." He insists that its primary meaning is descriptive. Against the view (found in Hare, cf. above) that such descriptive meaning as "good" may have only derives from the fact that certain people would commend certain things—e.g. that "a good wicket" describes one which comes up to the standards of cricket fans—Geach argues thus: "Somebody who did not care two pins about cricket, but fully understood how the game worked (not an impossible supposition), could supply a purely descriptive sense for the phrase 'good batting wicket' regardless of the tastes of cricket fans" (*GE*, p.68). More fundamentally, he contends that, even when we are not invoking generally accepted standards, but simply applying our own, we are not primarily commending: "if I call a man a good burglar or a good cut throat I am certainly not commending him myself. . . " (*ibid*). He will allow no plausibility at all to the view that the most fundamental meaning of "good" is other than descriptive.

In passing, we may note that at one point he makes what looks like a concession to the prescriptivist view that moral judgments guide actions or choices. What he says is a trifle complicated but I think it hinges on these two remarks:

(i)   "It ought to be clear that calling a thing a good A does not influence choice unless the one who is choosing happens to want an A" (*GE*, p.68).

(ii) "It belongs to the *ratio* of 'want', 'choose', and 'good' and 'bad', that, normally, and other things being equal, a man who wants an A will choose . . . an A that he thinks good and will not choose an A that he thinks bad" (*GE*, p.69).

In the former quotation, Geach appears to be saying that if, as a matter of contingent fact, the person to whom we are speaking wants an A and has to make a choice, then by calling X a good A we can commend X to him. In the second quotation, the reference to *ratio* seems to indicate that the point Geach is making is as follows: it is a test of whether or not a man is rational to ask whether, when he wants an A and can choose, he will choose an A that he thinks good, rather than one he thinks bad. From these considerations Geach concludes that the connection between calling a thing "a good A" and guiding actions or choices, though not analytic, is not "a mere rough empirical generalization" either (p.70). But this is not really a concession to prescriptivism. Geach remains adamant that such considerations take nothing from the fact that the primary meaning of "good" is descriptive. He insists that, in order to guide actions or choices, a value judgment does not need to be imperative, or to entail an imperative, as Hare supposed. It is possible for a purely indicative sentence to guide actions or choices. As Geach puts it, immediately after the former of the two quotations above, "'You have ants in your pants', which obviously has a primary descriptive force, is far closer to affecting action than many uses of the term 'good'" (*GE*, p.68). If an indicative sentence, such as that, can guide actions or choices, it follows that a value judgment could have all the connections Geach conceives it to have with guiding actions and choices, but still remain primarily descriptive in meaning. This is what he wishes to maintain against the prescriptivists.

"Man" as a Functional Noun

So far I have been thinking mainly of the way in which Geach's descriptivism is based on his opinion that "good" is an attributive adjective. But what now of his other fundamental opinion, that "man" is a functional noun? Geach contends that if I do not know what a thing like a hygrometer is *for*, I do not know what is meant by "a good hygrometer," and by the same token, that unless I know what men are *for*, I do not know what is meant by "a good man" (cf. *GE*, p.69).

In his book, *The Virtues* (Cambridge, 1977) he has an opening chapter entitled "Why Men Need the Virtues", in which he argues that the four cardinal virtues are necessary conditions of any man fulfilling that which he is *for*. Just as a knife is for cutting and a good knife, therefore, is one that cuts well, so a good man is one who evinces prudence, temperance, justice and courage because without these virtues no one can attain the true end or purpose for which men exist. Geach is alive to the kinds of objections commonly brought against this teleological conception of morality—e.g. that it supposes nature to have aims, or implies a purposive creator of the natural order—but he dismisses them as all "quite worthless." In his view, an Aristotelian type of ethic can be defended without recourse to any such beliefs. His argument to this effect runs as follows.

In biology, questions which take parts of the body to have functions—e.g. "What are teeth for?" or "What are hearts for?"—have heuristic value. Similarly, according to Geach, "it makes good sense to ask, 'What are men for?'" (*Virtues*, p.12). True, the answer may not be as easy to come by as some thinkers in antiquity supposed, but this does not render the question pointless. However, as we shall now see, it is a question that Geach himself manages to side-step.

One would have expected him, at this point, to give some specific account of what men are *for*, and then to derive from this the criteria of goodness in men. But his line of argument is different from that. Instead of asking us to take one specific function as the true end of man, he invites us to think of "any large-scale, worthy enterprise" that men might adopt and then to ask ourselves what would be the necessary conditions of its attainment. This, as he notes, gets us out of the difficult business of saying what man's specific function is—"in order to show that men need virtues to effect whatever men are for, it may turn out unnecessary to determine the end and the good of man" (*Virtues*, p. 13). In other words, we need not worry our heads about whether the final end of man is to glorify God, or promote evolution, or maximize happiness, or develop every human potentiality, etc., before we can adopt a teleological conception of moral goodness. All we need think about is what would necessarily be involved in the pursuit of any end or purpose that is large enough to involve more than one human being in some measure of common activity. If we consider this, we shall see at once that the human beings involved would need to have a certain amount of health and sanity, for without these the enterprise would be quite impossible. But more. On further reflection, we shall see that they would also need to have the four cardinal virtues; and that their success in attaining the end in question, whatever it might be, would be commensurate with the degree in which they possessed these virtues.

People may vary in their views as to the purpose or function for which men exist, but underlying all such differences, thinks Geach, there is a deeper consensus. Think, for instance, of how people with different religious beliefs and with none can cooperate in building and running a hospital. Or again, think how such peace and civilization as there is in the world subsists because there is some agreement in value judgments, below the level at which nations fight and scheme against each other. These deeper levels of agreement in value judgment serve as a background against which our moral disagreements are thrown into relief and they represent a consensus of opinion concerning the proper function of man, despite all the differences that arise on that score when people try to be more specific about it. The consensus to which reference has been made is to a large degree a recognition of the moral worth of the cardinal virtues. As Geach puts it:

> And on the basis of this consensus we can see the need of the four cardinal virtues to men: these virtues are needed for any large-scale, worthy enterprise, just as health and sanity are needed. We need prudence or practical wisdom for any large-scale planning. We need justice to secure cooperation and mutual trust among men, without which our lives would be nasty, brutish, and short. We need temperance in order not to be deflected from our long-term and large-scale goals by

seeking short-term satisfactions. And we need courage in
order to persevere in face of set-backs, weariness, difficulties and dangers. (*Virtues*, p.16)

Like Mrs. Foot, Geach finds a starting point for moral
philosophy in the question, "Why should I?" or "Why
shouldn't I?" and, like her, he thinks that any relevant
answer which is given to it must "relate to inclinations"
(*Virtues*, p.9). What men want, he insists, again like Mrs.
Foot, is not exclusively selfish; they may want things for
others as well as for themselves. But, whatever they want,
prudence, temperance, justice and courage will be necessary
to the attainment of it, and so a man always has good reason to live in accordance with these virtues.

Geach recognizes (*Virtues*, p.16) that there could conceivably be crazy people about, who do not participate in
the consensus to which he has referred. They would not
want to engage in any "large-scale, worthy enterprise."
They might even be in favour of destroying all hospitals and
wrecking all civilization. But he thinks such people should
be excluded from discussion when it comes to the question
of how we ought to live, just as we would exclude people
with crazy views (e.g. flat-earthers?, animists?) when we
are discussing physical nature. In matters of value, as in
matters of fact, there is a consensus of opinion to which we
must relate what we wish to say, if it is to make any sense.
And normal human beings, thinks Geach, can be shown
that what they really want is attainable only through the
practice of virtue.

He adds a comment on his use of the word "need." He
says that he has put it into the title of his chapter—"Why
Men Need The Virtues"—because it is important to distinguish between two senses of "want"—"namely, the 'desire'
sense and the 'need' sense." It is human wants in this latter
sense which he takes to be the key notion in his teleological
conception of morality.

The notion of needs certainly fits more completely into
the idea of a teleological ethic than that of mere desires.
The question "What do you desire that *for*?" could, in
certain circumstances, quite legitimately be dismissed with

the reply, "I don't desire it for anything. I just desire it." But a similar question with regard to something conceived as a need could not be similarly dismissed. We can never say, "I don't need it *for* anything. I just need it", since the word "need" implies a *telos*, as the word "desire" does not. So, it is quite appropriate for a teleological moralist, such as Geach, to point out that, in his view, morality has to do with needs, rather than simply desires.

Criticism of Geach

However, the account Geach gives of the *telos*, to which morality is a mean˜ ɔf fulfilment, leaves him particularly exposed to two lines of criticism, which I will indicate in a moment.

It will be remembered that he speaks of this *telos* as "any large-scale, worthy enterprise." The virtues, he thinks, are needed for the carrying out of such enterprises. True, Geach speaks of them as "worthy," but nothing seems to turn on this in his account of the virtues. If we glance back at his words about why we need the virtues, we shall see that it is the largeness of the relevant enterprises—the facts that these involve more than one person and require a good deal of effort to carry through—that explains why we need the virtues. He says that we need prudence to manage large-scale affairs; justice because these involve cooperation with others; temperance, so that we shall not be diverted by short-term aims; and courage, to keep us going when things get difficult. None of this implies moral worthiness in the enterprises concerned. Hitler would have needed to have these virtues just as much as Mother Teresa does.

The former of the two criticisms to which such an account of the virtues exposes Geach, is that it reduces morality to mere expediency. As he represents it our obligation to practise the virtues derives simply from the fact that it will pay us to do so. And that in heteronomous terms. The criticism is directed against Geach's point that we need the virtues, not in order to be morally worthy human beings, but in order to fulfil our large, cooperative enterprises, whatever these may be.

He takes a very short way with what he calls this "high Stoic line" of criticism, dismissing it as sophistical:

> It is mere sophistry to confuse the thesis that men need the cardinal virtues for their benefit—that we can see this without determining specifically what men are for—with the thesis that being brave or just must pay the individual brave or just man. Men need the virtues as bees need stings. An individual bee may perish by stinging, all the same bees need stings; an individual man may perish by being brave or just, all the same men need courage and justice. It is equally sophistical to write as if the alternatives were: moral virtue for its own sake, and selfishness. Men are so made that they do care what happens to others; quite apart from respect for Duty, that is the way men's Inclinations go. (*Virtues*, p.17)

But I think it is Geach himself who can be accused of sophistry. He writes here as if the point at issue between him and his critics were whether the "large-scale, worthy enterprises," for which men need the virtues, are selfish or other-regarding. But that is not what is at issue. What Geach's critics accuse him of is taking the point out of morality—robbing it of its distinctive obligation, reducing it to mere expediency—by representing the virtues simply as means to enterprises which may, or may not, be moral ones. Virtue, they insist, must be seen as its own reason and reward. It makes no difference from their point of view whether a non-moral enterprise, which virtue serves, is selfish or other-regarding. Hitler may well have cared for the success of the German people just as fervently as Mother Teresa cares for the comfort of the destitute in Calcutta. But would that have made him a virtuous man?

The second line of criticism is that Geach has abandoned the teleological theory of ethics in the process of defending it. There is a parenthesis in the above quotation which indicates that he thinks such a theory can be defended "without determining specifically what men are for." And indeed, his whole account of our need for the virtues proceeds on the assumption that we do not need to worry our heads about what man's *telos* is, because it can be shown that the virtues are necessary for "any large-scale worthy enterprise." He does not say that men have no *telos*; simply, that, so far as the virtues are concerned, we need not concern ourselves with what it is. Now, what does this amount to, if not an abandonment of the central idea of teleological ethics? The central idea is that one cannot know what one ought to do, unless and until one knows what one is *for*. It may be that this *telos*, or function, is hard to discern; it may be that Aristotle was vague about it; it may be that we shall never be intelligent or well-informed enough to understand what it is; but none of this would mean that teleological ethics can get on very well without it. Morality, according to a teleological theory of ethics, has to be read off from the *telos*. Is the latter to glorify God, to further evolution, to maximize happiness, to develop human potentialities, or what? Only when we know that, do we know how men ought to live. If you say, as Geach says, that the virtues are necessary to achieve man's *telos* whatever it may be, then you have made what it is irrelevant to morality. And that, one can justifiably say, is to abandon teleological ethics in the very process of defending them.

(II) STUART HAMPSHIRE ON THE CONNECTION BETWEEN ATTRIBUTIVE AND PREDICATIVE USES OF "GOOD"

Stuart Hampshire takes up the distinction between the attributive and predicative uses of "good" and interprets Aristotle's ethics in the light of it. In his paper "Ethics: A Defence of Aristotle" (*Freedom of Mind and Other Essays*, Princeton, N.J., 1971) he begins by giving his own account of the two uses of "good", offering "a good play" as his example of the attributive use and "good news" as his example of the predicative. In both these instances, he notes, reasons may be asked for the judgment; someone may say, "What is good about the play?", or "about the news?" In the former case, the answer "must be wholly found in the qualities, or features, of the play, and of nothing else" (*FM*, p. 66). That is to say, the criteria of goodness can be read off from the concept, play. This concept is not entirely static; playwrights do, on occasion, introduce innovations which modify it. But there is a continuity in its history; so goodness in a play could hardly, for instance, be said to depend on the brilliance of the lighting in the auditorium, or the price of the drinks at the bar. It must depend on the quality of things like the dialogue, the dramatic action, the characterization, and other such features which make a play a play. This, then, is the attributive use of "good". By contrast, it is not the case that the reasons given for calling something "good news" must be found within the concept, news. If one is asked what is good about the news, it will be in place to refer to certain interests or desires of oneself or others, which the news may be said to satisfy—e.g. "It's good news because it will enable me to pay my bills" or "because it will increase my department's prestige," etc. The range of such interests or desires is, of course, "vast and indefinite," says Hampshire; but some such reference there must be, if what is meant by "good news" is to be intelligible (*FM*, p. 67). This is the predicative use of "good."

The Nature of the Connection

Now, is there any connection between the two uses? Hampshire thinks so and he brings it out in terms of *choice* (or selection), *interest* (or desire) and *satisfaction* (or a thing to try to get).

To begin with, in *both* its uses, "good" evaluates; that is to say, it *chooses* (or selects) some things from among others because they come up to a certain standard.

In the case of the predicative use of "good," the standard is that they serve some human *interest* (or desire) and thereby give *satisfaction* (a thing to try to get) to some human being(s) or other. Well, can anything of the same kind be said about the attributive use of "good"? Hampshire's answer is that it can: " 'This is a good play' implies that, in the circumstances in which a man is *choosing* among plays, and while this *interest* overrides other interests that he may have, this is conspicuously one of the things for him *to try to get*" (*FM*, pp. 70–71 italics mine). He adds that, when a critic emphatically and confidently calls a play good, this commits him to the implication that anyone not satisfied by it would not really have an overriding interest in plays but an interest in something else which they are confusing with one in plays (*FM*, p. 72). So, in the attributive use, as Hampshire interprets its implications, there are the elements of choice, interest and satisfaction, just as there are in the predicative use.

What I have just been saying may seem to make the connection between the two uses of "good" very close. Consequently, this connection may appear to lend some plausibility to the view of those moral philosophers, who are so strongly opposed to moral theories like Stevenson's or Hare's—which make much of the predicative use—that they deny this predicative use altogether. Hampshire describes their view in these terms: "that every apparent absolute, unqualified and predicative use of the word 'good' is reducible, within a context, to a qualified and attributive use, or that it requires the specification of a particular interest . . . " (*FM*, p. 73). The standard or criterion of predicating goodness must, on this view, always be read off *from within* the context and refer either to the kind of thing to which goodness is attributed or to the specified interest that is expected to be satisfied by it; it cannot be read off from criteria that are brought *from outside* into the context by the person judging, as emotivists and prescriptivists have thought it can. For all his own hostility to emotivism and prescriptivism, Hampshire calls this view—that the predicative use of "good" can be reduced to the attributive— "a false doctrine."

His reason for that judgment is as follows. Unless there is what he calls "a distinct, non-elliptical, absolute, and predicative use of 'good'," there will *not* be "a possibility of arguing about the relative value of different human interests and purposes, and systematically relating this argument to the canons of excellence employed in evaluating particular kinds of things" (*FM*, p. 73). What I take him to mean is this. We must first have a way of evaluating the relative worth of human interests, when compared with one another; but once we have made this evaluation, it will affect our criteria of goodness, when we are deciding whether things which purport to satisfy these several interests are good of their kind. For example, it is easy to imagine how our (predicative) assessment of the value of play-going, when compared with other human interests and activities, might influence what we thereafter look for in a play, when deciding whether or not it is (attributively) good as a play. So far from the predicative use being reducible to the attributive, Hampshire appears to be saying, the attributive is parasitic upon the predicative.

How the Uses are connected in Aristotle

Hampshire's discussion of the predicative and attributive uses of "good" is, of course, conducted with a view to explaining and commending Aristotle's ethics and to this subject we must now turn. I think what Hampshire wished to say can be summarized like this. We need to distinguish clearly between the predicative and attributive uses of "good" so that we can understand just how that distinction "breaks down" in Aristotle's moral philosophy. Hampshire, if I read him aright, takes Aristotle to have agreed with his own distinction between the attributive and predicative uses, as illustrated by "a good play" and "good news"; and also with his connection of them in terms of choice, interest and satisfaction. Then again, Hampshire thinks that Aristotle would have accepted his account of the need for a predicative use of "good" in order to compare the relative value of human interests; and with the consequent effects of this on its attributive use. But, he goes on:

> Aristotle went further . . . ; he argued that, in explaining why such-and-such an activity is a good thing, I must finally indicate its relation to other activities in a whole system of activities, which taken as a whole, constitute a good, or the best, form of life for man. This allows Aristotle to give a clear and connected rational reconstruction of the type of arguments appropriate both to predicative judgments and to attributive judgments of value. More than that: it explains how the more reflective and critical uses of the word "good' in the attributive sense develop from those predicative uses which were

originally unreflective. Within this scheme, to explain why play-going is a good thing is to explain the wider interests that it uniquely serves. It shows how play-going fits in, as a contributory means, or as a by-product, or concomitant, of activities that are essential to excellence in men and to some form of life that is to be desired. So it becomes possible to explain, by reference to the part that play-going, or the enjoyment of drama, plays in the whole scheme of a way of life, why the criterion of excellence in plays is what it is. The connection is neat and clear—more clear, I think, as an approach to a rational reconstruction of moral argument than anything else in the literature. But it has familiar difficulties. (*FM*, pp. 77—78)

What all this means can perhaps be illustrated by a simple example. Take the two activities of play-going and philosophical reflection. Both can serve human interests. Play-going can divert our attention from oppressive cares and worries; and philosophical reflection can enlarge our understanding of morality, science, religion and other great matters. Now, suppose, by a predicative use of "good", we compare these two activities and come to the conclusion that philosophical reflection is better than play-going. Hampshire is quite right when he says that this may thereafter affect what we mean by "a good play." We may think of it, for instance, as a play that directs our attention away from our own anxieties, not simply by making us laugh, but by making us see how trivial our own concerns are, when compared with the nature of the universe, the highest moral good, the will of God, or some other such great matter. This, I think, will serve as an example of what Hampshire has in mind when he speaks of "how the more reflective and critical uses of the word 'good' in the *attributive* sense develop from those *predicative* uses which were originally unreflective." Of course, play-going and philosophical reflection are only two amongst countless interest-satisfying human activities; and something of the same kind may occur, if we compare any of these human activities evaluatively with one another, whether they are connected with our work or leisure, our life as members of families or circles of friends, our ambitions or aspirations, or anything else at all. Out of such comparisons, through a *predicative* use of "good," developments may occur in what we *attributively* mean when we speak of a good job, a good pastime, a good friend, a good parent, etc., just as we have supposed one to occur in what is meant by "a good play."

But here is the important point. The predicative use of "good" can bring about a development in its attributive use, only by *changing* the concept of that to which goodness is attributed. It will not suffice—to return to our example— if we simply suppose that the stimulation of philosophical reflection is one *possible* characteristic of plays, which we have selected as our criterion of goodness in plays; for then "good" is still being used predicatively. If an attributive use is to develop, the stimulation of interest in philosophical reflection must be thought of as a *necessary* characteristic of plays—as part of the *concept* of a play—for, as we saw above, the attributive use of "good" is logically dependent on the concept of that to which it is attributed.

Hampshire in the above quotation speaks of a "system of activities, which taken as a whole, constitute a good, or the best, form of life for man;" and he says that play-going and other activities can "fit in" to this system. What he evidently means is this. We can grade human activities—by the *predicative* use of "good"—into a hierarchy of value. We can develop in the process—by an *attributive* use of "good" —our conceptions of what it is to see a good play, have a good job, be a good friend, etc. And then these latter conceptions can be put together to form a "system" of what is "essential to excellence in men." Notice that this is, so to speak, a system made up of *attributively* good components. And so, it must itself be attributive. It consists, that is to say, of a conception of what it is to be a *man*, from which we can read off what it is to be a *good* man.

I think that is a fair account of what Hampshire takes to be the essence of Aristotle's teleological ethics. But, as he says, there are "familiar difficulties" in it and to some of these we must now turn.

The Difficulties Hampshire Finds in Aristotle's Ethics

The main difficulties that Hampshire finds in Aristotle's ethics are as follows. Firstly, Aristotle argued that there must be some norm of goodness, which can be read off from the concept, man, because otherwise we shall never have conclusive reasons for deeming any human activities or interests better than others. Against this line of argument Hampshire—of course rightly—points out that we cannot suppose there must be some such norm merely because it is a condition of conclusiveness in practical reasoning. Conceivably, such reasoning never is conclusive (cf. *FM*, pp. 78–79).

A second difficulty arises because Aristotle took the norm to be easily discoverable and to consist in the perfect development of human potentialities (or the complete satisfaction of human interests). But he made the considerable assumption (as Hampshire puts it) that, when fully developed (or satisfied), these potentialities (or interests) will all harmonize in "some single all-inclusive and final 'form of life' called the good for man." But, as has so frequently been pointed out, human beings have diverse potentialities (or interests)—for virtue and for vice, for kindness and cruelty, cooperation and self-aggrandizement, etc.—and this fact casts doubt on Aristotle's assumption. "That ends of action should be stated in a conjunctive form, and should permit conflicts that cannot always be settled by one overriding criterion, which is sufficiently definite to count as a criterion, is not in itself an unintelligible suggestion" (*FM*, p. 79), is Hampshire's restrained comment.

He has a third and more forthright criticism to the effect that Aristotle has begged the whole question at issue. Hampshire says:

> The judgment "A is a good man", interpreted as involving an ordinary attributive use of "good" is unlike all other critical judgments of similar form in one important respect; namely, that the interests of men cannot determine the appropriate standard, or criterion, to apply in discriminating good men from bad men: for this would

indeed be circular, and a begging of the question at issue.
(*FM*, pp. 79—80)

I take the point of this remark to be as follows. In an ordinary attributive use of "good," what is being said—as Hampshire pointed out with regard to "a good play"—is that, if
you have an overriding interest in the kind of thing concerned, then the thing called good will satisfy that interest.
The interest, be it noted, is in such cases, given or presupposed—a good play is one which will satisfy you, if you
already have an overriding interest in plays. But, when we
are considering what is meant by the expression "a good
man," we cannot start by asking what interests a man will
serve by being a good man. For what is really at issue is:
what interests will a man have, if he is good? We cannot
start our inquiry by presupposing that a good man will
have certain interests, for it is the *end* of the inquiry to
discover which he will have. Therefore, "good" in "a good
man" cannot be regarded as an ordinary attributive use,
without the meaning being viciously circular and the
essential question being begged.

We can see now why Hampshire said that in Aristotle
the distinction between the attributive and predicative uses
of "good" "breaks down." Even more clearly, we can see
why he called the idea that all uses of "good" are in the last
analysis attributive, rather than predicative, a "false doctrine." The very reverse would seem to be the case: attributive uses are parasitic in the last analysis upon predicative
ones. We do not know what an (attributively) good play is
unless we have compared play-going with other interest-
serving activities in respect of (predicative) goodness. And
even when we have fitted this idea of a good play into a
system of activities that are essential to excellence in men,
the system is still grounded at its base in predicative uses of
"good."

Hampshire goes on to say, however, that we must not
draw from the fact that Aristotle's ethic breaks down the
conclusion that it is altogether mistaken. Indeed, as we have
already noted, he considers it "more clear" than any other
attempt to illuminate moral thinking. There are, Hampshire

insists, "conceptual restrictions" on what can count as praise of a human being as a human being. He goes on: "But there is a wide range of choice, an unmarked area of different ideals that may be incompatible in practice, and that are plausible as ideals of an admirable, or praiseworthy, or completely satisfying form of life" (*FM*, p. 83). He thinks that any moral philosopher, who is not a pure meta-ethicist, and has some first order morality, necessarily commits himself to some kind of answer to the question that Aristotle forces upon us, namely: What is the activity of the human soul which constitutes the highest merit, or excellence, of men, considered merely as human beings, and apart from any excellencies or merits they have in subordinate roles?— i.e. as soldiers, scholars, or whatever.

Hampshire's conclusion seems to be that the great merit of Aristotle's ethics is that it showed us that there is a kind of dialectic between the predicative and attributive uses of "good" always going on in moral thinking. Neither can be taken for the fundamental meaning of "good" to the exclusion of the other. No doubt, if this is so, it is because Aristotle (see above) conceived of virtue as both the means to the realization of man's *telos* and part of that *telos* itself. We may read off atributively from our conception of man's *telos* what it is virtuous to do. But we can always predicatively call in question the moral judgments we thereby form. And if we revise them, we are thereby necessarily revising our conception of the *telos* itself.

(III) A. C. MACINTYRE ON "MAN" AS A FUNCTIONAL NOUN

I said, when introducing my remarks on Geach, that two opinions are fundamental to an Aristotelian type of ethic; one, that "good" is an attributive adjective; and the other, that "man" is a functional noun. We have just been seeing what Hampshire made of the former of these ideas. Now, I want to discuss what A. C. MacIntyre, another philosopher who advocates a return to the Aristotelian conception of morality, has to say about "man" as a functional noun.

In his book, *After Virtue* (London, 1981), he defines the idea which he takes to be central to the Aristotelian tradition, whether in its Greek or mediaeval versions, as "the concept of *man* understood as having an essential nature and an essential purpose or function" (*AF*, p. 56). The thesis he propounds is that the erosion and eventual loss of this teleological conception of human nature has vitiated moral philosophy from the time of the Enlightenment; and has now produced in our own day a state of affairs in which the language and appearances of morality persist, whilst its integral substance has to a large degree been fragmented and destroyed (cf. *AF*, p. 5). We still use moral expressions but we are strangers to the conceptual scheme which gives them meaning. Only a recovery of the idea that "man" is a functional noun—or, as MacIntyre puts it, "of man as having an essence which defines his true end" (*AF*, p. 52)— can restore to us a correct understanding of both the theory and practice of morality.

Aristotelian Analysis of Morality

In any Aristotelian analysis of morality, says MacIntyre, there are three elements. The first is a conception of "man as he happens to be" (or, as he alternatively calls it, "un-tutored human nature"). The second is a conception of "man as he could be if he realised his essential nature" (or, "human nature as it could be if it realised its *telos*"). And the third element is morality understood as "the science which is to enable men to understand how they make the transition from the former state to the latter" (or "the precepts of rational ethics" which "instruct us both as to what our true end is and as to how to reach it") (*AF*, pp. 50—51).

If the idea of man having an end, purpose, or function, is lost, then the second of the above three elements inevitably goes with it. And where does that leave morality? This is MacIntyre's answer:

> Since the whole point of ethics—both as a theoretical and a practical discipline—is to enable man to pass from his present state to his true end, the elimination of any notion of essential human nature and with it the abandonment of any notion of a *telos* leaves behind a moral

scheme composed of two remaining elements whose relationship becomes quite unclear. There is on the one hand a certain content for morality: a set of injunctions deprived of their teleological context. There is on the other hand a certain view of untutored-human-nature-as-it-is. Since the moral injunctions were originally at home in a scheme in which their purpose was to correct, improve and educate that human nature, they are clearly not going to be such that they could be deduced from true statements about human nature or justified in some other way by appealing to its characteristics. (*AF*, p. 52)

According to MacIntyre, the secular rejection of Catholic and Protestant theology and the philosophical rejection of Aristotelianism combined to eliminate from moral thinking the second of the three elements in his analysis. No notion of "human nature as it could be if it realised its *telos*" was able to survive the corrosive effects of scepticism and modernity. Philosophers who wanted to present a rational justification of morality were left with only the first and the third elements in the Aristotelian analysis. They attempted to give the desired justification in their different ways by fastening upon some feature in "untutored human nature" and representing morality as a set of rules which beings possessed of the relevant feature could be expected to accept and obey. Hume, for instance, looked to the passions in "man as he happens to be" for a justification of morality; Kant, to reason (*AF*, p. 50). But this whole enterprise was, in MacIntyre's submission, bound to fail. For, in so far as such thinkers had to work with only the first and third elements in the Aristotelian analysis, they were compelled to think in terms of two conceptions "which had been expressly designed to be discrepant with each other" (*AF*, p. 53). They inherited from the time before the Enlightenment only the conception of nature as it happened to be and of certain moral rules for making it into something else. Therefore, it was a misconception of the whole point of this moral content to suppose that it could be justified solely in terms of the untutored human nature which it was intended to educate to better things.

Fact and Value

MacIntyre thinks that the loss of the second element in his Aristotelian analysis accounts for the dogma that no argument can move validly from entirely factual premises to any moral or evaluative conclusion. This dogma, as everyone knows, has been very influential in moral philosophy for more than a couple of centuries. Hume can perhaps be taken simply to have raised the question as to whether "ought" can be deduced from "is"; but Kant laid it down that the moral law cannot be inferred from statements about human happiness, or God's will. This "is-ought gap" in MacIntyre's opinion, is simply the consequence of a change in the meaning of the key moral terms, which took place through the loss of the idea of "human nature as it could be if it realised its *telos*."

Factual statements cannot entail value judgments, where all thought of purpose or function is excluded. But "This watch tells the time accurately" entails "This is a good watch"; and "This farmer gets remarkably large crops from his land" entails "He is a good farmer." The premises are factual and the conclusions evaluative in such cases; and it is the concept of the subjects concerned as *functional*— watches and farmers indisputably exist *for* something—that makes the inference valid. So, MacIntyre contends that it is not a truth of logic that values can never be deduced from facts, as defenders of the "is—ought gap" sometimes claim. In modern moral philosophy, this claim is simply made because all thought of man as having a *telos* is ruled out. By contrast, within the Aristotelian tradition, " 'man' stands to "good man' as 'watch' stands to 'good watch' or 'farmer' to 'good farmer'." Aristotle took as his starting point in ethical inquiry the assumption that the relationship of "man" to "living well" is analogous to that of "harpist" to "playing the harp well." He thought of "man" as essentially a functional word (*AF*, p. 56).

It is important to see that MacIntyre's insistence that "man" is a functional noun seems to be based simply on the fact that it was so thought of in antiquity. He claims that in the classical tradition "every type of item which it is appropriate to call good or bad—including persons and actions—has, as a matter of fact, some given specific purpose or function" (*AF*, p. 57). And he draws the following inference: "To call something good therefore is also to make a factual statement." To say that a watch or a farmer is good is necessarily to say that in fact they perform their respective functions well. And so with men. To say that any act is right or good is to say that it is the kind of thing that would be done by a man who had progressed from human nature as it happens to be to human nature as it can be when it realizes its *telos*. And MacIntyre insists that "within this tradition, moral and evaluative statements can be called true or false in precisely the way in which all other factual statements can be so called" (*ibid*). It is only when the idea that "man" is a functional noun loses its hold upon us that we think it implausible to treat moral judgments as factual statements.

MacIntyre is, of course, quite right to say that Aristotle thought of man as *for* something. But he goes beyond mere exposition. The purpose of MacIntyre's book is to recommend an Aristotelian type of ethic; in his opinion, morality *needs* to be teleological. We are, therefore, entitled to ask what grounds there are for so regarding it. The mere reply that Aristotle so regarded it will not suffice. And, of course, MacIntyre says far more than that. He says that, for lack of a concept of "human nature as it could be if it realised its *telos*," morality has become confused and hesitant. But the fact, if it is a fact, that the recovery of Aristotelianism would make it less confused and hesitant is also not in itself a sufficient reason for embracing that type of ethic. The fact, or putative fact, just referred to could be merely an instance of how questions can be made easier to answer by oversimplifying them. If we take man to have a *telos*, it may well be that clear and distinct moral judgments will be easier to deliver. But the question remains: *does* man have a *telos* and, if so, *what* is it? Only if we have an affirmative answer to the first part of that question, and an informative one to the second part, are we entitled to conceive of morality teleologically. I do not think MacIntyre gives us more by way of answers than that Aristotle believed man to have a *telos* and that a morality which rejects this view is hesitant and uninstructive. And this invites the comment: what if morality has to be like that simply because man has no telos? Geach, as we saw above, thought it unnecessary to say what man's *telos* is, in order to have a teleological ethic. And MacIntyre observes that Aristotle himself left the question of what constitutes *endaimonia* open (*AF*, p. 139). Well, there may be some grounds for the opinion that we do not have to define man's *telos* too precisely, in order to conceive of him as having one. But what we surely do need to be given, before we can have good reason for embracing a teleological conception of morality, is some good ground for believing that man has a *telos*, whatever it may be. Given certain metaphysical or religious presuppositions, that view makes perfectly good sense. But if no such grounds are offered for it, why should anyone suppose it to be true? To reply that morality has traditionally supposed it to be true and that, in the absence of it, moral terms change their meaning, is not an adequate answer. Copernian revolutions can presumably take place in moral, as in scientific, discourse. And, if we find ourselves talking in new ways about what is right or good because we can no longer believe what was implicit in the old ways of talking, all we can do is make the best of it.

The Communal Character of the Telos

So much for scepticism about the whole idea of "man" as a functional being. But if we can surmount such scepticism, or temporarily lay it aside, the interesting question remains: what is man *for*? MacIntyre's account of that is as follows:

> . . . the use of 'man' as a functional concept is far older than Aristotle and it does not initially derive from Aristotle's metaphysical biology. It is rooted in the forms of social life to which the theorists of the classical tradition give expression. For according to that tradition to be a man is to fill a set of roles each of which has its own point and purpose: member of a family, citizen, soldier, philosopher, servant of God. It is only when a man is thought of as an individual prior to and apart from all

roles that 'man' ceases to be a functional concept. (*AF*, p. 56)

The loss of the idea that "man" is a functional noun, according to MacIntyre, must be seen as the consequence of a historical occurrence which he describes as the invention of the individual (*AF*, p. 59). This was not simply an intellectual occurrence, it was the consequence of many factors, practical and theoretical, at work in human history. Their combined effect was to break up the old social order and with it the old way of thinking about man and morality.

The communal character of man's purpose or function is brought out, according to MacIntyre, in what Aristotle had to say about the cardinal virtues. Notice, first, how he connected them with man's *telos*. The *telos* is *endaimonia* (or happiness, blessedness, prosperity). Now, says MacIntyre, "the virtues are precisely those qualities the possession of which will enable an individual to achieve *endaimonia* and lack of which will frustrate his movement toward that *telos*" (*AF*, p. 139). They must not, however, be thought of *simply* as means to that end. "For what constitutes the good for man is a complete human life lived at its best, and the exercise of the virtues is a necessary and central part of such a life, not a preparatory exercise to secure such a life. We thus cannot characterise the good for man adequately without already having made reference to the virtues" (*AF*, p. 140). In the light of this remark, we can understand MacIntyre's other remark that, whilst Aristotle's ethic was teleological, it was not consequentialist (*AF*, p. 141). Aristotle did not think of virtue as justified by the fact that it maximizes happiness (or not solely); he thought of it as an essential part of happiness; that is, of what man is *for*.

But notice also that Aristotle thought of a virtuous individual as one who fills his place in a virtuous community. As MacIntyre points out, "it is worth remembering Aristotle's insistence that the virtues find their place not just in the life of the individual, but in the life of the city and that the individual is indeed intelligible only as a *politikon zoon*" (*AF*, p. 141). Aristotle had much to say in his *Ethics* about the virtue of friendship and, as MacIntyre reminds us, "the type of friendship which Aristotle has in mind is that which embodies a shared recognition and pursuit of good." Just as, in Aristotle's view, one cannot possess any of the virtues in a developed form without possessing them all, so one cannot possess them except in so far as one finds one's place within a community and lives well as a parent, teacher, soldier, friend, or whatever such roles are marked out for one within one's community. MacIntyre sums up this communal conception of virtue in the following way:

> What education in the virtues teaches me is that my good as a man is one and the same as the good of those others with whom I am bound up in human community. There is no way of my pursuing my good which is necessarily antagonistic to you pursuing yours because *the* good is neither mine peculiarly nor yours peculiarly — goods are not private property. Hence Aristotle's definition of friendship, the fundamental form of human relationship, is in terms of shared goods. (*AF*, p. 213)

It was this notion of shared goods which broke up when the classical tradition was destroyed by what MacIntyre calls the invention of the individual. The most thoroughgoing expression of the break-up is to be found, according to MacIntyre, in the philosophy of Nietzsche. The latter, he says, saw that, once the concept of "human nature as it could be if it realised its *telos*" was lost, then attempts to find a justification for morality in "human nature as it happens to be" are futile. All there is left for morality to be is an expression of my will.

> There can be no place for such fictions as natural rights, utility, the greatest happiness of the greatest number. I myself must now bring into existence 'new tables of what is good.' 'We, however, *want to become those we are*—human beings who are new, unique, incomparable, who give themselves laws, who create themselves'

says MacIntyre, quoting and expounding Nietzsche (*AF*,

p. 107). Here there is a total rejection of the ideas that man is *for* something and that what he is for is realized in community. And MacIntyre sees the ultimate choice in morality as that between Aristotle and Nietzsche.

In our day, he sees emotivism and existentialism as evidence that the choice has gone the wrong way. Both these ethical theories reduce moral judgment to personal preference. Whatever criteria of moral judgment the emotivist or existentialist self may invoke, says MacIntyre, will be:

> expressions of attitudes, preferences and choices which are themselves not governed by criterion, principle or value, since they underlie and are prior to all allegiance to criterion, principle or value. But from this it follows that the . . . self can have no rational history in its transitions from one state of moral commitment to another. Inner conflicts are for it necessarily *au fond* the confrontation of one contingent arbitrariness by another. It is a self with no given continuities, save those of the body which is its bearer and of the memory which to the best of its ability gathers in its past. (*AF*, p. 31)

Given an emotivist or existentialist morality, MacIntyre contends, only two modes of social life are open to us. Either, one in which the free and arbitrary choices of individuals are sovereign; or one in which a bureaucracy, which limits these individual choices, is sovereign. Both are, in his opinion, worthless alternatives to the fulfilment of a virtuous individual within a virtuous community, which Aristotelian ethics was designed to produce. We are in a new dark ages, morally speaking, according to MacIntyre. Just as the classical tradition of the virtues was kept alive in monasteries during the last dark ages, so he sees our only hope to lie in "the construction of local forms of community within which civility and the intellectual and moral life can be sustained through the new dark ages which are already upon us." He concludes: "This time however the barbarians are not waiting beyond the frontiers; they have already been governing us for quite some time. And it is our lack of consciousness of this that constitutes part of our predica-

ment. We are waiting not for a Godot, but for another—
doubtless very different—St. Benedict" (*AF*, p. 245).

Critical Comment

I find it remarkable that MacIntyre regards the idea that
a man realizes his *telos* only in so far as he contributes to
the realization of the larger *telos* of his community, with
such uncritical approval; and that he considers what he
calls the invention of the individual, manifest in emotivist
and existentialist conceptions of morality, to have been
such an unqualified moral disaster. The doctrine that what
I am *for* is to fulfil the duties of a parent, a teacher, or
whatever, as these roles have been traditionally defined
within my community, has, in the course of human history,
spawned many repressive and repellent ideas and practices.
"The Italian nation is an organism with ends and means of
action superior to those of the individuals of which it is
composed," is the formulation that Mussolini, for example,
gave to it and some abominable implications were counten-
anced thereby. It may also be true, of course, that the
emotivist conception of moral judgments, as simply the
expressions of a speaker's pro- or con-attitudes, and the
existentialist idea that in delivering moral judgments we are
inventing, rather than realizing, what human nature can be,
may between them have given rise to some bizarrely egoistic
conceptions of the good for man. But the other side of this
coin is that they bear witness to the fact that there is a
critical element running through moral thinking. It may be
(as we shall find, in the next section, some philosophers
say) that moral judgments are unintelligible unless they
conform to certain traditional conceptions of virtue or vice;
but it is no less true that there is an openness in the moral
concepts which allows us always to inquire whether what
we have hitherto thought right or good really is so.

And not just that. There is a desirable diversity in what
people conceive to be right or good, which reflects their
individualism, as P. F. Strawson in his paper "Social Morality
and Individual Ideal" (*P* XXXVI, 1961, reprinted in his
collection *Freedom and Resentment*, London, 1974) has
pointed out. He concedes that in any society there has to

be some common recognition of certain virtues and obligations, for without these the society would disintegrate. But within that framework there can be—and in his opinion it is desirable that there should be—a wide diversity of what he calls "individual ideals." That is to say, of "images" or "pictures" or "ways of life" that dominate the ethical imaginations of different individuals. These conceptions of the good for man are certainly diverse and they may indeed conflict. A given individual may be held captive by one at a certain time in his life and by another at a different time. Or he may find himself at odds between more than one of them at the same time. Examples Strawson gives are: "The ideas of self-obliterating devotion to duty or to the service of others; of personal honour or magnanimity; of asceticism, contemplation, retreat; of action, dominance and power; of the cultivation of 'an exquisite sense of the luxurious'; of simple human solidarity and cooperative endeavour; of a refined complexity of social existence; of a constantly maintained and renewed sense of affinity with natural things—any of these ideas, and a great many others too, may form the core and substance of a personal ideal" (*Freedom and Resentment*, p. 26). I suppose if one believes, as Strawson does, that it is good for such diverse ideals to be pursued in one's society (even where one does not pursue most of them oneself and even if one finds some of them at variance with the ideals one does pursue) it would be logically possible to say that those who do pursue them are realizing their own *telos* only by realizing the good of their community. But it is surely nearer the mark to say that these diverse "idealists" are simply expressing their own individuality. The point I wish to make is merely that it is not as obvious as, on MacIntyre's line of argument, it ought to be, that such individualism undermines and destroys a society's morality. One does not need to approve of everything that goes on in the name of permissiveness to see that a society in which individuals "do their own thing" rather than conform to the traditional roles that society marks out for them, could thereby be enriching and renewing its moral life. But MacIntyre's version of Aristotelianism does not seem to allow for this possibility.

(IV) BASIL MITCHELL ON THE CONNECTION BETWEEN
MORALITY AND RELIGION

Running through all Aristotelian types of ethical theory, as we have seen, there is a conception of morality as the means whereby men may pass from what they happen to be to what they could be if they realized their *telos*. We noted that, in such types of theory, the practice of virtue is usually conceived, not simply as a means to self-fulfilment, but as itself an aspect of such fulfilment. It is part of what men are *for*. Nevertheless morality is thought of as teleological in the sense of having a point or purpose beyond itself. To use an expression made popular by Miss Anscombe in her paper, "Modern Moral Philosophy" (*P* XXXIII, 1958, reprinted in my *The Is—Ought Question*) morality is the way that leads to "human flourishing."

Now, it has seemed to some philosophers that it can only be coherently thought of in this way when certain metaphysical or religious beliefs about human nature are accepted. I take Basil Mitchell's Gifford Lectures, entitled *Morality: Religious and Secular* (Oxford, 1980), as an example of the kind of view that I have in mind (see particularly his pages 138—56).

Mitchell starts from the question, "Why should the individual acknowledge the authority of morality at all?". He notes G. J. Warnock's opinion in *The Object of Morality* (London, 1971) that rational beings as such do not *have* to regard moral reasons for action as compelling in themselves, much less as overriding all other kinds of reason. A rational being, for instance, could conceivably decide to let his wife and children starve, if this were a necessary condition of engaging in some activity which he preferred to earning enough money to take care of them. We could not say *simpliciter* that it would be against reason for anyone to behave in that way. What then, if anything, could we say? This is all that Warnock can offer by way of a reply: "One can want to acquire and exercise the settled disposition to comply with . . . (*sc.* moral) principles in one's judgment and conduct, to give due weight to the range of (*sc.* moral) reasons that those principles generate" (*Object of Morality*,

p. 165). In other words, though a rational man does not *have* to regard moral principles and reasons as compelling or over-riding, he may *want* to live as if they were. Like Mrs. Foot's later view (see above), this view grounds moral obligation in the contingent fact that those who feel it simply happen to have a certain disposition. Mitchell considers this a "somewhat lame" answer to the question why anyone should think and act in the light of moral considerations at all (*Morality*, p. 141).

He recognizes however, that the question is not an easy one to answer. It puts us in something of a dilemma. For if the answer we give is, in effect, that there is a heteronomous pay-off for being good that reduces morality to mere expediency or prudence; but, on the other hand, if we insist on the autonomy of morals and say that we ought to be moral simply because we morally ought, that is circular. Mitchell calls these, respectively, the "down to earth" and the "high-minded" answers to the question at issue. The former kind—e.g. "Honesty pays"—he considers "plainly untrue and not high-minded enough." What he says of the latter kind of answer takes us, I think, to the heart of his argument, and it goes as follows:

> But the high-minded contention that "virtue is its own reward" is doubly unsatisfying. If moral virtue is what we have all along supposed it to be, a principled concern for others' needs, then those needs matter or virtue so conceived is pointless. And if other men's happiness, at which the good man ought to aim, is distinct from their virtue, the good man's own happiness cannot consist in his virtue alone . . . There is need, as Kant saw, for some connection between virtue and happiness of a down to earth kind. Something can be done to bring the two positions together, the down-to-earth and the high-minded, by insisting with Plato and Aristotle on the contentment which attends the life of moral virtue, which is the highest and purest pleasure and flows from the recognition that one is achieving excellence as a man. But Aristotle, at least, saw that there is more to happiness than this; it may be an essential element in

human flourishing, but it is not the fullness of it. And it becomes apparent from the words of Christ: "If ye, then, being evil, know how to give good gifts unto your children, how much more shall your father which is in heaven give good gifts to them that ask him." No human father, if it was in his power to give his children more, would be satisfied with giving them only the opportunity to be virtuous and the contentment that flows from it. He would want them to enjoy all the happiness that life can afford. (*Morality*, pp. 142—43)

I say that this takes us to the heart of Mitchell's argument because it puts us on the track of an answer to the question, "Why should I be moral?", which, in his opinion, escapes both the reductionism of the "down to earth" view and the circularity of the "high minded" one. If I read him correctly, what Mitchell is doing, in the earlier part of the passage I have just quoted, is calling attention to two things we normally take for granted with regard to virtue, and then drawing out the implications of each of them. In the latter part of the quotation, he lines himself up with Aristotle on the subject of virtue and happiness.

The first of the two things he thinks we normally take for granted is that virtue is "a principled concern for others' needs." This seems true enough; if we were told that a man had no such concern, I think we would hesitate to call him virtuous, whatever else might be said in his favour. Now, implicit in this first thing we normally take for granted is the idea that virtue has an objective beyond itself without which it would lose its *raison d'etre* — if other men's needs did not "matter," virtue would be "pointless." The second of the two things, which Mitchell thinks we take for granted, is that "other men's happiness, at which the good man ought to aim, is distinct from their virtue." Here, again, this can hardly be doubted. It would be odd to say that a man could not be virtuous unless he had a concern for others' virtue to the exclusion of all else. We normally conceive of a virtuous man as concerned for the needs of others in a wider sense that that. From this Mitchell draws the inference that "the good man's own happiness cannot consist in his virtue alone."

I take him to mean that, if a good man has done his best to bring about the happiness, as well as the virtue, of others, but without success, this good man will necessarily feel some regret. He has done his best and so remorse (as distinct from regret) will be inappropriate; but, as a good man he will deeply desire the happiness of others, and so it will make him sad to think that he has not succeeded in making others happy. Since the good man's own happiness, therefore, consists in something more than the realization of virtue alone, it will not suffice to say that he simply believes "high-mindedly" in "virtue for virtue's sake."

In the latter part of the above quotation, as we noted just now, Mitchell relates his view to that of Aristotle. I am not absolutely certain that I have caught his drift and he may be saying more than I take him to be. But he appears to be lining himself up with Aristotle's view of morality as the means whereby we pass from "human nature as it happens to be" to "human nature as it could be when it realises its *telos*" and conceiving of the latter as, whilst including virtue, amounting to something more than that alone. This is the view that Mitchell, in the earlier part of the above quotation, found implicit in our ordinary conception of virtue.

If it is indeed implicit, then any justification of virtue, as it is commonly conceived—i.e. any satisfactory answer to the question, "Why should I be moral?"—must rest in the final analysis upon a belief that men have a *telos* that is other, or at any rate more, than the practice of virtue but to which such practice serves as a means of attainment.

Now, the connection which Mitchell finds between religion and morality appears to be this. Religion lends a foundation to morality in so far as it teaches that God has created men for a purpose which they can achieve through the practice of virtue, but which does not consist solely in such practice. It is comparatively easy for Mitchell to defend this view against the criticism of Richard Robinson, in his *An Atheist's Values*, that it reduces morality to prudence by offering as the reason for doing good simply the belief that it will bring one to heaven, and for not doing evil, that it would land one in hell. Mitchell's reply is that it is only in so far as men have some love of virtue for its own sake that they will be able to enjoy, and enter into, the blessedness of heaven (cf. *Morality*, p. 145).

But whether or not a religious account of morality's foundation is acceptable cannot be decided simply by considering whether or not it would fit neatly into an Aristotelian analysis of morality, if it were true. And Mitchell does not claim that. He simply insists that an Aristotelian type of ethic requires us to hold certain beliefs about the nature and destiny of man and observes that "if you believe that morality is in some way based upon the fundamental needs of men, you may concede to religion some say as to what the fundamental needs of men are" (*Morality*, p. 151). Warnock, who raised the question, "Why should I be moral?", remarks (but does not elaborate) that "one could do the trick with the help of a deity" (*Object of Morality*, p. 159). Mitchell, I think, has shown how it could be done in that way. Those who take the Aristotelian line are, of course, at liberty to show a more convincing way of doing it, if they can. But not simply to wave aside the question, "Does man have a *telos* and if so, what is it?"

(V) CONCLUDING COMMENT

A number of times in discussing Neo-aristotelian ethics, I have commented on the difficulty of answering the question, "What are men *for*?" Many philosophers would say that this question itself does not make sense; some would argue that it is an instance of the fallacy of composition in so far as it assumes that the human race as a whole must have a purpose because individual members of it have purposes. But even if philosophers are willing to take the question seriously, they find it hard to answer. Given certain metaphysical or religious beliefs, of course, it is easy to answer. If God exists and has a purpose, or if Nature as a whole can be conceived to have an aim, then what men are *for* can be thought of in terms of such a purpose or aim. But then the relevant metaphysical or religious beliefs themselves have to be justified and many philosophers would say that they cannot be. Neo-aristotelians, when they abjure such beliefs, are left with only human nature itself to contemplate and from such contemplation alone it is notoriously difficult to deduce what men are for.

Suppose we ask what is distinctive of human nature and try to proceed from that. We may say, for example, that human beings are distinguished from the rest of creation by a greater capacity for rational or social activity and that man's *telos* must therefore consist in developing these capacities to the full. But the trouble with this, if it is offered as guidance about how we ought to live, is that immoral conduct seems to offer just as great a scope for rational and social activity as moral behaviour does. This point was well taken by Hare against Geach's functional conception of human nature, which we considered above. "Geach", says Hare, "is the latest of a famous succession of thinkers who have systematically confused 'what a thing *can* (or, alternatively, *can typically*, or *does typically*) do', with the quite different notion 'what a thing *ought* to do (or, alternatively, what it is specifically *good* for it to do' ") (in P. Foot, *Theories of Ethics*, pp. 81—82n.). Hare goes on to say that the assimilation of these two conceptions of function is only justified if we accept the assumed premise *Natura (sive Deus) nihil facit inane*. And he warns anyone who feels attracted by Geach's use of this kind of reasoning to read Aristotle's *Politics* 1252a, where a similar premise is used to justify slavery and the subjection of women.

Against that sort of objection to deducing morality from function, teleological moralists sometimes invoke the concept of *health*. It stands for an ideal physical and mental condition, for the attainment of which certain standards of behaviour can be laid down. "Why then", a Neo-aristotelian might ask, "cannot we conceive of what men are *for* as an extension of this concept of health and of morality as laying down rules of conduct for its attainment?" The short answer, I think, is that we cannot do so because the two conceptions—health and *telos*—are radically different in a vital respect. Health can be thought of as a means; *telos* cannot.

Health is an ideal physical and mental condition which, in so far as it is attained, enables one to do certain things one wants to do more effectively than one otherwise could. What enables people to live longer, run faster, think more clearly, sleep more soundly, and so on? This is the kind of question that determines what counts as health. The states of mind or body which are identified, and prescribed, as constituting health are those which enable human beings to do such things as run faster, rest more easily, etc. These states of mind or body are fairly easy to define because there is a considerable consensus as to what people want to achieve through the exercise of their minds and bodies. True, some fanatics regard health as an end in itself; but most of us think and speak of it as a means to certain ends, such as longevity, the fulfilment of our ambitions, freedom from neurotic anxiety, etc., which we desire for ourselves or others. By contrast, what men are *for*, i.e. their *telos*, cannot be thought of as a means to something beyond itself. How could a final end be that? It must be conceived as man's true function, self-fulfilment, flourishing, or whatever other such description seems appropriate. And what all those descriptions have in common is that they mark an end-point to explanation and justification. Something, that is, which does not, like health, enable us to live well or to do what we want; but which determines what it is to live well and what we ought to want.

Neo-aristotelianism, as a version of the type of ethical theory called descriptivism, purports to deduce "ought" from "is." In effect, it represents the core of moral thinking thus: "If T *is* a man's *telos*, then he *ought* to do what will realize T." The way in which the bridge is built between this "is" and "ought" is commonly by invoking the concept of *needs*. Neo-aristotelians go along with the idea that a man is given a reason for action when he is shown the way to something he wants, but they deepen the concept of wanting and make it into that of needing. Just as a plant needs certain soil and air conditions in order to flourish, so human flourishing has its necessary conditions and these needs constitute the bridge notion between "is" and "ought." If T is a man's *telos*, and N is a necessary condition of realizing it, then a man ought to fulfil N. The question "Ought one to do what one wants to do?" is open. But "Ought one to do what one needs to do?" seems *prima facie* to admit only of an affirmative answer. So, if human flourishing can be represented as the fulfilment of human needs, it seems to entail an ought.

There is, however, an ambiguity in the word "need." I may need N, (i) in the sense that N is a necessary condition of existence *simpliciter* or (ii) in the sense that N is a necessary condition of *good existence*. If N is a need in sense (i), then the question "Is N good?" remains open; but if N is a need in sense (ii) then this question is self-answering in the affirmative.

The question which these considerations raise with regard to the notion of human flourishing is whether or not that notion is purely descriptive. Is the statement (as understood by Neo-aristotelians) "T is my *telos*" a purely factual statement? Or does it contain an implicit value judgment? Is whatever one takes to constitute the correct answer to the question "What are men *for*?" necessarily an indication, not only of what one thinks men *are*, but of what one considers that they *ought* to be? Reflection on this point seems to show that, just as there is an ambiguity in the word "need", so there is in the notions of man's *telos* or of human flourishing. It is the ambiguity between existence *simpliciter* and *good* existence. If, and only if, I attain my *telos*, do I *exist as a man*. But the derivation, "If T *is* what it is to exist as a man, then I *ought* to realize T" only has the appearance of a deduction of "ought" from "is" because at the heart of it there is equivocation on two ideas of "existence as a man." We may think of this as *existence simpliciter or as good existence*. "Exist as a man" is, in effect, conceived in the premise ("T is what it is to exist as a man") as a fact; but in the conclusion ("I ought to realize T") as a norm. This seems to be the defect at the heart of all teleological accounts of morality. What they take simply to be the *fact* that such-and-such is man's function or *telos* always involves an *evaluation* and so they beg the question whether "ought" can be deduced from "is" right from the start.

IV. MORALITY GROUNDED IN TRADITION

It may seem a little odd to call the type of ethical theory, with which I am now going to deal, a version of descriptiv-

ism. But I venture to do so because those who subscribe to
it take morality to have a certain restricted *content*. They
reject the prescriptivist idea that, in order to be moral, all a
judgment needs to have is a certain logical *form*—prescriptivity, universalizability, or whatever—and insist that what
makes it a moral judgment can only be the fact that it is in
accordance with generally accepted ideas of what is right or
wrong. They would contend, for example, that if I say, "I
ought to do act A because it has characteristic C," this
judgment could not be accounted a moral one purely on
the grounds that I assented to the entailed imperative, "Let
me do A," or agreed that if any other action also had
characteristic C, I ought to do that as well. In their opinion
my judgment would only be recognizable as a moral one, if
characteristic C showed act A to be an instance of a kind of
behaviour that is generally considered morally worthy or
obligatory. For example, some such characteristic as "courageous" would meet the case. If what I said were, "I ought
to do act A because it will be courageous," this would make
my judgment moral because it would bring it into accord
with the belief that one ought to act courageously and that
belief is part of the content of morality in our society.

Words like "courageous" are both descriptive and evaluative in meaning. Therefore, the view that "Act A is courageous" entails "Act A ought to be done" is not, perhaps,
as thorough-going a version of descriptivism as the other
theories considered in the present chapter. The fact that an
act will satisfy a want which all men have, or the fact that
it will enable one to attain one's true end, are purely factual
reasons for saying that the act referred to is obligatory; and
philosophers, who would take them to be good reasons for
such a moral judgment, are, therefore, descriptivists in a
more unequivocal sense than the members of the school of
thought I am now going to consider. For, the latter, as we
shall see, hold that moral thinking is logically grounded, not
simply on certain matters of putative fact—such as, that
some sorts of action satisfy our ultimate wants or maximize
happiness—but on an agreement in moral judgments, which
they take to be the basis of morality in their society. Nevertheless, what their ethical theory comes to is that, unless
courses of action or states of affairs can be described in

ways which classify them as instances of accepted virtues or vices, they cannot be the subjects of moral judgments. And this is why I call this type of ethical theory a version of descriptivism. The representatives of it whom I shall have in mind are Peter Winch, D. Z. Phillips and H. O. Mounce, R. W. Beardsmore and Richard Norman.

Agreement in Judgments

According to these philosophers, there is, in any given society at any given time, a range of moral concepts, such as courage, honesty, truthfulness, generosity, etc., which (together with their opposites) are generally regarded as virtues (or vices). And it is only when these concepts are invoked, explicitly or implicitly, as norms of positive (or negative) value, that judgments can be understood as moral ones. It is the acceptance, and application, of these traditional norms which gives moral judgments their point.

Phillips and Mounce bring this out in their paper, "On Morality's Having a Point" (*P* XL, 1965, reprinted in *The Is—Ought Question*). They agree with Mrs. Foot (see above) that, in order to have any point, a moral judgment needs a certain kind of "background." Her example, it will be remembered, was that of a man who thinks he ought to clench his hands persistently. This seems pointless unless some background is supplied which will show that, in so doing, the man safeguards certain interests or fulfils certain desires. It may be, for instance, that the recovery of the use of his fingers depends on this exercise and so it is in his own interest to perform it; or additionally that, unless he performs it, he will lose his powers as a pianist or a surgeon and so be unable to fulfil his desire to help or please other people. The former would be a good moral reason for doing it, according to Mrs. Foot's earlier views; the latter, according to her later ones. But, whilst they consider a background necessary to give moral judgments point, Phillips and Mounce do not think that it is supplied by such heteronomous considerations of interest or desire. They think the background has to be *moral*:

Such concepts as sincerity, honesty, courage, loyalty, respect, and, of course, a host of others, provide the kind of background necessary in order to make sense of rules as moral principles. It does not follow that all the possible features of such backgrounds need to be present in every case. The important point to stress is that unless the given rule has *some* relation to such backgrounds, we would not know what is meant by calling it a moral principle. (*I—OQ*, p. 230)

Their illustration is that of a man who thinks he ought to take off his shoes when he comes to a certain place. Conceived as a moral obligation, this makes no sense until we understand that it is regarded in his society as a mark of *respect* for holy ground. Phillips' and Mounce's insistence that the background, which gives moral judgments their point, must be a *moral* one is, of course, another example of the "high Stoic line" which they consistently take. To their way of thinking, virtue, which is its own reward, must also be its own reason. In the last analysis, actions or states of affairs can only be understood to have positive or negative moral value in so far as they instantiate virtues or vices.

Exponents of the type of ethical theory we are now considering are fond of quoting a remark of Wittgenstein's, which they take to support their point of view. It occurs in *Philosophical Investigations*, I.242: "If language is to be a means of communication there must be agreement not only in definitions but also (queer as this may seem) in judgments." In the context where this remark occurs, Wittgenstein points out that a definition of the word "red," such as " 'red' means the colour that occurs to me when I hear the word 'red'," would not be of any use for purposes of communication unless there were general agreement about what things are red. Similarly, he says, it would be of no use to have an agreed method of measuring unless there was a certain constancy in the results of measurement. Whether or not Wittgenstein would have wished to see the point he is making extended to moral communication is by no means certain. G. Hallett tells us in his erudite *Companion to Wittgenstein's Philosophical Investigations* (London, 1973, pp. 304—5) that in a hitherto unpublished manuscript Wittgenstein expressly denies that this point applies to aesthetically evaluative terms such as "beautiful" and "ugly;" and this, to say the least, raises doubts as to whether he would have applied it to moral terms such as "right" and "wrong." However, the philosophers whom we are now considering have no hesitation in doing so.

What they take Wittgenstein to be saying is, to quote Peter Winch ("Nature and Convention" in his collection, *Ethics and Action*, London, 1972, p. 60): "human rationality is essentially social in character." When I give a reason for what I say, it counts as a reason, not simply because I adhere to it consistently, but because it is the kind of thing that I and others have been brought up to appeal to, and accept, in the sort of context within which I happen to be speaking. Winch quotes Robert Oppenheimer to this effect with regard to natural science: "The deep things in modern physics, and probably in mathematics too, are not things you can tell about unless you are talking to someone who has lived a long time acquiring the tradition" (*ibid.*, p. 54). Exactly the same, in Winch's opinion, can be said about moral discourse. There is tradition which consists of "agreement in judgments" and unless reasoning conforms to this agreement, it will be unintelligible. He offers the following illustration:

> Suppose that two men, *A* and *B*, are arguing about a proposed relaxation of the divorce laws. *A* convinces *B* that the divorce laws as they exist generate much human misery and that the proposed relaxation would not bring with it any deleterious after-effects, such as a weakening in public respect for the institution of marriage. Suppose then that *B*, having accepted all this and without raising any counter-considerations of his own, then says that he has decided to oppose any relaxation in the law. Of course, we can imagine *B* acting like this; but I suggest that we should find what he was doing unintelligible. And if he were *always* to act like this, we should say he was incapable of rational decision. (*Ethics and Action*, p. 55)

Winch comments that morality cannot be logically grounded in *decisions* of principle, as prescriptivists have supposed, "for a decision can only be made within the context of a meaningful way of life and a moral decision can only be made within the context of a morality." What decisions are, and what are not, "possible," he contends, "will depend on the morality within which the issues arise; and not *any* issue can arise in a given morality" (*ibid.*). The key notion here is obviously that of *intelligibility*. The word "possible," just quoted, means understandable. The point which Winch is making is that, as with *A* and *B* in his illustration, people can only understand each other in moral discourse, if there is some agreement between them as to what counts as a reason for saying one thing rather than another. And this, in the last analysis, is an agreement in judgments as to what is right or wrong; what ought or ought not, to be done; what is virtuous or vicious.

We should perhaps pause for a moment on what I have called the key notion of intelligibility. Some one else's reasoning may be said to be unintelligible to me for either of two reasons. I may, first, not understand how anyone can count certain considerations so lightly (or *mutatis mutandis* so heavily) in arriving at a certain conclusion. For instance, I may say that it seems unintelligible to me that, in supporting unilateral disarmament, some people can give so little weight to the consideration that wars are caused by men who think they can win and, therefore, the way to prevent wars is to leave men who are likely to cause them in no doubt that they cannot win. But there is another, and a different, sense of "unintelligible." Suppose someone said he was in favour of unilateral disarmament because bombs are made of metal. My puzzlement would be, not as to why he counted this consideration so heavily, but as to why he counted it at all. Why is the fact that bombs are made of metal a reason for not making them? Nothing in my own ways of thinking will serve as an answer. This reasoning is not only different from mine; in my book, it is not reasoning at all. So, when Winch says that what decisions are "possible" will depend on "the *morality* within which they arise," or when he says that they "can only be made within the context of a meaningful *way of life*" (*Ethics and Action*, p. 55, italics mine), I take him to mean, by "morality" or "way of life" here, a system of thought based upon certain fundamental judgments which determine what, within that system, counts as a reason and what does not.

It is important to realize that this is not taken to imply, by proponents of the type of ethical theory we are considering, that morality is not morality unless it is conventional. R. W. Beardsmore emphasizes this in his *Moral Reasoning* (London, 1969). This book presents an admirably clear account of the version of descriptivism I am now discussing. Towards the end of it, Beardsmore reminds us that, in the context where Wittgenstein speaks of "agreement in judgments," he contrasts this with "agreement in opinions" (*MR*, p. 124); and he insists that some such contrast must be drawn with regard to morality. Agreement in "opinions" is what Beardsmore would call conventionalism. He offers, as an example of it, the remark of the Neo-hegelian moralist, F. H. Bradley, "to be moral is to live in accordance with the moral tradition of one's country" (*Ethical Studies*, 173). Bradley, it will be recalled, believed that any divergence from the generally accepted ideas of one's community, concerning what is right or wrong, takes one to the brink of immorality. Moral innovation is dangerous and must be discouraged. There must be agreement in "opinions." But this view is quite different, says Beardsmore, from what he—following Wittgenstein—means by "agreement in judgments." The latter is not an agreement "within" morality, but one which "gives (moral) language its sense" (*MR*, p. 125). The agreed judgments constitute a content in so far as they are judgments and not mere definitions. In Winch's illustration, the "agreement in judgments" between *A* and *B*—for lack of which *B*'s opinion was unintelligible to *A*—concerned such matters of substance as that what "generates human misery" is bad and what "does not weaken public respect for the institution of marriage" is good. The point of the illustration was not to show that *B*'s opinion was unconventional and therefore bad; but that *B* refused to appeal to, and accept, the judgments that he and *A* had been brought up to regard as settling moral issues. And, therefore, what *B* had to say could not be considered a contribution to moral discourse.

Tradition and Innovation

The criticism sometimes made of this type of ethical theory, which grounds morality in tradition, is that it affords no explanation of moral reform or innovation. There undoubtedly are moral reforms and innovations, but if moral judgments only make sense in so far as they rest upon "agreement in judgments," how can this be? Beardsmore's insistence upon the difference between agreement in "opinions" and in "judgments" opens the door to an answer and he offers one in a chapter entitled "The Rebel and Moral Traditions." Nietzsche is his example of a rebel.

Now, Nietzsche is certainly thought to have been a radical one. In his writings there are fierce attacks on such virtues as piety, truth-telling, and above all on humility. He calls all this "slave morality." But Beardsmore thinks there are at least two different ways in which Nietzsche's radicalism can be interpreted.

According to one, he was attacking the conventional morality of his day as a perversion of genuine morality. Nietzsche expresses contempt for "the servile mode of thought" whereby the good man is "the *safe* man . . . good-natured, easily deceived, perhaps a little stupid, *un bon-homme*" (*Beyond Good and Evil*, quoted by Beardsmore, *MR*, p. 56). He speaks derogatorily of what he evidently regards as current hypocrisy: "It is so *convenient* to be frank and honest. . . . It is wise for a people to pose and let itself be regarded as profound, clumsy, good-natured, honest and foolish" (*MR*, p. 58). All such remarks may be read, not as a rejection of morality, but as an exercise in it. Hypocrisy has been called the tribute vice pays to virtue and, on the present interpretation of Nietzsche, all he is doing is appealing for sincerity and integrity. Let people really practise the virtues, in which they profess to believe, and have done with pretence! If this is all Nietzsche was, in effect, saying, there is no reason for any traditional moralist to be disturbed.

However, the other interpretation Beardsmore thinks possible is that Nietzsche regarded "slave morality" as a genuine morality but was advocating its replacement by a different morality. He says that the virtues of "the gregari-

ous European man," such as "public spirit, kindness, defer-
ence, industry, temperance, modesty" are "only one kind
of human morality" and there are "many other moralities,
and above all *higher* moralities." Some things he says make
the higher morality he is evidently advocating sound exceed-
ingly alien to us; for instance, that it does not seek "to do
away with suffering" but wants it to be "worse and more
than it ever was" (*MR*, p. 61). The significant thing however
is that this is then said to be desirable as the means to an
increase of such virtues as courage, sensitivity, passion. On
this second interpretation, therefore, as on the first, says
Beardsmore, Nietzsche's "views are intelligible only because
he is able to support them with reasons which have some
sort of connection with accepted moral considerations"
(*MR*, p. 62). This, he goes on, is what differentiates the
views of a moral revolutionary from those of a moral
maniac, whose opinions are incomprehensible. A revolutionary differs from a conservative in his "opinions;" but a
maniac differs from both of them in his "judgments."

Public Norms

One of the best defences known to me of the logical
point at the foundation of this type of ethical theory is to
be found in Richard Norman's *Reasons for Actions* (Oxford,
1971). He criticizes both the prescriptivism that Hare represents and the type of descriptivism propounded by Mrs.
Foot, for making what he considers the same mistake,
namely that of grounding moral reasons for action in "some
psychological state of the agent" (*RA*, p. 15). Not the same
state, of course; Hare grounds them in the agent's pro- or
con-*attitudes*, Mrs. Foot in his ultimate *wants*.

Norman argues that, if they are to serve as reasons, attitudes and wants must have some connection with what Miss
Anscombe has called "desirability characterizations." He
makes the point mainly with regard to wants but I think it
can be extended to attitudes, decisions or choices as well.
Suppose a man, to take Miss Anscombe's example, expresses
a desire for, or a choice of, a saucer of mud. When we ask
him what he wants, or has chosen, it *for*, he replies, "Not
for anything. I just want it (or have chosen it)." We shall

feel that there *must* be something that makes it desirable or choice-worthy—"Does it serve as a symbol? Is there something delightful about it? Does the man want to have something to call his own?" (Anscombe, quoted by Norman, *RA*, p. 53). If no such questions are answerable in the affirmative, we shall conclude that the man does not have a reason for wanting or choosing his saucer of mud. "I just want it," or "I simply choose it," in themselves, will not serve as reasons.

Other examples of "desirability characterizations," mentioned by Miss Anscombe, are "comfortable," "pleasant," "fun," "it befits me," "it suits me." Things that are wanted or chosen may, of course, be consciously regarded simply as means to something else, as Mrs. Foot recognized in developing her earlier views. But what Norman is pointing out is that, even the other kind of wants for which Mrs. Foot said the question "Why do you want that?" does not make sense, are wanted, or chosen, because they have some "desirability characterization"—because, that is, they are comforting, interesting, or whatever. As Norman puts the point:

> Wants have to be backed up by reasons. Therefore, not just any assertion of the form "I want just X" (*sic*) can provide an ultimate reason-for-acting. If it does so, this will be because the description 'X' characterizes the thing wanted in such a way that no further reason is necessary. And in that case, it is the fact that the thing is desirable as 'X', not the fact that the thing is wanted, that constitutes the reason-for-acting. The notion of 'wanting' can be allowed to fall out altogether. (*RA*, p. 63)

If Norman is told that this simply puts wanting a stage further back, since we can ask of any "desirability characterizations," "Why do you want to be comfortable, interested, etc.?", he, in turn, can reply that any reason which is given will itself in due course depend upon some "desirability characterization," and so *ad infinitum* (*RA*, p. 65).

Turning his attention now to specifically moral reasons

for acting, Norman argues that these also depend in the last analysis on "desirability characterizations." In moral discourse these are descriptions such as "courageous," "dishonest," or whatever. The function of concepts such as courage or honesty etc. is "both to characterize an action as being of a certain kind, and at same time to indicate that its being of that kind constitutes a reason for performing it" (*RA*, p. 66). Since Norman, like Winch, thinks that rationality is essentially social in character, he considers that a reason for performing an action can be given to it only by bringing it under "a public norm." And that is precisely what a description such as "courageous" or "dishonest" does. Such "Janus words" (as Norman calls them, following P. H. Nowell Smith, *Ethics*, 100 ff.), "encapsulate" public norms and thereby "determine what counts as a rational action" (*RA*, p. 67). They represent that "agreement in judgments," that fundamental content to morality, which determines what it does, and does not, make sense to say within it. Janus-words, Norman says, are "in a very important sense . . . more fundamental" in morality than words like "good" or "evil," which merely express approval or disapproval without invoking any specific criteria. An expression of approval or disapproval cannot in itself be regarded as rational; it becomes so only if its object can be characterized by a Janus-word. This makes the intelligibility of purely evaluative words, like "good" or "evil," parasitic on the meaning of words which encapsulate public norms like "courageous" or "dishonest." And that is the "very important sense" in which Norman thinks these Janus-words are logically "more fundamental" than purely evaluative ones in morality. He thinks that there can be no question of norms being constituted by wants or choices because "it becomes possible to want the thing only when one has already learnt to see it in the relevant way" — i.e. in terms of a desirability characterization. He adds, by way of illustration, "I can value my house as a 'home' only because I have already learnt the concept of a 'home' and in learning the concept and its place within a form of social life I have learnt an evaluative norm" (*RA*, p. 76).

There is I think some confusion, in the type of ethical

theory which I have just been outlining, between the notions of intelligibility and rationality. The simple idea that my use of "rights," for example, will necessarily be *unintelligible* to you unless there is "agreement in judgments" between us as to what is right, seems plainly to be mistaken. You and I could both say that something was right but disagree fundamentally on the properties which make it right. We should certainly understand each other in the sense that we would each know that the other's use of "right" meant that he was evaluating the thing positively. Everything that could be inferred from such a positive evaluation would also be intelligible to us to the extent of our powers of inference.

If, however, we now consider *rationality* rather than mere intelligibility, it is true that, in order to regard each other's evaluative judgments as rational, we should need to share, to some extent, the same criteria of positive and negative value. These would not be simply linguistic rules but substantial moral judgments. For there to be reasoning between people, for what is said by one to the other to make sense as argument, reflection, the interchange of ideas—in Wittgenstein's word, as "communication"—some fundamental "agreement in judgments" would be necessary. With the proviso that such agreement was always open to revision, I think a prescriptivist such as Hare would not dissent from this opinion (cf. his *Moral Thinking*, p. 70).

CHAPTER 8. ANTI-UTILITARIANISM AND THE "TWO-LEVEL" THEORY

I. NEO-INTUITIONISM'S ATTACK ON UTILITARIANISM

As we noted earlier (p. 227), Hare claims that his pre-scriptivism provides "a formal foundation" for utilitarianism. And, if prescriptivity and universalizability are in fact necessary conditions of moral judgment, it certainly seems to follow that, unless a judgment commends the maximum possible satisfaction of the wants of all the affected parties, it cannot be a moral one. But many moral philosophers would now say that this implication is to the discredit of prescriptivism. For utilitarianism—whether represented as an aspect of the logic of moral discourse or as a correct substantial account of what is right—has come in for severe criticism of late from influential thinkers.

When John Stuart Mill popularized it more than a century ago—in his articles for *Fraser's Magazine*, 1861, now published as the essay *Utilitarianism*—he encountered fierce opposition from the ethical intuitionists (see my *A Century of Moral Philosophy*, London, 1980, Chapter 1). In recent times, there has been what may be described as a revival of intuitionism. I am not saying, of course, that these latter-day "intuitionists" have taken over lock, stock and barrel the ontology and epistemology of the classical intuitionists: I doubt if any of them would wish to say there are "non-natural" moral properties that actions or states of affairs can be known by intuition to possess. But what all of them do share is the opinion that, when a plain man consults his conscience, he will often find its deliverances at variance with those of the principle that an act is right, provided only that it will effect the greatest happiness of the greatest number.

Three Examples of Neo-Intuitionism

Miss Anscombe voices this opinion forthrightly. She points out that, in certain conceivable circumstances, utilitarianism would prescribe the judicial execution of an innocent man. It might be expedient that one man should die for the people. We could imagine conditions in which the greatest happiness of the greatest number could be effected by ignoring one man's innocence and treating him as if he were guilty. Since Henry Sidgwick, so Miss Anscombe affirms (in her much-quoted paper, "Modern Moral Philosophy", first published in *P* XXXIII, 1958) all the best known English academic moral philosophers have put out forms of ethical theory according to which this kind of thing could conceivably be right. Far more important than any differences between them, in her view, is the fact that they are all so completely at variance with what she calls "the Hebrew-Christian" ethic, according to which "there are certain things forbidden *whatever* consequences threaten, such as: choosing to kill the innocent for any purpose, however good; vicarious punishment; treachery (by which I mean obtaining a man's confidence in a grave matter by promises of trustworthy friendship and then betraying him to his enemies); idolatry; sodomy; adultery; making a false profession of faith." She speaks of such intuitionism as a kind of descriptivism: it is "the prohibition of certain things simply in virtue of their description as such-and-such identifiable kinds of action, regardless of any further consequences" (reprinted in my *The Is—Ought Question*, pp. 184—85). Her rejection of the utilitarian and prescriptivist idea, according to which it is sometimes morally and logically possible to evaluate actions of the kinds she has described as right, could not be more complete: "if someone really thinks . . . that it is open to question whether such an action as procuring the judicial execution of the innocent should be quite excluded from consideration—I do not want to argue with him; he shows a corrupt mind" (*ibid.*, p. 192. The words I have omitted are "in advance." In a footnote, the author explains that she has inserted them to allow for the possibility that a "normally tempted human being", might think this "in the concrete situation". But this qualification does not affect the point I am making.)

Another example of anti-utilitarian neo-intuitionism is to be found in the writings of Stuart Hampshire. His 1972 Leslie Stephen lecture "Morality and Pessimism" (published in S. Hampshire *et al., Public and Private Morality*, Cambridge, 1978) is a trenchant attack on the utility principle. He contends that the existence of "moral impossibilities," i.e. of "prohibitions" or "barriers to action," with regard to the taking of life and certain related matters, belongs to the very "notion of morality." That is to say, "a morality is, at the very least, the regulation of the taking of life and the regulation of sexual relations, and it also includes rules of distributive and corrective justice; family duties; almost always duties of friendship; also rights and duties in respect of money and property" (*PPM*, p. 7). This idea of what one cannot, or must not, do—e.g. "I can't leave him now," "I can't say that," etc.—is integral to morality, in Hampshire's estimation. He thinks the fatal error of the utilitarians is to have supposed that these "moral impossibilities"—or as he also calls them, "intuitive responses"—are (a) "systematically connected" and (b) "not absolute, but conditional" (*PPM*, p. 8). In other words, that they are subordinate to the utility principle. This opinion, that they are morally obligatory only in so far as they instantiate the general happiness principle, and serve as a means to its fulfilment, is, in Hampshire's judgment, totally mistaken. He will allow no room at all to the utilitarian contention that, in so far as they appear disconnected and absolute, these "moral impossibilities" merely perpetuate a primitive, or pre-rational, level of moral thinking.

He admits, of course, that their particular content varies in different moral codes, or as he calls them, "ways of life." It is not only their content, but also the weight placed upon them relatively to one another, that may vary. "A way of life is a complicated thing, marked by many details of style and manner, and also by particular activities and interests, which a group of people of similar dispositions in a similar social situation may share; so that the group may become an imitatable human type who transmit many of their habits and ideals to their descendants, provided that social change is not too rapid" (*PPM*, pp. 11—12). An individual may wish that he could combine prohibitions from many different ways of life but find it impossible to do so. However, individuals can, to some extent, create their own "mix" of "intuitive responses." Like different social groups, individuals may "recognise rather different moral necessities in the same essential areas of moral concern" (*PPM*, p. 15). So Hampshire sums up the position thus: "Each society, each generation within it, and in the last resort each reflective individual, accepts, and amends, an established morality expressed in rituals and manners, and in explicit prohibitions; and he will do this in determining what kind of person he aspires to be and what are the necessary features of a desirable and admirable way of life as he conceives it (*PPM*, p. 19).

Hampshire has a good deal to say about the "rational reflection" involved in deciding upon a "way of life" but I do not think he makes it crystal clear what he means by this. He is quite explicit about what he does *not* mean. To be rational is not, as a prescriptivist might say, to be willing to universalize one's moral judgments, any more than it is, as a utilitarian would think, to conform to the utility principle. It is neither of these kinds of consistency that Hampshire expects of a rational moralist; what he does expect he describes thus: "the connection, upon which a reasonable man reflects, is to be found in the coherence of a single way of life, distinguished by the characteristic virtues and vices recognised within it" (*PPM*, p. 11). But I am not sure in what he conceives this "coherence" to consist. That is made the harder to imagine by the fact, as we shall see, that Hampshire considers a conflict of obligations to be endemic to the moral life.

He is well aware that he may be accused by utilitarians of simply putting the clock back in all this talk of "intuitive responses" and "moral impossibilities," and he is therefore careful to dissociate himself from some classical versions of intuitionism: "there are no conclusive proofs, or infallible intuitions, which put a stop to the adducing of new considerations" (*PPM*, p. 15). Moreover, he recognizes that the prohibition of killing, or respect for human life, which he evidently considers the most fundamental of all "intuitive responses," has traditionally been conceived to rest on a religious foundation. But what if that foundation disappears? Hampshire insists that, even if "the idea that human life has a unique value has to be recognised as a a human invention" (*PPM*, p. 19), nevertheless "the prohibition against the taking of life, and respect for human life as such, may still be reaffirmed as absolute" (*PPM*, p. 17). How so? Of course, he rejects what he takes to be the utilitarian answer, viz. that "the horror of killing is only the horror of causing other losses, principally of possible happiness" (*ibid.*). For the answer that he himself gives he acknowledges his indebtedness to Aristotle and Spinoza. It is as follows: "One may on reflection find a particular set of prohibitions and injunctions, and a particular way of life protected by them, acceptable and respectworthy, partly because this specifically conceived way of life, with its accompanying prohibitions, has in history appeared natural, and on the whole feels natural, both to oneself and to others" (*PPM*, p. 21). If there are no overriding reasons for rejecting it, the "felt and proven naturalness" of this way of life is "one reason among others for accepting it" (*ibid.*). (On his indebtedness to Aristotle and Spinoza, see further in his *Two Theories of Morality*.)

My third example of neo-intuitionism is provided by the moral foundations of the political philosophy of John Rawls, as set out in his *A Theory of Justice* (first published 1971). He expressly intended to provide "a viable alternative to the utilitarian tradition," as the basis for his theory of justice. What he offers is a version of the social contract theory, to be found in Locke and Rousseau; but, in Rawls' case, this is not a contract to create the state, but to agree about what shall count as just and unjust.

He asks us to imagine an "original position," in which people get together to decide the principles of justice on which government shall be based. We must conceive of them doing so, as Rawls puts it, "behind a veil of ignorance."

That is to say, none of them knows who or what he is—they are all ignorant of their class, social status, wealth, natural endowments such as intelligence or physical strength, psychological propensities, and even of their own conception of what is good. All this makes it certain that, when they decide what is just, they will do so without knowing what would be to their own advantage, as distinct from that of others. Add the hypothesis that these people all have equal liberty, are self-interested and mutually disinterested, lack envy and are rational. And now ask: what principles of justice will people so placed choose?

Rawls consults his own intuitions and comes up with a twofold answer. He apparently considers this answer to be self-evident. He takes it for granted that this is how things must appear to his readers, when they, in turn, consult their own intuitions. In the "original position" behind the "veil of ignorance," any self-interested and rational being would assent to the following as the principles of justice, on which "social cooperation" and "forms of government" should be based:

(1) Each person is to have an equal right to the most extensive total system of equal basic liberties compatible with a similar system of liberty for all.

(2) Social and economic inequalities are to be arranged so that they are both: (a) to the greatest benefit of the least advantaged, consistent with a just savings principle, and (b) attached to offices and positions open to all under conditions of fair equality of opportunity. (*Theory of Justice*, p. 302)

The "just savings principle" is to the effect that each generation has a duty to bear its share of the burden of realizing and preserving a just society (*ibid*., pp. 284–293).

In so far as such examples of neo-intuitionism do not involve ontological or epistemological claims, they no doubt escape the kind of criticism of more traditional forms of intuitionism which was expressed in Chapter 3 (pp. 100–5). Miss Anscombe, Hampshire and Rawls appeal simply to what would be considered right or wrong by plain men;

and they reject utilitarianism for being at variance with what they take this to be. We must consider whether such criticism is well-founded.

Two Lines of Criticism

Utilitarianism, as expounded by Mill in his famous essay of that name, is based on two principles which are generally called, respectively, the Greatest Happiness principle and the Equity principle. The former is to the effect that the greatest possible amount of general happiness is the supreme good; and the latter, that, in assessing the general happiness, everybody is to be counted for one and nobody for more than one. Both these principles have been adversely criticized by opponents of utilitarianism, on the ground that they run counter to the consciences of plain men.

To begin with the greatest happiness principle: counter-examples to it of the following kind are commonly put forward by anti-utilitarians. In the eighteenth century, many families, travelling in the trail parties to the American West, were attacked by Indians. We are told of two such cases which had a lot in common. In both, the families concerned had gone into some sort of hiding from the Indians. And in both, they included among their members a baby at the breast. Yet again in both, it became apparent that the baby was going to cry at the wrong moment and give the family's whereabouts away to the Indians. Now, in one case, the mother put her hands round the baby's neck and strangled it before it could cry. As a result, all the rest of the family escaped with their lives. In the other case, the mother could not bring herself to kill her baby. It cried, the family was discovered, and all of them were killed.

Joseph Fletcher, who recounts these facts in his *Situation Ethics* (pp. 124–25), to which I referred above (p. 213), simply concludes his account with the question, "Which woman made the right decision?" Since the "situation ethics" he advocates is defined by him as declaring "that anything and everything is right or wrong, according to the situation" (*Situation Ethics*, p. 124), he would presumably have said that the answer depends on a number of factors, beyond the immediate circumstances as he has recorded them. But for those who do not subscribe to situation ethics —as do neither utilitarians nor anti-utilitarians of the kind we are considering—his example is a good test case.

According to the greatest happiness principle, there would seem to be only one answer to the question of which woman did right; namely, the mother who killed her baby. But is it self-evident that this is the correct answer? Even hardened utilitarians may have their doubts. They may, of course, seek to accommodate these doubts by the argument that the general happiness was better served by the mother who would not kill her child, because, although she and all her family died, such demonstrations of maternal love set an example, which reinforces the tendency of mothers to care for their children and, in the long run, contributes more to the general happiness than her survival and that of the other members of her family would have done. To this the anti-utilitarian is entitled to reply with the objection, "But suppose we build in the condition that no one would ever hear of the mother who refused to kill her baby. Would you then say that what she did was wrong?" Consistency would require a utilitarian to do so.

I have, from time to time, put this example to audiences and, although I have occasionally encountered among them very hardened utilitarians, who were prepared to say that the mother who decided not to strangle her baby did the wrong thing, most people have found themselves unable to say this. Utilitarians sometimes defend themselves against such examples by objecting that they are "fantastic" ones and insisting that the greatest happiness principle must be evaluated from more realistic situations.

Turning now to the equity principle, this rule lays it down that we ought not to distinguish between one person and another—at any rate on grounds which have nothing to do with increasing the general happiness—when we are deciding what we ought to do. If, for example, the life of only one person from amongst many can be saved there may be good utilitarian grounds for saving someone who is, let us say, a great scientist or a great composer, rather than any of the ordinary people who could not contribute anything like the same amount to the sum of human happiness as he could. But there are no good utilitarian reasons for saving someone just because he is, let us say, one's own child rather than someone else's. If, in both of two parallel cases, two children had an equal chance of happiness themselves in later life and their survival would give an equal amount of happiness to their relations and friends, then by the equity principle, one of the children, if it happened to be our own, would have no more moral claim upon us than the other child, if it happened to be someone else's. But is that how a plain man would see it?

Nicholar Rescher in his *Selfishness: The Role of the Vicarious Affects in Moral Philosophy and Social Theory* (Pittsburgh, 1975) thinks not. By a "vicarious affect" he means simply the affect which the happiness, or misery, of other people may have upon us. If our children or friends are happy, that in itself can make us happy; if they are unhappy, that in itself can make us unhappy. Conversely, if our enemies or rivals are happy, that in itself can make us miserable; but if they are miserable, that in itself can make us happy. Rescher calls the former kind of vicarious affect "positive" and "sympathetic;" and the latter kind, "negative" and "antipathetic." The positive kind—happiness at our loved ones' joy or success, and unhappiness at their failure or distress—Rescher thinks morally good. The latter kind—*Schadenfreude* at our enemies' or rivals' misfortune, misery at their well-being—he thinks morally bad. A man is a better man in so far as he takes delight in the happiness of those he loves, but a worse man in so far as he exults in the misery of those he hates. Rescher thinks that, in general, other people would agree with him in these opinions.

He argues that, in so far as they would, they must reject utilitarianism. And that for at least three reasons. Firstly, because the greatest happiness principle, in so far as it does not distinguish between *kinds* of happiness, admits the possibility of an act being right because it brings about negative vicarious affects. But our consciences cannot accept that. Secondly, because the equity principle excludes the possibility of an act being right simply because the vicarious affects it brings about are positive. But our consciences tell us that this could be so. Thirdly, because there is an internal contradiction in utilitarianism, brought to light by vicarious affects. In so far as vicarious affects increase happiness or misery, the greatest happiness principle bids us take account of them; but in so far as vicarious affects are concerned with whose happiness it is, the equity principle bids us ignore them.

Is Utilitarianism Self-defeating?

The third of Rescher's reasons, to which I have just referred, takes us beyond the simple empirical fact (if it is a fact) that the plain man's conscience approves of positive vicarious affects and disapproves of negative ones. This third reason calls in question the internal consistency of utilitarianism. And that makes us wonder whether it has any other self-defeating implications. Its contemporary critics have accused it of having at least two. The first is pointed out by Bernard Williams in his "A Critique of Utilitarianism" (in J. J. C. Smart and B. Williams, *Utilitarianism: For and Against*, Cambridge, 1973). Williams takes the example of a young scientist who is offered a research job in chemical and biological warfare. The young scientist has conscientious objections to such warfare. But, if he takes the job, the salary will make a very material difference to the happiness and well-being of his wife and children, which, so far as the young scientist can see, could not be obtained in any alternative way. We may take it that a utilitarian would tell him that he ought to forget his scruples and take the job, since that is obviously the right thing to do. Williams' comment is that many of us would not think this was the obviously right answer. And he goes on to say that it is not just a question of the rightness or obviousness of the answer:

It is also a question of what sort of considerations come into finding the answer. A feature of utilitarianism is that it cuts out a kind of consideration which for some others makes a difference to what they feel about such cases; a consideration involving the idea, as we may first and very simply put it, that each of us is specially responsible for what *he* does, rather than for what other people do. This is an idea closely connected with the value of integrity. It is often suspected that utilitarianism, at least in its direct forms, makes integrity as a value more or less unintelligible. I shall try to show that this suspicion is correct. (*Utilitarianism: For and Against*, p. 99)

The utilitarian solution to the young scientist's dilemma, which we took for granted above, was based on a calculation of satisfactions. Considered as a contribution to the sum of human happiness, did the satisfaction, which the young scientist's wife and children would get from having his salary to live on, outweigh the satisfaction which he would have got from abiding by his scruples and refusing the job? The ground for the utilitarian view that he ought to take the job was that this seems most likely; a greater sum of satisfaction would be achieved if he took the job than if he did not.

Now, Williams speaks of conscientious opinions, like that of the young scientist, as "projects." He does, however, differentiate them as "commitments," when comparing them with "projects" like those of the young scientist's wife and children, who simply wanted such things as food, clothing, shelter, etc. And then Williams makes this comment:

It is absurd to demand of such a man, when the sums come in from the utility network which the projects of others have in part determined, that he should just step aside from his own project and decision and acknowledge the decision which utilitarian calculation requires. (*ibid.*, p. 116)

Why is this absurd? In Williams' opinion because:

It is to alienate him in a real sense from his actions and the source of his action in his own convictions. It is to make him into a channel between the input of everyone's projects, including his own, and an output of optimific decision; but this is to neglect the extent to which *his* actions and *his* decisions have to be seen as actions and

decisions which flow from the projects and attitudes
with which he is most closely identified. It is thus, in the
most literal sense, an attack on his integrity. (*ibid.*,
pp. 116—17)

When Williams asks rhetorically, "How can a man, as a
utilitarian agent, come to regard as one satisfaction among
others, and a dispensable one, a project or attitude round
which he has built his life?" (*ibid.*, p. 116), I think he is
making, not just a psychological, but also a logical point.
The point is not simply that this is the idea of something
which a man would find it hard, if not empircally impossible, to do. But also, and more profoundly, that it is an
incoherent idea. How can a man be said to have a concern
for morality, if he counts the satisfaction of this concern as
"one satisfaction among others"? And "a dispensable one"
at that.' It *logically* must count with him more than the
others, if the man is to be a moral agent. For what is a
moral agent, if not someone who is concerned above all
other things to do what he sincerely believes to be right?
As an answer to "What ought one to do?", utilitarianism—
in so far as it takes the satisfaction of a man's "commitments" to be "one satisfaction among others, and a dispensable one"—robs the question of its point. In that sense, it is
self-defeating.

A second charge of self-stultification is levelled against
utilitarianism in D. H. Hodgson's *Consequences of Utilitarianism* (Oxford, 1967) and also by G. J. Warnock in *The
Object of Morality* (London, 1971). I will attempt to make
the essence of this criticism clear by taking a very simple
example.

The criticism of Hodgson and Warnock, in a nutshell, is
that the utilitarian account of the obligation to keep promises takes the point out of promising. As Hodgson observes,
"promising would be pointless unless a promisee sometimes
expected an. act which had been promised *more* than he
would have expected an act, if it had not been promised
but (say) merely mentioned as a possibility" (*Consequences
of Utilitarianism*, p. 40). In a *non*act-utilitarian society,
there would usually be good reason to have such an expecta-

tion, since promise-keeping is required by a conventional moral rule, which many people accept as a personal principle. But what if a society were composed *entirely* of act-utilitarians?

Suppose you and I belong to such an act-utilitarian society and I make you a promise. As an act-utilitarian, I will think myself obliged to keep this promise so long—but only so long—as I consider that doing so will have certain desirable consequences. You, knowing that I am an act-utilitarian, will know that this is how I regard my obligation to keep the promise. You will, therefore, have in mind that there is some possibility of my going back on it and so rely on it that much less. But I shall know that you are making some allowance for this possibility and so feel that much less compunction about breaking it. But you will know that this is the case and consequently place even less reliance upon my promise. I, in turn, will know that this is your reaction, and so feel even less compunction than before. But you will know that this is how I react . . . and so *ad infinitum*. A point will eventually be reached, along this continuum, at which you will be well advised to have no more expectation of my doing what I promised to do than if I had only said it was a possibility.

I have taken only one kind of obligation, that of promising, and only one kind of utilitarianism, namely act-utilitarianism, into consideration here. Warnock, and especially Hodgson, elaborate their criticism in much more detailed, complex terms. But I hope I have said enough to show what the essence of that criticism is. It is that, by making moral obligation dependent upon consequences, utilitarianism necessarily erodes it; and that, followed through to its logical conclusion, utilitarianism takes the point out of morality. Just as Williams argued that, in effect, it does so by undermining the idea of the integrity of a moral agent, so Hodgson and Warnock evidently think that it does so by taking the bindingness out of the idea of moral obligation.

Defence of Utilitarianism

Can utilitarianism be defended against the kinds of criticism that we have been considering in this chapter? In so far as they have turned on whether or not a plain man's conscience accords with the deliverances of the utility principle, a utilitarian can defend himself in either of two ways. He can, if he chooses, simply deny that this sort of evidence goes against him. Miss Anscombe may think that a plain man would not approve of the judicial execution of the innocent, and Rescher may suppose that he would approve of positive vicarious affects, and so on. But, against all that, your hard-nosed utilitarian may insist that a plain man judges actions by their felicific consequences and believes in an egalitarian distribution of happiness; and contend that, when things are put to the plain man clearly, he delivers utilitarian judgments. Who is right about the plain man's conscience—utilitarians or neo-intuitionists—is an empirical matter and if this is the utilitarian's defence, the strength of it could presumably be settled by some kind of public opinion poll.

Alternatively, a utilitarian could defend himself by first conceding that the neo-intuitionists are correct in their opinion that plain men would approve of the mother who refused to strangle her baby, and would disapprove of *Schadenfreude*, and so on; and by then contending that such judgments are simply the measure of the plain man's irrationality and benightedness. This utilitarian would have to acknowledge that such anti-utilitarian moral judgments, if sufficiently widespread, prove that the plain man is not a utilitarian; but, of course, it would still be open to him to contend that the plain man ought to be one.

Criticisms of utilitarianism which turn on the contention that it is internally incoherent, and therefore self-defeating, are not so easy for its defenders to dismiss.

Rescher's third reason for rejecting it (see above) can perhaps be countered. He said that utilitarianism contradicts itself because the utility principle implicitly bids us take account of vicarious affects, whilst the equity principle explicitly forbids us to do so. But does the equity principle really do that? Mill (*Utilitarianism*, Everyman edition, p. 7) and Sidgwick (*The Methods of Ethics*, seventh edition, pp. 241–42) together with many later utilitarians, have recognized that the greatest happiness may be achieved by people having a special regard for their friends and relations. So, it is arguable that the equity principle is not intended to forbid this but to ensure that the benefits of any consequent happiness are distributed as widely as possible. For example, if people took better care of those dear to them, the demands on the welfare state could be reduced. The equity principle may be thought of as simply prescribing that the good effects of the consequent saving in public expense should be equitably distributed. These effects should not, for instance, result in a decrease of income tax only for the rich—or alternatively, only for the poor.

Against Williams' criticism that utilitarianism "cuts out" integrity or makes it "more or less unintelligible" (see above), a utilitarian might reply that this is a complete misrepresentation. As a theory of what ought to be done, utilitarianism rates the satisfaction of the desire to do what one ought as highly as any alternative theory; but it does not consider every individual's own conception of what he ought to do to be sacrosanct. People can be mistaken about that, and when they are, we should try to put them right. In the case of the young scientist the utilitarian, who advised him to take the job, must have considered his scruples about doing so to be misconceived. In inviting him to discard them, this utilitarian was not saying that the satisfaction of doing what one thinks one ought to do is just one amongst many satisfactions and therefore dispensable. He was intent, not upon getting the young scientist to ignore his conscience, but to enlighten it. When convictions are mistaken, one is entitled—indeed, obliged—to confront the conscientious with a demand that they be set aside.

As for the criticism that utilitarianism evades moral obligation and, if carried to its logical conclusion, takes the point out of promise-keeping, truth-telling, and other such duties, I suppose a utilitarian could say that this might be true; just as, for instance, it is also true that we can never know what all the possible consequences of our actions will be. But, just as it would be unreasonable to say that, because we cannot see what all the consequences of some act will be, we should not judge it by those consequences we can see, so it is unreasonable to say that, because utilitarianism

carried to its logical conclusion might be self-defeating, it is
of no use, when applied well short of that conclusion. In
all kinds of ways, we know that we can rely upon people
only so far, and they know we know, and we know they
know we know . . . But it would be absurd to say that
because, if we went on thinking along these lines, we should
eventually conclude that they cannot be relied on at all, it
is therefore impossible, or alternatively irrational, not to
arrive at that conclusion. As a guide in practical affairs—a
utilitarian might say with some justice—act—(or any other
form of) utilitarianism should not be judged by what it
would make us think, if we carried it to its logical conclusion, but by how well it works as a way of solving moral
problems.

The claim most commonly made for the utility principle
is that it enables us to resolve conflicts of obligation. If we
go by our intuitions we shall often find them at variance
with one another. But utilitarianism provides us with an
overriding principle that can always be invoked to show us
what we ought to do. So, it is not surprising to find that, in
rejecting this principle, many neo-intuitionists abandon
with it the hope of avoiding moral conflict. Indeed, writers
like Hampshire and Williams regard conflict as of the essence
of the moral life. Hampshire says, for example, "a conflict
of moral claims is natural to us;" "unavoidable conflict of
principles of conduct, and not a harmony of purposes, is
the stuff of morality, as we ordinarily experience it" (*PPM*,
pp. 42–43). Williams, in a similar vein, speaks of the "moral
cost, as opposed to costs of some other kind (such as utility)
which have to be considered in arriving at the moral decision" ("Ethical Consistency", *PAS* Supplementary volume,
No. 39, 1965, p. 65). By "moral cost" he evidently means
the remorse which goes with having to ignore some obligations for the sake of fulfilling others. He considers it a
defect in utilitarianism that it takes no account of this
moral cost. Whether or not the plain man's moral life is as
fraught with conflict and burdened with guilt as Hampshire
and Williams appear to think is, one would have supposed,
an empirical question. Neo-intuitionist anti-utilitarians
sometimes talk as if they think that it necessarily *must* be

so fraught and so burdened because there is no single over-riding moral principle. But even so, the test of what they say is empirical. To prove they are right, they will have to show that, on the whole, when plain men, having in some morally demanding situation done the best they can, sleep soundly in their beds untroubled by remorse or conflict, they have not been thinking with sufficient care about what they ought to do. Unless this contention is made true by definition—an illegitimate move—I should think it would be a very hard thing to show.

In his recent writings, R. M. Hare attempts to reconcile what I have been calling neo-intuitionism with his own prescriptivist utilitarianism in a "two-level" theory of moral thinking. In my final section, I shall deal with this attempt.

II. HARE'S RECENT MORAL PHILOSOPHY

In Chapter 5 we considered R. M. Hare's moral theory as it is contained in his two books *The Language of Morals* (1952) and *Freedom and Reason* (1963). In 1981 he published another book called *Moral Thinking*. The question that I shall now consider is: what new developments, if any, in his moral theory does this recent book introduce?

There are no radical departures from the prescriptivism of his earlier writings but there are, I think, at least two developments, both of which are of interest and the latter of which is particularly important. Both these developments may be seen as off-shoots of the rationalism in Hare's moral theory. The former of them brings out the element of constraint in rationalism; the latter, the element of criticism. I shall treat them both below as consequences of a conviction which seems to grip Hare even more firmly in his recent writings than in the earlier ones. It is the conviction, in his own words, that "the freedom which we have as moral thinkers is a *freedom to reason*, i.e. to make rational moral evaluations" (*MT*, pp. 6–7, italics mine).

Constraint and criticism both seem to me to be essential elements in the concept of rationality (cf. my "Learning to be Rational" in *Proceedings of the Philosophy of Education Society of Great Britain*, XI, 1977, where I speak of "conformity" rather than "constraint" but mean much the same).

On the one hand, it is part of our concept of rational thinking (and of the behaviour it directs) that it should conform to certain constraints, or rules, of correct procedure. Such thinking marches towards its conclusions step by justified step; and the justifications always consist in conformity to some appropriate canons. These canons will, of course, vary in some degree according to the discipline within which one is operating; but the very notion of rationality implies adherence to some such standards. That is the sense in which I conceive of rationality as essentially subject to *constraints*. But it is also essentially subject to *criticism*. As we normally use the word "rational," a person is entitled to that description only if he is open to the suggestion, not simply that others may be mistaken, but that he himself may. His own mistakes can, broadly speaking, be of two kinds. First, the conclusions he reaches may be erroneous because of the limitations of his own intelligence or the defectiveness of his own observations. The cleverest and most perceptive of us often get things wrong. But then again, a person's mistakes may run deeper than that. The very rules of procedure in accordance with which he has been taught to think may be inadequate to their subject-matter. In such case, something in the nature of a Copernican revolution alone will put things right. It is the mark of a rational man that he is open-minded enough to conceive of the possibility that he is mistaken on either count. That is the sense in which I say that rational thinking is essentially critical.

In some remarks on rationality, towards the end of *Moral Thinking*, Hare refers to: ". . . the thought-processes one has to go through if one is going to be rational, and the sorts of criticism to which these thought-processes are open . . ." (*MT*, p. 215). The particular point he is making in the context is that the said "thought-processes" and "sorts of criticisms" will both differ if one is asking what one ought to do from what they would be if one were simply asking what to do. But I quote Hare's words here merely because they seem to me to draw exactly the same kind of distinction as that which I have just been drawing between being subject to constraints and being subject to criticism. This brief quotation encapsulates the two matters concerning which there is some development of thought in Hare's latest book. On the one hand, to use his own expression, he "screws up" more tightly. the "thought-processes" involved in rational moral thinking and thereby brings out the element of constraint in it. On the other hand, he marks out more clearly the place which "sorts of criticism" have in such thinking and thereby highlights the element of criticism within it. We must look more closely at each of these developments in turn.

(I) THE CONSTRAINT OF "LOGIC AND THE FACTS"

According to Hare, moral thinking is subject to constraint in the sense that it must be done in the light of "logic and the facts." He has, of course, always held this view. We noted above (p. 157) that he started writing moral philosophy with the intention of replacing emotivism with "a rational kind of non-descriptivism." Without denying the emotivist's view that in morality we are free to decide for ourselves what principles to live by, he insisted in his early writings that, once these decisions of principle are made, morality requires us to be rational in our adherence to them. And for Hare that has always meant at least two things. One, that we should try to see as clearly as we can what the logical rules are, in accordance with which our principles must be adopted if they are to qualify as moral ones; the other, that we should try to discover as accurately as possible what the relevant and available facts of a situation are, when considering whether or not it comes under any of our principles. The phrase "logic and the facts" which, as we shall see, rings like a refrain through *Moral Thinking*, is no new note in Hare's philosophy. But I think it is sounded even more clearly in his latest book than it was in the earlier ones.

What, then, does he say about "logic and the facts"in *Moral Thinking*? By "logic" he means the logical properties of the distinctive concepts in terms of which moral judgments are framed, and, in particular, those connected with

the word "ought." By "the facts" he means the relevant
and available ones in any situation upon which a moral
judgment is being passed, especially those about how what
is done will affect all the people concerned. In Hare's view,
rational moral thinking requires a command of both these
kinds of consideration.

So far as the logical properties of the moral concepts are
concerned, the account which he gives of these in *Moral
Thinking* is virtually the same as that which he gave in *The
Language of Morals* and *Freedom and Reason*. The two properties which do all the work are prescriptivity and universalizability. What Hare means by these expressions was explained at
length in Chapter 5; but let me briefly recapitulate. First, as to
prescriptivity, it is characteristic of the moral "ought" that
it guides actions or choices. This is apparent from the fact
that we should think it very odd for anyone to say, "You
ought to do such-and-such an act but don't do it!" Normally, moral judgments entail imperatives and that is the
sense in which they are prescriptive. Second, as to universalizability, it is also characteristic of moral judgments that we
must be prepared to give reasons for them. It would be very
odd if anyone said, "You ought to do so-and-so but I have
no reason for saying this." It is of the very nature of a
reason to be universal; that is to say, as long as we regard it
as a reason, we must be prepared to do so consistently. But,
as I explained above (pp. 185–88) mere consistency is not
enough; the reasons given for moral judgments must, according to Hare, have an especially high degree of universality.
They must be what he calls U-type, i.e. ones which do not
contain any reference to a particular individual. When
anyone has delivered a moral judgment, he must be prepared
to universalize it with regard to both the agent and the
recipient of the action concerned. Suppose I say that I
ought to give Smith money because he is poor. I may be
asked "Would you say the same if you were one of your
own dependents or creditors?" or "Would you say the same
if it were Jones, not Smith, who was poor?" So, when
prescriptivity and universalizability are put together, it
follows, according to Hare, that, if I am considering what
I ought to do, I have to ask myself, concerning any possible

answer that occurs to me, whether I would be prepared to act in accordance with it (prescriptivity) and also whether I am willing that it should be done in any relevant circumstances of which I can conceive (universalizability). As he puts it in *Freedom and Reason*, universalizability requires me to go "the round of all the affected parties . . . giving equal weight to the interests of all;" and prescriptivity, to ask myself, "How much (as I imagine myself in the place of each man in turn) do I want to have this, or to avoid that?" (where "this" and "that" refer to the content of the relevant imperative entailed by the judgment) (*FR*, p. 123). Through this exercise of the imagination I shall be able to weigh the cumulative satisfaction of certain affected parties, if I do not help Smith, against that of the other affected parties, if I do. The side on which the scales come down will indicate what I ought to do. Hare acknowledges (*MT*, p. 21) that not all moral judgments need to be prescriptive; some simply describe actions or states of affairs as being in accordance with generally accepted moral standards. And again, he recognizes that some other-than-moral judgments are universalizable; for instance, aesthetic ones. Nevertheless, he affirms that prescriptivity and universalizability "suffice to govern the reasoning" (*MT*, p. 54) of our moral judgments so long as the latter are "confined to situations where the interests of others are affected." Though he concedes that all moral judgments are not so confined, he thinks that they predominantly "turn on people's interests" and so in the majority of cases prescriptivity and universalizability will tell us which moral principles to adopt and which to reject.

So far as what is meant by "the facts" is concerned, Hare says that we must take cognizance of these where the logic of the moral concepts makes them relevant and they are, in practice, available to us. Whenever a reason is given for a moral judgment, the question may be asked as to whether or not the factual claims that it makes are veridical. Suppose someone says that a certain act ought to be performed because it would fulfil a promise. Questions may be raised as to whether the promise was in fact made and whether the act referred to would in fact fulfil it. These questions arise simply from the terms of the reason itself.

But if Hare's view of the logical properties of the moral concepts is correct, further factual questions are made relevant. Universalizability, in requiring us to go the round of all the affected parties, brings in the question of who in fact would be affected by the act under consideration. Prescriptivity, in requiring us to identify ourselves with the preferences of the affected parties raises the question of what these preferences, in fact, are. Hare does not suggest that every such relevant fact can be known; rational moral thinking simply requires us to take into account all of them that we can discover.

This then, briefly stated, is what I believe Hare takes moral thinking in the light of "logic and the facts" to be. The "freedom to reason," which as moral thinkers we enjoy, is the freedom to think in conformity to the correct logical canons, as these are determined by the meanings of moral words, and with as full an awareness as we can attain of the facts of the given situation, which these canons make relevant. Now, one way in which Hare "screws up" more tightly his account of the constraints within which we exercise our freedom is by saying a time or two—I think more explicitly than he did in his earlier books—that, in so far as we think within these constraints, we shall all be led to the same conclusions. For instance, he writes: "if we assumed a perfect command of logic and the facts, they would constrain so severely the moral evaluations that we can make, that in practice we would be bound all to agree to the same ones" (*MT*, p. 6). Sadly, such a "perfect command" is in actual practice beyond us. Hare puts his point in a more explicit way, as we shall see when we come to his "two-level" theory, by saying that we could all manage to "say the same thing" only "to the extent that we manage to think like archangels" at the 'critical" level (*MT*, p. 46).

But it is very important not to misunderstand what he has in mind when he says such things as these; and, in particular, not to suppose that he intends to retract in any degree the view expressed in his earlier writings, that there is an "irreducibly *evaluative* or *prescriptive*" element in moral thinking (*MT*, p. 6). Perhaps the best way of understanding what he does intend is by recalling the comparison, which he drew in *Freedom and Reason* between K. R. Popper's account of scientific thinking and his own account of moral thinking. On Popper's account of the former, people are free to dream up any hypothesis they like in science; but having done so they must then submit their hypothesis to the logic of scientific discovery and the facts of the natural world. Only if it comes through unscathed can it be welcomed into the corpus of what is commonly called scientific knowledge. Similarly, it has always been—and still is—Hare's view that people are free to propose their own evaluative or prescriptive principles (in the reasons they give for their moral judgments) provided only that they are prepared, before committing themselves irrevocably to any such principle, to examine it in the light of "logic and the facts," as this expression has been interpreted above. In all this, he most certainly does *not* intend to replace his prescriptivist theory by one of what is commonly called the objectivist kind. He is *not* saying that a moral judgment is any kind of descriptive statement, such that we only need to get at certain objective facts (whether of a logical, moral or empirical kind, and whether apprehended by perception, intuition, or ratiocination) in order to know whether our moral judgments are true or false. We must consider below the criticism that Hare has inadvertently landed himself in a form of descriptivism by his remarks on the constraint of "logic and the facts;" but whatever our opinion of that criticism, there can be no doubt that Hare himself does not consider what he has to say, about "logic and the facts" leading us all to the same moral evaluations, to be a surrender to objectivism or descriptivism.

Fanaticism and Utilitarianism

It comes as no surprise, in view of what Hare says about the prescriptivity and universalizability of moral judgments, to find that, in his opinion, these moral evaluations—to which "logic and the facts" would lead us all if we were what he calls "archangels" (see below)—are such as a utilitarian might hold. But, in order to understand precisely what he means by this, it may be useful to see how it has affected his views about fanaticism in his latest book.

In *Freedom and Reason* he defined a fanatic as someone "who has whole-heartedly espoused . . . an ideal" and "does not mind if people's interests—even his own—are harmed in the pursuit of it" (*FR*, p. 105). The "ideal" referred to was a moral one; that is to say, the fanatic thinks of it as something at which he ought to aim. Examples of such "ideals" which Hare gave were the extermination of all Jews, which some fascists would regard as their duty, and the closing down of all strip clubs, which some puritans would think they ought to try to effect. The consequent suffering of the Jews, or the frustration of people who enjoy going to strip clubs, do not deter such "fanatics" from their moral purpose. In so far as fanaticism is a form of moral thinking, a fanatic has to go the round of all the affected parties and to weigh in his imagination the satisfaction he finds in the thought e.g. of all Jews being exterminated, or of all strip clubs being closed, or whatever, against the cumulative satisfaction he finds in the thought of escaping extermination (after putting himself in the place of each Jew in turn) or of being able to go to strip clubs (after putting himself in the place of each patron in turn) etc. In order to arrive at the moral judgment that he ought to exterminate all Jews, try to close all strip clubs, etc., he has to find that the satisfaction he feels in the former thought in each case outweighs that which he feels in the latter. To the question "Is it possible for him to do so?" Hare's answer was that it is logically, but not empirically, possible (see above p. 228). We can conceive of someone, who is so fanatical that he would find more satisfaction in the thought of a world without Jews than in that of one in which existing Jews survived, even after putting himself imaginatively in the place of each of the latter in turn; but empirically human nature is not like that. Hare thought we are so made that it would be psychologically impossible for anyone to come up with this result, if he really went through the exercise in imaginative sympathy which moral thinking demands of him.

In *Moral Thinking*, he does not go back on any of this, but he expands his ideas about fanaticism in certain ways. For one thing, he is careful to distinguish fanaticism from what he calls amoralism. An amoralist is someone who refuses to think in moral terms at all. Hare sees nothing logically impossible in this. Like Mrs. Foot (cf. above), he takes the view that "on the whole morality pays" (*MT*, p. 196) and for much the same reasons as she; at the very least, anyone who refuses to be guided by moral considerations is likely to suffer personal inconvenience as a result of social disapproval and its effects. Realizing this, an amoralist may, of course, set out to give the impression that he has a conscience even when he has not. This, he will find, calls for a degree of ingenuity that few if any of us possess; as Hare has it, "by far the easiest way of seeming to be upright is to be upright" (*ibid.*). But when that has been said, it remains true, in Hare's opinion, that one could be an amoralist without committing any logical errors. What we must *not* do, however, is to confuse amoralism with fanaticism. Fanaticism is a way of thinking morally and, in all that is said of it, must be conceived as such.

Hare draws a distinction in his latest book between "impure" and "pure" fanatics. "Impure" ones are those who, through perversity or prejudice, will not think as clearly and honestly as they could about what they ought to do. "Pure" fanatics, by contrast, are those who do think as clearly and honestly as they can about their duty. "Impure" fanaticism is not only a possibility; there are, in fact, a great many representatives of it about. But is "pure" fanaticism possible? Hare's answer is that a "pure" fanatic is not an *empirical* possibility; we do not meet such people in real life. Nevertheless, the "pure" fanatic is a logical possibility, *provided* we conceive him to hold moral opinions which are "not, after all, inconsistent with utilitarianism" (*MT*, p. 171). And this proviso can be fulfilled. A "pure" fanatic could conceivably expose his moral judgments to the light of "logic and the facts" and still retain them. This, at first blush, may strike us as an extraordinary conclusion for Hare to have reached. We may wonder how a fanatic, who by definition (see above) ignores his own and other people's interests in the pursuit of his "ideal", can be conceived to have arrived at his moral opinions (as Hare says he must have done, if he is to be regarded as a moral thinker) by going the round of all the affected parties, putting himself in the place of each in turn, and calculating what will maximize satisfactions. But perhaps I can make Hare's point a little clearer in terms of an example he himself uses.

In his earlier writings, his examples of fanaticism were all repellent—Jew-baiting Nazis or sanctimonious kill-joys—and he is sensitive to the objection that this kind of example loads the dice from the start against people who have moral ideals which they are prepared to pursue even if their own or other people's interests are harmed in the process. Now he admits that, in point of fact, some very nice people are fanatics. So he takes as his example of pure fanaticism, a doctor, who believes that he ought to keep his patients alive as long as possible, even if in some cases this means that they will have to suffer a week or two of unnecessary pain. This doctor is an excellent person, who holds the honourable belief, whether on religious grounds or not, that life is sacred and it his job to treat it as such. He has arrived at this moral conviction under the constraint of "logic and the facts." In his imagination he has weighed the satisfaction he finds in the thought of keeping his patients alive as long as possible against that which he finds (after putting himself in the place of each in turn) in the thought of them escaping unnecessary suffering. Quite sincerely, he cannot evade the conclusion that the former satisfaction outweighs the latter. Hare evidently thinks that we would be entitled to point out to this doctor that, if only he could get rid of his conviction, he could give his patients the satisfaction of escaping unnecessary suffering without having to endure any consequent dissatisfaction himself from a guilty conscience; and this would result in a much greater balance of satisfaction over dissatisfaction than is achieved by the doctor satisfying his conviction at the expense of his patients' suffering. So, according to Hare, we would be justified in asking the doctor to subject his conviction to critical re-examination in order to see if he really is committed to it completely. But supposing, after carefully and responsibly consulting his conscience, this doctor declares that he still finds more satisfaction in the thought of keeping his patients alive as long as possible than in letting them escape unnecessary suffering, even after putting himself in the place of each in turn. In such case, we would be back at square one; there would be nothing left for us to say. And why? Simply because the doctor's conclusion would be "not, after all, inconsistent with utilitarianism." That is to say, it would be a conclusion to the effect that the action which maximizes satisfactions ought to be done.

Summary So Far

I hope I have given a clear, though brief, account of what I mean by saying that there is a strong emphasis in *Moral Thinking* on the constraints imposed by reason. But it is perhaps appropriate to warn the reader yet again not to jump to the wrong conclusions. Some may feel a temptation to do so. They may think that Hare's emphasis on *reason* in *Moral Thinking* is incompatible with what he had to say in his earlier books about the place of *freedom* in moral thinking. In particular, they may feel that, since Hare goes so far as to assert that, if we all did our moral thinking in the full and unclouded light of "logic and the facts," we should all "say the same thing," he must be—wittingly or unwittingly—going back on opinions such as that expressed in his early book, *The Language of Morals*, p. 73 to the effect that morality "regains its vigour when ordinary people have learned afresh to decide for themselves what principles to live by." How can moral thinking require us *both* to "decide for ourselves" *and* all "say the same thing"?, his critics may ask. But it is a mistake to suppose that this rhetorical question reveals an inconsistency in Hare. His response—or part of it—would be that *both* freedom *and* reason play their parts in moral thinking in the following way. We are free to think up principles by which we might live and to work out for ourselves whether we ought to adopt them; but the process of working this out requires us to examine the said principles by such light from "logic and the facts" as we can gain. Because in the nature of the case the light each of us has is limited we may arrive at different conclusions about any given principle. But, if we all had perfect light, we should all arrive at the same conclusions— at least about principles which concern actions that affect others besides ourselves. And these conclusions would, according to Hare, be "not inconsistent with utilitarianism."

Linguistic and Moral Intuitions

It occurs to me that the cumulative effect of all I have been saying about Hare on "logic and the facts" may have left some readers with the impression that he thinks moral conclusions can be deduced from purely linguistic premises. So, I must make it clear that this is emphatically *not* the case. When he says that, in the measure of our command of the logic of the moral concepts and the relevant and available facts, we shall all move towards the same moral conclusions, he is not saying that substantial moral judgments can be inferred from the meaning of moral words, any more than that they can be deduced from matters of natural fact. Very early in *Moral Thinking* (pp. 10–20) he draws a very clear distinction between what he calls our moral and linguistic intuitions.

Hare recognizes that our linguistic intuitions—i.e. how we think words should be used—"can support theses in empirical linguistics and, in a subtler way, in philosophical logic." And he explains that they can support the former kind of thesis because the native speakers of a language are authorities on how it should be spoken; and the latter kind of thesis, because the intention of any speaker as to how his words should be taken—i.e. what they imply—is authoritative. Since the main purpose of language is communication, those who use any language will usually be agreed on how the words within it should be used and on what they imply. But individual speakers can always use words differently from the way others use them; and provided they stipulate their own definitions clearly, no confusion or contradiction need ensue.

Now, the point which Hare is concerned to make—especially I think against descriptivists like Searle (see above) and neo-intuitionists like Professor Anscombe (see above)—is that linguistic intuitions "can *never* yield either statements or precepts of substance about morals" (*MT*, p. 11).

To see what he means, suppose I enunciate the substantial moral principle that we ought to do what we have promised to do. I might point out that when I say somebody has promised to do something, I always intend to imply that he ought to do it. That is how I use the verb "to promise." As a native speaker of English, I am an authority on the meaning of words in that language; and as an individual speaker of any sort, I am an authority on what I intend to imply by the words I use. Do not these facts, then, suffice to establish the correctness of my initial judgment that when people have promised to do something, they ought to do it?

Not for a moment!, is Hare's reply. And if *all* users of English share my view of the meaning of "to promise" and use it intending to imply the same as I would, that makes no difference, according to him. Descriptivists and neo-intuitionists may argue that "Smith ought to do X" can be validly deduced from "Smith promised to do X"; and so perhaps it can, if "to promise" in ordinary English usage has both evaluative and descriptive meaning. But this leaves wide open the substantial moral issue of whether Smith, or anyone else, ought to do what he has promised to do. If anyone says that a person who has promised to do something is under no obligation to do it, he is not talking nonsense, as he would be if the matter were settled by the way in which words are generally used. He is differing from the rest of us on a matter of moral principle, not on a logical or linguistic point. Ordinary English usage permits him to raise the question of whether one really ought to do what one has promised. Nothing can be settled concerning substantial moral questions, such as this, from purely linguistic considerations according to Hare. Nothing I have said about his recent moral philosophy is intended to imply that he thinks it can.

Some Criticisms of Hare on "Logic and the Facts"

It may help to clarify Hare's views even further and to enable us to assess them, if I now turn to some of the main criticisms that have been levelled against his account of what it means to be constrained by "logic and the facts" in one's moral thinking. I have three such criticisms in mind and will take them in turn.

First, there is the objection that, if the logical properties of the moral concepts required us to go the round of all the affected parties before delivering a moral judgment, in the way that Hare supposes, they would require us to do the logically impossible. In order to "imagine myself in the place of each man in turn"—i.e. precisely in his place—I should have to identify myself completely with each in turn. But it is self-contradictory to suppose that I could become somebody else and so this requirement can never be met. Hare recognizes that difficult problems concerning personal identity are raised by his universal prescriptivism but attempts to deal with them in the following way (*MT*, pp. 119—21).

Let us concede that it is self-contradictory to suppose that two given individuals could have all their defining characteristics in common; that they could, for instance, both have been born to the same parents at exactly the same point in time and space. Each given individual may be said to have an essence which he does not share with any other individual. However, whilst this makes it impossible for Smith to become Jones, it does not make it impossible for him to imagine being Jones, for the sufficient reason, as Hare puts it, that " 'I' is tied to no 'essence' ". He explains this remark: ". . . putting myself in somebody else's shoes does not involve supposing myself to have simultaneously two incompatible sets of properties; it involves merely supposing that I might lose one set and acquire the other." It is therefore not incoherent for Smith to say to himself, "Suppose I were Jones."

In order to imagine that he is Jones, the main thing Smith would have to do, according to Hare (*MT*, pp. 96—99), is to imagine himself with Jones' preferences. When I put myself in somebody else's shoes, whatever else this may involve, it involves having a considerably greater concern for the satisfaction of their preferences than I otherwise should. To think of someone else (past or future as well as present) as myself is to have now the preferences that I think he has (or had or will have). When it is said that I have his preferences, what this means is that I am already prescribing their satisfaction. My identification with him is thus at bottom a *prescriptive* identification. From the contention that "I" is tied to no essence—or to put the same point in different terms, that it is "not wholly a descriptive word"—Hare has now moved to the further contention that " 'I' has a prescriptive element in its meaning" (*MT*, p. 221). When "I" is brought into use, this involves the ascription of no essential properties to the individual so designated but it does identify the individual referred to with certain prescriptions. When I put myself in someone's else's place, I identify with his preferences and so necessarily with his prescriptions. Therefore, when Hare speaks of a rational moral thinker going the round of all the affected parties and putting himself in the place of each in turn, what is in his mind (*MT*, pp. 222–23) is as follows. Since morality, unlike mere prudence, is concerned with the interests of others (or, as Hare puts it, "admits no relevant difference between 'I' and 'he' ") it obliges us to prescribe the satisfaction of those preferences we would call "his" no less than of those we would call "mine". This may be a psychologically hard thing to do but it is not logically impossible.

A second criticism, which is sometimes levelled against Hare's moral theory, is that it falsely assumes all satisfactions (or dissatisfactions) to be homogeneous as to their moral significance. All we have to do is calculate *how much* cumulative satisfaction (or dissatisfaction) we would experience, if we were in the place of the affected parties, in order to arrive at what we ought to do. But, it is objected, for purposes of moral judgment satisfactions cannot be quantified in that way since they differ in their moral character. Let me offer two examples of how this objection might be put. One is as follows. The satisfaction you may find in having a harmonious and affectionate relationship with your spouse and children has a different moral quality from the satisfaction I may find in consuming large quantities of food and drink. And so, we are not entitled to assume that, if a certain act would spoil your family relationships to a small extent, it ought nevertheless to be done, provided only that it would also greatly replenish my larder and cellar. Family harmony is a worthier sort of satisfaction than gastronomic repletion.

Another example is provided by the doctor who was referred to a short time ago. His satisfaction in keeping his patients alive as long as possible was that of a man doing what he believed to be his duty. Now, does it make sense to say that this doctor—when he is thinking morally about what he ought to do—should throw the thought of this satisfaction, which he finds in keeping his patients alive for as long as possible, into the scales of his imagination along with thoughts of satisfactions such as that which his patients would find in being spared unnecessary suffering? The former kind of satisfaction is that of a moral conviction; the latter, that of a physical desire. If they are to be regarded as homogenous, then the doctor is in effect being asked to ignore moral considerations in the very act of attempting to make a moral decision. And is not that an incoherent, if not a plainly self-contradictory, request? How can he be expected to sit so lightly to his sense of duty—or as we saw above to what some moral philosophers (e.g. Bernard Williams) would call his own integrity—when deciding what he ought to do?

Hare would defend himself against such criticism, I think, in either of two ways. The one is perhaps particularly appropriate to the former kind of example and the other to the latter kind.

In reply to the former kind of example, he might say that he has never denied that satisfactions are of different kinds. Of course, the fulfilment people find in family relationships is a different kind of experience from that which they find in eating or drinking. But the question we can ask ourselves with regard to satisfactions of whatever kind is: how much do I *prefer* this satisfaction to others of the same, or different, kinds? Suppose, to return to the first example, I could do something which would only marginally diminish your domestic bliss but enable me to dine and wine lots of people lavishly, ought I to do it? On Hare's account of moral thinking, what I would have to ask myself is: would I prefer the cumulative satisfaction of my replete guests, if I were in their places, to the avoidance of some coolness within your family, if I were in yours? Presumably, I would know which I prefer, whatever differences there might be between the kinds of satisfaction compared.

Hare would say, in reply to the second kind of example—
that of the doctor—that it puts the cart before the horse.
If we regard any form of satisfaction as morally more
worthy (or unworthy) than any other, then we have to that
extent begged the moral question before we start. Appeal
to "logic and the facts", if it is conceived to be the correct
way of forming moral judgments, cannot involve any such
petitio. A method of deciding what ought to be done is
otiose to the extent to which it proceeds on the assumption
that the answer to that question is (in part at least) already
known. As Hare has it: "If the doctor says, 'My initial
preference is based on moral conviction, so it has to prevail,'
he is taking the argument in the wrong order; it is an argument whose purpose is to *arrive at* a moral conviction by
critical thought. To insist on the *prior* authority of the
moral intuitions that one starts with is simply to refuse to
think critically" (*MT*, p. 179). The references to "moral
intuitions" and "critical thought" here point forward to
what will be said about Hare's "two-level" theory of moral
thinking. In order to understand his reply, we need to know
that he regards "moral intuitions" as the "cart", so to speak,
and "critical thinking" as the "horse". The way in which he
thinks that the latter should "come before" the former will
be discussed at some length below.

A third criticism which has recently been made of Hare
(see e.g. H. M. Robinson's "Is Hare a Naturalist?", *PR*, XCI,
1982) is to the effect that his account of the constraints of
"logic and the facts" lands him in the very kind of theory
he has always been most anxious to refute, namely, descriptivism or naturalism.

Hare takes ethical descriptivism to be the theory that, in
the case of moral judgments, as in that of descriptive statements, their meaning determines their truth-conditions (cf.
MT, p. 218); and ethical naturalism, to be the theory that
solely from certain factual statements certain moral judgments can be validly deduced (cf. *MT*, p. 186). He rejects
the accusation that he has landed himself in either.

As an example of both descriptivism and naturalism,
we may recall Mrs. Foot's early view that morality is
logically grounded in "wants that all men have." (We saw
that by "wants" here, she means interests or desires.) To

her mind, the value judgment that an act, A, ought to be done was equivalent in meaning to—or at least entailed by—the factual statement that A would satisfy certain wants that all men have. Her descriptivism is evident from her belief that this meaning (or entailment) determines the truth-conditions of the value judgment—it is true that act A ought to be done, if it satisfies certain wants that all men have, and false if it does not. And her naturalism was apparent from her belief that a moral judgment follows from a descriptive statement alone—the mere fact that A satisfies certain wants implies that it ought to be done.

What Hare has to defend himself against, then, is the criticism that he has offered an account of moral thinking which is, in principle, indistinguishable from that of descriptivists and naturalists, such as Mrs. Foot. There may appear to be some *prima facie* plausibility in this criticism. If moral thinking is subject to the constraints of "logic and the facts", as explained above, does not this mean that moral judgments follow logically from certain matters of fact, which the logic of the moral concepts makes relevant? And is not this a version of naturalism and descriptivism? According to an unequivocal descriptivist or naturalist of the early Mrs. Foot's kind, the logic of the moral concepts is such that to say of an act that it ought to be done is to say that it will satisfy certain wants. If, therefore, we (a) understand the logic of the moral word "ought" and (b) assent to the factual statement that a given act will satisfy the said wants, then we cannot (logically) refuse to say that the act in question ought to be done (in the absence of countervailing obligations, of course). Now, what Hare's critics want to know is how all his talk of "logic and the facts" differs, in principle, from this kind of theory. According to Hare, the logic of the moral concepts is (putting it summarily) such that to say of an act that it ought to be done is to say that, of all conceivable acts in the given situation, it is the one which the person judging thinks will maximize preference-satisfactions among the affected parties. Does it not follow—in parallel to the case of Mrs. Foot just quoted—that if we (a) understand the logic of the moral word "ought" and (b) assent to the factual statement that a given act will maximize the preference-satisfactions of the affected parties, then we cannot (logically) refuse to say that this act ought to be done? And in that case is not Hare as much of a descriptivist or naturalist as Mrs. Foot?

Such, briefly stated, is the criticism Hare has to meet. He has two kinds of reply to it (*MT*, pp. 218—26). One recalls what he has said about the logical possibility of amoralism. Hare writes:

> The admission that amoralism can be a consistent position marks a departure from descriptivism . . . for if logic cannot compel us to abjure amoralism, provided that it is consistently followed, that leaves it open to us, when any universal prescription or prohibition is proposed, either to accept it, if it is consistent with the other prescriptions that our preferences commit us to, or, if we are an amoralist, to reject it. (*MT*, p. 219)

Hare speaks of the amoralist as having "a possible escape-route from the form of moral argument which I have been advocating" (*MT*, p. 183). And he spells out the nature of this escape-route in terms of the following example:

> Suppose that *A* is proposing to do something to *B* which *B* prefers should not be done. By the method we have been pursuing, it is possible to bring *A* to reject the moral judgment that he ought to do it, because, having thought what it would be like to be in *B*'s position, he will not accept the universal prescription that this be done in such circumstances. But having rejected this universal prescription, he is not compelled to accept a universal prohibition on such acts. He can, instead, refuse to accept any universal prescription, affirmative or negative, for such situations, and this leaves it open for him to say that it is neither the case that he ought to do it, nor the case that he ought not. (*ibid.*)

We can, therefore, according to Hare, think in accordance with "logic and the facts" but when we find that this is leading us to prescriptions or prohibitions which would not harmonize with others to which we are committed, we can always opt out of the process. I think what he means is more than that we can, as a matter of empirical fact, simply bring our moral thinking to a stop, if we are uneasy about where it is leading us. After all, on a descriptivist or naturalist account of moral thinking, that empirical possibility would also exist. I think Hare is saying that there is the *logical* possibility of an "escape-route", given his prescriptivism, which is lacking in descriptivism or naturalism. From *within* moral thinking, so to speak, this escape-route is open, given Hare's prescriptivism.

But how so? his critics may ask. If it is a fact that a given act will maximize the preference-satisfactions of the affected parties, how, on Hare's account of the logic of the moral concepts, can we escape the implication that it ought to be done? This is where Hare brings in his second kind of reply to the present criticism. He recalls what he has said about preferences being expressed by prescriptions. Remember that the criticism he is facing at this point is that he, no less than naturalists like Mrs. Foot, infers moral value judgments from matters of empirical fact; that he takes what would in fact maximize the preference-satisfactions of the affected parties to determine what ought to be done. In reply to this accusation, Hare asks what it means to go the round of all the affected parties, imaginatively identifying oneself with the preferences of each in turn, as moral thinking on his account of it requires us to do. He says that this does *not* mean to describe certain facts, but to assent to certain prescriptions. To work out what would maximize the satisfaction of such preferences is not to describe a state of affairs, but to give one's assent to a cumulative prescription. So, to say that it follows from this latter prescription that a certain act ought to be done is *not* to be guilty of descriptivism or naturalism. For it is perfectly consistent with Hare's universal prescriptivism to infer a moral judgment from such a prescription.

(II) THE "TWO-LEVEL" THEORY

I turn now to the second main development in Hare's

Moral Thinking (and in a number of papers which pre-
ceded its publication).[1] We have been considering so far the
element of constraint—what Hare called "the thought-
processes one has to go through"—in rational moral thinking.
Now we come to the element of criticism—what Hare called
"the sorts of criticism to which these thought-processes are
open."

What constitutes this critical element in rational moral
thinking? Hare approvingly quotes (*MT*, p. 214) R. B. Brandt's
remark that a moral judgment is rational if it can survive
"maximal criticism by facts and logic." The operative word
is "maximal". In so far as a moral judgment deserves to be
called rational it will, according to Hare, at some time and
in some place, have been made by someone who was attempting to think in accordance with "logic and the facts."
That is so, whether we are thinking of the moral judgments
a person has made for himself or of those which form part
of the morality he has inherited from his parents or teachers.
But in either case, it is always possible that whoever made
the judgment was to some extent muddled in his logic or
mistaken as to the facts. There is, therefore, always room
for reappraisal. Is this judgment really in accordance with
"logic and the facts"? That question is for ever open and
it belongs to the very concept of a rational moral being that
he keeps it in mind.

I remarked above that a rational thinker will be mindful,
not only that he himself may be mistaken, through lack of
intelligence or perception, in the particular conclusions at
which he arrives, but that the very rules of procedure, in
accordance with which he has been taught to work things

---

[1] E.g. "Principles" in *Proceedings of the Aristotelian Society*,
LXXIII, 1972–3; "Utiliarianism and the Vicarious Affects" in *The
Philosophy of Nicholas Rescher*, edited by E. Sosa; "Ethical Theory
and Utilitariansim" in *Contemporary British Philosophy*, vol. 4,
edited by H. D. Lewis (London, 1976); "Justice and Equality" in
Justice and Economic Distribution, edited by J. Arthur and W. Shaw,
1978; "Moral Philosophy" in B. Magee, *Men of Ideas* (London,
1978).

out, may be mistaken. If he is a moral thinker, that is to
say, there will be two sorts of question he can ask himself,
viz. (i) Am I correct in the moral opinions I at present hold?
and (ii) Am I correct in what I take the logic of the moral
concepts to be? As we noted in the Introduction, these are
commonly differentiated as the *ethical* and *meta-ethical*
questions respectively. Hare's extensive writings in defence
of his prescriptivism show that he is fully alive to the latter
question. But it is with the need to answer the former
question that he is concerned in what he calls his "two-level"
theory.

What, then, are these "two levels"? Before we come to
them notice first, that from within the *meta-ethical* point
of view, Hare differentiates two elements in any *ethical*
system, such as utilitarianism for example. These two elements he calls respectively, the "formal" (or "abstract")
and the "material" (or "substantial"). To keep to our
example, the *formal* element in utilitarianism is the principle of impartial benevolence; and the *substantial* element
is whatever is believed to fulfil this principle, given the facts
of the world, and in particular of human nature, as they are.
Now we can go on to identify the two levels in what Hare
calls his "two-level" theory. Within the "substantial" element in ethical thinking, or as he calls it, within "substantial normative ethics"—that is to say, within the moral
thinking about what they ought, in practice, to do in
which people at any time engage—Hare draws a distinction
between what he calls respectively "intuitive" and "critical"
thinking. And these are the "two levels", the nature of
which I am concerned in this section to explain.

The need for reappraisal, in our efforts to decide how we
ought to live, is what Hare, as a rationalist, is concerned to
high-light by his "two-level" theory. In his most recent
writings, he does not deny that descriptivists in general, and
neo-intuitionists in particular, are correct in many of the
things they say. Morality could not do without generally
accepted criteria of right and wrong. That is to say, it needs
its intuitive level. It is perfectly true that in a great deal of
moral thinking, we are directed, like Professor Anscombe
(see above) by convictions about which we do not want to

argue; that is, by intuitive responses, or moral impossibilities, as Hampshire (see above) would call them. The exigencies of everyday life are such that we should be morally lost without these unequivocal injunctions; and the requirements of moral education, such that it would be impossible unless there were some simple non-contentious guide-lines to point out to the young. Much of our moral thinking, therefore, is indeed intuitive and descriptive. But that is only one level, the level of received opinion, of unquestioned principle. At that level, moral doubts and dilemmas may occur; occasions may arise when we cannot but wonder whether we are right in the convictions we have hitherto held. As rational thinkers, we will then need a vantage point from which to reappraise them. Hare claims, as the merit of his universal prescriptivism, that it can show us where this rational requirement is to be found. Namely, at another level of moral thinking, where there is not the same danger of conflict or confusion.

We shall see clearly how the "two levels" differ from each other, and what constitutes each of them, if we note what Hare says about "proles" and "archangels". He takes these names from Orwell and Godwin respectively. Proles are conceived as moral beings who think entirely at the intuitive level; archangels as ones who think entirely at the critical level.

An "archangel" (*MT*, pp. 44–5). get things completely and instantly right in his moral thinking. He does everything "by reason in a moment of time", because he is "a being with superhuman powers of thought, superhuman knowledge and no human weaknesses ...." Hare goes on: "When presented with a novel situation, he will be able at once to scan all its properties, including the consequences of alternative actions, and frame a universal principle (perhaps a highly specific one) which he can accept for action in that situation, no matter what role he himself were to occupy in it. Lacking, among other human weaknesses, that of partiality to self, he will act on that principle, if it bids him act." The points to notice in this description are as follows. Firstly, the "archangel" is omniscient and so will be fully apprised of whatever facts are relevant to his moral judgments. Secondly, he is free from any defects of intellect or character which might inhibit a lesser man from seeing which judgments he would be prepared to universalize and prescribe. Perfect command of "logic and the facts" is therefore characteristic of the archangel. In consequence, the moral judgments which he forms can be relied on to be correct. As Hare has it: " . . . archangels, at the end of their critical thinking, will all say the same thing, . . . on all questions on which moral argument is possible, . . . and so shall we, to the extent that we manage to think like archangels." These archangelic judgments may be very specific. There is a difference between generality and universalizability and between specificity and particularity (see Hare's "Principles" in *Proceedings of the Aristotelian Society*, LXXIII, 1972–3). A moral principle may be extremely specific yet still universalizable. The more carefully thought out and the better informed a person's moral judgments are, the more likely it is that they will be specific, i.e. will prescribe what ought to be done in certain kinds of situation as distinct from others. An archangel does not go in for sweeping generalizations; he is very sensitive to all the intricacies of circumstances which alter cases, when it comes to what people ought to do.

A "prole" (*ibid*.) is the very opposite of an archangel. He lacks all those powers which enable the latter to "reason in a moment of time." So devoid is the prole of knowledge and acumen that his only hope of being in accord with logic and the facts is to go by what other people have told him. Through the influence of his parents and teachers, he will have been brought up to believe that certain sorts of action are right or wrong—e.g. that it is right to tell the truth, wrong to be unkind, etc. These principles of conduct will have disposed him to behave in certain ways and to have feelings of virtue or guilt in consequence of keeping to them or failing to do so. Such habits of mind, social conventions, intuitions—or whatever else one chooses to call them—are the prole's only hope of making correct moral judgments.

Hare's point in all this is not that the archangel and the prole are rivals, or alternatives, within morality, except in a schematic sense. In point of fact, we are all, according to him, part archangel and part prole. Some of us are more the one; others more the other; but we are all both in limited and varying degrees. That is to say, we all think to some extent intuitively, and to some extent critically. On the one hand, most of us most of the time live by such "intuitive" principles of conduct as we have acquired in consequence of our education and experience. We have not the time or capacity to think out from scratch every moral judgment that we are called upon to make. But occasions do arise when we have to subject these intuitions to reappraisal and then "critical" thinking is required of us. There is no fixed rule as to when it is appropriate to think like an archangel and when like a prole, any more than there are fixed rules in other walks of life about when to act as one usually does without further thought and when to consider carefully whether some new kind of behaviour would be more appropriate.

But one can identify, according to Hare, at least three kinds of circumstance in which critical, rather than intuitive, thinking is called for ("Ethical Theory and Utilitarianism" *op. cit.*, p. 124). One is when our moral intuitions conflict; a second is when the situation which confronts us is so unusual that our moral intuitions seem wholly inadequate to the facts of the case; and the third is when we have to decide what to include in the moral education of the next generation. On such occasions it is obviously very appropriate to take a critical look at what we are accustomed to regard as right or wrong and to ask ourselves whether or not it really is so.

It will be evident that one must not simply conclude that Hare is in favour of critical moral thinking but against intuitive. In his opinion both are desirable; both have their part to play in real life morality. We need intuitive principles that are comparatively simple and general (*prima facie* ones, as Hare calls them, borrowing the expression from W. D. Ross, cf. above p. 92) because the realities of life are such that we very often cannot find the time or energy to think things out more specifically and because we need to give our children some guidance in how they ought to live that will be sufficiently clear and straightforward for them to understand it. But then again, the realities of life are such that, if morality is to be adequate to the complicated situations in which we sometimes find ourselves, it will have to allow, on occasion, for critically thought-out judgments in accordance with very specific principles. The two levels of moral thinking are complementary, not mutually exclusive.

The Relationship between the "Two Levels" of Moral Thinking

But how exactly does Hare conceive of their relationship with one another? I think the key to this matter is to be found in his remark: "Because *intuitive* moral thinking *cannot be self-supporting*, whereas *critical* thinking *can be and is*, the latter is epistemologically prior" (*MT*, p. 46, italics mine). On the same page, he happily uses a quotation from Aristotle's *Nichomachean Ethics* to make the point that intuitive moral thinking must "listen to reason (i.e. to critical moral thinking) as to a father." What, then, is the nature of this "support", which the critical level lends to the intuitive? What constitutes the epistemological priority, or rational paternalism, that the critical level exercises over the intuitive?

I think the place to begin our answer to these questions is with Hare's conception of *overridingness*. He thinks that *moral* evaluative principles can be differentiated from those of other kinds by the fact that the former are not only prescriptive and universalizable, but also overriding (*MT*, pp. 24, 53—62). And he defines what he means by an overriding principle in the following terms: "To treat a principle as overriding then is to let it always override other principles when they conflict with it and, in the same way, let it override all other prescriptions, including non-universalizable ones (e.g. plain desires)" (*MT*, p. 56).

Hare recognizes that if a moral principle is overriding in this sense, then it is impossible for it to be overridden by another moral principle or by any nonmoral prescription; yet he notes that "both of these cases occur" (*MT*, p. 57). That is to say, there are what we call "moral conflicts"; and what may be called "moral holidays". The former are resolved by letting one moral principle override another; and the latter occur when someone allows a nonmoral prescription (or plain desire) to override one or more of his moral principles. Well, how does Hare defend what looks like a contradiction in his account of the overridingness of moral principles? How does he think it can be impossible for them to be overridden and yet possible for this to occur? It will be best, if I first give what I take to be his answer in his own words, and then make some comments upon it.

> If we think of the whole structure of moral thinking with its two levels, "moral" can be defined, in the sense in which we are using it, . . . as follows. The class of a man's moral principles consists of two sub-classes: (1) those universal prescriptive principles which he does not allow to be overridden; these will be what I called "critical moral principles" and are therefore capable of being made so specific and so adapted to particular cases that they do not need to be overridden; (2) those *prima facie* principles which, although they can be overridden, are selected . . . by critical thinking, in the course of which use is made of moral principles of the first sub-class. (*MT*, p. 60)

Hare goes on to say that, when we want to know whether people are treating a principle as a moral one, we have first to ask whether they would ever, in any circumstances, let it be overridden. If they say they would not, we know they are treating it as a principle of the first (i.e. critical) sub-class, referred in the above quotation. But if they say they can conceive of circumstances in which they would let the said principle be overridden, Hare thinks it may, nevertheless still be a moral principle, though of the second (i.e. intuitive) sub-class. But how so? He explains that what we must ask anyone, who says he can conceive of circumstances in which he would be prepared to see one or more of his moral principles overridden, is how in such case he *justifies* thinking of it as a moral one; and at this point he introduces his notion of "acceptance utility" as the only feasible justification. He writes in this way of the person, whom we have just imagined ourselves asking to justify a principle, that can be overridden, as a moral one:

> . . . if he says that it would be on the basis of critical thinking, in that this was a principle whose general acceptance would lead to people's actions and dispositions approximating to the greatest extent to the deliverances of a perfectly conducted critical thinking (i.e. to the moral principles of the first sort that such critical thinking would arrive at), then this principle too will count as a moral principle, but of the second class. (*MT*, p. 61)

The point may be put like this. Moral principles are of two kinds, which may be described as *derived* and *underived* respectively. The underived kind are deliverances of a moral thinker's critical thinking. They are the principles which he would not allow to be overridden in any conceivable circumstances. A moral thinker's principles of the derived kind by contrast, are the ones which he considers to have what Hare calls "acceptance utility". That is to say the thinker concerned considers that their general acceptance would be useful as a means to the fulfilment of his underived moral principles. To take the simplest of examples, suppose a moral thinker had arrived by critical thinking at the conclusion that we ought always to do what we think will maximize happiness. He might then consider that, if everyone told the truth, except in abnormal circumstances, that would contribute significantly to the maximization of happiness. In such a case, this moral thinker's underived principle would be the maximization of happiness; and his derived principle, truth-telling.

So, the relationship between Hare's "two levels" of moral thinking has become clear. The intuitive level has to do with derived principles; the critical level with underived ones. Only those of the latter kind have absolute overridingness. Those of the former kind—intuitive or derived principles—do not have any overridingness in their own right. But they have been selected by critical thinking for their "acceptance utility," as means to the ends of underived principles. It is, therefore, the overridingness of the deliverances of critical thinking which, in the last analysis, makes derived principles moral, just as it makes underived ones so.

I think we are able now to see what Hare's answers would be to the questions posed at the beginning of this sub-section, about the nature of the "support" which critical moral thinking lends to intuitive; and about the nature of the epistemological priority and rational paternalism which the former exercises over the latter. It is only the deliverances of critical thinking that are overriding. And so everything in morality is in the end dependent upon, and subordinate to, critical thinking. It is the overridingness of its deliverances which holds the "two levels" together and makes them both part of *moral* thinking.

The idea that there are two levels of moral thinking is not, of course, peculiar to Hare, as he would be the first to point out. Many philosophers have drawn some such contrast. Plato differentiated "knowledge" from "right opinion". Aristotle, in turn, contrasted the "that" of morality with the "why". In more recent times, William Whewell spoke of a level on which morality is directed by "subordinate rules" and a level on which there is only one "supreme rule": Henry Sidgwick spoke of a level on which moral principles are "germinal" and another on which they are "adult"; W. D. Ross differentiated *prima facie* obligations from obligations *sans phrase*; J. O. Urmson contrasted "standard using" with "standard setting", etc. John Rawls drew a distinction between "justifying a principle" and "justifying a particular action falling under it", and in a lengthy footnote he lists parallels to this distinction in Hume, John Austin, Mill, Toulmin, Quinton, and Nowell-Smith (see "Two Concepts of Rules", *PR*, 64, 1955 reprinted in P. Foot, *Theories of Ethics*).

I am not suggesting, of course, that all these other philosophers anticipated, or duplicate, Hare in detail. But it lends credibility to his theory to find that so many others have come, in their various ways, to the conclusion that moral thinking has two tiers. What I think Hare has done is to present a clear and thoroughly rationalist account of each of the two levels and of the relationship between them; and to show how each is an aspect of that "freedom to reason" which he takes to be fundamental to moral thinking.

Freedom and Reason

Hare's argument in *Moral Thinking* is subtle and complicated. This is not surprising since he is dealing with issues which are themselves complex. But it lays him open to the possibility of misunderstanding and some readers may find it hard to hold all the strands of his argument together in their minds. I do not know whether Hare would approve of the way in which I am going to summarize his ideas and I must make it clear that I am speaking only for myself, but I think one useful way of bringing the elements of his argument together is by considering how they bear upon the relationship between reason and freedom in moral thinking as he conceives of it. At the beginning of my account of his later moral philosophy, I remarked that some readers of his most recent book may feel that what he has to say in it about *reason* goes back on some of the things he had to say about *freedom* in his earlier writings. Hare himself, as we noted, denies explicitly that this is so. What I wish to suggest, in concluding my attempt to introduce the reader to the latest developments in his type of moral theory, is that, in order to understand him, one should hold in mind first, what has been said about the place he gives to reason in moral thinking; and then see how this is compatible with freedom. As we saw above he does not regard anything he has said about the constraint of "logic and the facts" as a denial, or qualification, of the "irreducibly *prescriptive* or *evaluative*" element in moral thinking.

For my own part, I think there are two ways in which Hare may be said to have left room for freedom in moral thinking. The former is perhaps best summed up in his remark "we remain free to prefer what we prefer" (*MT*, p. 225). There are, I would say, three points in Hare's analysis of moral thinking at which he claims that we have this freedom.

First, when we bring any principle (proposed reason) into the light of "logic and the facts," in order to see if we can adopt it as a moral one, we never *have* to bring it. Our preferences, in the widest sense, will determine the sorts of reasons for moral judgments that we are prepared to consider. If any such proposed reason does not fit in with our preferences in general, it will not get through, even as a candidate for moral status. The parallel Hare draws between his own account of moral thinking and Popper's account of scientific thinking, safeguards our freedom "to prefer what we prefer", so to speak, at the very source of moral thinking.

Secondly, what Hare says about the "escape-route" of amoralism preserves our freedom "to prefer what we prefer" in the midstream of moral thinking. If logic cannot compel us to abjure amoralism, Hare affirms, "that leaves it open to us, when any universal prescription or prohibition is proposed, either to accept it, *if it is consistent with the other prescriptions that our preferences commit us to*, or, if we are an amoralist, to reject it" (*MT*, p. 219 italics mine). Here again, we are constrained to assent to the conclusions to which "logic and the facts" lead us, only if they fit in with "what we prefer."

Thirdly, the same is true, even when the constraint of "logic and the facts" has run its course. "We must remember", says Hare, "that what will determine our final moral judgment is our total system of preferences" (*MT*, p. 225). Think again of the fanatical doctor to whom reference was made above. When all that "logic and the facts" required of him had been accomplished (going the round of the affected parties, as the universality and prescriptivity of moral judgments require; taking full cognizance of who is, or will be, affected and precisely how) the total system of his preferences was still dominated by the preference to keep his suffering patients alive as long as possible. So that was that. There was no more that reason could do in order to get him to think he ought to let them die. Moral thinking had run its course to a conclusion which was "not inconsistent with utilitarianism." But the doctor remained "free to prefer what he preferred."

What any moral thinker prefers expresses itself in prescriptions. So, the "irreducibly prescriptive" element in moral thinking is there at the beginning, there in the midstream, and there at the conclusion of moral judgment. We are free, all the way through, to prescribe what we do prescribe. So at the end of *Moral Thinking* Hare is no less of a prescriptivist than he was at the beginning of *The Language of Morals*.

The latter of the two ways in which, I think, Hare leaves room for freedom in moral thinking is in what he says of its critical level. This level provides, so to speak, a base for freedom within reason itself. Critical thinking was defined above by Hare following Brandt, as "maximal" exposure to "logic and the facts." And we noted that there is no limit to the scope for re-appraisal of our moral judgements. However assured we may be of a moral principle, circumstances may arise which call it in question. Then we are free to criticize it. Does it *really* conform to the logic of the moral concepts? Are the factual beliefs involved *really* true? To these questions we are always free to return. They provide the dynamism in moral thinking; the freedom that self-conscious moral beings have to re-examine their own convictions. It is, as I endeavoured to say at the beginning, in the very nature of rationality that it not only places us under the constraint of logic and the facts, but also opens up to us the freedom of criticism. And this is so in moral thinking as in every other rational kind. Hare's "two-level" theory, in according an overriding place to criticism in moral reasoning, preserves the place of freedom, as I say, from within reason itself. So far from his later moral philosophy excluding freedom from moral thinking, it provides it with a rational base.

INDEX